ALSO BY STEPHEN GREENBLATT

Hamlet in Purgatory

Practicing New Historicism (with Catherine Gallagher)

Marvelous Possessions: The Wonder of the New World

Learning to Curse: Essays in Early Modern Culture

Shakespearean Negotiations:
The Circulation of Social Energy in Renaissance England

Renaissance Self-Fashioning: From More to Shakespeare

Sir Walter Ralegh: The Renaissance Man and His Roles

Three Modern Satirists: Waugh, Orwell, and Huxley

EDITED BY STEPHEN GREENBLATT

The Norton Anthology of English Literature (general editor)

The Norton Shakespeare (general editor)

New World Encounters

Redrawing the Boundaries:
The Transformation of English and American Literary Studies

Representing the English Renaissance

Allegory and Representation

Will in the World

HOW SHAKESPEARE
BECAME SHAKESPEARE

Stephen Greenblatt

JONATHAN CAPE
London

Published by Jonathan Cape 2004

2 4 6 8 10 9 7 5 3

Copyright © Stephen Greenblatt 2004

Stephen Greenblatt has asserted his right under the Copyright, Designs
and Patents Act 1988 to be identified as the author of this work

First published in the United States in 2004 by W. W. Norton & Company

First published in Great Britain in 2004 by
JONATHAN CAPE
Random House, 20 Vauxhall Bridge Road,
London SW1V 2SA

Random House Australia (Pty) Limited
20 Alfred Street, Milsons Point, Sydney,
New South Wales 2061, Australia

Random House New Zealand Limited
18 Poland Road, Glenfield,
Auckland 10, New Zealand

Random House South Africa (Pty) Limited
Endulini, 5A Jubilee Road, Parktown 2193, South Africa

The Random House Group Limited Reg. No. 954009
www.randomhouse.co.uk

A CIP catalogue record for this book is available from the British Library

ISBN 0-2240-6276-X

Papers used by Random House are natural,
recyclable products made from wood grown in sustainable forests;
the manufacturing processes conform to the environmental
regulations of the country of origin

Printed and bound in Great Britain by
Clays Ltd, St Ives plc

TO JOSH AND AARON, ONCE AGAIN,
AND NOW TO HARRY

Contents

Preface

A YOUNG MAN from a small provincial town—a man without
independent wealth, without powerful family connections, and
without a university education—moves to London in the late 1580s and,
in a remarkably short time, becomes the greatest playwright not of his
age alone but of all time. His works appeal to the learned and the unlettered, to urban sophisticates and provincial first-time theatergoers. He
makes his audiences laugh and cry; he turns politics into poetry; he reck-
lessly mingles vulgar clowning and philosophical subtlety. He grasps with
equal penetration the intimate lives of kings and of beggars; he seems at
one moment to have studied law, at another theology, at another ancient
history, while at the same time he effortlessly mimes the accents of country bumpkins and takes delight in old wives' tales. How is an achievement of this magnitude to be explained? How did Shakespeare become
Shakespeare?

Theater, in Shakespeare's time as in our own, is a highly social art
form, not a game of bloodless abstractions. There was a type of drama in
the age of Elizabeth and James that did not show its face in public;
known as closet dramas, these were plays never meant to be performed or

even printed. They were for silent reading in the privacy of small, preferably windowless rooms. But Shakespeare's plays were always decisively out of the closet: they were, and are, in the world and of the world. Not only did Shakespeare write and act for a cutthroat commercial entertainment industry; he also wrote scripts that were intensely alert to the social and political realities of their times. He could scarcely have done otherwise: to stay afloat, the theater company in which he was a shareholder had to draw some 1,500 to 2,000 paying customers a day into the round wooden walls of the playhouse, and competition from rival companies was fierce. The key was not so much topicality—with government censorship and with repertory companies often successfully recycling the same scripts for years, it would have been risky to be too topical—as it was intensity of interest. Shakespeare had to engage with the deepest desires and fears of his audience, and his unusual success in his own time suggests that he succeeded brilliantly in doing so. Virtually all his rival playwrights found themselves on the straight road to starvation; Shakespeare, by contrast, made enough money to buy one of the best houses in the hometown to which he retired in his early fifties, a self-made man.

This is a book, then, about an amazing success story that has resisted explanation: it aims to discover the actual person who wrote the most important body of imaginative literature of the last thousand years. Or rather, since the actual person is a matter of well-documented public record, it aims to tread the shadowy paths that lead from the life he lived into the literature he created.

Apart from the poems and plays themselves, the surviving traces of Shakespeare's life are abundant but thin. Dogged archival labor over many generations has turned up contemporary allusions to him, along with a reasonable number of the playwright's property transactions, a marriage license bond, christening records, cast lists in which he is named as a performer, tax bills, petty legal affidavits, payments for services, and an interesting last will and testament, but no immediately obvious clues to unravel the great mystery of such immense creative power.

The known facts have been rehearsed again and again for several centuries. Already in the nineteenth century there were fine, richly detailed, and well-documented biographies, and each year brings a fresh crop of them, sometimes enhanced with a hard-won crumb or two of new archival findings. After examining even the best of them and patiently sifting through most of the available traces, readers rarely feel closer to understanding how the playwright's achievements came about. If anything, Shakespeare often seems a drabber, duller person, and the inward springs of his art seem more obscure than ever. Those springs would be difficult enough to glimpse if biographers could draw upon letters and diaries, contemporary memoirs and interviews, books with revealing marginalia, notes and first drafts. Nothing of the kind survives, nothing that provides a clear link between the timeless work with its universal appeal and a particular life that left its many scratches in the humdrum bureaucratic records of the age. The work is so astonishing, so luminous, that it seems to have come from a god and not a mortal, let alone a mortal of provincial origins and modest education.

It is fitting, of course, to invoke the magic of an immensely strong imagination, a human endowment that does not depend upon an "interesting" life. Scholars have long and fruitfully studied the transforming work of that imagination on the books that, from evidence within the plays themselves, Shakespeare must certainly have read. As a writer he rarely started with a blank slate; he characteristically took materials that had already been in circulation and infused them with his supreme creative energies. On occasion, the reworking is so precise and detailed that he must have had the book from which he was deftly borrowing directly on his writing table as his quill pen raced across the paper. But no one who responds intensely to Shakespeare's art can believe that the plays and poems came exclusively from his reading. At least as much as the books he read, the central problems he grappled with as a young man—What should I do with my life? In what can I have faith? Whom do I love?— served throughout his career to shape his art.

One of the prime characteristics of Shakespeare's art is the touch of the real. As with any other writer whose voice has long ago fallen silent and whose body has moldered away, all that is left are words on a page, but even before a gifted actor makes Shakespeare's words come alive, those words contain the vivid presence of actual, lived experience. The poet who noticed that the hunted, trembling hare was "dew-bedabbled" or who likened his stained reputation to the "dyer's hand," the playwright who has a husband tell his wife that there is a purse "in the desk / That's covered o'er with Turkish tapestry" or who has a prince remember that his poor companion owns only two pairs of silk stockings, one of them peach-colored—this artist was unusually open to the world and discovered the means to allow this world into his works. To understand how he did this so effectively, it is important to look carefully at his verbal artistry—his command of rhetoric, his uncanny ventriloquism, his virtual obsession with language. To understand who Shakespeare was, it is important to follow the verbal traces he left behind back into the life he lived and into the world to which he was so open. And to understand how Shakespeare used his imagination to transform his life into his art, it is important to use our own imagination.

Acknowledgments

IT IS A TOKEN of the special delight Shakespeare bestows on everything that even the many debts I have incurred in writing this book give me deep pleasure to acknowledge. My remarkably gifted colleagues and students at Harvard University have been an unfailing source of intellectual stimulation and challenge, and the university's fabled resources—above all, its celebrated libraries and their accomplished staff—have enabled me to pursue even the most arcane questions. The Mellon Foundation gave me the precious gift of time, and the Wissenschaftskolleg zu Berlin provided the perfect setting to complete the writing of this book. I am grateful for the opportunities I had to try out my ideas at the Shakespeare Association of America, the Bath Shakespeare Festival, New York University, the Lionel Trilling Seminar at Columbia University, the Leo Lowenthal Memorial Conference, Boston College, Wellesley College, Hendrix College, the Einstein Forum, and, on multiple occasions, Marlboro College and the Marlboro Music Festival.

The idea of *Will in the World* originated years ago during conversations I had with Marc Norman, who was then in the early stages of writing a film script about Shakespeare's life. The script was the germ of a celebrated movie, *Shakespeare in Love*, but my own project lay dormant until my wife, Ramie Targoff, gave me the sustained encouragement, intellectual and emotional, to pursue it. Crucial advice and assistance came from Jill Kneerim, and my friends Homi Bhabha, Jeffrey Knapp, Joseph Koerner, Charles Mee, and Robert Pinsky each gave me more of their time, learning, and wisdom than I can ever hope to repay. I have benefited too from the help and probing questions of many other friends, including Marcella Anderson, Leonard Barkan, Frank Bidart, Robert Brustein, Thomas Laqueur, Adam Phillips, Regula Rapp, Moshe Safdie, James Shapiro, Debora Shuger, and the late Bernard Williams. Beatrice Kitzinger, Kate Pilson, Holger Schott, Gustavo Secchi, and Phillip Schwyzer have been tireless and resourceful assistants. With exemplary patience and insight, my editor, Alane Mason, continued to work on the manuscript of my book through the course of her pregnancy, and, by something of a miracle, she somehow managed to finish on her due date.

My deepest and most richly pleasurable debts are closest to home: to my wife and my three sons, Josh, Aaron, and Harry. Only the youngest, by virtue of being a toddler, has been spared endless conversations about Shakespeare and has not directly contributed his ideas. But Harry, who came into the world 104 years after the birth of his namesake, my father, has taught me how breathtakingly close we are to lives that at first sight seem so far away.

A Note to the Reader

AROUND 1598, still relatively early in Shakespeare's career, a man named Adam Dyrmonth, about whom next to nothing is known, set out to list the contents of a collection of speeches and letters that he had transcribed. Evidently, his mind began to wander, because he began to scribble idly. Among the jottings that cover the page are the words "Rychard the second" and "Rychard the third," along with half-remembered quotations from *Love's Labour's Lost* and *The Rape of Lucrece*. Above all, the scribbler repeatedly wrote the words "William Shakespeare." He wanted to know, it seems, what it felt like to write that particular name as one's own. Dyrmonth might have been the first to be driven by this curiosity, but he certainly was not the last.

As Dyrmonth's scribblings suggest, Shakespeare was famous in his own lifetime. Only a few years after Shakespeare's death, Ben Jonson celebrated him as "the wonder of our Stage" and the "Star of poets." But at the time such literary celebrity did not ordinarily lead to the writing of biographies, and no contemporary seems to have thought it worthwhile to collect whatever could be found out about Shakespeare while his memory was still green. As it happens, more is known about him than about most professional writers of the time, but this knowledge is largely the consequence of the fact that England in the late sixteenth and early seventeenth century was already a record-keeping society and that many of the records survived, to be subsequently combed over by eager scholars. Even with this relative abundance of information, there are huge gaps in knowledge that make any biographical study of Shakespeare an exercise in speculation.

What matters most are the works, most of which (the poems excepted) were carefully assembled by two of Shakespeare's longtime associates and friends, John Heminges and Henry Condell, who brought out the First Folio in 1623, seven years after the playwright's death. Eighteen of the thirty-six plays in this great volume, including such masterpieces as *Julius Caesar, Macbeth, Antony and Cleopatra*, and *The Tempest*, had not appeared in print before; without the First Folio they might have vanished forever. The world owes Heminges and Condell an immense debt. But beyond noting that Shakespeare wrote with great facility—"what he thought," they claimed, "he uttered with that easiness that we have scarce received from him a blot in his papers"—the editors had little or no interest in furthering biography. They chose to arrange the contents by genre—Comedies, Histories, and Tragedies—and they did not bother to note when and in what order Shakespeare wrote each of his plays. After many decades of ingenious research, scholars have reached a reasonably stable consensus, but even this time line, so crucial for any biography, is inevitably somewhat speculative.

So too are many of the details of the life. The Stratford vicar John Bretchgirdle noted in the parish register the baptism of "Gulielmus filius Johannes Shakspere" on April 26, 1564. Though anything can be called into question, that much seems beyond a reasonable doubt, but the scholars who subsequently fixed Shakespeare's date of birth as April 23—on the assumption that there was ordinarily a three-day interval at the time between birth and baptism—were engaged in speculation.

One further and potentially more consequential example will give readers a sense of the scope of the problem. From 1571 to 1575 the schoolmaster in the Stratford grammar school was Simon Hunt, who had received his B.A. from Oxford in 1568. He would thus have been

William Shakespeare's teacher from the age of seven to eleven. Around July 1575, Simon Hunt matriculated at the University of Douai—the Catholic university in France—and became a Jesuit in 1578. This would seem to indicate that Shakespeare's early teacher was a Catholic, a detail that is consistent with a whole pattern of experiences in his youth. But there is no hard-and-fast proof that Shakespeare attended the Stratford grammar school—the records for that period do not survive. Moreover, another Simon Hunt died in Stratford in or before 1598, and it is at least possible that this second Simon Hunt, rather than the one who became a Jesuit, was the schoolmaster. Shakespeare almost certainly attended the school—where else would he have acquired his education?—and the coincidence of the dates and the larger pattern of experiences make it highly likely that the schoolmaster from 1571 to 1575 was the Catholic Hunt. But in these details, as in so much else from Shakespeare's life, there is no absolute certainty.

Will in the World

CHAPTER 1

Primal Scenes

L ET US IMAGINE that Shakespeare found himself from boyhood fascinated by language, obsessed with the magic of words. There is overwhelming evidence for this obsession from his earliest writings, so it is a very safe assumption that it began early, perhaps from the first moment his mother whispered a nursery rhyme in his ear:

> Pillycock, pillycock, sate on a hill,
> If he's not gone—he sits there still.

(This particular nursery rhyme was rattling around in his brain years later, when he was writing *King Lear*. "Pillicock sat on Pillicock-hill," chants the madman Poor Tom [3.4.73].) He heard things in the sounds of words that others did not hear; he made connections that others did not make; and he was flooded with a pleasure all his own.

This was a love and a pleasure that Elizabethan England could arouse, richly satisfy, and reward, for the culture prized ornate eloquence, cultivated a taste for lavish prose from preachers and politicians, and expected even people of modest accomplishments and sober sensibilities to write poems. In one of his early plays, *Love's Labour's Lost*, Shakespeare created a ridiculous schoolteacher, Holofernes, whose manner is a parody of a classroom style that most audience members must have found immediately recognizable. Holofernes cannot refer to an apple without adding that it hangs "like a jewel in the ear of *caelo*, the sky, the welkin, the heaven" and that it drops "on the face of *terra*, the soil, the land, the earth" (4.2.4–6). He is the comical embodiment of a curriculum that used, as one of its key textbooks, Erasmus's *On Copiousness*, a book that taught students 150 different ways of saying (in Latin, of course) "Thank you for your letter." If Shakespeare deftly mocked this manic word game, he also exuberantly played it in his own voice and his own language, as when he writes in sonnet 129 that lust "Is perjured, murd'rous, bloody, full of blame, / Savage, extreme, rude, cruel, not to trust" (lines 3–4). Concealed somewhere behind this passionate outburst are the many hours a young boy spent in school, compiling long lists of Latin synonyms.

"All men," wrote Queen Elizabeth's tutor, Roger Ascham, "covet to have their children speak Latin." The queen spoke Latin—one of the few women in the realm to have had access to that accomplishment, so crucial for international relations—and so did her diplomats, counselors, theologians, clergymen, physicians, and lawyers. But command of the ancient tongue was not limited to those who actually made practical, professional use of it. "*All* men covet to have their children speak Latin": in the sixteenth century, bricklayers, wool merchants, glovers, prosperous yeomen—people who had no formal education and could not read or write English, let alone Latin—wanted their sons to be masters of the ablative absolute. Latin was culture, civility, upward mobility. It was the language of parental ambition, the universal currency of social desire.

So it was that Will's father and mother wanted their son to have a proper classical education. John Shakespeare himself seems to have had at most only partial literacy: as the holder of important civic offices in Stratford-upon-Avon, he probably knew how to read, but throughout his life he only signed his name with a mark. Judging from the mark she made on legal documents, Mary Shakespeare, the mother of England's greatest writer, also could not write her name, though she too might have acquired some minimal literacy. But, they evidently decided, this would not suffice for their eldest son. The child no doubt began with a "hornbook"—a wooden tablet with the letters and the Paternoster printed on a piece of parchment covered with a thin sheet of transparent horn—and with the standard primary school text, *The ABC with the Cathechism*. (In *The Two Gentlemen of Verona*, a lover sighs "like a schoolboy that had lost his ABC"[2.1.19–20].) Thus far he was only acquiring what his father and possibly even his mother may have possessed. But probably starting at age seven, he was sent to the Stratford free grammar school, whose central educational principle was total immersion in Latin.

The school was called the King's New School, but it was not new and it had not been founded by the king who was honored in its name, Elizabeth's short-lived stepbrother Edward VI. Like so many other Elizabethan institutions, this one wore a mask designed to hide origins tainted with Roman Catholicism. Built by the town's Guild of the Holy Cross in the early fifteenth century, it was endowed as a free school by one of its Catholic chaplains in 1482. The schoolhouse—which survives more or less intact—was a single large room above the guildhall, reached by a flight of external stairs that were at one time roofed with tile. There may have been partitions, particularly if an assistant teacher was teaching very young children their ABCs, but most of the students—some forty-two boys, ranging in age from seven to fourteen or fifteen—sat on hard benches facing the schoolmaster, sitting in his large chair at the head of the room.

By statute, the Stratford schoolmaster was not allowed to take money for his instruction from any of the students. He was to teach any male child who qualified—that is, anyone who had learned the rudiments of reading and writing—"be their parents never so poor and the boys never so unapt." For this he received free housing and an annual salary of twenty pounds, a substantial sum at the high end of what Elizabethan schoolmasters could hope to make. The town of Stratford was serious about the education of its children: after the free grammar school there were special scholarships to enable promising students of limited means to attend university. This was not, to be sure, universal free education. Here as everywhere else, girls were excluded from both grammar school and university. The sons of the very poor—a large proportion of the population—also did not go to school, for they were expected to begin work at a young age, and, besides, though there was no fee, there were some expenses: students were expected to bring quills for pens, a knife for sharpening the quills, candles in winter, and—an expensive commodity—paper. But for the sons of families of some means, however modest, a rigorous education, centered on the classics, was accessible. Though the Stratford school records from the time do not survive, Will almost certainly attended this school, fulfilling his parents' desire that he learn Latin.

In the summer the school day began at 6 A.M.; in the winter, as a concession to the darkness and the cold, at 7. At 11 came recess for lunch—Will presumably ran home, only three hundred yards or so away—and then instruction began again, continuing until 5:30 or 6. Six days a week; twelve months a year. The curriculum made few concessions to the range of human interests: no English history or literature; no biology, chemistry, or physics; no economics or sociology; only a smattering of arithmetic. There was instruction in the articles of the Christian faith, but that must have seemed all but indistinguishable from the instruction in Latin. And the instruction was not gentle: rote memorization, relentless drills, endless repetition, daily analysis of texts, elaborate exercises in imitation and rhetorical variation, all backed up by the threat of violence.

Everyone understood that Latin learning was inseparable from whipping. One educational theorist of the time speculated that the buttocks were created in order to facilitate the learning of Latin. A good teacher was by definition a strict teacher; pedagogical reputations were made by the vigor of the beatings administered. The practice was time-honored and entrenched: as part of his final examination at Cambridge, a graduate in grammar in the late Middle Ages was required to demonstrate his pedagogical fitness by flogging a dull or recalcitrant boy. Learning Latin in this period was, as a modern scholar has put it, a male puberty rite. Even for an exceptionally apt student, that puberty rite could not have been pleasant. Still, though it doubtless inflicted its measure of both boredom and pain, the King's New School clearly aroused and fed Will's inexhaustible craving for language.

There was another aspect of the very long school day that must have given Will pleasure. Virtually all schoolmasters agreed that one of the best ways to instill good Latin in their students was to have them read and perform ancient plays, especially the comedies of Terence and Plautus. Even the clergyman John Northbrooke, a killjoy who in 1577 published a sour attack on "dicing, dancing, vain plays or interludes with other idle pastimes," conceded that school performances of Latin plays, if suitably expurgated, were acceptable. Northbrooke stressed nervously that the plays had to be performed in the original language, not in English, that the students should not wear beautiful costumes, and, above all, that there should be no "vain and wanton toys of love." For the great danger of these plays, as the Oxford scholar John Rainolds noted, was that the plot may call for the boy who is playing the hero to kiss the boy who is playing the heroine, and that kiss may be the undoing of both children. For the kiss of a beautiful boy is like the kiss of "certain spiders": "if they do but touch men only with their mouth, they put them to wonderful pain and make them mad."

In fact it is almost impossible to expurgate Terence and Plautus: take out the disobedient children and sly servants, the parasites, tricksters, whores, and foolish fathers, the feverish pursuit of sex and money, and you have virtually nothing left. Built into the curriculum, then, was a kind of recurrent theatrical transgression, a comic liberation from the oppressive heaviness of the educational system. To partake fully of the liberation, all you needed, as a student, was a histrionic gift and enough Latin to get the point. By the time he was ten or eleven, and perhaps earlier, Will almost certainly had both.

No surviving records indicate how often the Stratford teachers during Will's school years had the boys perform plays or which plays they assigned. Perhaps there was a time, a year or so before Will left school, when the teacher—Oxford-educated Thomas Jenkins—decided to have the boys perform Plautus's frenetic farce about identical twins, *The Two Menaechmuses*. And perhaps on this occasion, Jenkins, recognizing that one of his students was precociously gifted as both a writer and an actor, assigned Will Shakespeare a leading role. There is hard evidence from later in his life that Shakespeare loved this particular play's combination of logic and dizzying confusion, the characters constantly just missing the direct encounter and the explanation that would resolve the mounting chaos. When he was a young playwright in London casting about for the plot of a comedy, he simply took over *The Two Menaechmuses*, added a second set of twins to double the chaos, and wrote *The Comedy of Errors*. The comedy was a great success: when it was performed at one of London's law schools the students rioted trying to get seats. But for the talented schoolboy in the King's New School, this future triumph would have seemed almost as implausible as the zany events depicted in the play.

In Plautus's opening scene, Menaechmus of Epidamnum squabbles with his wife and then goes off to visit his mistress, the courtesan Erotium (women's parts as well as men's would have been played by the boys in Will's class). Before Menaechmus knocks at her door, it swings open and Erotium herself appears, ravishing his senses: "Eapse eccam exit!" ("Look, she's coming out herself!"). And then in this moment of rapture—the sun is bedimmed, he exclaims, by the radiance of her lovely body—Erotium greets him: "Anime mi, Menaechme, salve!" ("My darling Menaechmus, welcome!").

This is the moment that anxious moralists like Northbrooke and Rainolds most feared and hated: the kiss of the spider boy. "Beautiful boys by kissing," writes Rainolds, "do sting and pour secretly in a kind of poison, the poison of incontinency." It is easy to laugh at this hysteria, but perhaps it is not completely absurd—on some such occasion as this, it is possible that the adolescent Shakespeare felt an intense excitement in which theatrical performance and sexual arousal were braided together.

Long before performances in school, Will may already have discovered that he had a passion for playacting. In 1569, when he was five, his father, as the bailiff—that is, the mayor—of Stratford-upon-Avon, ordered that payments be made to two companies of professional actors, the Queen's Men and the Earl of Worcester's Men, which had come to town on tour. These traveling playing companies would not have been an especially impressive sight: some six to a dozen "strowlers" carrying their costumes and props in a wagon, compelled by circumstances, as one contemporary observer wryly put it, "to travel upon the hard hoof from village to village for cheese and butter-milk." In fact the usual rewards would have been slightly more substantial—a pound or two in cold cash, if they were fortunate—but not so great as to make the players turn up their noses at whatever free cheese and buttermilk they could cadge. Yet to most small boys it would all have been unspeakably thrilling.

The arrival in provincial towns generally followed a set pattern. With a flourish of trumpets and the rattle of drums, the players swaggered down the street in their colorful liveries, scarlet cloaks, and crimson velvet caps. They proceeded to the house of the mayor and presented the letters of recommendation, with wax seals, that showed that they were not vagabonds and that a powerful patron protected them. In Stratford in 1569 they would have come to Henley Street, to the boy's own house, and they would have spoken to his father with deference, for it was he who would decide whether they would be sent packing or allowed to post their bills announcing the performances.

The first performance was known as the Mayor's Play, and it was usually free to all comers. Stratford's bailiff would certainly have been expected to attend this, for it was his privilege to determine the level of the reward to be paid out of the city coffers; he would, presumably, have been received with great respect and given one of the best seats in the guildhall, where a special stage had been erected. The excitement of this occasion was not limited to small boys: municipal records in Stratford and elsewhere routinely recorded broken windows and damage to chairs and benches caused by mobs of unruly spectators jostling for a good view.

These were festive events, breaks in the routines of everyday life. The sense of release, always bordering on transgression, was why some stern town officials occasionally turned the players away, particularly in times of dearth, sickness, or disorder, and why the players were not permitted to perform on Sundays or during Lent. But even the most puritanical mayors and aldermen had to think twice about annoying the aristocrats whose liveries the players proudly wore. After all, at the end of each performance in these country towns, the players would kneel down solemnly and ask everyone present to pray with them for their good lord and master—or, in the case of the Queen's Men, for the great Elizabeth herself. Hence, even when they were forbidden from performing, the troupes were often sent off with a gratuity, bribed in effect to go away.

John Shakespeare, the records indicate, did not send the players on their way. He permitted them to play. But would he have taken his five-year-old son to see the show? Certainly other fathers did. In his old age, a man named Willis, born the same year as Will, recalled a play (now lost), called *The Cradle of Security*, that he saw in Gloucester—thirty-eight miles from Stratford—when he was a child. On arriving in town the players, Willis wrote, followed the usual routine: they presented themselves to the mayor, informed him what nobleman's servants they were, and requested a license for performing in public. The mayor granted the license and appointed the company to give their first performance before the aldermen and other officials of the town. "At such a play," Willis remembered, "my father took me with him and made me stand between his legs, as he sat upon one of the benches, where we saw and heard very well." The experience was a remarkably intense one for Willis: "This sight took such impression in me," he wrote, "that when I came towards man's estate, it was as fresh in my memory as if I had seen it newly acted."

This is probably as close as it is possible to get to Will's own primal scene of theatricality. When the bailiff walked into the hall, everyone would have greeted him and exchanged words with him; when he took his seat, the crowd would have grown quiet in the expectation that something exciting and pleasurable was about to happen. His son, intelligent, quick, and sensitive, would have stood between his father's legs. For the first time in his life William Shakespeare watched a play.

What was the play that the Queen's Men brought to Stratford in 1569? Records do not show, and perhaps it does not matter. The sheer magic of playing—the fashioning of an imaginary space, the artful impersonations, the elaborate costumes, the flood of heightened language—may have been enough to capture the young boy forever. There was, in any case, more than one occasion for the spell to be cast. Troupes came repeatedly to Stratford—the Earl of Leicester's Men in 1573, for example, when Will was nine years old, the Earl of Warwick's Men and the Earl of Worcester's Men in 1575, when he was eleven—and each time the thrilling effect, initially enhanced by the child's sense of his father's importance and power, may have been renewed and strengthened, the clever devices stored away as treasured memories.

For his part, Shakespeare's contemporary Willis remembered all his life what he had seen at Gloucester: a king lured away from his sober, pious counselors by three seductive ladies. "In the end they got him to lie down in a cradle upon the stage," he recalled, "where these three ladies, joining in a sweet song, rocked him asleep, that he snorted again; and in the meantime closely conveyed under the cloths wherewithal he was covered, a vizard, like a swine's snout, upon his face, with three wire chains fastened thereunto, the other end whereof being holden severally by those three ladies; who fall to singing again, and then discovered his face, that the spectators might see how they had transformed him." The spectators must have found it very exciting. Some of the older ones probably remembered the swinish face of Henry VIII, and all in the audience knew that it was only under special circumstances that they could publicly share the thought that the monarch was a swine.

Young Will is likely to have seen something similar. The plays in repertory in the 1560s and '70s were for the most part "morality plays," or "moral interludes," secular sermons designed to show the terrible consequences of disobedience, idleness, or dissipation. Typically, a character—an embodied abstraction with a name like Mankind or Youth—turns away from a proper guide such as Honest Recreation or Virtuous Life and begins to spend his time with Ignorance, All-for-Money, or Riot.

> Huffa, huffa! Who calleth after me?
> I am Riot, full of jollity.
> My heart is light as the wind,
> And all on riot is my mind.
> (*The Interlude of Youth*)

It is rapidly downhill from here—Riot introduces Youth to his friend Pride; Pride introduces him to his glamorous sister Lechery; Lechery lures him to the tavern—and it looks like it will all end badly. Sometimes it does end badly—in the play Willis saw, the king who is transformed into a swine is later carried away to punishment by wicked spirits—but more typically, something happens to awaken the hero's slumbering conscience just in time. In *The Interlude of Youth*, Charity, reminding the sinner of Jesus's great gift to him, frees him from the influence of Riot and restores him to the company of Humility. In *The Castle of Perseverance*, Penance touches Mankind's heart with his lance and saves him from his wicked companions, the Seven Deadly Sins. In *Wit and Science*, the hero Wit, asleep in the lap of Idleness, is transformed into a fool, complete with cap and bells, but he is saved when he catches sight of himself in a mirror and realizes that he looks "like a very ass!" Only after he is sharply whipped by Shame and taught by a group of strict schoolmasters—Instruction, Study, and Diligence—is Wit restored to his proper appearance and able to celebrate his marriage to Lady Science.

Relentlessly didactic and often clumsily written, morality plays came to seem old-fashioned and crude—any summary of them will make them sound boring—but they were in vogue for a long period of time, extending into Shakespeare's adolescence. Their blend of high-mindedness and exuberant theatrical energy pleased an impressively broad range of spectators, from the unlettered to the most sophisticated. If these plays had little or no interest in psychological particularity or social texture, they often had the canniness of folk wisdom along with a strong current of subversive humor. That humor could take the form of a swine-snouted king, but it more often centered on the stock character known generally as the Vice. This jesting, prattling mischief-maker—bearing in different interludes names such as Riot, Iniquity, Liberty, Idleness, Misrule, Double Device, and even, in one notable instance, Hickscorner—embodied simultaneously the spirit of wickedness and the spirit of fun. The audience knew that he would in the end be defeated and driven, with blows or fireworks, from the stage. But for a time he pranced about, scorning the hicks, insulting the solemn agents of order and piety, playing tricks on the unsuspecting, plotting mischief, and luring the innocent into taverns and whorehouses. The audience loved it.

When Shakespeare sat down to write for the London stage, he drew upon those rather creaky entertainments that must have delighted him as a child. He learned from them to give many of his characters emblematic names: the whores Doll Tearsheet and Jane Nightwork and the sergeants Snare and Fang in *2 Henry IV*, the drunken Sir Toby Belch and the puritanical Malvolio ("ill will") in *Twelfth Night*. On rare occasions he went further and brought personified abstractions directly onto his stage—Rumour, in a robe painted full of tongues, in *2 Henry IV,* and Time, carrying an hourglass, in *The Winter's Tale.* But for the most part his debt to the morality plays was more indirect and subtle. He absorbed their impact early, and they helped fashion the foundations, largely hidden well beneath the surface, of his writing. That writing builds upon two crucial expectations the morality plays instilled in their audiences: first, the expectation that drama worth seeing would get at something central to human destiny and, second, that it should reach not only a coterie of the educated elite but also the great mass of ordinary people.

Shakespeare also absorbed specific elements of his stagecraft from the moralities. They helped him understand how to focus theatrical attention on his characters' psychological, moral, and spiritual life, as well as on their outward behavior. They helped him fashion physical emblems of this inner life, such as the withered arm and hunchback that mark the crookedness of Richard III. They helped him grasp how to construct plays around the struggle for the soul of a protagonist: Prince Hal poised between his sober, anxious, calculating father and the irresponsible, seductive, reckless Falstaff; the deputy Angelo, in *Measure for Measure*, given the reins of power and put to the test by his master the duke; Othello torn between his faith in the celestial Desdemona and the obscene suggestions of the demonic Iago. And above all, they provided him with a source for a theatrically compelling and subversive figure of wickedness.

The Vice, the great subversive figure of the moralities, was never far from Shakespeare's creative mind. With mingled affection and wariness, Hal refers to Falstaff as "that reverend Vice, that grey Iniquity" (*1 Henry IV*, 2.5.413); the mordantly funny, malevolent Richard III likens himself to "the formal Vice, Iniquity" (3.1.82); and Hamlet describes his wily, usurping uncle as "a vice of kings" (3.4.88). The word "vice" does not have to be directly invoked for the influence to be apparent: "Honest Iago," for example, with his air of camaraderie, his sly jokes, and his frank avowal of villainy, is heavily indebted to this figure. It is no accident that his diabolical plot against Othello and Desdemona takes the form of a practical joke, an unbearably cruel version of the tricks played by the Vice.

It may seem strange at first that the lovable Falstaff should find himself in the company of cold-hearted murderers like Claudius and Iago. But Shakespeare learned something else essential to his art from the morality plays; he learned that the boundary between comedy and tragedy is surprisingly porous. In figures such as Aaron the Moor (the black villain in *Titus Andronicus*), Richard III, and the bastard Edmund in *King Lear*, Shakespeare conjures up a particular kind of thrill he must have first had as a child watching the Vice in plays like *The Cradle of Security* and *The Interlude of Youth*: the thrill of fear braided together with transgressive pleasure. The Vice, wickedness personified, is appropriately punished at the end of the play, but for much of the performance he manages to captivate the audience, and the imagination takes a perverse holiday.

The authors of the morality plays thought they could enhance the broad impact they sought to achieve by stripping their characters of all incidental distinguishing traits to get to their essences. They thought their audiences would thereby not be distracted by the irrelevant details of individual identities. Shakespeare grasped that the spectacle of human destiny was, in fact, vastly more compelling when it was attached not to generalized abstractions but to particular named people, people realized with an unprecedented intensity of individuation: not Youth but Prince Hal, not Everyman but Othello.

To achieve this intensity, Shakespeare had as much to free himself from the old morality plays as to adapt them. He felt free to discard many aspects of them altogether and use others in ways their authors could never have imagined. At times he greatly intensified the fear: Iago is immeasurably more disturbing—and more effective—than Envy or Riot. At other times he greatly intensified the laughter: the Vice's trickery and delight in confusion turns up in Puck in *A Midsummer Night's Dream*, but the wickedness has been entirely leached away, leaving only the mischievousness. So too if the ass's head placed on Bottom strikingly recalls the swine's snout placed on the face of the king, the heavy weight of moral instruction has been entirely lifted. Bottom, to be sure, is asinine, but it takes no magical transformation to reveal that fact. Indeed, what is revealed is not so much his folly—he does not have one moment of embarrassment or shame, and his friends do not laugh at him—as his intrepidity. "This is to make an ass of me," the ass-headed Bottom stoutly declares, when his friends have all run away in terror at his appearance, "to fright me, if they could; but I will not stir from this place, do what they can" (3.1.106–8). He is surprised at the Fairy Queen's passionate declaration of love, but he takes it in his stride: "Methinks, mistress, you should have little reason for that. And yet, to say the truth, reason and love keep little company together nowadays" (3.1.126–28). And he is entirely at ease in his new body: "Methinks I have a great desire to a bottle of hay. Good hay, sweet hay, hath no fellow" (4.1.30–31). When the ass's head is finally taken from him, he does not experience a moral awakening; rather, as Puck puts it, he merely peeps at the world once again with his own fool's eyes.

Here, and throughout his career, Shakespeare altogether scrapped the piety that marked the plays he saw in his youth. The underlying structure of those plays was religious. Hence they often climaxed in a moment of vision that signaled the protagonist's redemption, a vision that pointed beyond the everyday and what was familiar to a truth that exceeded mortal understanding. In the words of St. Paul's Epistle to the Corinthians, words deeply familiar to Shakespeare and his contemporaries from endless repetitions in church, "The eye hath not seen, and the ear hath not heard, neither have entered into the heart of man" those things that God has prepared (1 Corinthians 2:9, from the Bishops' Bible [1568], the version Shakespeare knew and used most often). "I have had a most rare vision," Bottom begins, when he is returned to his human shape. And then, in a series of fits and starts, he tries to recount it:

I have had a dream past the wit of man to say what dream it was. Man is but an ass if he go about t'expound this dream. Methought I was—there is no man can tell what. Methought I was, and methought I had—but man is but a patched fool if he will offer to say what methought I had. The eye of man hath not heard, the ear of man hath not seen, man's hand is not able to taste, his tongue to conceive, nor his heart to report what my dream was. (4.1.199–207).

This is the joke of a decisively secular dramatist, a writer who deftly turned the dream of the sacred into popular entertainment: "I will get Peter Quince to write a ballad of this dream. It shall be called 'Bottom's Dream,' because it hath no bottom, and I will sing it in the latter end of a play" (4.1.207–10). The joke reaches out a long way—to the solemnities of the pulpit, to the plays that the professional playing companies took to the provinces when Shakespeare was a boy, to the amateur actors who performed cruder versions of these plays, and perhaps to the young, awkward Shakespeare himself, filled with visions his tongue could not conceive and eager to play all the parts.

There must have been many such moments in Will's life at home. The very young boy could have amused his family and friends by imitating what he had seen on the raised platform of the Stratford town-hall stage or on the back of the traveling players' cart. And as he grew older and more independent, his exposure to playacting was not restricted to Stratford: the touring companies crisscrossed the Midlands, performing in neighboring towns and manor houses. A stage-struck youth could have seen most of the great actors of the time performing within a day's ride of his home.

Theatrical life in the region by no means depended solely upon the visits of professional troupes. Towns in the vicinity of Stratford, as in the rest of the country, had seasonal festivals, when the members of guilds and fraternities donned costumes and performed in traditional plays. For an afternoon, ordinary folk—carpenters and tinkers and flute makers and the like—paraded before their neighbors as kings and queens, madmen and demons. Coventry, eighteen miles away, was particularly vital; when he was young, Will could have been taken to see the Hock Tuesday play there. The second Tuesday after Easter, Hock Tuesday traditionally initiated the summer half of the rural year and was celebrated, in many places, by women tying up passersby with ropes and demanding money for charity. In

Coventry the men and women had a special way of marking the festival: they staged a rowdy commemoration of an ancient English massacre of the Danes, an event in which Englishwomen were said to have displayed particular valor. The annual reenactment enjoyed considerable local fame and may have drawn, among its spectators, the Shakespeare family.

In late May or June, in the time of long, sweetly lingering twilights, they could also have seen one of the great annual Corpus Christi pageants, plays presenting the whole destiny of mankind from the creation and the Fall to the redemption. These so-called mystery cycles, among the great achievements of medieval drama, had survived into the later sixteenth century in Coventry and in several other cities in England. Associated originally with a grand procession to honor the Eucharist, the production of a mystery cycle was a major civic enterprise, involving large numbers of people and significant expenditure. At various places in the city, usually on specially built scaffolds or carts, a part of the cycle—the story of Noah, the angel of the Annunciation, the raising of Lazarus, Jesus on the Cross, the three Marys at the tomb, and so forth—was performed by pious (or simply exuberantly histrionic) townspeople. Particular guilds usually assumed the costs and the responsibility for the individual pieces of the cycle, at times with particular appropriateness: the shipwrights undertook Noah, the goldsmiths the Magi, the bakers the Last Supper, and the pinners (men who made pins and needles) the Crucifixion.

Protestant reformers were understandably hostile, for they wished to dismantle the traditional Catholic culture and rituals out of which these pageants arose, and they campaigned hard to put the performances to an end. But the plays were not strictly Catholic, and the civic pride and pleasure in them was intense, so they lingered, in the teeth of opposition, into the 1570s and '80s. In 1579, when Will was fifteen, he and his family could still have seen them performed at Coventry. Something of their power—their way of constructing a shared community of spectators, their confidence that all things in the heavens and the earth can be represented onstage, their delicious blending of homeliness and exaltation—left its mark upon him.

These events were particularly spectacular instances of seasonal festivities that shaped Will's sense of the year and conditioned his later understanding of the theater. Many of the traditional holidays had with-ered under attacks, both from those who thought the calendar offered working people too many occasions to play and from those who thought that particular customs were tinged with Catholicism or paganism. But the moralists and the religious reformers had not yet managed to disci-pline the festive year into relentless sobriety. "I came once to a place, rid-ing on a journey homeward from London," wrote the great Protestant bishop Hugh Latimer in 1549,

> and I sent word over night into the town that I would preach there in the morning because it was holy day. . . . The church stood in my way, and I took my horse, and my company, and went thither. I thought I should have found a great company in the church, and when I came there, the church door was fast locked. I tarried there half an hour and more, at last the key was found, and one of the parish comes to me and says: "Sir, this is a busy day with us, we cannot hear you, it is Robin Hood's Day. The parish are gone abroad to gather for Robin Hood. . . ." I was fain there to give place to Robin Hood.

A traditional May game probably kept the parish busy that day—on May Day people had long celebrated the legend of Robin Hood, with raucous, often bawdy rituals.

Thirty-four years later an irascible polemicist, Philip Stubbes, reiter-ated the complaint:

> Against May, Whitsunday, or other time, all the young men and maids, old men and wives, run gadding overnight to the woods . . . where they spend all the night in pleasant pastimes, and in the morning they return, bringing with them birch and branches of trees. . . . But the chiefest jewel they bring from thence is their Maypole, which they bring home with great veneration, as thus: they have twenty or forty yoke of oxen, every ox having a sweet nosegay of flowers placed on the tip of his horns; and these oxen draw home this Maypole (this stinking idol, rather) which is cov-

ered all over with flowers and herbs, bound round about with
strings from the top to the bottom, and sometimes painted with
variable colors, with two or three hundred men, women, and children following it with great devotion. And thus being reared up
with handkerchiefs and flags hovering on the top, they strew the
ground round about, bind green boughs about it, set up summer
halls, bowers, and arbors hard by it. And then fall they to dance
about it, like as the heathen people did at the dedication of the
idols, whereof this is a perfect pattern, or rather the thing itself.

Stubbes was writing in 1583, when Will was nineteen. Even if Stubbes
sullenly exaggerated the pervasiveness and vitality of the ancient folk customs—customs whose attractiveness comes across despite his pious horror—he was not making it up: traditional festivities, though constantly
under attack, endured throughout the late sixteenth century and beyond.

What might Will have participated in, growing up in Stratford and
its surrounding countryside? Men and women and children, their faces
flushed with pleasure, dancing around a Maypole, decked with ribbons
and garlands. A coarse Robin Hood show, with a drunken Friar Tuck and
a lascivious Maid Marion. A young woman garlanded with flowers as the
Queen of the May. A young boy dressed as the bishop and paraded
through the streets with mock gravity. A belching, farting Lord of Misrule who temporarily turned the world upside down. Topsy-turvy days
when women pursued men and schoolboys locked the teachers out of the
classroom. Torchlight processions featuring men dressed as fantastic animals, "wodewoses" (wild men), and giants. Leaping morris dancers—from
their supposed Moorish origin—with bells around their knees and ankles,
cavorting with dancers wearing the wickerwork contraption known as the
Hobbyhorse. Bagpipers, drummers, and fools dressed in motley carrying
baubles and pigs' bladders. Drinking contests, eating contests, and singing
contests at sheep-shearing and harvest-home festivals. Most interesting of
all, perhaps, at Christmastime there was the mummers' play, featuring a
madman, his five sons—Pickle Herring, Blue Breeches, Pepper Breeches,
Ginger Breeches, and Mr. Allspice—and a woman named Cicely (or, on
occasion, Maid Marion). The madman first fights with the hobbyhorse

and with a "wild worm," that is, a dragon. The sons then decide to kill their father; interlocking their swords around his neck, they force him to kneel down and make his will, before dispatching him. One of the sons, Pickle Herring, stamps his feet upon the ground and brings the father back to life. The play—or perhaps, with its seasonal occasion, primordial rhythms, and indifference to realism, it should be called a ritual—lurches toward its end with the father and sons wooing Cicely together and then with grotesque sword dances and morris dances.

These folk customs, all firmly rooted in the Midlands, had a significant impact upon Shakespeare's imagination, fashioning his sense of theater even more than the morality plays that the touring companies brought to the provinces. Folk culture is everywhere in his work, in the web of allusions and in the underlying structures. The lovers who meet in the Athenian woods in *A Midsummer Night's Dream* are reminiscent of May Day lovers; the deposed Duke Senior in the Forest of Arden in *As You Like It* is likened to Robin Hood; the drunken Sir Toby and, still more, Falstaff are Lords of Misrule who turn the order of things topsy-turvy; and, as queen of the feast, the garlanded Perdita in *The Winter's Tale* presides over a rustic sheep-shearing festival, complete with dancing swains and maidens and a sly, light-fingered peddler.

The author of *The Winter's Tale* was not a folk artist, and he made it clear in many ways that he was not. A sheep-shearing festival performed on the stage of the Globe as part of a sophisticated tragicomedy was not in fact a sheep-shearing festival; it was an urban fantasy of rural life, informed by knowing touches of realism but also carefully distanced from its homely roots. Shakespeare was a master of this distancing; if he had a sympathetic understanding of country customs, he also had ways of showing that they were no longer his native element. The Athenian lovers are not in fact in the woods to celebrate the May; Duke Senior bears no real resemblance to Robin Hood; the queen of the sheep-shearing festival is not a shepherd's daughter but the daughter of a king; and if an old, mad father becomes the object of murderous attack by his children, it is not in the grotesque comedy of the mummers' play but in the sublime tragedy of *King Lear*. No one can stamp upon the ground and make Lear or his daughter Cordelia spring back to life. Sir Toby and Falstaff come closer to the actual way in which Lords of Misrule functioned—they do for a limited time overturn sobriety, dignity, and decorum—but Shakespeare went out of his way to depict them after their disorderly reign is over: "What, is it a time to jest and dally now?" Prince Hal shouts in a rage, throwing the bottle of sack at Falstaff (*1 Henry IV*, 5.3.54). "I hate a drunken rogue," moans Sir Toby, beaten and hungover (*Twelfth Night*, 5.1.193–94).

But there was nothing defensive in the ways Shakespeare distanced himself, no stiff-necked insistence on his sophistication or learning, no self-conscious embrace of the urban or the courtly. He had deep roots in the country. Virtually all of his close relatives were farmers, and in his childhood he clearly spent a great deal of time in their orchards and market gardens, in the surrounding fields and woods, and in tiny rural hamlets with their traditional seasonal festivals and folk customs. When he was growing up, he seems to have taken in everything about this rustic world, and he did not subsequently seek to repudiate it or pass himself off as something other than what he was. The cultivated Elizabethan literary critic George Puttenham writes snobbishly of "boys or country fellows" who listened with delight to blind harpers and tavern minstrels singing old romances and who enjoyed the carols sung at Christmas dinners and at the old-fashioned wedding feasts known as bridales. Will was almost certainly one of those country fellows. He doesn't seem to have been anxious about such pleasures, though he subsequently moved in circles that laughed at their rusticity. He simply took them with him to London, as his possession, to be used as much or as little as he liked.

Shakespeare was anything but indifferent to being counted as a gentleman. But his concern for his station in life, his longing for social success, and his fascination with the lives of aristocrats and monarchs did not entail the erasure of the world from which he came. Perhaps he simply loved the world too much to give any of it up. Instead, he used his boyhood experiences—as he used virtually all of his experiences—as an inexhaustible source of metaphor.

In one of his earliest history plays, *2 Henry VI* (written around 1591), Shakespeare has the ambitious, conniving Duke of York explain that he has lured the headstrong Kentish peasant Jack Cade into rebellion. "In

Ireland have I seen this stubborn Cade" fight against a troop of soldiers,
York remarks,

> And fought so long till that his thighs with darts
> Were almost like a sharp-quilled porcupine;
> And in the end, being rescued, I have seen
> Him caper upright like a wild Morisco,
> Shaking the bloody darts as he his bells.
>
> (3.1.360, 362–66)

Shakespeare himself had in all likelihood not served in the wars and had
never seen a soldier's thighs pierced with arrows, but, as a country boy, he
had certainly seen his share of spiny hedgehogs and, as an adult, he may
have seen the porcupine that Queen Elizabeth kept in her small
menagerie near the Tower. He had also almost certainly seen his share of
morris dancers—"wild Moriscos"—leaping about in a kind of ecstasy.
From such sights he constructed his astonishing image of the unstoppable Cade. More important, from the accumulation of such sights and
sounds and rituals he constructed his sense of the magic of the theater.

But it was not only these traditional folk rituals, with their illusory
but compelling air of timelessness, that exercised a powerful imaginative
influence upon him; a particular event in his neighborhood, widely noted
at the time, seems to have strongly marked his vision of the theater. In the
summer of 1575, when Will was eleven, the queen had gone to the Midlands on one of her royal progresses—journeys, accompanied by an enormous retinue, on which, bejeweled like a Byzantine icon, she displayed
herself to her people, surveyed her realm, received tributes; and all but
bankrupted her hosts. Elizabeth, who had already visited the area in 1566
and again in 1572, was the supreme mistress of these occasions, at once
thrilling and terrifying those who encountered her. In 1572 she was
greeted officially by the Recorder of Warwick, Edward Aglionby, a local
dignitary whom the Shakespeares would probably have known. Aglionby
was a learned and imposing figure, but in the presence of the queen he
trembled. "Come hither, little Recorder," the queen said, holding out her
hand for him to kiss. "It was told me that you would be afraid to look

upon me or to speak so boldly; but you were not so afraid as I was of you."
No one, least of all the "little Recorder" himself, would have believed that
polite fiction from the daughter of Henry VIII.

The climax of the 1575 progress was a nineteen-day stay—from July
9 to 27—at Kenilworth, the castle of the queen's favorite Robert Dudley,
the Earl of Leicester. Kenilworth is located some twelve miles northeast
of Stratford, which would have been caught up, like the entire region, in
the feverish preparations for the visit. John Shakespeare, a Stratford
alderman at the time, was too insignificant a figure to have got very close,
in all likelihood, to the elaborate entertainments that were staged for the
queen by the man she called her "eyes," but it is certainly conceivable that
he took his son Will to glimpse what they could of the spectacles: the
grand arrival of the queen, greeted with speeches by Sibylla, Hercules, the
Lady of the Lake, and (in Latin) an emblematic poet; fireworks; a dialogue between a Savage Man and Echo; a bearbaiting (a "sport" in which
mastiffs attacked a bear chained to a stake); more fireworks; a display of
acrobatics by an Italian; and an elaborate water pageant.

Leicester, whose hold on the queen's favor had been slipping and who
clearly regarded this as an occasion on which nothing should be omitted
that might conceivably bring her pleasure, also arranged for a set of rustic
shows. The shows were the equivalent of the mock-authentic cultural performances done in our own time for visiting dignitaries or wealthy tourists;
they included a bridale and morris dance, a quintain (a sport of tilting at
targets), and the traditional Coventry Hock Tuesday play. These folk entertainments were of the kind that had been attacked by moralists and strict
reformers, as Leicester understood perfectly well. He also understood that
the queen took pleasure in them, was hostile to their puritanical critics, and
would be sympathetic to an appeal to allow them to continue.

Will may have watched these pieces of his own local culture staged
for the grand visitors. He would at the very least have heard the events
described in loving detail, and he is also likely to have encountered an
elaborate written description of them in a marvelous long letter by a
minor official— "clerk of the council chamber door"—Robert Langham,
or Laneham. The letter, inexpensively printed and widely circulated,
would have been useful reading for anyone who was in the business of

trying to entertain the queen—and Shakespeare was shortly to go into that business.

Langham's letter makes clear that the performance of the Hock Tuesday play was a carefully stage-managed piece of cultural politics. Certain "good-hearted men of Coventry," led by a mason named Captain Cox, had learned that their neighbor, the Earl of Leicester, was entertaining the queen. Knowing that he was eager to make his sovereign "gladsome and merry" with all pleasant recreations, the Coventry artisans petitioned that they might renew their old show. They thought that the queen would particularly enjoy the commemoration of the ancient massacre because it showed "how valiantly our English women for love of their country behaved themselves." This appeal to the queen's special interest was part of a defensive strategy that Langham conveniently summarizes: "The thing, said they, is grounded on story, and for pastime wont to be played in our city yearly, without ill example of manners, papistry, or any superstition, and else did so occupy the heads of a number that likely enough would have had worse meditations." The claims here turn out to be ones that would be repeated again and again throughout Shakespeare's lifetime, both in the justification of particular plays and in defense of the stage in general: the play in question is based on history ("grounded on story"), it is a traditional form of entertainment, it is free from ideological contamination and immorality, and it is a distraction from potentially dangerous thoughts, "worse meditations." That is, members of the audience who might otherwise be plotting mischief—brooding on injustice, for example, or longing for the old religion, or hatching rebellion—would have their minds safely occupied by the spectacle of the ancient massacre of the Danes.

What was the problem, then? Why did the Hock Tuesday play, which had "an ancient beginning and a long continuance," need to be defended at all? Because, the artisans acknowledged, it had been "of late laid down"— that is, banned. The men scratched their heads and said they could not quite understand it: "They knew no cause why." Then, as if it suddenly occurred to them, they came up with an explanation: "unless it were by the zeal of certain of their preachers, men very commendable for behavior and learning, and sweet in their sermons, but somewhat too sour in preaching away their pastime." The performance at Kenilworth, then, was not simply a way of amusing the queen; or rather, in any attempt to amuse the queen there was always a half-hidden agenda. Here the agenda was to get the queen to pressure the local clergy to halt the campaign against a beloved local festivity: "they would make their humble petition unto her highness that they might have their plays up again."

Despite the careful planning for the Hock Tuesday performance—the show took place directly below the queen's window—the occasion was botched. Too many things were going on at once—the bridale and the dancing drew away the queen's attention, and she was further distracted by "the great throng and unruliness" of the crowd that had been allowed into the courtyard (into which an eleven-year-old boy may have made his way). Elizabeth managed to see only a bit of the play. After all their rehearsals and strategizing, the men of Coventry must have been crushed. But then, unexpectedly, all was saved—the queen commanded that the performance be repeated on the following Tuesday. It was a success: "Her Majesty laughed well." The town players, rewarded with two bucks upon which to feast and with five pieces of silver, were ecstatic: "What, rejoicing upon their ample reward, and what, triumphing upon the good acceptance, they vaunted their play was never so dignified, nor ever any players afore so beatified." And in the Coventry records for the next year there is a crucial confirmation of their triumph: "Thomas Nicklyn Mayor. . . . This year the said mayor caused Hock Tuesday, whereby is mentioned an overthrow of the Danes by the inhabitants of this city, to be again set up and showed forth."

"Her Majesty laughed well." Said to have cost Leicester the staggering sum of a thousand pounds a day, the Kenilworth festivities were an enormous machine designed to produce those laughs—along with admiration, wonder, and delight—from the remarkable, unpredictable, dangerous woman who ruled the country. The spectacles were elaborate and arresting, but the attention of the Earl of Leicester—and no doubt of many others in the crowd—would have been intensely focused on a single person. If a wide-eyed young boy from Stratford did see her, arrayed in one of her famously elaborate dresses, carried in a litter on the shoulders of guards specially picked for their good looks, accompanied by her gorgeously arrayed courtiers, he would in effect have witnessed the greatest theatrical spectacle of the age. As the queen once candidly remarked of herself, "We princes are set on stages in the sight and view of all the world."

Shakespeare continued to be fascinated throughout his entire career by the charismatic power of royalty—the excitement awakened in crowds, the trembling in otherwise strong men, the sense of awesome greatness. Long after he had come to understand the dark sides of this power; long after he had taken in the pride, cruelty, and ambition that it aroused, the dangerous plots that it bred, the greed and violence that it fostered and fed upon, Shakespeare remained in touch with the intoxicating pleasure and excitement royalty aroused. At the close of his creative life, in the play originally called *All Is True* and known today as *Henry VIII*, he still drew on this excitement, imagining the birth of the radiant queen whom he may have first glimpsed at Kenilworth in 1575. For there *was* a first time that he glimpsed her—if not at Kenilworth, then somewhere else, in a procession or a grand entertainment or a court reception—and his imagination was certainly fired by what he saw. And the events at Kenilworth, whether young Will saw them for himself or listened to eyewitness accounts of them or simply read Langham's letter, seem to have left traces in his work.

In the single most extravagant entertainment Leicester staged for the queen during her long stay, a twenty-four-foot-long mechanical dolphin rose up out of the waters of the lake adjacent to the castle. On the back of the dolphin—in whose belly was concealed a consort of wind instruments—sat the figure of Arion, the legendary Greek musician, who sang, as Langham put it, "a delectable ditty" to the queen. "The ditty in metre so aptly endited to the matter," Langham recalled,

> and after by voice so deliciously delivered; the song by a skilful artist into its parts so sweetly sorted; each part in its instrument so clean and sharply touched; every instrument again in its kind so excellently tunable; and this in the evening of the day, resounding from the calm waters, where presence of her Majesty and longing to listen had utterly damped all noise and din; the whole harmony conveyed in time, tune, and temper thus incomparably melodious. With what pleasure . . . with what sharpness of conceit, with what

lively delight this might pierce into the hearers' hearts, I pray you imagine yourself as you may, for so God judge me, by all the wit and cunning I have, I cannot express, I promise you.

Years later, Shakespeare seems to have remembered this luminous spectacle in *Twelfth Night*, when the sea captain tries to reassure Viola that her brother may not have drowned in the shipwreck: "like Arion on the dolphin's back," he tells her, "I saw him hold acquaintance with the waves" (1.2.14–15).

More strikingly, in *A Midsummer Night's Dream* (written in the mid-1590s, when Shakespeare was about thirty), the playwright's imagination drew on the scene at Kenilworth in crafting a gorgeous compliment to Elizabeth. The queen probably attended one of the early performances of the comedy—perhaps the earliest, if, as many scholars think, it was written for an aristocratic wedding that she graced with her presence—and the company obviously felt that a piece of flattery was called for. But Shakespeare did not simply break the illusion and have the players turn to address the queen. Instead, he slipped in a passage of prince-pleasing mythology that takes the form of a memory. The memory—of an occasion when Cupid took aim at the "fair vestal thronèd by the west" (2.1.158)—clearly alludes to Leicester's attempt, some twenty years earlier, to charm the queen. "Thou rememb'rest," the Fairy king Oberon asks his principal assistant, Puck,

> Since once I sat upon a promontory
> And heard a mermaid on a dolphin's back
> Uttering such dulcet and harmonious breath
> That the rude sea grew civil at her song
> And certain stars shot madly from their spheres
> To hear the sea-maid's music?
>
> (2.1.148–54)

It is worth reading the last three lines aloud for oneself to see how perfectly they serve as an exquisite instance of "dulcet and harmonious breath." Eerily beautiful, they conjure up, across the gap in time, the fireworks visible from afar—as far as twenty miles away, according to one observer—along with a fantastical version of the water pageant. The speech goes on to bow graciously toward the aging Elizabeth's cult of virginity: Cupid's arrow missed its mark, and "the imperial vot'ress passèd on, / In maiden meditation, fancy-free" (2.1.163–64). Having delivered this exquisite compliment to the queen, the play resumes its momentarily suspended plot. The arrow intended for the fair vestal, Oberon explains to Puck, fell instead on a little western flower. When placed on the eyelids of a sleeping man or woman, the juice of this flower will make the person dote on the next live creature that he or she sees. It is this device, love juice, mistakenly applied to the wrong eyelids, that occasions the wild confusions of the play.

The glimpse of the dolphin's back is only an isolated moment in *A Midsummer Night's Dream*, a decorative flourish. But the lines about the mermaid's song, though irrelevant to the plot, speak to something deeply important in the play and in the playwright's imagination. The memory of Kenilworth served to evoke the power that song has to create hushed order and to excite an almost frenzied attention. This paradox—art as the source both of settled calm and of deep disturbance—was central to Shakespeare's entire career. As a dramatist and a poet, he was simultaneously the agent of civility and the agent of subversion. This double vision in him might well reach back to the astonishing spectacle, mounted close to his home when he was eleven years old: a huge, restive sea of spectators quieted by the queen's presence, with everyone straining intently to listen to the song of Arion, the primordial poet.

What Shakespeare articulated in *A Midsummer Night's Dream* was a deep cultural fantasy that Leicester's entertainments extravagantly tried to embody. The fantasy was of a world of magical beauty, shot through with hidden forces and producing a free-floating, intense erotic energy to which all creatures, save one alone—the "fair vestal thronèd by the west"—had to succumb. Reality could never have approached this dream: the fireworks were hardly stars starting from their spheres; there was no sea, only an unruly crowd by the castle lake; the fair vestal was a middle-aged woman with rotting teeth; the mechanical dolphin would have looked no better than expensive floats usually look; and the figure on the dolphin's back was neither Arion nor a mermaid but a singer named Harry Goldingham. As an unpublished contemporary account of the festivities relates, the singer was not in good voice:

> There was a Spectacle presented to Queen Elizabeth upon the water, and amongst others, Harry Goldingham was to represent Arion upon the Dolphin's back, but finding his voice to be very hoarse and unpleasant when he came to perform it, he tears off his Disguise, and swears he was none of Arion, not he, but even honest Harry Goldingham; which blunt discovery pleased the Queen better than if it had gone through in the right way.

The queen's gracious response managed to salvage the enchantment of the afternoon, even in the face of its apparent crumbling. Something similar could be said about any production of *A Midsummer Night's Dream*: the spectators do not see fairies flying through the moonlit woods near Athens; they see a troupe of all-too-human actors tramping about onstage. But the risk of disillusionment only seems to enhance the experience of wonder.

Leicester got the effect he wanted by means of an enormous capital outlay. Shakespeare offered a vastly less expensive magic: the players in *A Midsummer Night's Dream* entertain the wild hope that they might be rewarded with a pension of sixpence per day apiece. For the playwright relied not on elaborate machinery but on language, simply the most beautiful language any English audience had ever heard:

> I know a bank where the wild thyme blows,
> Where oxlips and the nodding violet grows,
> Quite overcanopied with luscious woodbine,
> With sweet musk-roses, and with eglantine.
> There sleeps Titania sometime of the night,
> Lulled in these flowers with dances and delight.
>
> (2.1.249–54)

Shakespeare, who had already written such plays as *The Taming of the Shrew* and *Richard III*, was capable of a very different kind of dramatic speech, altogether tougher and leaner, but in *A Midsummer Night's Dream* he gave full scope to what is, to borrow one of the adjectives he uses here, luscious poetry.

Among Shakespeare's plays, *A Midsummer Night's Dream* is one of the very few for which scholars have never located a dominant literary source; its vision of moonlit, fairy-haunted woods evidently sprang from more idiosyncratic and personal imaginative roots. Shakespeare was able to tap into his close-up knowledge of "the barky fingers of the elm" or "a red-hipped humble-bee on the top of a thistle" (4.1.41, 11–12). He was also, if this account of his childhood is correct, able to tap into firsthand experiences of the swirling delights of May Day and Hock Tuesday and into memories of the lavish, visionary entertainments Leicester staged in order to please his royal guest.

If Shakespeare's sense of the transforming power of theatrical illusions may be traced back to what he heard about or saw for himself in 1575 at Kenilworth, his sense of the coarse reality that lies beneath the illusions may very well go back to the same festive moment. Virtually the whole last act of *A Midsummer Night's Dream* is given over to a hilarious parody of such amateur theatrical entertainments, which are ridiculed for their plodding ineptitude, their naïveté, their failure to sustain a convincing illusion. The Hock Tuesday play, performed by the Coventry artisans for the queen and her courtiers, is transmuted into "A tedious brief scene of young Pyramus / And his love Thisbe: very tragical mirth" (5.1.56–57), performed by the Athenian artisans for the highborn couples joining in wedlock. The newlyweds, and the audience of *A Midsummer Night's Dream*, take pleasure in laughing at the grotesque absurdities of the play and the spectacular incompetence of the players, "Hard-handed men that work in Athens here, / Which never laboured in their minds till now" (5.1.72–73). One of the blundering artisans in *A Midsummer Night's Dream*, Snug the Joiner, even seems to mimic Harry Goldingham's "blunt discovery" of his actual identity. The dim-witted Snug, cast as a lion, has from the start been worried about the role, and all of the players are concerned that he will frighten the ladies. Hence, when he plays his part, he pulls a Harry Goldingham:

> You, ladies, you whose gentle hearts do fear
>> The smallest monstrous mouse that creeps on floor,
> May now perchance both quake and tremble here
>> When lion rough in wildest rage doth roar.
> Then know that I as Snug the joiner am
> A lion fell. . . .
>
> (5.1.214–19)

Sure enough, the comic ineptitude pleases the ruler. "A very gentle beast," says Duke Theseus, "and of a good conscience" (5.1.222). The performance gets what these performances always longed to get: the smile of the great. "Her Majesty laughed well."

A Midsummer Night's Dream—written some twenty years after the Kenilworth festivities—marks the adult playwright's access to some of the most memorable scenes of his childhood, and at the same time it marks the distance he had traveled from home. By 1595, Shakespeare clearly grasped that his career was built on a triumph of the professional London entertainment industry over traditional amateur performances. His great comedy was a personal celebration of escape as well as of mastery. Escape from what? From tone-deaf plays, like Thomas Preston's *A Lamentable Tragedy, Mixed Full of Pleasant Mirth, Containing the Life of Cambises, King of Persia*, whose lame title Shakespeare parodied. From coarse language and jog trotting meter and rant pretending to be passion. From amateur actors too featherbrained to remember their lines, too awkward to perform gracefully, too shy to perform energetically, or, worst of all, too puffed up with vanity to perform anything but their own grotesque egotism. The troupe of artisans who perform "Pyramus and Thisbe"—the weaver Nick Bottom, the bellows-mender Francis Flute, the tinker Tom Snout, the joiner Snug, the tailor Robin Starveling, and their director, the carpenter Peter Quince—are collectively an anthology of theatrical catastrophes.

The laughter in act 5 of *A Midsummer Night's Dream*—and it is one of the most enduringly funny scenes Shakespeare ever wrote—is built on a sense of superiority in intelligence, training, cultivation, and skill. The audience is invited to join the charmed circle of the upper-class mockers onstage. This mockery proclaimed the young playwright's definitive passage from naïveté and homespun amateurism to sophisticated taste and professional skill. But the laughter that the scene solicits is curiously tender and even loving. What saves the scene of ridicule from becoming too painful, what keeps it delicious in fact, is the self-possession of the artisans. In the face of open derision, they are unflappable. Shakespeare achieved a double effect. On the one hand, he mocked the amateurs, who fail to grasp the most basic theatrical conventions, by which they are to stay in their roles and pretend they cannot see or hear their audience. On the other hand, he conferred an odd, unexpected dignity upon Bottom and his fellows, a dignity that contrasts favorably with the sardonic rudeness of the aristocratic spectators.

Even as he called attention to the distance between himself and the rustic performers, then, Shakespeare doubled back and signaled a current of sympathy and solidarity. As when borrowing from the old morality plays and folk culture, he understood at once that he was doing something quite different and that he owed a debt. The professions he assigned the Athenian artisans were not chosen at random—Shakespeare's London theater company depended on joiners and weavers, carpenters and tailors—and the tragedy they perform, of star-crossed lovers, fatal errors, and suicides, is one in which the playwright himself was deeply interested. In the period he was writing the "Pyramus and Thisbe" parody, Shakespeare was also writing the strikingly similar *Romeo and Juliet*; they may well have been on his writing table at the same time. A more defensive artist would have scrubbed harder in an attempt to remove these marks of affinity, but Shakespeare's laughter was not a form of renunciation or concealment. "This is the silliest stuff that ever I heard," Hippolyta comments, to which Theseus replies, "The best in this kind are but shadows, and the worst are no worse if imagination amend them." "It must be your imagination, then, and not theirs," is her rejoinder (5.1.207–10)—the spectators' imagination and not the players'—but that is precisely the point: the difference between the professional actor and the amateur actor is not, finally, the crucial consideration. They both rely upon the imagination of the spectators. And, as if to clinch the argument, a moment later, at the preposterous suicide speech of Pyramus—

> Approach, ye furies fell.
>   O fates, come, come,
>   Cut thread and thrum,
>   Quail, crush, conclude, and quell
>   (5.1.273–76)

—Hippolyta finds herself unaccountably moved: "Beshrew my heart, but I pity the man" (5.1.279).

When in *A Midsummer Night's Dream* the thirty-year-old Shakespeare, drawing deeply upon his own experiences, thought about his profession, he split the theater between a magical, virtually nonhuman element, which he associated with the power of the imagination to lift itself away from the constraints of reality, and an all-too-human element, which he associated with the artisans' trades that actually made the material structures—buildings, platforms, costumes, musical instruments, and the like—structures that gave the imagination a local habitation and a name. He understood, and he wanted the audience to understand, that the theater had to have both, both the visionary flight and the solid, ordinary earthiness.

That earthiness was a constituent part of his creative imagination. He never forgot the provincial, everyday world from which he came or the ordinary face behind the mask of Arion.

CHAPTER 2

The Dream of Restoration

A STRATFORD LEGEND, recorded around 1680 by the eccentric, gossipy biographer John Aubrey, held that Will Shakespeare, apprenticed to be a butcher like his father, occasionally took a turn at slaughtering the animals: "When he killed a calf, he would do it in a high style, and make a speech." The inquisitive Aubrey, trying to find out how young Shakespeare solved the problem of work and discovered his vocation, wanted to know what happened between the time that he left school, presumably at some point in the late 1570s or early 1580s, and the time, in the early 1590s, that he was first noted as a professional actor and playwright in London.

The mystery of what Shakespeare was up to in what scholars have dubbed the "Lost Years"—the years when he dropped from sight and left no traces in the documents of a notably record-keeping society—has generated mountains of speculation. Legends, some more or less plausible, began to emerge about seventy-five years after his death, that is, when those who could possibly have known him personally had all died off but people were still alive who could, in their younger years, have encountered his contemporaries and sought out information about him.

Though Aubrey's story about butchery is implausible—John Shakespeare was not a butcher and would not have been permitted by trade regulation to slaughter animals—it is a safe bet that from boyhood on Will had helped his father in the family business, the making and selling of gloves from the shop that occupied part of the family's handsome double house on Henley Street.

No doubt he wrote poems in his spare moments, but his family would hardly have toiled to subsidize his idleness. Paper was expensive. A pack of paper that, neatly folded and cut, yielded about fifty small sheets would have cost at least fourpence, or the equivalent of eight pints of ale, more than a pound of raisins, a pound of mutton and a pound of beef, two dozen eggs, or two loaves of bread. Perhaps young Will carved his verses, like Orlando in *As You Like It*, on trees. All the same, he would have been expected to work. Indeed, there is an odd trace of the kind of contribution to the glove trade his special talents as a poet offered. Alexander Aspinall came to Stratford in 1582 to be master at the King's New School, shortly after Will had finished his schooling there but when his younger brothers presumably were in attendance. In the seventeenth century, someone wrote down in a commonplace book—a notebook in which it was customary to record memorable or curious things—verses that accompanied a pair of gloves sent by Master Aspinall to the woman he was then courting:

> The gift is small, the will is all.
> Alexander Aspinall

The gloves were presumably bought at John Shakespeare's shop, for the posy was noted as a trace of the famous poet: "Shaxpaire upon a pair of gloves that master sent to his mistress." Instead of making a career writing plays, Will could have stayed at home and eked out a living as the writer of personalized jingles into which he slyly inserted his own name.

He did not, in fact, leave it all completely behind: gloves, skins, and leather show up frequently in the plays, in ways that seem to reflect an easy intimacy with the trade. Romeo longs to be a glove on Juliet's hand, so that he could touch her cheek. The peddler in *The Winter's Tale* has scented gloves in his pack "as sweet as damask roses" (4.4.216). "Is not parchment," asks Hamlet, "made of sheepskins?" "Ay, my lord," replies Horatio, "and of calf-skins too" (5.1.104–5). The officer in *The Comedy of Errors* wears a calf-skin uniform—he resembles "a bass viol in a case of leather" (4.3.22); Petruchio, in *The Taming of the Shrew*, has a bridle made of sheep's leather; the cobbler in *Julius Caesar* resoles shoes made of neat's leather; tinkers, according to *The Winter's Tale*, carry sow-skin bags. When Shakespeare wanted to convey the fantastical world of the fairies in *A Midsummer Night's Dream*, he played with miniaturized versions of this trade: the "enamelled skin" shed by snakes is "wide enough to wrap a fairy in," and the Fairy Queen's followers war with bats "for their leathern wings / To make my small elves coats" (2.1.255–56, 2.2.4–5).

For Shakespeare, leather was not only a means of providing vivid detail but also the stuff of metaphor; it evidently came readily to mind when he was putting together his world. "A sentence is but a cheverel glove to a good wit," quips the clown Feste in *Twelfth Night*, remarking on the ease with which language can been twisted, "how quickly the wrong side may be turned outward" (3.1.10–12). Young Will, assisting his father in the glover's shop, no doubt observed the qualities of good "cheverel"—fine kidskin valued for its elasticity and pliability—and they made a strong impression on him: "O, here's a wit of cheverel," Mercutio teases Romeo, "that stretches from an inch narrow to an ell broad [big stretch: an ell was forty-five inches]" (*Romeo and Juliet*, 2.3.72–73). "Your soft cheveril conscience," the reluctant Anne Boleyn is told in *Henry VIII*, would receive the king's gifts, "If you might please to stretch it" (2.3.32–33).

John Shakespeare bought and sold wool as well as leather. Here he was violating the laws that restricted this business to authorized wool merchants. But the illegal trade, called wool brogging, was potentially lucrative, and he had the range of contracts both in the town and in the countryside to make it seem worth the risk. To make his deals, John would have had to travel to sheep pens and rural markets, and he is likely to have taken his eldest son with him. Here too Will's imagination seems to have borne the imprint long after. We are constantly "handling our ewes," says the shepherd in *As You Like It*, explaining why he and his fellows do not kiss their hands in the manner of courtiers, "and their fells, you know, are greasy" (3.2.46–47). And when the rustic in *The Winter's Tale* carefully reckons how much his shearing is likely to bring, he uses terms—"wether," meaning a castrated ram; "tod," meaning twenty-eight pounds of wool—that Will would have heard as a child at his father's side: "Let me see. Every / 'leven wether tods, every tod yields pound and odd shilling. Fifteen hundred shorn, what comes the wool to?" (4.3.30–32). When in the nineteenth century the wing of the house that had served as John Shakespeare's shop needed a new floor, fragments of wool were found embedded in the soil beneath the floorboards.

Other traces of the shop on Henley Street and the surrounding countryside are preserved in the plays and poems. A legal document, dated three years before Will's birth in 1564, describes his father as an "agricola," Latin for farmer. Long after he settled in Stratford, John Shakespeare not only dealt in agricultural commodities but also continued to buy and lease farmland around Stratford. Will must have been out in the country with his father and his mother all the time. (An inhabitant of Elizabethan Stratford, a town with only some two thousand inhabitants, was, in any case, only a short stroll away from the surrounding farms and woods.) One of the most beautiful and appealing aspects of his imagination is the ease, delicacy, and precision with which he enters into the lives of animals and describes the vagaries of the weather, the details of flowers and herbs, and the cycles of nature. He enters deftly as well into the business cycles of nature. "I am shepherd to another man," says Corin in *As You Like It*, explaining to his visitors why he cannot offer them hospitality, "And do not shear the fleeces that I graze." This is not an urban fantasy of shepherds piping melodies on oaten flutes, but an altogether more realistic world. "My master is of churlish disposition," the shepherd adds.

> Besides, his cot, his flocks, and bounds of feed
> Are now on sale, and at our sheepcote now
> By reason of his absence there is nothing
> That you will feed on.
>
> (2.4.73–75, 78–81)

Though he had intimate knowledge of the country—he had seen the inside of a shepherd's "cot" (cottage) and knew that the grazing rights, the "bounds of feed," would have been sold along with the flocks— William Shakespeare was not essentially a countryman, nor, despite his origins, was his father. Indeed, the son was powerfully struck less by his father's rural wisdom than by his moneylending, for which he was twice taken to court in 1570, and by his property transactions, the real-world model for the maps, deeds, and conveyances that figure so frequently in the plays. The core biographical records of the poet's adult life are real estate documents. Biographers have often lamented the plethora of these documents in the place of something more intimate, but Shakespeare's lifelong interest in property investments—so unlike that of his fellow playwrights—may be more intimate a revelation than has been readily understood to be.

Will's early years, in any case, must have been strongly marked by his father's impressive entrepreneurial energy and ambition. John Shakespeare, the son of a tenant farmer from the small village of Snitterfield, was rising in the world. In the late 1550s he had made his first decisive move upward by wedding Mary Arden, the daughter of the man from whom his father had rented land. The Arden name was itself a significant piece of social capital: the family was one of Warwickshire's most distinguished, tracing its lineage back to the Domesday Book, the great record of property holdings compiled for William the Conqueror in 1086. The Arden properties occupy four long columns in that record, and the great expanse of forest to the north and west of Stratford was still in Shakespeare's time known as the Forest of Arden.

Mary's father, Robert, was by no means a prominent member of this family; he was simply a prosperous farmer who kept seven cows, eight oxen for the plough, two bullocks, and four weaning calves. If the inventory made at the time of his death is any indication, the household had no table knives, forks, or crockery—domestic signs of social distinction in a period when ordinary folk ate with their fingers from wooden plates— and owned no books. In the Arden household, the most visible marks of culture were "painted cloths" —the low-cost equivalent of tapestries, typically captioned with sententious mottoes—of which the inventory lists two in the hall, five in the chamber, and four in the bedroom. (When he wrote *The Rape of Lucrece,* Shakespeare ironically recalled their homely lessons: "Who fears a sentence or an old man's saw / Shall by a painted cloth be kept in awe.") It is not clear that anyone in the household could read the mottoes on their painted cloths; perhaps they simply liked the effect of the writing on the walls.

In a world that took kinship seriously, it meant something to be related, if only distantly, to such a distinguished and wealthy man as Edward Arden of Park Hall, the great house near Birmingham. Arden was a name for anyone with social ambition to conjure with, and a name was by no means all the riches that Mary's dowry held. Though she was the youngest of eight daughters, Mary was her father's favorite. When he died in 1556—commending his soul, like a good Catholic, "to Almighty God, and to our blessed Lady Saint Mary, and to all the holy company of heaven"—he left his youngest daughter a tidy sum of money and his most valuable property, a farm called Asbies in the village of Wilmcote, along with other lands. John Shakespeare married well.

There is no record of precisely when John decided to leave the farm in Snitterfield and move to Stratford, where he must have apprenticed himself to a glover, but his neighbors were quick to recognize his virtues. In 1556, when he was still in his twenties, he was elected an ale-taster for the borough, one of the inspectors of bread and ale. The position was for people deemed "able and discreet," who would not "let for favor or for hatred but do even right and punish as their minds and consciences would serve." In the following years he held a steady succession of municipal offices: constable, in 1558–59 (responsible for keeping the peace); affeeror (responsible for fixing fines not set by statute); chamber-lain, from 1561 to 1565 (responsible for the property of the corporation, including collecting revenues and paying debts and overseeing building repairs and alterations); alderman, in 1565; bailiff, in 1568–69; and chief alderman, in 1571.

This is the record of an impressively solid citizen and a locally dis-tinguished public man, someone liked and trusted. In the patriarchal world of Tudor Stratford none of these positions was taken lightly. The constables in the year John Shakespeare served struggled to maintain order at a time of intense suspicion and the risk of communal violence between Catholics and Protestants. The aldermen looked into the lives of residents who were said to be living "immorally"; they could order the arrest of servants who had left their masters or apprentices who ventured out of doors after the curfew hour of 9 P.M.; they decided whether a wife who was said to be a "scold" should be tied to the "cucking stool" and ducked in the waters of the Avon. And the Elizabethan bailiff had powers that are hardly conveyed by our notion of a mayor: no one could receive a stranger into his house without the bailiff's permission. Several of John Shakespeare's offices involved regular contact with the magnates of the region: the lord of the manor, the Earl of Warwick, whose ancestors had held Stratford as a feudal fiefdom in the Middle Ages; wealthy gentlemen like Sir Thomas Lucy, who entertained the queen at his house in nearby Charlecote; the influential and learned bishop of Worcester, Edwin Sandys. Stratford was not directly ruled by any of these imposing figures; it was an independent town, having been incorporated as a royal borough in 1553. But the big men exercised considerable power as well as prestige, and local officials would have had to possess great skills of tact and cunning in order to uphold their rights. John Shakespeare must have been good at the task; he would not otherwise have been entrusted with his offices.

Then, around the time Will reached his thirteenth year, things began to turn sour for his buoyant, successful father. One of the fourteen aldermen of Stratford, John Shakespeare had been marked absent from council meetings only once in thirteen years. Abruptly, beginning in 1577, he ceased to attend meetings. He must have had very good friends on the council, for they repeatedly exempted him from fines, reduced his assessments, and kept his name on the roster. At one time he had given generously to the poor, but now his situation had changed. When in 1578 the corporation voted to levy every alderman fourpence per week for poor relief, "Mr John Shaxpeare" among the sitting aldermen was exempted. The exemption was an exceptional gesture of kindness—not all aldermen in financial difficulties were treated with comparable consideration. It was repeated when he was given an extremely low assessment for the expenses of equipping the town's constabulary: four men with bills, three men with pikes, and one man with a bow and arrow. There must have been something unusually appealing and useful about the man, something that kept his colleagues hoping that he would somehow or other right himself and return to public affairs. But still he did not resume attending meetings, and still he seems to have had difficulty paying his dues, even the reduced levies. Finally, in 1586, after years of nonattendance, Shakespeare's name was struck from the roll; he had by that time ceased to be a person who counted for much in Stratford. His public career had ended, and his private situation had clearly deteriorated.

John Shakespeare needed money. He needed it urgently enough by November 1578 to do what Elizabethan families dreaded and resisted doing: he sold and mortgaged property. And not just any property: in a few years' time he disposed of virtually all of his wife's inheritance. Piece by piece, in exchange for ready cash, the properties she brought to the marriage slipped through the fingers of her improvident husband. An interest in land in Snitterfield, where his father had farmed, was sold for four pounds; Asbies was let for a nominal rent, presumably in exchange for a payment up front; and in 1579 another house and fifty-six acres at Wilmcote were mortgaged for forty pounds to his wife's brother-in-law, Edmund Lambert, of Barton-on-the-Heath. This cash evidently vanished quite quickly. When the borrowed money came due the next year, John was unable to repay it, and the property was lost. Years later, he twice sued to try to get the land back, claiming that he had in fact proffered payment, but the courts found for Lambert. All Will's mother, Mary, had left of what she brought to the marriage was the Arden name.

The most striking glimpse of John Shakespeare's financial situation is provided by evidence of the inquisitive eyes of the queen's officers. The government was anxious to enforce religious uniformity. Though the queen had declared that she did not want to rip open each individual's soul and inquire into private beliefs, she wanted to pressure as many of her subjects as she could to observe at least the outward forms of official Protestant belief. Once a month at a minimum, everyone was expected to attend Sunday services of the Church of England, services in which the Protestant Book of Common Prayer would be used and in which the ministers would deliver one of the homilies, or state-sponsored sermons, written by the central religious authorities. People who broke the law requiring regular church attendance were subject to fines and other punishments. The fines were relatively small and manageable until 1581; thereafter, in the wake of a systematic crackdown on religious dissidents, they became astronomical.

In the autumn of 1591 the government ordered the commissioners of every shire in the land to draw up a list of those who did not come monthly to church. John Shakespeare's name turns up on the list prepared by the local officials, but in a category set apart by a note: "We suspect these nine persons next ensuing absent themselves for fear of processes." Some months later the commissioners filed their report and reiterated the explanation: "It is said that these last nine come not to church for fear of process for debt." If the explanation is accurate and not a cover for religious dissent, then the onetime bailiff of Stratford and justice of the peace was staying in his house on Sundays—and, presumably, many other days as well—to avoid arrest. The public man had become a very private man.

By 1591, when John Shakespeare was making himself scarce, his eldest son had almost certainly flown the coop: the next year he is first mentioned as a London playwright. But his father's humiliating position was only the latest scene in a drama that had been long unfolding and that must have shaped Will's entire adolescence. As he came of age, Will would have been keenly aware that something had gone seriously wrong. He could not have been indifferent to what he saw; his father's standing in the world was sinking exactly at the time when he, the oldest son and heir, was about to emerge as an adult.

What was the cause of the decline? Then, as now, there were business cycles—the last decades of the sixteenth century were particularly difficult in the Midlands—and in hard times people are obviously less likely to purchase luxury goods like elegant gloves. But many prominent merchants in comparable situations weathered hard times and personal disasters. Another Stratford chamberlain, Abraham Sturley, lost his house in a fire that swept through several streets of the town on September 22, 1594, and never fully recovered financially, but he managed to keep his eldest son, Henry, at Oxford and to send his second son, Richard, to

Oxford the next year. Another prominent Stratford citizen, William Parsons, lost his house in the same fire, but he too managed to send his son to Oxford and to serve as alderman and magistrate. John Shakespeare's debts, mortgages, fines, and losses and his sudden and precipitous disappearance from public life suggest something more than the consequences of a cyclical downturn in the glove trade.

A far likelier cause was a sharp government crackdown on one of the key sources of his income. In the wake of wool shortages in the mid-1570s, the authorities decided that the fault lay with the "broggers," men like John Shakespeare, who had already been twice denounced for illegal transactions. In October of 1576 the queen's principal advisers, the Privy Council, ordered wool traders in for questioning; in November they temporarily suspended all wool trading; and in the following year they required all known wool broggers to post bonds of one hundred pounds—a very large sum—as a surety against any further illegal dealings. This was all terrible news for John Shakespeare.

Matters were made worse by another financial blow. In 1580 the Crown issued a long list of names—over two hundred—and demanded that everyone listed appear on a specified day in June at the Queen's Bench in Westminster to be bound over to "keep the peace towards the queen and her subjects." John Shakespeare's name was on the list. "Binding over"—roughly equivalent to a restraining order—was a key low-level policing and crime-prevention method in the sixteenth and seventeenth centuries. Upon someone's swearing an oath that he feared for his life or well-being or the well-being of the entire community, the court could issue an order requiring the suspected malefactor to appear in order to guarantee his good behavior and to post a bond—a surety—to this end. The surviving records do not reveal who swore an oath against John Shakespeare or why. Was it because of his wool brogging, or some drunken quarrel for which he had been denounced, or a suspicion that he held the wrong religious beliefs? He somehow managed to find four guarantors for his appearance, and he agreed reciprocally to serve as guarantor for one of them. But on the June date neither John nor his guarantors appeared—again their absence has never been explained—and they forfeited their money. John was fined twenty pounds for himself and twenty pounds for John Audley, the Nottingham hatmaker for whom he had agreed to pledge. In the wake of his other difficulties, this was money he could not spare.

The impact upon his family appears to have been severe. Unlike the sons of Sturley and Parsons, Will conspicuously did not go to Oxford, nor did John Shakespeare's other sons. In the early eighteenth century the Shakespeare biographer and editor Nicholas Rowe wrote that John Shakespeare sent his eldest son to the Stratford grammar school, where he learned some Latin, "but the narrowness of his Circumstances, and the want of his assistance at Home, forc'd his Father to withdraw him from thence, and unhappily prevented his further Proficiency in that Language." Rowe believed, incorrectly, that John Shakespeare had had ten children, and the rest of the account may be equally incorrect. But the story of the son's being taken out of school in order to help at home would certainly be consistent with the documented financial straits of the late 1570s. At a certain point it may have seemed an absurd luxury to have his eldest son parsing Latin sentences.

"My father charged you in his will to give me good education," Orlando complains to his wicked brother in the pastoral comedy *As You Like It*. "You have trained me like a peasant, obscuring and hiding from me all gentleman-like qualities" (1.1.56–59). A good education marked the difference between a gentleman and a peasant. And yet Shakespeare did not, from all appearances, harbor any regrets about failing to attend Oxford or Cambridge; he did not show signs of a frustrated vocation as a scholar. For that matter, nothing in his works suggests any very sentimental feeling about school: Jaques' vision in the same comedy of "the whining schoolboy with his satchel / And shining morning face, creeping like snail / Unwillingly to school" does not convey nostalgia for a lost happiness (2.7.144–46). Nor does the scene of Latin instruction in *The Merry Wives of Windsor*, a scene that must have come quite close to Shakespeare's own direct memories of the King's New School. "My husband says my son profits nothing in the world at his book," Mistress Page complains to the Welsh pedagogue Sir Hugh Evans, whereupon Evans—in the Welsh accent that struck English ears as funny—puts little William through his paces:

EVANS: What is "*lapis*," William?
WILLIAM: A stone.
EVANS: And what is "a stone," William?
WILLIAM: A pebble.
EVANS: No, it is "*lapis*." I pray you remember in your prain.
WILLIAM: "*Lapis*."
EVANS: That is a good William.

(4.1.11–12, 26–32)

The tedium of rote learning is deftly recalled, as is the punning—preferably, obscene punning—that must have been the schoolboy Shakespeare's principal psychic relief from this tedium. This language lesson manages to turn the genitive into the genitals and to make us hear the word "whore" in the Latin for "this":

EVANS: What is your genitive case plural, William?
WILLIAM: Genitive case?
EVANS: Ay.
WILLIAM: *Genitivo: "horum, harum, horum."*
MISTRESS QUICKLY: Vengeance of Jenny's case! Fie on her! Never name her, child, if she be a whore.

(4.1.49–54)

These dirty jokes surfaced in abundance whenever Shakespeare gave a thought to Latin lessons or indeed to any language lessons at all. "Comment appelez-vous les pieds et la robe?" asks the French princess in *Henry V*, trying to learn the English words "feet" and "gown." Her tutor's reply discombobulates her: "*De foot*, madame, et *de cown*." In "foot" she and the audience (or at least the members of the audience in on the joke) hear the French word *foutre*, "fuck," and in the slightly mangled pronunciation of "gown" she hears *con*, "cunt."

CATHERINE: *De foot* et *de cown*? O Seigneur Dieu! Ils sont les mots de son mauvais, corruptible, gros, et impudique, et non pour les dames d'honneur d'user. [O Lord God! Those are evil-sounding words, easily misconstrued, vulgar, and immodest, and not for respectable ladies to use.]

(3.4.44–49)

If this stuff is not, in truth, infinitely amusing, it still can generate chuckles after four hundred years, and it would have served to lighten the burden of an exceedingly long school day. But it is certainly not the glimpse of a lost vocation. Ben Jonson wrote scholarly footnotes to his Roman plays and his classicizing masques; Shakespeare laughed and scribbled obscenities.

The end of his formal schooling must have meant more time for Will in the glove trade, getting to know the qualities of cheverel and deerskin. All the Shakespeare children probably helped in the family business. But after the late 1570s, there may not have been much of a business left to help in. Will's younger brother Gilbert, born in 1566, is described in town records as a "haberdasher," and Edmund, born in 1580, followed Will to London and became an actor. No records survive of how a third brother, Richard, born in 1574, spent his almost forty years of life. He too probably did not become a glover; if he had something to do with the father's business, and certainly if he had been a success at it, he is likely to have left a trace.

It often happens, Hamlet tells Horatio, that there is "some vicious mole of nature" in men (1.4.18.8), some inborn propensity or weakness, that ruins what would otherwise be an altogether admirable life. The particular fault on which Hamlet focuses his brooding attention is heavy drinking, a Danish national custom, he says, "More honoured in the breach than the observance" (1.4.18). Other nations call us drunkards, Hamlet complains, and with this charge sully our reputation:

> and indeed it takes
> From our achievements, though performed at height,
> The pith and marrow of our attribute.

(1.4.18.4–6)

Hamlet's extended meditation on this fault makes for a rather strange passage—extraordinarily intense, as if the thoughts were forcing themselves into speech, but at the same time oddly irrelevant, since his crafty, calculating uncle and his confederates are not elsewhere in the tragedy notably depicted as drunkards. One of the texts of *Hamlet* simply cuts the lines, as if they represented a false start, an idea Shakespeare decided not to pursue.

Is this a further clue to the cause of the father's decline? Did the man who served in 1556 as the borough ale-taster drink himself into deep personal trouble? In the mid-seventeenth century, when the public began to be curious about the life of their greatest playwright, Thomas Plume, archdeacon of Rochester, jotted down something he had been told about the Stratford glover, "a merry-cheeked old man" whom someone had seen once in his shop and questioned about his celebrated son. "Will was a good Honest Fellow," the father is said to have replied and then added, as if he had been challenged, "but [I] durst have cracked a jest with him at any time." The anecdote comes too late to be reliable as an eyewitness account, but does it contain a trace of the actual person, genial, good-natured, at once proud of his son and a touch competitive with him, and, possibly, "merry-cheeked" from something more than good humor or advancing age?

Throughout his career, Shakespeare kept thinking about drunkenness. He registered the disgust eloquently voiced by Hamlet. But he was also fascinated by the delicious foolishness, the exuberant cracking of jests, the amiable nonsense, the indifference to decorum, the flashes of insight, the magical erasure of the cares of the world. Even when he depicts the potentially disastrous consequences of alcohol, Shakespeare never adopts the tone of a temperance tract, and in *Twelfth Night* the drunk and disorderly Sir Toby Belch delivers the decisive put-down of the puritanical Malvolio: "Dost thou think because thou art virtuous there shall be no more cakes and ale?" (2.3.103–4). In a luminous scene in one of the greatest of the tragedies, *Antony and Cleopatra*, the rulers of the world become soused, join hands, and dance "the Egyptian bacchanals" (2.7.98). Even grave, calculating Caesar is caught up, against his will, in the muddle-headed revelry: "It's monstrous labour when I wash my brain, / An it grow fouler." "Gentle lords, let's part," he says, looking at the faces of those about him and feeling his own flushed face. "You see we have burnt our cheeks" (2.7.92–93, 116–17).

If Caesar's cold sobriety marks him as likely to prevail in the struggle for power, it also marks him as far less appealing than the riotous, great-spirited Antony. True nobility in *Antony and Cleopatra*—nobility not of blood alone but of character—has an affinity with excess, a perception that extends to many of Shakespeare's plays and carries the force of a conclusion drawn from life. John Shakespeare may have never seemed more like a nobleman to his observant, imaginative child than when he was in his cups, his cheeks burning.

But heavy drinking is associated in the plays with clowns, buffoons, and losers as well as kings. And an early play, *The Taming of the Shrew*, brings drunkenness literally close to home in the figure of Christopher Sly, who is noisy, impotently belligerent, and entirely unwilling to pay for the glasses he has broken. When the tavern hostess calls him a rogue and threatens to call the constable, the drunken beggar grandly stands on his family honor—"The Slys are no rogues. Look in the Chronicles—we came in with Richard Conqueror" (Induction 1, lines 3–4)—and then promptly falls asleep. A few moments later, a nobleman decides to trick the beggar into thinking he is a lord, and the baffled Sly clutches at a more homely sense of his identity: "What, would you make me mad? Am not I Christopher Sly—old Sly's son of Burton Heath, by birth a pedlar, by education a cardmaker, by transmutation a bearherd, and now by present profession a tinker? Ask Marian Hacket, the fat ale-wife of Wincot, if she know me not." (Induction 2, lines 16–20).

Shakespeare wrote this comedy shortly after he moved to London, and it bears vivid traces of the district around Stratford: Barton-on-the-Heath, where his cousins the Lamberts lived; Wincot, where dwelled a Hacket family he probably knew; perhaps Sly himself, since there was a Stephen Sly living in Stratford. It must have amused Shakespeare, in a quiet, private way, to introduce these familiar details onto the urban stage in order to give a realistic air to his depiction of rustic folly. Perhaps, like his comic character, he too felt dazed by his recent transmutation. He had gone from a provincial nobody to a professional actor and playwright in the great city of London, and he used the details to remind himself of who he was—old John Shakespeare's son of Stratford. The character of Christopher Sly is hardly a depiction of his father—a man whose accomplishments and social standing were far higher—but perhaps the drunkenness, the family pride, the mounting debts, and the unwillingness or inability to pay seemed as reminiscent of home as the familiar place-names Barton-on-the-Heath and Wincot.

Shakespeare's greatest representation of drunkenness is Sir John Falstaff, the grotesquely fat knight whose reiterated call for a white wine imported from Spain and the Canaries serves virtually as his motto: "Give me a cup of sack." In the second part of *Henry IV*, Falstaff delivers an ecstatic rhapsody to the virtues of "sherry-sack"—that is, sack from Jerez, in Andalusia—a mock-scientific analysis of its power to inflame both wit and courage:

> A good sherry-sack hath a two-fold operation in it. It ascends me into the brain, dries me there all the foolish and dull and crudy vapours which environ it, makes it apprehensive, quick, forgetive, full of nimble, fiery, and delectable shapes, which, delivered o'er to the voice, the tongue, which is the birth, becomes excellent wit. The second property of your excellent sherry is the warming of the blood, which, before cold and settled, left the liver white and pale, which is the badge of pusillanimity and cowardice. But the sherry warms it, and makes it course from the inwards to the parts' extremes; it illuminateth the face, which, as a beacon, gives warning to all the rest of this little kingdom, man, to arm; and then the vital commoners and inland petty spirits muster me all to their captain, the heart; who, great and puffed up with his retinue, doth any deed of courage. And this valour comes of sherry. (4.2.86–101)

Of course, the playwright could have heard the prototype of this encomium to drink in the alehouse or made it all up from scratch. But in the context of the trajectory that led the once prosperous bailiff to hide in his house from creditors, the end of this speech is striking: "If I had a thousand sons, the first human principle I would teach them should be to forswear thin potations, and to addict themselves to sack" (4.2.109–11). Perhaps in the wake of the family's financial decline, this was what Will took to be his father's first principle, the legacy the crumbling glover had decided to leave him.

But this did not mean that Will had to accept the legacy. One of the earliest anecdotes about Shakespeare reports that though he was good company, he was not a "company keeper"—he "wouldn't be debauched, and if invited to, writ: he was in pain." Aubrey recorded this around 1680, many years after the playwright's death, but it is peculiar enough as a recollection to suggest that it might be authentic. "He was in pain." Stories of drinking contests with village boozers or drunken flights of wit at the Mermaid Tavern or thousand-pound gifts from enamored aristocrats are far more the stuff of legend than a propensity to decline invitations with a polite excuse and to stay at home. A certain steadiness, in any case, rings true: it would be hard otherwise to imagine how Shakespeare could have done what he did—learn his parts and perform them onstage, help to manage the complex business affairs of the playing company, buy and sell country real estate and agricultural commodities, compose exquisitely crafted sonnets and long poems, and for almost two decades write on average two stupendous plays a year.

Shakespeare depicted heavy drinkers from close-up—he noted the unsteadiness of their legs, the broken veins in their nose and cheeks, their slurred speech—and he did so with an unusual current of understanding, delight, even love. But his sympathy was braided together with other elements, including the overwhelming sense of waste that Hamlet articulates. He saw in Sir Toby Belch a parasite who sponges off his niece, ruthlessly gulls his supposed friend Sir Andrew, and richly deserves the thrashing he receives at the hands of the effeminate boy he thought he could bully. He saw in Falstaff something roughly similar—a gentleman sinking into mire—but darker and deeper: a debauched genius; a fathomlessly cynical, almost irresistible confidence man; a diseased, cowardly, seductive, lovable monster; a father who cannot be trusted. The drunkenness that in both cases seems linked to gaiety, improvisational wit, and noble recklessness is unnervingly disclosed at the same time to be part of a strategy of cunning, calculation, and ruthless exploitation of others. Invariably, a failed strategy: the grand schemes, the imagined riches, the fantasies about the limitless future—all come to nothing, withering away in an adult son's contempt for the symbolic father who has failed him. "God save thee, my sweet boy!" exclaims Falstaff, when he sees Hal in triumph in London. "I know thee not, old man," Hal replies, in one of the most devastating speeches Shakespeare ever wrote.

> Fall to thy prayers.
> How ill white hairs become a fool and jester!
> I have long dreamt of such a kind of man,
> So surfeit-swelled, so old, and so profane;
> But being awake, I do despise my dream.
>   (*2 Henry IV*, 5.5.41, 45–49)

These are words written deep within the history play, words spoken by the newly crowned king of England to his exceptionally amusing, exceptionally dangerous friend. Yet it is difficult to register the overwhelming power and pathos of the relationship between Hal and Falstaff without sensing some unusually intimate and personal energy.

HOW DID THE SON of the failing glover make it into the theater? In the absence of any documentary traces, the principal evidence, pored over for clues by generations of ardent admirers, is the huge body of work that Shakespeare left behind, the plays and poems that spark the interest in the life in the first place and provide tantalizing hints of possible occupations he might have followed.

The strong presence of legal situations and terms in his plays and poems—used, for the most part, accurately, and infiltrating scenes where one would least expect them—has led to the recurrent speculation that he worked in the office of a local attorney, someone who handled minor lawsuits, title searches, and the like. No doubt much of the work would have been boring, but it would have put food on the table and would have fed his appetite for new words and fanciful metaphors. It is easy to imagine the law clerk, engaged in the humdrum task of sealing documents, letting his imagination wander—as the schoolboy had done over his Latin lessons—and conjuring up erotic visions. A few years later, the visions, still carrying the traces of their modest origin, take the form of the goddess of love in hot pursuit of the beautiful young huntsman. "Pure lips, sweet seals in my soft lips imprinted," says panting Venus, pleading for another kiss,

> What bargains may I make still to be sealing?
> To sell myself I can be well contented,
> So thou wilt buy, and pay, and use good dealing;
>   Which purchase if thou make, for fear of slips
>   Set thy seal manual on my wax-red lips.
>   (*Venus and Adonis*, lines 511–16)

The image of the imprint in wax might, in this account of Shakespeare's life, represent not only the imagined kiss but also the hard impact of his months or years of legal work on the poet's imagination.

Perhaps. But the strong presence in his work of terms from the leather trade seems a convincing personal trace only because of the objective likelihood that Will worked in his father's shop. Once we get away from the near certainty of this experience, we run into Shakespeare's uncanny ability to absorb vocabulary from a wide range of pursuits and his lightning transformation of technical terms into the intimate registers of thoughts and feelings. It is true that the absorption is not uniform—though in the course of his life he bought and sold houses, for example, he picked up relatively few terms from architecture and the building trades—but the general phenomenon is broad enough and intense enough to defy using language as a clue to any occupation he formally pursued. He undoubtedly took in legal language and concepts, but he also was remarkably attuned to theological and medical and military language and concepts. Was he directly involved in all of these professions too? A young man without prospects, he could have run off to the army fighting a nasty campaign in the Netherlands—so some, impressed by his theatrical command of military jargon, have speculated. He could, from his evident fascination with sea voyages, have found a place on a ship bound for America—"To seek new worlds," as Sir Walter Ralegh put it, "for gold, for praise, for glory." But the actuarial likelihood of his making it back home from such adventures was exceedingly small. And none of these possible professions adequately accounts for the trajectory that led from Stratford to London. Indeed, each seems only to lead away from the place that most matters in his life, the theater.

The most obvious access to the theater companies for a talented young man was through apprenticeship. But Will's marriage license places him securely in Stratford in November 1582, at the age of eighteen, and the baptismal records of his children —Susanna, christened on May 26, 1583, and the twins Hamnet and Judith, christened on February 2, 1585— strongly suggest that he still lived there or at the very least continued to make regular visits. Apprentices were usually taken on as adolescents and were not allowed to marry (let alone to father children in their late teens). Still, the skills that theatrical apprentices acquired provide a clue to some of the things that the young Shakespeare must have been learning to do, however he earned his living, in the years after he left school.

The last will and testament of Augustine Phillips, one of Shakespeare's fellow actors, business partners, and friends (he left his "fellow" Shakespeare a "thirty-shilling piece in gold") provides some sense of these skills: "I give to Samuel Gilborne, my late apprentice, the sum of forty shillings, and my mouse-coloured velvet hose, and a white taffety doublet, a black taffety suit, my purple cloak, sword and dagger, and my bass-viol. I give to James Sands, my apprentice, the sum of forty shillings, and a cittern, a bandore, and a lute, to be paid and delivered unto him at the expiration of his term of years in his indenture of apprenticeship." Money was only part of the bequest. Both the former apprentice Gilborne and the current apprentice Sands also received valuable tools of the trade: costumes, weapons, and musical instruments. The fact that James Sands had to wait for his bequest until his term of service was up suggests Phillips had his company's interests uppermost in mind: he did not want the young actor, inherited money and musical instruments in hand, to offer his services to a rival troupe.

The terms of Phillips's will indicate something of the expectations playing companies had of their actors. First, actors were supposed to be gifted musicians, able to play at least the impressive range of string instruments that Phillips evidently played—the guitar-like cittern, the mandolin-like bandore (from which we get the word "banjo"), the immensely popular lute, and the bass viol. Second, they were expected to be able to fight—or at least convincingly to mime fighting—with sword and dagger. More generally, they had to be agile: there is often dancing, as well as fighting, in Elizabethan drama, and all performances of plays, whether tragic or comic, ended with complex dances. (It takes some adjustment to imagine the players in *Hamlet* or *King Lear* brushing off the stage blood at the play's end, joining hands, and performing a set of elaborate figures, but so they did.) Third, as the bequests strongly imply, they were expected to wear clothes gracefully: Phillips's "mouse-coloured velvet hose" were no doubt designed to show off his legs—in this period of long dresses, it was men's legs, rather than women's, to which eyes were drawn.

The musical ability, sword fighting, and above all the costly clothing of velvet and silks (for taffeta in this period referred to a kind of plain-woven silk) together point to what was probably the most significant aspect of the Elizabethan actor's training: players were supposed to be able to mime convincingly the behavior of gentlemen and ladies. That is, boys and men, drawn almost entirely from the 98 percent of the population that were not "gentle," had to assume the manner of the upper 2 percent. Not all the parts in the plays, of course, were of the gentry, and some actors no doubt specialized in lower-class roles, but these were repertory companies in which most of the actors were expected to play a range of social types. And it is clear from the budgets of the playing companies that they were willing to invest a great deal of money in making the impersonation of the gentry convincing. Their single largest expense, apart from the physical building itself, was the cost of costumes—the gorgeous, elaborate clothes that audiences expected to see gracing the bodies of the actors playing the parts of lords and ladies.

There is a paradox here. Actors were classified officially as vagabonds; they practiced a trade that was routinely stigmatized and despised. As "masterless men"—men without a home of their own or an honest job or an attachment to someone else's home—they could be arrested, whipped, put in the stocks, and branded. (This is why they described themselves legally as the servants of aristocrats or as guild members.) And yet the heart of their enterprise was a representation of the upper classes persuasive enough to delight a discriminating audience that included real gentlemen and ladies. Augustine Phillips was bequeathing to his apprentices the tools of a trade that much of the time required them to learn how to look and act like their betters. Phillips himself evidently wanted to carry the performance outside the walls of the playhouse: he simply bought a coat of arms to which he had no claim at all, an act for which he was subsequently attacked by an official of the College of Heralds known grandly (after the badge of office that he wore) as the Red Dragon Pursuivant.

We scarcely know for ourselves, let alone for a person who lived four hundred years ago, how someone acquires a particular vocational desire. Will's love of language, his sensitivity to spectacle, and a certain erotic thrill in make-believe may all have played a part in drawing him to the stage. But, in the light of Shakespeare's family circumstances—a mother who could trace her family to the important Ardens of Park Hall, a father who had risen in the world only to sink down again—the focus of Elizabethan theatrical impersonation is deeply suggestive. Will may have been attracted to the trade of acting in part because it so centrally involved the miming of the lives of the gentry. As a practical strategy, this was, of course, absurd: becoming an actor or even a playwright was probably the worst imaginable route toward social advancement, something like becoming a whore in order to become a great lady. But as the legends of whores who become great ladies suggest, there is at work in certain professions a powerful mimetic magic. Onstage Shakespeare could be the person that his mother and father said he was and that he felt himself to be.

Even without a formal theatrical apprenticeship, Will must have acquired much of what he needed during his Stratford adolescence. Local talent abounded; filled with linguistic exuberance and rich fantasy, Will could have studied the lute with one of his accomplished neighbors, dancing with another, swordsmanship with still another. Observing his reflection in a glass or his shadow on a wall, he could have recited grand-sounding speeches and practiced courtly gestures. And with his mother's link to the Ardens of Park Hall and his father's faded but still notable distinction, he could have arrived at the sense that he could confidently carry off the role of a gentleman and fulfill his parents' dreams.

John Shakespeare had once had great expectations, a vision of the arrow of the family's fortunes that his accomplishments would propel toward a glorious future. At the height of his wealth and prestige—in 1575 or '76, just before his downward slide began—he had applied to the College of Heralds for a coat of arms, an expensive process a person undertook not only to confer honor on himself but also to enhance the status of his children and grandchildren. To be granted a coat of arms—not to buy one on the sly, as Phillips tried to do, but to obtain one officially—was to rise above playacting to the thing itself.

Elizabethan society was intensely, pervasively, visibly hierarchical: men above women, adults above children, the old above the young, the rich above the poor, the wellborn above the vulgar. Woe betide anyone who violated the rules, forgetting to cede place to someone above him or attempting to pass through a door before his betters or thoughtlessly sitting somewhere at church or at a dinner table where he did not belong. William Combe, the squire of a town near Stratford, sent a person named Hicox to Warwick Jail and refused bail because he "did not behave himself with such respect in his presence it seemeth he looked for." The social elite lived in a world of carefully calibrated gestures of respect. They demanded constant, endlessly reiterated signs of deference from those below them: bowing, kneeling, doffing hats, cringing. There was virtually no respect for labor; on the contrary, it was idleness that was prized and honored. Dress was the opposite of democratizing—nothing could be further from Shakespeare's world than a culture in which magnates and workmen often wear the same clothes. It wasn't simply a question of money. By royal proclamation, silks and satins were officially restricted to the gentry. Actors were exempted, but outside of the playhouse they could not legally wear their costumes. In general, treatment by government officials and by the courts was drastically different for the upper classes than it was for those at the bottom. Even executions were distinct: hanging for the base, beheading for the elite.

To pass from the status of yeoman—the term used to describe John

Shakespeare, even after he had left the land and established himself in business—to the status of gentleman was a major step, a virtual transformation of social identity. There were many fine gradations in Elizabethan society, but the key division was between the gentry and the "common," or "baser," sort. The division was routinely mystified as a matter of blood, an immutable, inherited characteristic. But at the same time it was possible to cross the boundary, and everyone knew the ways it could be done. "As for gentlemen," writes one canny contemporary observer, Sir Thomas Smith,

> they be made good cheap in England. For whosoever studieth the laws of the realm, who studieth in the universities, who professeth the liberal sciences, and, to be short, who can live idly and without manual labor and will bear the port, charge, and countenance of a gentleman, he shall be called master, for that is the title which men give to esquires and other gentlemen. . . . And, if need be, a King of Heralds shall also give him for money arms newly made and invented, the title whereof shall pretend to have been found by the said herald in the perusing of old registers.

"Who studieth in the universities": not only was this something inconceivable for the yeoman and glover John Shakespeare, but it was also something he conspicuously failed to see that his eldest son do. But all was not lost. The key requirement, if you are climbing into the ranks of the elite, is to live like a gentleman—that is, you have to "live idly" and to maintain a certain level of conspicuous expenditure. The next requirement is to hide the ladder—that is, you have to pretend that you are already there. You do so, Smith notes, by acquiring a coat of arms from an institution, the College of Heralds, which was in the peculiar business of concealing social mobility by reinventing the past. In exchange for money, the herald pretends that he has discovered in the old registers what he—or the applicant—is in fact fabricating.

It was not quite as simple as Smith's wry account suggests. To be an "armiger," someone entitled to bear a heraldic device, one had to meet certain requirements overseen by a bureaucracy headed by the Garter King-of-Arms, the chief of the College of Heralds. In John Shakespeare's case, it was civic office that helped to confer eligibility: "If any person be advanced into an office or dignity of public administration," one expert on these matters held, "be it either Ecclesiastical, Martial, or Civil . . . the Herald must not refuse to devise to such a public person, upon his instant request and willingness to bear the same without reproach, a coat of Arms." The bailiff of Stratford was just such a "public person," and accordingly, when he submitted a sketch for his arms to the college, John Shakespeare must have been confident that his application would be granted. But though you could not legitimately simply buy a proper coat of arms—one that you and your descendants could proudly bear forever, as an acknowledged right—you most definitely had to pay for it. The heralds' fees were high. When his financial circumstances worsened, ascent to the status of gentleman must have seemed a hopeless extravagance or perhaps a mockery, like a beggar dreaming of a crown. John Shakespeare's application was shelved and forgotten.

But not, it seems, by his oldest son. Decades later, in October 1596, the process was renewed. The old sketch—"Gould. On A Bend Sables, a Speare of the first steeled argent. And for his Creast or Cognizance a falcon, his winges displayed Argent. Standing on a wrethe of his Coullors. Suppourting a Speare Gould. Steeled as aforesaid sett uppon a helmett with mantelles & tasselles"—was pulled off the shelf, where it had gathered dust; once again John Shakespeare's claim was reviewed and, this time round, approved. Who reinstituted the application, provided the necessary information, and paid the fees to the notoriously greedy, arrogant, and irascible head of the London College of Heralds, Sir William Dethick? Not the elderly glover and his wife, whose financial situation had not, in all likelihood, greatly improved, and not, with any likelihood, the provincial haberdasher Gilbert, the apparent nonentity Richard, the unsuccessful actor Edmund, or the unmarried sister Joan. The obvious answer is William, already prospering handsomely in the London theater.

Why should he have gone to the trouble? Most obviously, by helping his father complete the process, the playwright, in an act of prudential, self-interested generosity, was conferring gentle status on himself and his children. Will had by this time no doubt played gentlemen onstage, and he could carry off the part outside the playhouse as well, but he and others would always know he was impersonating someone he was not. He now had the means to acquire legitimately, through the offices his father had once held, a role he had only played. He could legally wear outside of the theater the kinds of clothes he had been wearing onstage. For a man singularly alert to the social hierarchy—and Shakespeare spent most of his professional life imagining the lives of kings, aristocracy, and gentry—the prospect of this privilege must have seemed sweet. He would sign his last will and testament "William Shakespeare, of Stratford upon Avon in the county of Warwick, gentleman." His heirs and their offspring would be ever further from the glover's shop and, for that matter, the playhouse; they would have the luxury of taking their gentility for granted and laying claim without irony to the motto that someone— again, in all probability, Will himself—had devised to accompany the shield and crest: *Non sanz droict.*

"Not without right." Is there a touch of defensiveness in that motto, a slight sense that the claim to gentlemanly status might raise eyebrows? If so, the insecurity would not belong to the impecunious glover but to his successful playwright son. For whatever John Shakespeare's problems—drink or foolish loans or whatever—he did in fact legitimately possess the social standing, through the offices he had held in Stratford, to lay claim to the status of a gentleman. Not so his son. There were few occupations for an educated man more stigmatized socially than player. That Shakespeare was acutely aware of the stigma can be surmised from the sonnets, where he writes that, like the dyer's hand, he has been stained by the medium he has worked in. It was with such a consciousness of social shame—the sense of what it means to go up and down, making oneself a motley to the view—that he may have come up with the family motto, half-defiant, half-defensive.

The clerk who wrote down the words on the draft of the grant of arms made a telling mistake—either unconsciously or with sly sarcasm— that he had to strike out: he twice wrote "Non, Sanz Droict." The comma in effect turns the motto into an official rejection: "No; without justification." The correction was made, the motto was finally written correctly, and the arms were granted. But for Will the insecurity—or at least the sense of incongruity—is unlikely to have vanished, for there were jokes and unpleasant reminders. Most manifestations of social policing—raised eyebrows, wry faces, ironic witticisms, teasing—are evanescent and hardly outlast a day or two, let alone four hundred years. But in this case, perhaps because the volume of insult was high, perhaps because Will was sufficiently a public figure, traces of it survive. In the satiric comedy *Every Man Out of his Humour*, performed at the newly erected Globe by the Lord Chamberlain's Men in 1599, Ben Jonson has a rustic buffoon named Sogliardo pay thirty pounds for a ridiculous coat of arms, to which an acquaintance mockingly proposes the humiliating motto "Not Without Mustard." As a member of the Lord Chamberlain's Men, Will would have listened to this insult again and again in rehearsal and in performance. He probably laughed uncomfortably —how else does someone get through this kind of teasing?

In 1602 his discomfort would have been renewed when a disgruntled genealogist, the York herald Ralph Brooke, filed a formal complaint against the Garter King-of-Arms, Sir William Dethick, for abusing his authority by elevating base people to a status they did not merit. Brooke drew up a list of twenty-three such cases. "Shakespear ye Player" was the fourth name on the list.

Shakespeare was a witty mocker of pretensions and must have known that he would be exposing himself to this embarrassment. He may have felt that the social cachet was worth wincing for, but a further key to his action may lie in the specific remarks penned on the drafts that Dethick drew up in granting the renewed request on behalf of John Shakespeare. These remarks must have been based on information provided by the person paying for the application, information that could then be verified, if the officials were acting responsibly, by the College of Heralds. There is, of course, no reference to the glover's shop or the illegal trade in wool and other commodities. Along with a vague reference to the distinction of the petitioner's ancestor, who allegedly did "faithful and valiant service" to King Henry VII, though no record of this service or its reward has emerged, Dethick notes that "the said John hath married the daughter and one of the heirs of Robert Arden of Wilmcote," that he had served as a justice of the peace and the bailiff of Stratford, and that he had "lands and tenements of good wealth and substance," worth five hundred pounds.

By 1596 this was all something of a dream, akin to Christoper Sly's "we came in with Richard Conqueror." John Shakespeare was hardly destitute—despite his losses, he still had possessions—but he had ceased to be what the application claimed he was: a "man of good substance." The story Will likely told the Garter King-of-Arms—a story about a man whose ancestors had served the king, a man who had married an heiress bearing a distinguished name, a man who had risen to high civic office, in short a man of good substance—erased or undid the man who mortgaged away his wife's property, who could not leave his house for fear of arrest for debt, and whose relations with his fellow townspeople had so deteriorated by 1582 that in that year he petitioned for sureties of the peace against four men "for fear of death and mutilation of his limbs." In this application, John Shakespeare had not only been restored to his lost position; he had been raised to a position he never quite held.

The dream of restoration haunted Shakespeare throughout his life. In *The Comedy of Errors*, a merchant of Syracuse, in search of his lost twins, is arrested in the rival city of Ephesus and is threatened with death if he cannot pay a heavy fine. At the end of a zany tangle of confused identities, in which one of his sons is arrested for debt by a leather-clad officer (of the type that used to accompany the bailiff John Shakespeare), the father is reunited with the twins and with their mother, the beloved wife from whom he had been separated in a shipwreck thirty-three years before. The merchant's life is spared, his fine is forgiven, the son's debt is settled, and the family is magically restored. In *The Merchant of Venice*, a wealthy merchant loses all of his wealth in a series of shipwrecks and is about to be carved up by a merciless Jewish creditor, until, through a clever interpretation of the law, he regains everything he has lost and acquires the creditor's money as well. In *Twelfth Night*, the son and daughter of a nobleman are separated from one another and shipwrecked on the coast of Illyria. The son wanders through his life as if he is in a dream. The daughter takes a new name and pretends she is a young man, Cesario. In her assumed identity, she has suffered a steep loss in social standing—Cesario is a servant—but even in her disguise she clings to her origins. "What is your parentage?"

asks the proud countess, and the servant replies, "Above my fortunes, yet my state is well. / I am a gentleman." The countess is smitten:

> I'll be sworn thou art.
> Thy tongue, thy face, thy limbs, actions, and spirit
> Do give thee five-fold blazon.
>
> (1.5.247–49, 261–63)

"Five-fold blazon": in his speech, looks, movements, though not in his clothes or occupation, Cesario bears a gentleman's coat of arms. And when the brother and sister finally encounter one another by chance, they lay claim to their displaced identities:

> SEBASTIAN: What countryman? What name? What parentage?
> VIOLA: Of Messaline. Sebastian was my father.
>
> (5.1.224–25)

Not only are they restored to their proper social identities, but they each make a marriage above their station, the young woman to the Duke of Illyria, the young man to a great heiress.

In none of these cases is restoration entirely straightforward. The Syracusan merchant gets back a family that had, because of the disastrous shipwreck, never actually lived as one. The Venetian merchant, who despises usury, not only recoups his maritime losses; he is also given "in use" half the accumulated wealth of the Jewish moneylender. The twin brother and sister are not so much restored to one another or to their lost identities as they are linked through their new spouses, Viola marrying the duke who has long been madly in love with the countess, Sebastian's immensely wealthy bride. And the social-climbing success is strangely shadowed by the figure of the countess's steward Malvolio, who dreams of making the match that Sebastian succeeds in making.

Malvolio serves as the shadow side of Shakespeare's own fascination with achieving the status of a gentleman. He is, says the waiting gentlewoman Maria, who hates him, "an affectioned ass that cons state without book and utters it by great swathes"—that is, he memorizes and recites the dignified and high-flown language of his betters. And he is a narcissist: "the best persuaded of himself, so crammed, as he thinks, with excellencies, that it is his grounds of faith that all that look on him love him" (2.4.132-35). He suffers from what Shakespeare in the sonnets characterizes as his own besetting "Sin of self-love": "Methinks no face so gracious is as mine. / No shape so true, no truth of such account" (62.1, 5–6). Out of these qualities, Malvolio's enemies will work their revenge, which will be to make him a "common recreation" (2.3.121).

What is ridiculed in Malvolio, then, is not simply ill nature or puritanical severity but rather the dream of acting the part of a gentleman. And the ridicule comes very close to describing the process by which any actor, including Shakespeare himself, must have learned his trade. "He has been yonder i' the sun," Maria tells her fellow conspirators, "practising behaviour to his own shadow this half-hour" (2.5.14–15). When he comes close enough to be overheard, what the mockers witness is someone rehearsing a fantasy: "To be Count Malvolio!" "Now he's deeply in," one of the conspirators whispers. "Look how imagination blows him" (2.5.30, 37–38). The audience is then invited to watch someone enter a part—"deeply in"—and improvise a scene, complete with costume, props, dialogue, and what actors call a backstory:

> Having been three months married to her, sitting in my state . . .
> Calling my officers about me, in my branched velvet gown, having come from a day-bed where I have left Olivia sleeping . . .
> And then to have the humour of state and—after a demure travel of regard, telling them I know my place, as I would they should do theirs—to ask for my kinsman Toby. . . . Seven of my people with an obedient start make out for him. I frown the while, and perchance wind up my watch, or play with my —
> [*touching his chain*] some rich jewel. (2.5.39–54)

Malvolio is about to be lured into the trap that has been laid for him, the trap that will lead to yellow cross-garters, inappropriate smiling, imprisonment as a madman, and cruel humiliation. One of the greatest comic plots in all of Shakespeare, it draws deeply on the playwright's inner life, including a strong current of ironic laughter at the whole project—his own and that of his parents—of laying claim to a higher status.

Shakespeare found the pleasures and ironies of restoration inexhaustibly fascinating, even in his tragedies and tragicomedies. At the climax of *King Lear*, the old king's wicked daughters are defeated, and, after all his losses and his atrocious sufferings, the king is restored to "absolute power" (5.3.299). But it is too late: his beloved daughter Cordelia is dead in his arms, and he dies in an agony of despair mixed with the delusive hope that she might still be alive. A similar fate befalls Timon of Athens, who finds when he has lost his wealth that he has no friends and goes off to live alone in the woods. Digging in the earth for roots to eat, he finds gold, the last thing he desires, and once again becomes, to his virtually fatal disgust, an immensely wealthy man. And in *The Winter's Tale*, King Leontes, after sixteen years, recovers the wife and daughter whom his paranoid jealousy had seemed to destroy. But the wide gap in time is not so simply erased: his wife, Leontes remarks, "was not so much wrinkled, nothing / So agèd" as the woman he has recovered (5.3.28–29), and other victims of his jealousy—his only son, Prince Mamillius, and his faithful counselor Antigonus—do not miraculously return from the grave. The emotion of restoration is powerfully present—the sense that what was seemingly irrevocably lost has been reclaimed against all hope and expectation—but the recovery is never quite what it seems: the past that is recovered turns out to be an invention or a delusion or, in the worst case, an intensification of loss.

Near the very end of his career Shakespeare returned one more time to this plot structure, giving it in almost pure form in *The Tempest*: a ruler is thrust from his dukedom, cast out to sea in a leaky boat with his infant daughter, and shipwrecked on a strange island; years later, through the exercise of his magic, he triumphs over his enemies and recovers his lost realm. These are familiar, highly traditional motifs, and yet the peculiar intensity with which Shakespeare repeatedly embraces the fantasy of the recovery of a lost prosperity or title or identity is striking.

There is no direct relation between the staging of various forms of restoration in Will's plays and the renewal of the lapsed application for the status of gentleman. Art rarely emerges so transparently from the circumstances of life and would be far less compelling if it did. Shakespeare was in the business of reaching thousands of people, none of whom had any reason to be interested in the business affairs and social status of a Stratford glover. But there were many ways in which he might have tried to reach his audience, and his fascination with a particular set of stories—his sense that these might work and, still more, that he might have it in him to work with them—does not seem entirely random. Though his imagination soared to faraway places, the fantasies that excited his imagination seem often to have had their roots in the actual circumstances of his life or rather in the expectations and longings and frustrations generated by those circumstances. Hence, in settings as remote as the mythical Athens of *A Midsummer Night's Dream* or the romantic Bohemia of *The Winter's Tale*, there are notes that take us back to the young man who grew up on Henley Street in Stratford and dreamed that he was a gentleman. Sometime in his late adolescence, the young man awoke to find that the dream had fled, along with his mother's dowry and his father's civic stature. But, as we have seen, he did not give it up, either in his life or in his art.

Again and again in his plays, an unforeseen catastrophe—one of his favorite manifestations of it is a shipwreck—suddenly turns what had seemed like happy progress, prosperity, smooth sailing into disaster, terror, and loss. The loss is obviously and immediately material, but it is also and more crushingly a loss of identity. To wind up on an unknown shore, without one's friends, habitual associates, familiar network—this catastrophe is often epitomized by the deliberate alteration or disappearance of the name and, with it, the alteration or disappearance of social status. Shakespeare's characters repeatedly have to lay claim to a gentility that is no longer immediately apparent, all of its conventional signs having been swept away by the wild waves.

In Will's imagination his father's failure might have seemed a shipwreck, but the Shakespeares had no secure grasp of gentlemanly status to begin with. The family was at best only just about to become gentle, acquiring the coat of arms for which his father had applied. It is possible, of course, that his mother had filled her eldest son with tales of the Ardens of Park Hall or even of Turchill of the Forest of Arden, the lordly ancestor whose lands merited four columns in the Domesday Book. In that case, Will could have dreamed that the family was just about to recover, through his father's civic offices, the status that had at one time belonged by birthright to the Ardens. This dream too seems to have stayed with him. In 1599, three years after the old application for the coat of arms was revived, almost certainly at his instigation and expense, Will was in all likelihood the person behind another successful application to the College of Heralds, this time for the right to add (the technical term is "impale") the Arden arms to what is now described as "the Ancient coat of Arms" of the Shakespeares. In the end only the Shakespeare arms appeared on his funeral monument, but the symbolic statement is clear: I am not someone who can be treated like a hired servant or whipped like a vagabond; I am someone who does not merely pretend onstage to be a gentleman; I am a true gentleman, entitled to bear arms both by virtue of my father's distinguished service to the queen and by virtue of my mother's distinguished family. And, half-concealed, another symbolic statement: I have with the fruits of my labor and my imagination returned my family to the moment before things began to fall apart; I have affirmed the distinction of my mother's name and restored my father's honor; I have laid claim to my lost inheritance; I have created that inheritance.

CHAPTER 3

The Great Fear

EVEN IF WILL in his late teens or early twenties had decided clearly that he wanted to become an actor, he was in fact not likely simply to have headed off to London to seek his fortune onstage, stopping along the way to pick up a few pennies for food and lodging by singing and juggling. A person uprooted from his family and community in Elizabethan England was generally a person in trouble. This was a society deeply suspicious of vagrancy. (Shakespeare would later make much in his works of the tribulations of the uprooted and unprotected.) The age of questing knights and wandering minstrels was over—if indeed it ever existed except as a fantasy. Itinerant friars and pilgrims had certainly existed, and within living memory, but the religious orders had been dissolved by the state and the pilgrimage sites had been shut down and smashed by zealous reformers. There were wanderers on the roads, but they were exceedingly vulnerable. Unaccompanied, unprotected women could be attacked and raped almost with impunity. Unaccompanied men were less desperately at risk, but they too needed all the protection they could get. Trades that required travel were heavily regulated—every peddler and tinker was required to have a license from two justices of the shire in which he resided, and anyone not so licensed could be officially or unofficially victimized. An able-bodied beggar or idle vagrant could by statute be seized and brought before the local justice of the peace for interrogation and punishment. Being able to sing and dance, juggle or recite speeches was no excuse: among those who were to be classed as vagrants, the Vagabond Act of 1604, continuing earlier statutes, includes players of interludes, fencers, bearwards, minstrels, begging scholars and sailors, palmists, fortune-tellers, and others. If the vagrant could not show that he had land of his own or a master whom he was serving, he was tied to a post and publicly whipped. Then he was either returned to his place of birth—to resume the work he was born to do—or put to labor or placed in the stocks until someone took him into service.

A very small number of people lived lives of privileged idleness, but most inhabited a society of scarcity with no patience for anyone who did not, as Shakespeare put it, commit his body to painful labor. And the fruits of that labor, in theory at least, were supposed to be earned by people who knew and kept their place. Social regulations were amazingly harsh: lest the whip and the stocks seem too lenient, a mid-sixteenth-century statute ordered that vagabonds were to be branded and put to forced labor as slaves. Even if such draconian statutes were not strictly enforced—and the evidence is too scanty to be certain—this clearly was not a culture in which a provincial young man uncertain of his future and in need of an income to feed his wife and three small children would venture off fancy-free to the big city in the hope that, as Dickens's Mr. Micawber puts it, something would turn up.

The seventeenth-century gossip John Aubrey jotted down something that strongly suggests that Will did not immediately find a place in a theater company or move directly from Stratford to London in search of employment. "He had been in his younger years," Aubrey wrote, "a schoolmaster in the country." Most of Aubrey's gossip about Shakespeare needs to be taken with a grain of salt, but this particular item has more authority than most, for he noted its source as the actor William Beeston. Beeston was the son of Shakespeare's former colleague in the Lord Chamberlain's company, Christopher Beeston. This, therefore, is a piece of biographical information that can be traced directly back to someone who actually knew Shakespeare. (They acted together, records show, in the 1598 production of *Every Man in His Humour*.) No one has been able to establish with certainty where "in the country" Shakespeare was a teacher, but many scholars have come to take seriously a controversial claim, first made in 1937, that he spent a period of time, perhaps two years, in Lancashire, employed by an immensely wealthy Catholic gentleman, Alexander Hoghton, and then, upon Hoghton's death, by his friend Sir Thomas Hesketh, of nearby Rufford.

The vicious, murky world of Tudor religious conflict will help to explain why an adolescent boy, fresh from school, might have ventured from the Midlands of England to the north, how he could have had a connection with a powerful Catholic family there, and why that family would have bothered to employ someone like him rather than a licensed schoolmaster with an Oxford or Cambridge education.

Stratford had nominally become Protestant, like the rest of the kingdom, when in 1533 Henry VIII—bent on getting a divorce and on seizing the enormous wealth of the monasteries—had himself declared "Supreme Head of the Church in England." Officially, England had decisively broken away from Rome. But in matters of religious belief, families in early-sixteenth-century England were characteristically fractured, and many individuals were similarly fractured inwardly. It would have been an unusual extended kin group that did not have at least some of its members holding on to the old faith, an unusual convert to Protestantism who did not feel on occasion at least some residual Catholic twinges, and an unusual lay Catholic who did not feel a current of national pride and loyalty when Henry VIII defied papal authority. This ambivalence remained true even during the reign of Henry's son, Edward VI, from 1547 to 1553, when England's ruling elite moved decisively to a serious embrace of Protestant doctrine and practice. But significant steps were taken in these years to make a return to Catholicism, even in imagination, more difficult.

Salvation, the leaders of the new English church said, came not through the Mass and the other rituals of Roman Catholicism, but through faith and faith alone. Now it was not only the venerable monasteries and the celebrated pilgrimage sites that came under attack. The altarpieces, statues, crucifixes and frescoes that filled the churches were declared to be idols, designed to lure the people into ignorance and superstition. They were defaced, whitewashed over, or smashed, and the zealous vandals went on to attack other time-honored ways of acting out the faith, including rituals, pageants, and plays.

The most exalted moment in the Catholic service had been the Elevation of the Host. The gorgeously arrayed priest, his back to the congregation and partly concealed behind a screen surmounted by a large crucifix, would lift up the consecrated wafer. At that moment, a bell was rung, and the faithful would look up from their private prayers and strain to see the piece of bread that had miraculously been transformed into the body and blood of God. Protestant polemicists had a range of hostile nicknames for the Host—"Round Robin," "Jack in the Box," "Worms' Meat," and the like—and comparably insulting terms for the Mass, including "the Pope's Theater."

The Mass was an impressive performance, they conceded, but it was all a histrionic fake, a tissue of lies and illusions. The theater might have its value—zealous Protestants like John Bale, who wrote anti-Catholic plays, clearly thought so—but it had no business infecting worship. There was no miraculous transformation of the substance of the bread, as the Catholics claimed, only a solemn act of commemoration, which should be conducted not at an altar but at a table. Faith should rest not on a gaudy spectacle but on the word of God, not on alluring images but on texts. The only certain guide was Scripture. It was a scandal, religious reformers repeatedly complained, that the Holy Bible had been deliberately kept out of the hands of lay men and women (English translations deemed heretical had been burned in great bonfires by the Catholic authorities) and thereby confined to a Latin translation mumbled by priests. In the 1520s, aided by the printing press, Protestants moved to make an English version, shaped by the principles of the Reformation, widely available and to encourage the literacy that would give ordinary people access to what they called the plain, unvarnished truth. They moved as well to translate the liturgy into English and promulgate the Book of Common Prayer, so that all believers would understand the service and pray in unison in their own mother tongue.

This was the crucial moment in the development of the English language, the moment in which the deepest things, the things upon which the fate of the soul depended, were put into ordinary, familiar, everyday words. Two men above all others, William Tyndale and Thomas Cranmer, rose to the task. Without them, without the great English translation of the New Testament and the sonorous, deeply resonant Book of Common Prayer, it is difficult to imagine William Shakespeare.

The achievement did not come lightly. Too radical for the doctrinally conservative Henry VIII, Tyndale was driven in the 1520s to the Continent, where eventually he was captured and garroted to death by the Catholic authorities. During the reign of Edward VI, Cranmer, as archbishop of Canterbury, led the Protestant reforms, but when the sickly Edward died in 1553 the throne passed to his sister, the Catholic Mary Tudor. Mary moved at once to reverse direction, and Cranmer, along with other leading Protestants who had not managed to escape to Germany or Geneva, was burned at the stake at Oxford in 1556. The memory of these executions—which formed the core of John Foxe's great Protestant *Book of Martyrs*—haunted the later sixteenth century and sharpened the violently anti–Roman Catholic sentiments of the committed reformers.

When Mary died childless in 1558, the wheel turned once again: the twenty-five-year-old Elizabeth quickly made it clear that she would return the country to the religious course upon which it had embarked under the reign of her father and, still more, that of her brother. Though cautious about unleashing extreme reforms, the queen signaled her Protestant views at a procession on January 14, 1559, the day before her coronation. At the Little Conduit in Cheapside, she took the English Bible proffered to her by an allegorical figure of Truth, kissed the book, held it aloft, and then clasped it to her breast. When some days later at Westminster Abbey monks bearing incense, holy water, and candles approached to offer her their blessings, she dismissed them roughly: "Away with those torches," she commanded; "we can see well enough by daylight." In the months that followed, altarpieces and statues that had been reerected were taken down, altars were again transformed into simple tables, and the ancient Catholic liturgy was replaced by the Book of

Common Prayer. The Catholic priests who had emerged from what they regarded as the nightmare years under Edward VI were compelled either to conform to the Protestant doctrine or to vanish once again. Either they fled into exile abroad, or, more dangerously, they took on disguises and hid themselves in the houses of Catholic gentlemen.

At first repression was relatively mild. Queen Elizabeth made it clear that she was interested more in obedience and conformity than in purity of conviction. She had, as Bacon said, neither the desire nor the intention to "make windows into men's hearts and secret thoughts." What she wanted was an outward act of adherence to her authority and to the official religious settlement. Specifically, she wanted regular attendance at the state-sanctioned church services, whereupon the authorities would abstain from asking such questions as, Do you inwardly long for the old Catholic sacraments? Do you believe in the existence of purgatory? Do you think that priests have the power to grant absolution? Do you think that if a mouse eats a consecrated communion wafer, it has eaten the body and blood of Christ? Her officials generally followed suit, if sometimes grudgingly, until the moment came in which they felt that the Protestant religious settlement was in danger.

That moment came when William Shakespeare was six years old. In May 1570 a well-to-do Catholic, John Felton, nailed to the door of the bishop of London's house a papal bull excommunicating Queen Elizabeth. The pope, Pius V, added an order to all her Catholic subjects "that they presume not to obey her, or her monitions, mandates, and laws," lest they too be excommunicated. Felton was tortured, convicted of treason, and executed. English Catholics were regarded with greatly intensified suspicion.

Why should the pope—who was subsequently beatified and made a saint—have put the faithful in such an impossible position? Because in his view and that of many others, Elizabeth was the only serious obstacle to the return of wayward England to the Catholic faith. He was confident that most ordinary English men and women retained their ancient religious loyalty, and his agents had conducted a survey in 1567 that disclosed that fifty-two of the English peers were either staunch Catholics or well disposed to the Catholic Church and only fifteen were firmly committed

Protestants. The question was whether this religious loyalty could be turned into political action, and the pope decided that it could. The papal bull initiated a nightmarish sequence of conspiracy and persecution, plot and counterplot that continued throughout Elizabeth's long reign.

STRATFORD EXPERIENCED THE SAME sudden shifts, tensions, and ambiguities that marked much of the realm all through the sixteenth century. The monasteries and nunneries in the area had been sacked in the 1530s and '40s, and certain local families—among them the Lucys of Charlecote—had enriched themselves with the spoils. Then in the 1550s, when John Shakespeare moved to Stratford, the surrounding area was dotted with pyres on which local Protestant leaders— Laurence Saunders, at Coventry; John Hooper, at Gloucester; Hugh Latimer, at Oxford; among many others—were burned to death by the resurgent Catholics under Queen Mary. At the accession of Elizabeth, Catholic leaders were now in their turn in serious trouble, though in the first years of her reign the queen, both by temperament and policy, preferred fines, dismissal, and imprisonment to judicial murder. In Stratford the Catholic priest Roger Dyos, who had baptized the Shakespeares' first child, Joan, was dismissed, replaced by the staunchly Protestant John Bretchgirdle. It was Bretchgirdle who on April 26, 1564, christened the Shakespeares' first son, "Gulielmus filius Johannes Shakspere." Religious upheaval aside, it was not a propitious moment to enter the world: by July the town was ravaged by bubonic plague, killing fully a sixth of the population before the winter. Nearly two-thirds of the babies born that year in Stratford died before they reached their first birthday. Perhaps Mary Shakespeare packed up and took her newborn to the country for several months, away from the pestiferous streets.

For parents of John and Mary Shakespeare's generation, the world into which they brought their children must have seemed strange, unsettling, and dangerous: within living memory, England had gone from a highly conservative Roman Catholicism—in the 1520s Henry VIII had

fiercely attacked Luther and been rewarded by the pope with the title
"Defender of the Faith"—to Catholicism under the supreme headship of
the king; to a wary, tentative Protestantism; to a more radical Protestantism; to a renewed and militant Roman Catholicism; and then, with
Elizabeth, to Protestantism once again. In none of these regimes was
there a vision of religious tolerance. Each shift was accompanied by
waves of conspiracy and persecution, rack and thumbscrew, ax and fire.

Most people found it possible to keep their heads down, do what
they had to do in order to conform to the official line, and reconcile their
conscience to the shifts in doctrine and practice. Accommodation in the
interests of survival led some to acquire a certain skeptical detachment
from the strong claims made by both sides, claims made in the name of
love and yet enforced by torture and execution. But for those who
believed that the fate of their eternal souls depended upon the precise
form of worship—and that, after all, is what the strong claims were
about—the shifts in official belief and regulated practice must have been
excruciating. Local communities were ruptured, friendships were broken,
families were torn asunder—parents against children, wives against husbands—and inner lives tormented with pity and fear.

It was not only the pious who found it difficult to keep their heads
down (or, more precisely, their heads on); it was also the ambitious. Major
figures—powerful aristocrats, important magnates, members of the
queen's Privy Council—were of course expected to stand up and be
counted, and so too were small-scale civic leaders like John Shakespeare.
As a constable in 1558–59, he had to keep the peace between Catholics
and Protestants in the tense year of transition from the reign of the
Catholic Mary to that of the Protestant Elizabeth. No doubt he had difficult moments, but at least he could maintain, if he wished, an air of
studied neutrality. But as chamberlain, alderman, and bailiff, he had to
act to carry out the policies of the regime, and that meant something
more than keeping the peace.

A few months before Will's birth and in the years that followed,
Chamberlain John Shakespeare oversaw the "reparations" of Stratford's
fine Guild Chapel. "Reparations" here was a euphemism. What it meant
was that he paid the workmen who went in with buckets of whitewash

and ruined the medieval paintings—St. Helena and the Finding of the Cross, St. George and the Dragon, the murder of St. Thomas à Becket, and, above the arch, the Day of Judgment—that covered the church walls. Their task was not quite finished: the workmen also broke up the altar, putting a simple table in its place, and pulled down the rood loft— a gallery, surmounted by a cross, that separated the nave from the choir and displayed to the faithful the image of the crucified God. Town authorities proceeded to sell off the gorgeous vestments worn by the Catholic priests who had once celebrated the mystery of the Mass. It is worth pausing over these acts: John Shakespeare did not directly do any of them, and, in all likelihood, he did not single-handedly make the decision to have them done, but he was responsible for them, answerable both administratively—in the form of signed accounts presented on January 10, 1564, March 21, 1565, and February 15, 1566—and morally.

What were the changes for which he was paying? They were the material manifestations of the reformed religion, calculated acts of symbolic violence against the traditional Catholic religious observance, ways of compelling the community to acknowledge the new order and to observe its practices. Somewhere within the actions there is a theology, subtle doctrinal and philosophical arguments by relentlessly sober intellectuals. But the deeds in Stratford, for which the chamberlain disbursed the payments, were not subtle: men with hammers, awls, and grappling hooks violently changed the appearance of the church and the form of worship that would take place within it.

Paymaster for the ideological vandals, John Shakespeare acted officially as a committed Protestant, the agent of the Reformation in Stratford. On the town council, he voted to dismiss the Catholic steward Roger Edgeworth and to hire the Protestant Bretchgirdle—an unusually well-educated man, with a library that contained humanist classics as well as theology—to replace the Catholic curate. It is difficult to gauge how earnestly John Shakespeare oversaw these actions. He could have regarded them with the enthusiasm of a zealot, and yet the picture as a whole suggests a more complicated attitude.

The same town council that hired the new vicar Bretchgirdle also hired for the King's New School a succession of impressively learned schoolmasters who had surprisingly strong Catholic connections. The schoolmasters would have had to put in an appearance of conformity to the Anglican church—for such appointments would have been officially approved by the staunchly Protestant Earl of Warwick and the bishop of Winchester—but each evidently harbored loyalty to the ancient faith. Judging from their choices, John Shakespeare and his colleagues cannot have been too eager to identify old believers or apply any ideological test to those who would teach Stratford's children. On the contrary, they allowed—winked at or perhaps even connived at—the teaching of the young not merely by those who might have had some residual regard for the cult of the saints or the Virgin but by those who evidently possessed a deep Catholic commitment. Originally from Lancashire, in the north of England, where the old faith was clung to most tenaciously, Simon Hunt, Will's teacher between the ages of seven and eleven, took the drastic step of leaving Stratford in 1575 for the Continent to attend the Catholic seminary at Douai and, eventually, to become a Jesuit. Why drastic? Because the decision meant that he would either spend the rest of his life in exile or return to England in secret, knowing that the authorities would hunt him down, if they could, and execute him as a seditious traitor. During his years as Stratford schoolmaster, Hunt evidently did not keep his convictions entirely to himself. He seems to have taken at least one of the students from the school with him to Douai— Robert Debdale, who was about seven or eight years older than Will. The Debdales from nearby Shottery were a Catholic family, and Hunt may have had his eye out for other promising children of recusants. He may have taken an interest in William Shakespeare, whose mother was related, albeit distantly, to one of the area's major Catholic families and may even have been related to the Debdales.

The defection of Hunt and Debdale did not seem to deter the Stratford authorities when they chose the next schoolmaster: Thomas Jenkins, a graduate and fellow of St. John's College, Oxford, had a letter of recommendation from the Catholic founder of that college, Sir Thomas White. Like all other Oxford and Cambridge colleges, St. John's was officially Protestant—no other affiliation would have been permitted in an educational institution—but it had the reputation of welcoming

Catholics who were willing to conform and profess loyalty to the queen. This double consciousness—a tenaciously held inward Catholic faith coupled with a steadfast public adherence to the official religious settlement—was widespread in England, where there were many so-called church papists. Jenkins, who would have known and may have studied with the brilliant Catholic scholar Edmund Campion, also a fellow at St. John's, is likely to have been adept at maintaining this delicate balance. The pious Campion himself managed to stay for several years within the bounds of conformity—during which time he deeply impressed the Protestant Earl of Leicester and Queen Elizabeth herself with his brilliance—but in 1572 he embarked for Douai on a course that led him to the priesthood, enlistment in the Jesuits, a teaching post in Prague, and a return to England as a clandestine missionary.

Thomas Jenkins taught in Stratford for four years, from 1575 to 1579, and hence must have been, together with Simon Hunt, a significant schoolteacher in Will's life. Then, at about the time Will would have left the King's New School, Jenkins resigned his post and was succeeded by another Oxford graduate, John Cottam. Like Simon Hunt a native of Lancashire, Cottam, who presumably taught Shakespeare's younger brothers and whom Will certainly came to know, also had strong Catholic connections. His younger brother, Thomas, had gone abroad, after graduating from Oxford, and taken orders as a Catholic priest.

In June 1580 the schoolmaster's brother secretly returned to England as part of the mission led by Campion and a fellow Jesuit, Robert Parsons. Thomas Cottam was intending to go to the neighborhood of Stratford—specifically, to the village of Shottery. He carried a letter of introduction from his close friend and fellow priest, Robert Debdale, who had only five years earlier attended the Stratford grammar school. Debdale had entrusted Cottam with several Catholic tokens—a medal, several Roman coins, a gilt crucifix, and strings of rosary beads—for his family and urged them in his letter to "take counsel" from the messenger "in matters of great weight."

Cottam never reached Shottery. He had made the mistake on the Continent of confiding in a fellow English Catholic named Sledd. Sledd turned out to be an informer, and he provided a precise description of

Cottam to the authorities. "Searchers," as they were called, were watching for him at the ports, and he was arrested as soon as he disembarked at Dover. He had a brief moment of remission: the man in whose custody he was placed to be brought to London turned out to be a secret Catholic, and he let his prisoner escape. But in December 1580, when this custodian in turn was threatened with imprisonment, Thomas Cottam turned himself over to the authorities.

Determined to pry from Cottam his innermost secrets, officials in the Tower employed one of their most horrible devices, the scavenger's daughter. This instrument of torture was a hoop of iron that slowly closed around the prisoner's spine, bending it almost in two. Evidently, the government did not get enough from their interrogation to warrant an immediate trial. Instead, they kept their prisoner in the Tower almost a year, until they had captured other members of the mission. Cottam was then arraigned as a traitor, together with the others, in November 1581. On May 30, 1582, he was executed in the grisly way designed to demonstrate the full rage of the state: he was dragged on a hurdle through the muddy streets to Tyburn, past jeering crowds, and then hanged, taken down while he was still alive, and castrated; his stomach was then slit open and his intestines pulled out to be burned before his dying eyes, whereupon he was beheaded and his body cut in quarters, the pieces displayed as a warning. Robert Debdale met the same fate a few years later.

The Stratford council must have been shaken by the arrest of Thomas Cottam. It was one thing to have quietly hired three Catholic schoolmasters in succession; quite another to have a Catholic priest, suspected of treason, apprehended on his way to the neighborhood, in all likelihood to visit his schoolmaster brother as well as the Debdales. In December 1581, a month after Thomas's arraignment, John Cottam resigned from his position at the King's New School in Stratford and returned to the north. The council may informally have suggested that he leave, or, alternatively, he may simply have felt more comfortable back in Catholic Lancashire, at a safe distance from the vigilant Warwickshire sheriff, Sir Thomas Lucy, who had long been active in ferreting out priests in disguise and their recusant allies.

Why would the state have been so concerned about a young Oxford-educated priest carrying a few beads? From the perspective of the Catholics, such a person was a heroic idealist, abandoning all prospect of tranquility, career, honor, comfort, and family and risking his life daily to serve the embattled community of the faithful. Ordained at a seminary on the Continent and then smuggled back into a kingdom that had become the mortal enemy of his religion, a priest like Cottam would hope to elude informers and find shelter in the house of a sympathetic Catholic. There, disguised as a domestic servant or a child's tutor, he would preach, celebrate communion at a clandestine altar, hear confession, administer last rites to the dying, and perhaps, as Robert Debdale did, conduct exorcisms. From the perspective of the Protestants, he was at best a poor, deluded fool and, more likely, a dangerous fanatic, a conspirator in the service of a foreign power. He was, that is, a traitor, directed by his sinister masters in Rome and willing to do anything to return England to the power of the pope and his allies.

Protestant fears were not ungrounded. The Roman Catholic Church had invited English Catholics to rebel, and the meaning of this invitation was made explicit in 1580, when Pope Gregory XIII proclaimed that the assassination of England's heretic queen would not be a mortal sin. The proclamation was a clear license to kill. It was precisely at this time that the priest Thomas Cottam, with his small packet of Catholic tokens, was arrested on his way to the vicinity of Stratford. Small wonder that his brother's tenure as the town's schoolmaster was abbreviated: John Shakespeare and his fellow council members—and particularly those who had close Catholic kin—must have felt queasy. The trail could quite easily have led to them.

Such fears might seem absurd, for the schoolmaster John Cottam had done nothing wrong. But it will not do to underestimate the mood of paranoia and the reality of threat all through these dangerous years. The assassination of Elizabeth, early in her reign, would almost certainly have changed everything in the religious climate of England. And if it was in hindsight unreasonable to fear, as many people did, that thousands of English Protestants would be massacred as the French Huguenots had been, it was by no means irrational to suspect conspiracies—there *were* many—or to fear that some English Catholics would welcome and support a foreign invasion. The widespread persecution of Catholics made such support virtually inevitable; from this distance, what seems extraordinary is how many pious English Catholics remained loyal to a regime that was intent on crushing them.

Already by the acts that established the Church of England, the Mass was outlawed; it was made illegal to hold any service, except those contained in the Book of Common Prayer. A fine of one shilling was imposed for failure regularly to attend the parish church. In 1571, after the papal bull of excommunication, Parliament made it treason to bring into the country any papal bull or to call the queen a heretic. It was also illegal to go abroad for ordination or to bring into England or to receive any devotional object, "tokens, crosses, pictures, beads or other such like vain things from the Bishop of Rome." In 1581, in the wake of the Jesuits' clandestine mission, Parliament made it treason to reconcile oneself or anyone else to the Catholic Church with the aim of dissolving allegiance to the monarchy. By 1585 it was treason to *be* a Catholic priest, and by law it was illegal (and after 1585 a capital offense) to harbor priests or, knowingly, to give a priest aid or comfort. The penalty for failure to attend Protestant services in the local parish was raised to an astronomical twenty pounds per week. Though the fine cannot have been imposed very often, it hung, as a threat of ruin, over everyone who stayed away from church. Even the very few who could afford to pay such a penalty began to imitate poorer Catholic families: once their children reached the age of sixteen—the age at which the fines took effect—parents would send them to distant neighborhoods, where they were less likely to be caught by the oppressive system.

If Thomas Cottam had been apprehended in Stratford, there might well have been house-to-house searches, conducted by the sheriff. His arrest in London spared the local Catholic population that full-scale terror, but the Jesuit mission of 1580 and the tangled conspiracies of the ensuing years led to intensified rumormongering, spying, and sporadic raids on suspect recusant houses. Many of those houses harbored secrets that close scrutiny could have uncovered, and the house on Henley Street might not have been exempt. For example, if Will's mother, Mary, was a pious Catholic, like her father, she may have kept religious tokens—a rosary, a medal, a crucifix—very much like those seized on the person of the priest. And if the searchers had done a thorough job—and they were on occasion notoriously thorough, ripping open virtually everything in every room—they might have found a highly compromising document to which John Shakespeare had apparently set his name: a piously Catholic "spiritual testament," belying his public adherence to the Reformed faith.

The original document is lost—its contents are known only through a transcript—but given the risks attending such a declaration of faith, the survival of any trace of it at all is remarkable. In the eighteenth century a master bricklayer, retiling the house that had once belonged to the Shakespeares, found the six-leaf manuscript, sewn together with thread, between the rafters and the tiling. The manuscript, minus the first page, eventually reached the great editor of Shakespeare Edmond Malone, who published it but then, subsequently, had doubts about its authenticity, noting certain anomalies in the handwriting and spelling. That authenticity, though it remains open to question, was considerably bolstered by the discovery in the twentieth century of the document's source, a formulary written by the great Italian statesman and scholar Cardinal Carlo Borromeo. The Jesuits Campion and Parsons stayed with Borromeo in Milan, on their way to England, and could have received the text directly from him then. Translated and printed, with spaces left blank for the insertion of the names of the faithful, copies were smuggled into England and secretly distributed. Campion himself may have given them out when he passed through the Midlands, stopping in Lapworth, twelve miles from Stratford, where his host was the staunch Catholic Sir William Catesby, a relative by marriage of the Ardens. John Shakespeare could have received his copy from any number of people involved in the clandestine network of Jesuit sympathizers whom Lucy and the other Warwickshire officials were attempting to destroy.

The "spiritual testament" conflicts wildly with the iconoclastic violence that Chamberlain John Shakespeare authorized and paid for. What this suggests is that for Will, when he was growing up, there was not only a split between his father and mother, the former the active agent of the

Reformation in Stratford, the latter in all likelihood a Catholic, but also a split within his father. One side of him was the alderman who voted to dismiss Stratford's priest and replace him with a Reformed minister, the official who signed off on the whitewashing of the old frescoes and the smashing of the altar, the smiling public man who negotiated on behalf of the city with zealous Protestants like Thomas Lucy. The other side of him was the man whose name appeared on the "spiritual testament," who prayed for the special protection of the Virgin Mary and his personal saint, St. Winifred, who expressed an intense sense of his unworthiness as a "member of the holy Catholic religion." This was presumably the official who helped to hire the Catholic schoolmasters Hunt, Jenkins, and Cottam; and perhaps it was even the recusant who stayed away from church services and had his friends on the council cover his absence with the claim that he was worried about arrest for debt.

Perhaps the secret Catholic was the real John Shakespeare, and the Protestant civic officer was only the worldly, ambitious outward man. Alternatively, perhaps John Shakespeare, securely Protestant for most of his adult life, only briefly returned (during an illness, say, or simply to placate his wife) to the Catholicism he had left behind. Did John Shakespeare's eldest son know the truth? Could he have been sure which was the "real" father—the one who was moving up in the world or the one who kept the peace at home and perhaps in his heart by succumbing to the old fears and longings? He might have sensed that his father was playing a part, without ever knowing securely where the boundary lay between fiction and reality. He might have overheard whispered arguments between his father and mother and observed furtive acts. And at some point—to continue this line of speculation—he might have reached a strange but plausible conclusion: his father was both Catholic and Protestant. John Shakespeare had simply declined to make a choice between the two competing belief systems. Many of the people Will had encountered—the schoolmasters Simon Hunt, Thomas Jenkins, and John Cottam were presumably all examples—lived double lives: they outwardly conformed to the official Protestant religious settlement, at least enough to secure their jobs, but they inwardly adhered to the old faith. But John Shakespeare, his son may have observed, was something else. He wanted to keep both his options open—after all, he had seen enough of the world to know that there might be a drastic change of direction again; he wanted to cover himself in relation both to this life and to the afterlife; he was convinced that both positions, however incompatible they might seem to be, were possible to hold at once. He had not so much a double life as a double consciousness.

And Will? By the time he was leaving school in 1579–80, when he was fifteen or sixteen years old, had he come to acquire a comparable double consciousness? Shakespeare's plays provide ample evidence for doubleness and more: at certain moments—*Hamlet* is the greatest example—he seems at once Catholic, Protestant, and deeply skeptical of both. But though the adult Shakespeare was deeply marked by the religious struggles, what the adolescent believed (if he himself even knew what he believed) is wholly inaccessible. Out of a tissue of gossip, hints, and obscure clues a shadowy picture can be glimpsed, rather as one can glimpse a figure in the stains on an old wall.

It is odd and striking that several of Stratford's schoolmasters had connections to distant Lancashire, the part of the country where adherence to Catholicism remained particularly strong. John Cottam's family property there was only ten miles from one of the principal residences of the wealthy and influential Catholic Alexander Hoghton. As the scholar Ernst Honigmann and others have suggested, Cottam could have been asked by the Hoghtons to recommend a promising young man to be a teacher to their children—not a licensed schoolmaster, someone who would have to be certified as a Protestant by the local bishop, but a private tutor for a large household. He could have proposed Will Shakespeare, who had just left school and who, since his father's financial difficulties precluded his attending university, was looking for employment. Cottam would have been careful not only to find someone who possessed sufficient educational accomplishments—as it happened, he hit upon the most staggeringly talented young man in the kingdom—but also to find a good Catholic. For the devout Hoghtons almost certainly illegally harbored priests, along with illegal ritual objects and a large collection of banned or suspect books, and they would have wanted as servants only those whom they could trust to keep their dangerous secrets.

The small clue that Shakespeare sojourned in Lancashire has nothing in any obvious way to do with religion, Catholic or Protestant. Instead, it points to the theater. In his last will and testament, dated August 3, 1581, the dying Alexander Hoghton bequeathed all his "instruments belonging to musics [*sic*], and all manner of play clothes" to his brother Thomas, or, if Thomas does not choose to keep and maintain players, to Sir Thomas Hesketh. The will added, "And I most heartily require the said Sir Thomas to be friendly unto Fulk Gyllome and William Shakeshafte now dwelling with me and either to take them unto his service or else to help them to some good master." "Shakeshafte" is not "Shakespeare," and skeptics have pointed out that many local people were surnamed Shakeshafte. But in a world of notoriously loose spelling of names—in various records Marlowe is also Marlow, Marley, Morley, Marlyn, Marlen and Marlin— it is close enough, in conjunction with the Cottam-Hoghton connection, Shakespeare's future profession, and other small hints to have convinced many scholars that it refers to Stratford's Will.

The precocious adolescent—recommended by Cottam as intelligent, reasonably well educated, discreet, and securely Catholic—would have come north in 1580 as schoolmaster. The terms of the will suggest that he soon began to perform, at first probably only recreationally and then with increasing seriousness, with the players that Alexander Hoghton kept. Whatever his skills as a teacher, those he possessed as a player would have immediately brought him to the special attention of the household and its master, and the charismatic appeal of the young player would have enabled him—like Cesario in *Twelfth Night*—quickly to overleap other, older servants and become one of the trusted favorites. After Hoghton died in August 1581, Shakespeare could have passed briefly into the service of Hesketh and then might have been commended—as Hoghton had requested—to someone else. The likeliest candidate is a powerful neighbor of Hesketh's who was even more interested in drama. That neighbor, Henry Stanley, the fourth Earl of Derby, and his son Ferdinando, Lord Strange, (a poet whose gifts were celebrated by Edmund Spenser) employed a talented, professionally ambitious group of players who were licensed by the Privy Council as Lord Strange's Men. The principal players—Will Kempe, Thomas Pope, John

Heminges, Augustine Phillips, and George Bryan—formed the core of the London company with which Shakespeare would later be associated, the Lord Chamberlain's Men. The precise chronology of Shakespeare's link with this group cannot be determined, but the link eventually formed the center of his professional career, and it is at least possible that the initial contact—a momentous acquaintance to be renewed later—was made in the north of England in 1581.

Will's life, if he actually sojourned in the north, would have been a peculiar compound of theatricality and danger. On the one hand, a life of open, exuberant display, where for the first time Will's talents—his personal charm, his musical skills, his power of improvisation, his capacity to play a role, and perhaps even his gifts as a writer—were blossoming in performances beyond the orbit of his family and friends. His performances would not have been exactly public, but neither were they simply private after-dinner entertainments. The Heskeths were immensely wealthy, while the Hoghtons and, still more, the Stanleys were feudal magnates. They were representatives of a world of riches, power, and culture that had not yet been completely assimilated into the centralizing, hierarchical scheme of the Tudor monarchy, just as they had not yet been assimilated into the state religion. With small armies of retainers and followers; with crowds of allies, relations, and tenants; with pride fed by the obsequious deference of all around them; and with generosity reinforced by their craving for reputation as "householders," they entertained large companies of guests in banqueting halls that could easily serve as theaters. The brilliance of the performances in those halls redounded to the credit of the magnanimous host. Fulk Gyllome's improvisational skills and gifts as an actor are unknown, but William Shakespeare's proved sufficient to get him a place a few years later in London's leading playing company. As for his imaginative power, if only the smallest fraction began to show itself in the halls of the wealthy Lancashire gentlemen, its intensity would more than explain the dying Hoghton's benevolence.

On the other hand, Will would have lived a life of secrets, where even the lowliest servant knew things—a locked cabinet containing the chalice, books, vestments, and other objects with which to celebrate Mass; mysterious strangers bearing ominous rumors of Mary, Queen of

Scots, or of Spanish armies; mutterings of conspiracies—that could, if revealed, bring disaster upon the family. Lancashire in this period was tense with expectation, suspicion, and anxiety. The moment that Will is likely to have sojourned there is precisely the moment that the Jesuit Campion headed in the same direction, seeking the relative security afforded by the most stubbornly Catholic of the queen's subjects. Lancashire, in the view of the queen's Privy Council, was "the very sink of popery, where more unlawful acts are committed and more unlawful persons held secret than in any other part of the realm." On August 4, 1581, the day after Alexander Hoghton commended Shakeshafte to his friend Sir Thomas Hesketh, the Privy Council ordered a search for Campion's papers "at the house of one Richard Hoghton"—Alexander's cousin—"in Lancashire." And later that year, at a time when Will may have been in his service, Hesketh was thrown into prison for failing to suppress recusancy in his household. The atmosphere at the entertainments in which Will would have performed was compounded of festivity and paranoia.

The mission, led by Campion and Robert Parsons, had aroused the piety of Catholics and deeply alarmed the government. Not only had the pope effectively sanctioned the assassination of the queen, but an expeditionary force led by a Catholic Englishman, Nicholas Sander, had recently landed in Ireland in an attempt to spark an uprising against the Protestant colonists. The attempt had failed miserably: after unconditionally surrendering on November 10, 1580, some six hundred Spanish and Italian troops and their Irish allies, including several women and priests, were all massacred by English soldiers led by Walter Ralegh. The cold-blooded ferocity of the English response was presumably meant to chill any future invasion plans, but no one could doubt the determination of the pope and his allies to topple the Elizabethan regime and reclaim the realm. Even those English Catholics who were steadfastly loyal to Elizabeth—and there were many—must have felt some stirring of hope that the slow, relentless strangulation of their faith might somehow be reversed by the missionary piety and heroic determination of the Jesuits.

Catholics throughout the country secretly read and circulated a remarkable document that came to be known as "Campion's Brag," in which the onetime Oxford don, the object of an intense national search, explained his mission. "In this busy, watchful and suspicious world," he wrote in a tone of almost jaunty resignation, it was likely enough that he would eventually be caught and pressed to reveal his designs. Therefore, to save everyone time and trouble, he offered in advance a plain confession. He had not been sent to meddle in politics; his charge was "to preach the Gospel, to minister the Sacraments, to instruct the simple, to reform sinners, to confute errors." He knew, of course, that the authorities would claim that these activities, undertaken by a Catholic priest, were precisely what it meant to meddle in politics, and he knew that their response would be violent. But he and his companions were "determined never to give you over, but either to win you heaven, or to die upon your pikes." As for the charges of an international conspiracy, a sinister "enterprise" to invade and conquer England, he boldly played with them:

> And touching our Society, be it know to you that we have made a league—all the Jesuits in the world, whose succession and multitude must overreach all the practices of England—cheerfully to carry the cross you shall lay upon us, and never to despair your recovery, while we have a man left to enjoy your Tyburn, or to be racked with your torments, or consumed with your prisons. The expense is reckoned, the enterprise is begun; it is of God, it cannot be withstood. So the faith was planted: so it must be restored.

The sublime confidence that Campion exuded here was evident also in the challenge that gave his pamphlet its nickname: though he would be loath, he wrote, to say anything that would sound like an "insolent brag," he was confident enough of the transparent truth of the Catholic faith that he would undertake to debate any Protestant alive. His words have an odd ring to them, as if he were living not in a world of conspiracies, spies, and torture chambers but in a world in which scholars mount their books and ride out to chivalric contests: "I am to sue most humbly and instantly for the combat with all and every of them, and the most principal that may be found: protesting that in this trial the better furnished they come, the better welcome they shall be."

For Campion, the cruelty of the English Protestant authorities was a sign of their fear of open debate and hence a sign of their despair. He followed up his challenge with a longer, more scholarly work in Latin—the *Ten Reasons*—which he originally intended to call *Heresy in Despair*. This work he somehow planned during months in which he managed to evade the agents sent to capture him, months of shifting disguises, frequent moves from house to house, terrifying alarms, narrow escapes. He wrote it during the only period and in the only place in which he had enough time, protection, and access to books to sit and write: in the late winter and early spring of 1581 in Lancashire. And even there, in the north, he was forced every few days to make sudden shifts in his hiding place in order to confound the government spies and informers. Dressed as a servant, he scurried from one recusant household to another, guided by a former student and his wife. "By them," writes Campion's fine nineteenth-century biographer Richard Simpson, "he was led to visit the Worthingtons, the Talbots, the Southworths, the Heskeths, Mrs. Allen the widow of the Cardinal's brother, the Houghtons, the Westbys, and the Rigmaidens—at whose house he spent the time between Easter and Whitsuntide (April 16)."

The Heskeths and the Hoghtons: it is altogether possible, then, that in the guarded spaces of one or the other of these houses Will would have seen the brilliant, hunted missionary for himself. Campion's visits were clandestine, to be sure, but they were not narrowly private affairs; they brought together dozens, even hundreds of believers, many of whom slept in nearby barns and outbuildings to hear Campion preach in the early morning and to receive communion from his hands. The priest— who would have changed out of his servant's clothes into clerical vestments—would sit up half the night hearing confessions, trying to resolve moral dilemmas, dispensing advice. Was one of those with whom he exchanged whispered words the young man from Stratford-upon-Avon?

Let us imagine the two of them sitting together then, the sixteen-year-old fledgling poet and actor and the forty-year-old Jesuit. Shakespeare would have found Campion fascinating—even his mortal enemies conceded that he had charisma—and might even have recognized in him something of a kindred spirit. Not in piety, for though Will (in this ver-

sion of events) was a staunch enough Catholic at this point in his life to
be trusted with dangerous secrets, there is no sign in his voluminous later
work of a frustrated religious vocation. But Campion—a quarter century
older than Will—was someone who came from a comparably modest
family; who attracted attention to himself by his eloquence, intelligence,
and quickness; who loved books yet at the same time was drawn to life in
the world. His was a learned but not an original mind; rather he was brilliant at giving traditional ideas a new life through the clarity and grace of
his language and the moving power of his presence. Witty, imaginative,
and brilliantly adept at improvisation, he managed to combine medita-
tive seriousness with a strong theatrical streak. If the adolescent knelt
down before Campion, he would have been looking at a distorted image
of himself.

The Jesuit too, perhaps, even in a brief encounter, might have noticed
something striking in the youth. Campion was a gifted teacher who had,
in safer times, written a discourse on education. The ideal student, Campion wrote, should be born of Catholic parents. He should have a mind
"subtle, hot, and clear; his memory happy; his voice flexible, sweet, and
sonorous; his walk and all his motions lively, gentlemanly, and subdued;
and the whole man seeming a palace fit for wisdom to dwell in." His
years at school should plunge him into the classics: he must become intimate with "the majesty of Virgil, the festal grace of Ovid, the rhythm of
Horace, and the buskined speech of Seneca." And the good student is not
merely the passive receptacle of high culture; he is an accomplished musician, a budding orator, and a gifted poet. In short, he is—if the harried
fugitive Campion had occasion to observe him at all closely—the young
Shakespeare.

Well, not quite. For Shakespeare was not on his way to the further
studies—in philosophy, mathematics, astronomy, Hebrew, and, above all,
theology—that Campion's scheme of education envisaged. Moreover, in
one key respect he had already no doubt violated the spirit of the plan,
and he would go on to violate it as completely as possible. The ideal student is to study and to write poetry, Campion said, but with one significant exception: he is never to read or to write love poetry.

For his part, whether he actually met Campion in person or only heard about him from the flood of rumors circulating all through 1580 and 1581, Will may have registered a powerful inner resistance as well as admiration. Campion was brave, charismatic, persuasive, and appealing; everyone who encountered him recognized these qualities, which even now shine out from his words. But he was also filled with a sense that he knew the one eternal truth, the thing worth living and dying for, the cause to which he was willing cheerfully to sacrifice others as well as himself. To be sure, he did not seek out martyrdom. It was not his wish to return to England; he was doing valuable work for the church, he told Cardinal William Allen, in his teaching post at Prague. But he was a committed soldier in a religious order organized for battle, and when his general commanded him to throw his body into the fight, against wildly uneven odds, he marched off serenely. He would have taken with him young Shakespeare or anyone else worth the taking. He was a fanatic or, more accurately, a saint. And saints, Shakespeare understood all his life, were dangerous people.

Or perhaps, rather, it would be better to say that Shakespeare did not entirely understand saints, and that what he did understand, he did not entirely like. In the huge panoply of characters in his plays, there are strikingly few who would remotely qualify. Joan of Arc appears in an early history play, but she is a witch and a whore. King Henry VI has a saintly disposition—"all his mind is bent to holiness / To number Ave-Maries on his beads" (2 Henry II, 1.3.59–60)—but he is pathetically weak, and his weakness wreaks havoc on his realm. The elegant young men in the court of Navarre swear to live a "Still and contemplative" existence, the lives of ascetic soldiers who war against "the huge army of the world's desires" (1.1.14, 10), but Love's Labour's Lost shows them quickly succumbing to charms of the princess of France and her ladies. The severe Angelo in Measure for Measure is a man who "scarce confesses / That his blood flows" (1.3.51–52), but he soon finds himself contriving to compel the beautiful Isabella, a novice in a nunnery, to sleep with him. Isabella, for her part, is impressively true to her chaste vocation, but her determination to preserve her virginity, even at the cost of her brother's life, is something less than humanly appealing.

There are many forms of heroism in Shakespeare, but ideological hero-

ism—the fierce, self-immolating embrace of an idea or an institution—is
not one of them. Nothing in his work suggests a deep admiration for the
visible church. Several of his conspicuously Catholic religious figures—Friar
Laurence in *Romeo and Juliet* is an example—are fundamentally sympathetic, but not because they are important figures in the church hierarchy.
On the contrary, Shakespeare's plays almost always depict powerful prelates
as disagreeable, and his little-known history play *King John*, though set in
the early thirteenth century, attacks the pope in highly charged, anachronis-
tically Protestant terms. How dare the pope, King John indignantly asks the
papal legate, attempt to impose his will upon a "sacred king"?

> Thou canst not, Cardinal, devise a name
> So slight, unworthy, and ridiculous
> To charge me to an answer, as the Pope.
> Tell him this tale, and from the mouth of England
> Add thus much more: that no Italian priest
> Shall tithe or toll in our dominions;
> But as we, under God, are supreme head,
> So, under him, that great supremacy
> Where we do reign we will alone uphold
> Without th'assistance of a mortal hand.
>
> (3.1.74–84)

This coarsely explicit piece of Protestant pope-baiting is by no means
the sum of Shakespeare's mature attitude toward the Catholicism in
which he had been immersed as a young man. And it certainly cannot tell
us what the young man felt if and when he stood in the presence of the
fugitive Jesuit. But the only sainthood in which Shakespeare seems passionately to have believed throughout his life derives precisely from the
subject matter and emotions that Campion wished his students at all
costs to avoid: erotic sainthood.

> ROMEO: O then, dear saint, let lips do what hands do:
>   Then pray; grant thou, lest faith turn to despair.
> JULIET: Saints do not move, though grant for prayers' sake.

ROMEO: Then move not while my prayer's effect I take.
   [*He kisses her*]
   Thus from my lips, by thine my sin is purged.
JULIET: Then have my lips the sin that they have took.
ROMEO: Sin from my lips? O trespass sweetly urged!
   Give me my sin again.
   [*He kisses her*]
JULIET: You kiss by th' book.
                        (1.5.100–107)

There are traces of Catholicism here, of a kind that Campion would immediately have recognized, but the theology and the ritual practice have been wittily turned into desire and its fulfillment.

The beautiful, playful lines from *Romeo and Juliet* were written in the mid-1590s, some fifteen years after the moment when Shakespeare may have encountered Campion. But the sly blend of displacement and appropriation, the refashioning of traditional religious materials into secular performance, and the confounding of the sacred and the profane are characteristic of virtually the whole of Shakespeare's achievement as dramatist and poet. In *A Midsummer Night's Dream*, written relatively early in his career, the beds of the newly wed couples are blessed, as they would have been in a popular Catholic practice outlawed by the Protestants, but it is not with holy water; rather, the fairies sprinkle them with "field-dew consecrate" (5.2.45). And in *The Winter's Tale*, written near its end, there is an ecstatic description of a solemn ritual conducted by priests dressed in "celestial habits," but the "grave wearers" of those habits are not celebrating the Mass; rather, what is being described is the Delphic oracle:

                     I shall report,
For most it caught me, the celestial habits—
Methinks I so should term them—and the reverence
Of the grave wearers. O, the sacrifice—
How ceremonious, solemn, and unearthly
It was i'th' off'ring!
                        (3.1.3–8)

This is not a parody of the Mass, but it is also not exactly a sly tribute, slipped under the censor's eye. Instead, the lines and much else like them in Shakespeare's work suggest how completely he had absorbed Catholicism for his own poetic purposes. Those purposes were light-years from Campion's, and the distance might already have been apparent even—or perhaps especially—in Lancashire in 1581.

There is not only the matter of Will's temperament—a lack of religious vocation, a skeptical distance from the missionary's ardent faith, an adolescent's awareness of the claims of his own flesh. Though he was only a young servant, Will could easily have noticed something beyond its religious conviction about the strange, dangerous world he had come to inhabit. The north was a traditional site of resistance to the centralizing authority of the Crown, and the families in whose houses he lived and worked skirted close to treason. All of Shakespeare's early history plays—the plays with which he made a name for himself in London in the early 1590s—were concerned with rebellion, which he consistently conceived of as a family affair. These plays were safely set in the England of the fifteenth century, and the events were taken from the chronicles, but Shakespeare had to draw upon more than his reading to give his characters the touch of reality. His imagination was populated by powerful, restive, ambitious men and women who were willing to take extreme risks in playing the dangerous games of power. His image of these people could well have been taken from the families he would have closely observed during a sojourn in the north.

What this suggests is that if he actually saw Campion in 1581 Shakespeare would even then probably have shuddered and recoiled inwardly, pulling away from the invitation, whether implicit in the saint's presence or directly and passionately urged, to shoulder the cross and join in a pious struggle for the Catholic faith. Will had, as Hoghton's will suggests, been making a mark—probably for the first time in his life—as an actor; he had begun to sense what he was capable of doing and what he had within him. And he was not going to get caught up in a glorious, treasonous, suicidal crusade. If his father was both Catholic and Protestant, William Shakespeare was on his way to being neither.

Shakespeare—assuming that he is the Shakeshafte of Hoghton's will—stayed in Lancashire at least until August 1581, before heading back to Stratford. Campion had left the area earlier; he had been ordered by Parsons to return to the vicinity of London to oversee the secret printing of his *Ten Reasons*. Working hurriedly and in great danger, the printers managed to finish the task in time for the Oxford University commencement on June 27: the students and fellows who filed into St. Mary's Church found hundreds of bound copies waiting for them on their seats. A few weeks later, on his way back to Lancashire, Campion was trapped, arrested, taken to the Tower, and thrust into a cell aptly nicknamed "Little Ease." After four days of painful confinement—the cell did not permit the prisoner either to stand or to lie flat—he was suddenly taken out, carried under guard to a boat, and rowed to the mansion of the immensely powerful Earl of Leicester, the man who had been poised years before to be his patron. Leicester was joined by the Earl of Bedford and two secretaries of state. More astonishing still, Queen Elizabeth herself was in the room. They asked him why he had come to England. For the salvation of souls, he answered, whereupon Elizabeth asked him directly if he acknowledged her as his queen or no. "Not only as my queen," Campion replied, "but also as my most lawful governess." That word "lawful" did not escape the queen's attention; could the pope, she asked, "lawfully" excommunicate her? Could he discharge her subjects of their obedience? These were what Campion described as "bloody questions, and very pharisaical, undermining of my life." He could not, he grasped at once, give the answers she was demanding, the answers that would not only enable him to go free but would also, as the queen made clear, bring him riches and honors. He was taken back to the Tower, where he was interrogated, tortured on the rack, tried for treason, and then, with Thomas Cottam and the others, executed.

Will would only have been able to follow these terrible events through rumor and perhaps through the government's highly distorted printed reports. He would certainly have heard of Campion's capture— that was national news—and he would have heard too, no doubt with special anxiety, that Campion had, under torture, revealed the names of many of his hosts. (The extent of his confession, much trumpeted by the authorities, is still in dispute, though the pattern of subsequent arrests in

Lancashire and elsewhere, along with Campion's own words on the scaffold, indicates that he revealed more than he would have wished.)

Shakespeare might also have heard or read about an extraordinary event that intervened between the Jesuit's capture and his execution. The authorities clearly had been nettled by Campion's "brag"—his challenge to debate anyone on the merits of Catholicism—and by the clandestine publication of *Ten Reasons*. One day at the end of August, Campion was taken from his cell without warning and brought into the chapel of the Tower. There, in the presence of the guards, other Catholic prisoners, and such privileged members of the public as could crowd in, he was confronted with two Protestant theologians, Alexander Nowell, the dean of St. Paul's, and William Day, the dean of Windsor. The theologians, seated at a table piled with books and notes, were celebrated debaters. At another table two other distinguished but hardly neutral figures, William Chark, the preacher of Gray's Inn, and William Whitaker, the Regius Professor of Divinity at Cambridge, were poised to act as notaries. The prisoner would get his debate, but the government would set the stage and the rules.

Campion objected that he had had no time to prepare, had no notes and no books, and that he had been subjected to "hellish torture." The lieutenant of the Tower, Sir Owen Hopton, had the effrontery to declare that the prisoner "was scarce pinched and that it might rather be termed a cramping than racking." Responding with dignity that he himself "could best report, and be most truest judge, because he felt the smart," Campion accepted—as he had no choice but to accept—the grossly unfair terms of the debate. He then proceeded, by what appears to be a near-universal consensus, to annihilate his opponents. The authorities were chagrined. In the weeks that followed, bringing in fresh debaters and sharply restricting the scope and form of Campion's answers, they staged three further debates—this time without permitting any Catholic auditors—until they were satisfied that they could declare victory. They then brought Campion to the scaffold at Tyburn, hanged him, and chopped his body in quarters before a huge crowd of observers. One of the bystanders, a Protestant named Henry Walpole, was close to the place where the hangman was throwing the pieces of Campion's body into a vat of boiling water. A drop of the water mixed with blood splashed out upon his clothes, and Walpole felt at once, he said, that he had to convert to Catholicism. He left for the Continent, became a Jesuit, and was sent back to England, where he too was arrested and executed as a traitor. Such are the works of saints and martyrs.

Not surprisingly, Shakespeare never referred openly to Campion. Perhaps in *King Lear* there is a disguised recollection of the fugitive priest and his fellow missionaries in the figure of the innocent Edgar, viciously slandered by his bastard brother and forced to assume a disguise and flee for his life. "I heard myself proclaimed," the outlawed Edgar declares;

> And by the happy hollow of a tree
> Escaped the hunt. No port is free; no place,
> That guard, and most unusual vigilance,
> Does not attend my taking. Whiles I may 'scape,
> I will preserve myself. . . .
>
> (2.3.1–6)

But Edgar is not a missionary, and Shakespeare may have felt, more than anything else, the desire to distance himself from what had in the winter and spring of 1581 come dangerously close, and an overwhelming relief that he had not been drawn into the nightmare of persecution, torture, and death.

By the next year, Will was back in Stratford. Perhaps he had, after all, agreed to take one small risk, something to do with the unfortunate Thomas Cottam and whatever matters of "great weight" he had intended to convey to the family of Robert Debdale in the village of Shottery, two miles from Stratford. For shortly after he returned home, Will evidently began to walk along the path that led through the fields to Shottery. Did he have a secret message for the parents of the fugitive priest? It is impossible to say. But that the eighteen-year-old boy was in the village is certain, for there he met the eldest daughter of an old acquaintance of his father, a staunchly Protestant farmer named Richard Hathaway, who had died the year before. Anne Hathaway was twenty-six years old. In the summer of 1582—as if to mark his decisive distance from Campion, from the deep piety and the treasonous murmurs, from the scavenger's daughter and the horrible scaffold—Will was making love to her. To this secret life too there were momentous consequences, of a very different kind. By November they were married, and six months later their daughter Susanna was born.

CHAPTER 4

Wooing, Wedding, and Repenting

I F WILL RETURNED to Stratford in 1582 in the wake of a tense sojourn in Lancashire, if he agreed to go to Shottery that summer to convey a risky message or pass along a secret religious token to the Debdales, then his wooing of Anne Hathaway was manifestly a rebellion against the empire of fear. Anne's world was the diametrical opposite of the dangerous world to which he may have been exposed: the powerful all-male bonds formed by Simon Hunt, the schoolmaster who had gone off to the seminary with his student Robert Debdale; the conspiracy to protect Campion, Parsons, Cottam, and the other Jesuit missionaries; the secret sodality of pious, suicidal young men. But even if the circumstances were far less dire, even if Will were merely an inexperienced Stratford adolescent whose principal social points of reference had been his family and the boys at the King's New School, Anne Hathaway must have represented a startling alternative. Will's family almost certainly leaned toward Catholicism, and Anne's almost certainly leaned in the opposite direction. In his will, Anne's father, Richard, asked to be "honestly buried," the code phrase for the simple, stark burials favored by Puritans. Anne's brother Bartholomew also asked for such a burial, "hoping to arise at the Latter Day and to receive the reward of His elect." "His elect": these are people far different from Campion or, for that matter, the Catholic Ardens to whom Shakespeare's mother was related.

Anne Hathaway represented an escape in another sense: she was in the unusual position of being her own woman. Very few young, unmarried Elizabethan women had any executive control over their own lives; the girl's watchful father and mother would make the key decisions for their daughter, ideally, though not always, with her consent. But Anne—an orphan in her midtwenties, with some resources left to her by her father's will and more due to her upon her marriage—was, in the phrase of the times, "wholly at her own government." She was independent, in a way virtually ordained to excite a young man's sexual interest, and she was free to make her own decisions. Shakespeare's lifelong fascination with women who are in this position may have had its roots in the sense of freedom Anne Hathaway awakened in him. He would have felt a release from the constraints of his own family, a release too, perhaps, from the sexual confusion and ambiguity that Elizabethan moralists associated with playacting. If the imaginary schoolboy performance of Plautus had any equivalent in reality—if Will ever experienced a disturbing erotic excitement in acting a love scene with another boy—then Anne Hathaway offered a reassuringly conventional resolution to his sexual ambivalence or perplexity.

Quite apart from this imaginary resolution—whose appeal, albeit temporary, is not to be underestimated—Anne offered a compelling dream of pleasure. So at least one might conclude from the centrality of wooing in Shakespeare's whole body of work, from *The Two Gentlemen of Verona* and *The Taming of the Shrew* to *The Winter's Tale* and *The Tempest*. Lovemaking, not in the sense of sexual intercourse but in the older sense of intense courting and pleading and longing, was one of his abiding preoccupations, one of the things he understood and expressed more profoundly than almost anyone in the world. That understanding may not have had anything to do with the woman he married, of course, and, theoretically at least, it need not have had anything to do with his lived experience at all. But the whole impulse to explore Shakespeare's life arises from the powerful conviction that his plays and poems spring not only from other plays and poems but from things he knew firsthand, in his body and soul.

The adult Shakespeare is very funny about the love antics of rustic youths. In *As You Like It*, for example, he mocks the besotted bumpkin so in love with a milkmaid that he kisses "the cow's dugs that her pretty chapped hands had milked" (2.4.44–45). But somewhere lurking behind the laughter may be a distorted, wry recollection of Shakespeare's own fumbling adolescent efforts, efforts that were perhaps more amply rewarded than he had anticipated. By the summer's end, Anne Hathaway was pregnant.

Shakespeare's marriage has been the subject of almost frenzied interest, ever since a great nineteenth-century bibliophile, Sir Thomas Phillipps, found an odd document in the bishop of Worcester's registry. The document, dated November 28, 1582, was a bond for what was in the period a very large sum of money, forty pounds (twice the annual income of the Stratford schoolmaster; eight times the annual income of a London clothworker), put up in order to facilitate the wedding of "William Shagspere" and "Anne Hathwey of Stratford in the Dioces of Worcester maiden."

The couple—or someone close to the couple—wanted the marriage to take place without delay. The reason for the haste was not specified in the bond, but for once there is a properly documented explanation: the baptism six months later—on May 28, 1583, to be exact—of their daughter Susanna. The language of the bond notwithstanding, a "maiden" Anne Hathaway of Stratford in the diocese of Worcester was definitely not.

Normally, a wedding ceremony could take place only after the banns—the formal declaration of an intent to marry—had been publicly proclaimed on three successive Sundays in the local parish church. The interval that this process necessarily entailed could be compounded by the vagaries of canon law (the code of ecclesiastical rules and regulations), which did not permit the reading of banns during certain periods in the church calendar. In late November 1582 such a prohibited period was fast approaching. By submitting a sworn assurance that there were no impediments of the sort that the banns were designed to bring to light, it was possible, for a fee, to obtain a dispensation, enabling a marriage license to be issued at once. But to back up the sworn assurance, there had to be a way to indemnify the diocesan authorities and to guarantee that something—a prior contract to marry, for example, or the objection of a parent to the marriage choice of a minor, or a covenant not to marry until the end of a term of apprenticeship—would not unexpectedly turn up, solemn oaths notwithstanding, and send the whole business into court. Hence the bond, which would become void if no impediment surfaced.

It is not known if Will's parents approved of the marriage of their eighteen-year-old son to the pregnant twenty-six-year-old bride. Then as now, in England eighteen would have been regarded as young for a man to marry; the mean age upon marriage for males in Stratford in 1600 (the earliest date for which there are reliable figures) was twenty-eight. And it was unusual for a man to marry a woman so much his senior; women in this period were on average two years younger than their husbands. The exceptions were generally among the upper classes, where marriages were in effect property transactions between families and very young children could be betrothed. (In such cases, the marriages were not consummated until years after the wedding, and the newlyweds often waited a very long time before they began to live together.) In the case of Anne Hathaway, the bride had something of an inheritance, but she was hardly a great heiress—in his will her father had stipulated that she was to receive six pounds thirteen shillings fourpence on her marriage—and a financially embarrassed, communally prominent John Shakespeare might have hoped that his son's bride would bring a larger dowry. Had they bitterly objected, Shakespeare's parents could have made a legal fuss, since their son was a minor. (The age of majority was twenty-one.) They did not do so, perhaps because, as legal records show, Shakespeare's father had been acquainted with Anne's father. Still, it is likely that in the eyes of John and Mary Shakespeare, Will was not making a great match.

And Will? Through the centuries eighteen-year-old boys have not been famously eager in such situations to rush to the altar. Will might, of course, have been an exception. Certainly, he was able as a playwright to imagine such impatience. "When and where and how / We met, we wooed, and made exchange of vow / I'll tell thee as we pass," Romeo tells Friar Laurence on the morning after the Capulet ball; "but this I pray, / That thou consent to marry us today" (2.2.61–64).

Romeo and Juliet's depiction of the frantic haste of the rash lovers blends together humor, irony, poignancy, and disapproval, but Shakespeare conveys above all a deep inward understanding of what it feels like to be young, desperate to wed, and tormented by delay. In the great balcony scene, though they have only just met, Romeo and Juliet exchange "love's faithful vow" with one another. "If that thy bent of love be honourable, / Thy purpose marriage," Juliet tells Romeo at the close of the most passionate love scene Shakespeare ever wrote, "send me word tomorrow." When she knows "Where and what time thou wilt perform the rite," she declares, "All my fortunes at thy foot I'll lay, / And follow thee, my lord, throughout the world" (2.1.169, 185–86, 188–90).

Hence the urgency of Romeo's visit to the friar early the next morning, and hence the wild eagerness of Juliet for the return of her nurse, whom she has sent to get Romeo's response. "Old folks, many feign as they were dead," the young girl complains, "Unwieldy, slow, heavy, and pale as lead." When the nurse finally trundles in, Juliet can scarcely pry the all-important news from her:

> NURSE: I am a-weary. Give me leave a while.
>   Fie, how my bones ache. What a jaunce have I!
> JULIET: I would thou hadst my bones and I thy news.
>   Nay, come, I pray thee speak, good, good Nurse, speak.
> NURSE: Jesu, what haste! Can you not stay a while?
>   Do you not see that I am out of breath?
> JULIET: How art thou out of breath when thou hast breath
>   To say to me that thou art out of breath?
>   The excuse that thou dost make in this delay
>   Is longer than the tale thou dost excuse.
>   . . . .
>   What says he of our marriage—what of that?
>
>   (2.4.16–17, 25–46)

Exasperated impatience has never been more deftly and sympathetically chronicled.

Romeo's urgency is sketched rather cursorily; it is Juliet's that is given much fuller scope and intensity. Similarly, it is eminently likely that Anne, three months pregnant, rather than the young Will, was the prime source of the impatience that led to the bond. To be sure, this was Elizabethan and not Victorian England: an unmarried mother in the 1580s did not, as she would in the 1880s, routinely face fierce, unrelenting social stigmatization. But the shame and social disgrace in Shakespeare's time were real enough; bastardy was severely frowned upon by the community, as the child would need to be fed and clothed; and the six pounds thirteen shillings fourpence would only be given to Anne when she found a husband.

The substantial bond to hurry the marriage along was posted by a pair of Stratford farmers, Fulke Sandells and John Rychardson, friends of the bride's late father. The young bridegroom and father-to-be may have been grateful for this handsome assistance, but it is far more likely that he was a reluctant, perhaps highly reluctant, beneficiary. If the playwright's imagination subsequently conjured up an impatient Romeo, eager to wed, it also conjured up a series of foot-dragging bridegrooms shamed or compelled to wed the women with whom they have slept. "She is two months on her way," the clown Costard tells the braggart Armado, who has seduced a peasant girl. "What meanest thou?" Armado demands, trying to bluster his way out of the situation, but Costard insists: "She's quick. The child brags in her belly already. 'Tis yours" (*Love's Labour's Lost*, 5.2.658–63). Armado is no romantic hero; like Lucio in *Measure for Measure* and Bertram in *All's Well That Ends Well*, he is treated with irony, distaste, and contempt. But these may have been precisely the feelings evoked in Shakespeare when he looked back upon his own marriage.

In one of his earliest works, the *1 Henry VI*, he had a character compare a marriage by compulsion to one made voluntarily:

> For what is wedlock forcèd but a hell,
> An age of discord and continual strife,

> Whereas the contrary bringeth bliss,
> And is a pattern of celestial peace.
>
> (5.7.62–65)

The character is an earl, cynically persuading the king to make what will be a bad match, but the dream of bliss seems valid enough, along with the sense that "wedlock forcèd" is an almost certain recipe for unhappiness. Perhaps at the time he wrote those lines, in the early 1590s, Shakespeare was reflecting on the source of his own marital unhappiness. Perhaps too there is a personal reflection in Richard of Gloucester's sly observation "Yet hasty marriage seldom proveth well" (*3 Henry VI*, 4.1.18) or in Count Orsino's advice in *Twelfth Night*:

> Let still the woman take
> An elder than herself. So wears she to him;
> So sways she level in her husband's heart.
>
> (2.4.28–30)

Of course, each of these lines has a specific dramatic context, but they were all written by someone who at eighteen years of age had hastily married a woman older than himself and then left her behind in Stratford. How could he have written Orsino's words without in some sense bringing his own life, his disappointment, frustration, and loneliness, to bear upon them?

Suspicion that Will was dragged to the altar has been heightened by another document. The bond for the grant of a marriage license to Willam Shagspere and Anne Hathwey is dated November 28, but the Worcester archives also record a marriage license dated one day earlier, November 27, for the wedding of William Shaxpere and Anne Whatley of Temple Grafton. As there were other Shakespeares in Warwickshire, a different William could conceivably have happened to wed at just this time. Assuming, however, that such a coincidence would be unlikely, who on earth is Anne Whatley of Temple Grafton, a village about five miles west of Stratford? A woman Will loved and was hastening to marry until he was strong-armed by Sandells and Rychardson into wedlock with the pregnant Anne Hathaway?

The possibility has a novelistic appeal: "And so he was still riding to Temple Grafton in cold November," wrote Anthony Burgess in a fine flight of fancy, "winter's first harbingers biting. Hoofs rang frosty on the road. Hard by Shottery two men stopped him. They addressed him by name and bade him dismount." But most scholars have agreed with Joseph Gray, who concluded in 1905, after extensive study, that the clerk who entered the names on the license simply became confused and wrote Whatley instead of Hathaway. Most scholars imagine too that Will was in some measure willing. But the state of his feelings at the time of his wedding is not known, and his attitude toward his wife during the subsequent thirty-two years of marriage can only be surmised. Between his wedding license and his last will and testament, Shakespeare left no direct, personal trace of his relationship with his wife—or none, in any case, that survives. From this supremely eloquent man, there have been found no love letters to Anne, no signs of shared joy or grief, no words of advice, not even any financial transactions.

A sentimental nineteenth-century picture shows Shakespeare at home in Stratford, reciting one of his plays to his family—his father and mother listening from a distance, a dog at his feet, his three children gathered around him, his wife looking up at him adoringly from her needlework—but such a moment, if it ever occurred, would have been exceedingly rare. For most of his married life he lived in London, and Anne and the children apparently remained in Stratford. That in itself does not necessarily imply estrangement; husbands and wives have often been constrained for long periods to live at a considerable distance from one another. But it must have been exceptionally difficult in Shakespeare's time to bridge this distance, to keep up any intimacy. All the more difficult, of course, if, as seems likely, his wife Anne could not read or write. Of course, most of the women in his world had little or no literacy, but the commonness of the condition does not change the fact: it is entirely possible that Shakespeare's wife never read a word he wrote, that anything he sent her from London had to be read by a neighbor, that anything she wished to tell him—the local gossip, the health of his parents, the mortal illness of their only son—had to be consigned to a messenger.

Perhaps the optimists are right and their relationship, notwithstanding the long years apart, was a good one. Biographers eager for Shakespeare to have had a good marriage have stressed that when he made some money in the theater, he established his wife and family in New Place, the fine house he bought in Stratford; that he must have frequently visited them there; that he chose to retire early and return permanently to Stratford a few years before his untimely death. Some have gone further and assumed that he must have had Anne and the children stay with him for prolonged periods in London. "None has spoken more frankly or justly of the honest joys of 'board and bed,'" wrote the distinguished antiquarian Edgar Fripp, pointing to lines from *Coriolanus*:

> I loved the maid I married; never man
> Sighed truer breath. But that I see thee here,
> Thou noble thing, more dances my rapt heart
> Than when I first my wedded mistress saw
> Bestride my threshold.
>   (4.5.113–17)

But if these lines were, as Fripp thought, a recollection of the dramatist's own feelings many years before, the recollection was far more bitter than sentimental: they are spoken by the warrior Aufidius, whose rapt heart dances at seeing the hated man he has long dreamed of killing.

It is, perhaps, as much what Shakespeare did *not* write as what he did that seems to indicate something seriously wrong with his marriage. This was an artist who made use of virtually everything that came his way. He mined, with very few exceptions, the institutions and professions and personal relationships that touched his life. He was the supreme poet of courtship: one has only to think of the aging sonneteer and the fair young man, panting Venus and reluctant Adonis, Orlando and Rosalind, Petruccio and Kate, even twisted, perverse Richard III and Lady Anne.

And he was a great poet of the family, with a special, deep interest in the murderous rivalry of brothers and in the complexity of father-daughter relations: Egeus and Hermia, Brabanzio and Desdemona, Lear and the fearsome threesome, Pericles and Marina, Prospero and Miranda. But though wedlock is the promised land toward which his comic heroes and heroines strive, and though family fission is the obsessive theme of the tragedies, Shakespeare was curiously restrained in his depictions of what it is actually like to be married.

To be sure, he provided some fascinating glimpses. A few of his married couples have descended into mutual loathing: "O Goneril!" cries the disgusted Albany, in *King Lear*. "You are not worth the dust which the rude wind / Blows in your face." "Milk-livered man!" she spits back at him. "That bear'st a cheek for blows, a head for wrongs: . . . Marry, your manhood! mew!" (4.2.30–32, 51–69). But for the most part, they are in subtler, more complex states of estrangement. Mostly, it's wives feeling neglected or shut out. "For what offence," Kate Percy asks her husband, Harry (better known as Hotspur), in *1 Henry IV*, "have I this fortnight been / A banished woman from my Harry's bed?" She has in point of fact committed no offence—Hotspur is deeply preoccupied with plotting a rebellion—but she is not wrong to feel excluded. Hotspur has chosen to keep his wife in the dark:

> But hark you, Kate.
> I must not have you henceforth question me
> Whither I go, nor reason whereabout.
> Whither I must, I must; and, to conclude,
> This evening must I leave you, gentle Kate.
> (2.4.32–33, 93–97)

The rebellion is a family affair—Hotspur has been drawn into it by his father and his uncle—but though the fate of his wife will certainly be involved in its outcome, the only knowledge she has of it is from words she has overheard him muttering in his troubled sleep. With bluff, genial misogyny Hotspur explains that he simply does not trust her:

I know you wise, but yet no farther wise
Than Harry Percy's wife; constant you are,
But yet a woman; and for secrecy
No lady closer, for I well believe
Thou wilt not utter what thou dost not know.
And so far will I trust thee, gentle Kate.

(2.4.98–103)

The words are all good-humored and exuberant, in the way most of the things Hotspur says are, but the marriage they sketch is one at whose core is mutual isolation. (The same play, *1 Henry IV*, gives another, more graphic vision of such a marriage in Edmund Mortimer and his Welsh wife: "This is the deadly spite that angers me: / My wife can speak no English, I no Welsh" [3.1.188–89].)

Shakespeare returned to the theme in *Julius Caesar*, where Brutus's wife, Portia, complains that she has been deliberately shut out of her husband's inner life. Unlike Kate Percy, Portia is not banished from her husband's bed, but her exclusion from his mind leaves her feeling, she says, like a whore:

Am I yourself
But as it were in sort or limitation?
To keep with you at meals, comfort your bed,
And talk to you sometimes? Dwell I but in the suburbs
Of your good pleasure? If it be no more,
Portia is Brutus' harlot, not his wife.

(2.1.281–86)

The question here and elsewhere in the plays is the degree of intimacy that husbands and wives can achieve, and the answer Shakespeare repeatedly gives is very little.

Shakespeare was not alone in his time in finding it difficult to portray or even imagine fully achieved marital intimacy. It took decades of Puritan insistence on the importance of companionship in marriage to change the social, cultural, and psychological landscape. By the time Milton published *Paradise Lost*, in 1667, the landscape was decisively differ-

Mr. WILLIAM

SHAKESPEARES

COMEDIES,
HISTORIES, &
TRAGEDIES.

Published according to the True Originall Copies.

Martin Droeshout sculpsit London.

LONDON
Printed by Isaac Iaggard, and Ed. Blount. 1623.

Though Martin Droeshout (c. 1601–c. 1650) was only fifteen when Shakespeare died and thus unlikely to have seen him in person, his engraving on the title page of the First Folio (1623) must have seemed sufficiently accurate to satisfy the editors, who knew Shakespeare well. *By courtesy of W. W. Norton & Company.*

Gloves, of the kind that Shakespeare's father made, were often elaborate luxury items, such as this early seventeenth-century pair made of leather, satin, and gold bobbin lace. *By courtesy of V & A Images/V & A Museum.*

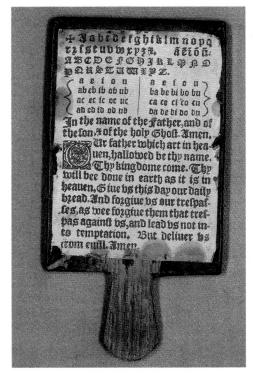

Young Will probably learned his letters from what was known as a hornbook: a printed sheet of parchment or paper mounted on wood and covered with a transparent sheet of animal horn.
By courtesy of the Folger Shakespeare Library.

The nave of Stratford's Guild Chapel, with the remains of the medieval wall painting of Christ and the Last Judgment, whitewashed over in 1563 on instructions from the town chamberlain, John Shakespeare. *By courtesy of Maya Vision International.*

P. EDMVNDVS CAMPIANVS Q PR̄ E SOC IESV LONDINI
PRO CAT⁰ FIDE MARTYR̄ CONSVMAVIT P̄ DEC ·1581·

In this copy of a portrait painted shortly after his execution in 1581, Edmund Campion, carrying the palm of martyrdom, is about to be crowned by an angel. Crowning by the Catholic Church took longer: beatified by Pope Leo XIII on December 9, 1886, Campion was canonized by Pope Paul VI in 1970. *By courtesy of Stonyhurst College, Lancashire.*

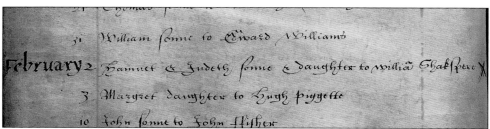

Record in the Stratford parish register of the christening, on February 2, 1585, of William and Anne Shakespeare's twins, Hamnet and Judith, named after their neighbors Hamnet and Judith Sadler. When, three years later, the Sadlers had a son, they named him William. *By permission of the Shakespeare Birthplace Trust.*

In this painting, attributed to Robert Peake (c. 1551–1626), Queen Elizabeth is carried in procession like a bejeweled idol. *By permission of the Bridgeman Art Library.*

Shakespear ye Player
by garter

The Shakespeare coat of arms, roughly sketched in 1602 by an official who claimed that "Shakespeare yᵉ Player" should not have been allowed to claim the status of a gentleman. *By courtesy of the Folger Shakespeare Library.*

...RITANNIÆ URBS, EM...

LONDON

S. Paules Church

...AMESIS

The Bear Garden   The Globe

Sou...

A detail from Claes Jansz. Visscher's engraving of London Bridge, showing the heads of traitors stuck on pikes. *By courtesy of the Folger Shakespeare Library.*

Panoramic view of early seventeenth-century London by the Amsterdam engraver Claes Jansz. Visscher (1587–1652), showing such sights as St. Paul's Church, the Globe Theater, the bear garden, and London Bridge. *By courtesy of the Folger Shakespeare Library.*

In this miniature, painted by Nicholas Hilliard (c. 1547–1619), the twenty-year-old Henry Wriothesley, third Earl of Southampton, displays the long auburn hair for which he was famous. *By permission of the Bridgeman Art Library.*

No portrait of Christopher Marlowe with a strong claim to authenticity survives, but the dating and provenance of this late sixteenth-century painting, at Corpus Christi College, Cambridge, makes it at least possible that it depicts the playwright as a brooding undergraduate. *By courtesy of Corpus Christi College, Cambridge.*

ent. Marriage was no longer the consolation prize for those who did not have the higher vocation of celibacy; it was not the doctrinally approved way of avoiding the sin of fornication; it was not even principally the means of generating offspring and conveying property. It was about the dream of long-term love.

But it is not clear how much of this dream could have been envisaged when Will agreed, whether eagerly or reluctantly, to marry Anne Hathaway. It is no accident that Milton wrote important tracts advocating the possibility of divorce; the longing for deep emotional satisfaction in marriage turned out to depend heavily upon the possibility of divorce. In a world without this possibility most writers seemed to agree: it was better to make jokes about endurance, pass over most marriages in discreet silence, and write love poetry to anyone but your spouse. Dante wrote the passionate *La vita nuova* not to his wife, Gemma Donati, but to Beatrice Portinari, whom he had first glimpsed when they were both children. So too Petrarch, who was probably ordained as a priest, wrote the definitive European love poems—the great sequence of sonnets—to the beautiful Laura, and not to the unnamed, unknown woman who gave birth to his two children, Giovanni and Francesca. And in England, Stella, the star at which Sir Philip Sidney gazed longingly in his sonnet sequence *Astrophil and Stella*, was Penelope Devereux, married to someone else, and not his wife, Frances Walsingham.

It was reasonable to hope for stability and comfort in marriage, but not for much more, and if you did not find anything that you wanted, if relations deteriorated into sour-eyed bitterness, there was no way to end the marriage and begin again. Divorce—even as an imagined solution, let alone a practical one—did not exist in 1580 in Stratford-upon-Avon, not for anyone of Shakespeare's class, scarcely for anyone at all. Like everyone who wedded at that time, he married for life, whether the marriage turned out to be fulfilling or disastrous, whether the person he had chosen (or who had chosen him) continued after a year or so to touch his heart or filled him with revulsion.

Yet diminished cultural expectations can at best only partially explain Shakespeare's reluctance or inability to represent marriage, as it were, from the inside. For he did in fact register the frustrated longing for spousal intimacy, though he attributed that longing almost exclusively to women. Along with Kate Percy and Portia, there is Shakespeare's most poignant depiction of a neglected wife, Adriana in *The Comedy of Errors*. Since *The Comedy of Errors* is a farce and since it is based on a Roman model that has absolutely no emotional investment in the figure of the wife—Plautus jokingly has her put up for sale at the close of his play—it is all the more striking that Shakespeare registered so acutely her anguish:

> How comes it now, my husband, O how comes it
> That thou art then estrangèd from thyself?—
> Thy 'self' I call it, being strange to me
> That, undividable, incorporate,
> Am better than thy dear self's better part.
> Ah, do not tear away thyself from me;
> For know, my love, as easy mayst thou fall
> A drop of water in the breaking gulf,
> And take unmingled thence that drop again
> Without addition or diminishing,
> As take from me thyself, and not me too.
>
> (2.2.119–29)

The scene in which these words are spoken is comical, for Adriana is unwittingly addressing not her husband but her husband's long-lost identical twin. Yet the speech is too long and the pain too intense to be altogether absorbed in laughter.

Though the comedy rushes on to madcap confusion and though at the play's end Adriana is blamed (erroneously, as it happens) for her husband's distracted state— "The venom clamours of a jealous woman / Poisons more deadly than a mad dog's tooth" (5.1.70–71)—her suffering has an odd, insistent ring of truth. The situation seized Shakespeare's imagination, as if the misery of the neglected or abandoned spouse was something he knew personally and all too well. Amid the climactic flurry of recognitions, the play does not include, as it would have been reasonable to expect, a scene of marital reconciliation. In *The Comedy of Errors,* as in most of his plays, the substance of such a reconciliation—what it would mean fully to share a life—seems to have eluded him.

Occasionally, as in *The Winter's Tale*, there is a glimpse of something more than a frustrated craving for intimacy. Hermione, nine months pregnant, manages lightly to tease her husband, Leontes, and her teasing discloses marital emotions that go beyond anxious dependence. Leontes, who has been trying unsuccessfully to persuade his best friend to extend his already lengthy visit, enlists his wife's aid. When his wife succeeds, Leontes pays her a hyperbolic compliment whose potential awkwardness Hermione immediately seizes upon:

> LEONTES: Is he won yet?
> HERMIONE: He'll stay, my lord.
> LEONTES: At my request he would not.
>   Hermione, my dearest, thou never spok'st
>   To better purpose.
> HERMIONE: Never?
>
> (1.2.88–91)

As befits a play fantastically sensitive to intonation, there is nothing on the surface of these simple lines to suggest that anything is going wrong. But perhaps Hermione has already sensed something slightly edgy in Leontes' response, and she instinctively tries to turn it into marital playfulness:

> HERMIONE: Never?
> LEONTES: Never but once.
> HERMIONE: What, have I twice said well? When was't before?
>   I prithee tell me. Cram's with praise, and make's
>   As fat as tame things.
>
> (1.2.91–94)

There is here, as so often in the ordinary conversation of husbands and wives, at once nothing and everything going on. As befits convention,

Hermione calls Leontes her lord, but she speaks to him on easy, equal footing, mingling sexual banter and gentle mockery, at once welcoming her husband's compliment and making fun of it. Grasping his initial misstep, Leontes quickly qualifies what he has said, turning "Never" into "Never but once," and then gives his pregnant wife what she says she longs for:

> Why, that was when
> Three crabbèd month had soured themselves to death
> Ere I could make thee open thy white hand
> And clap thyself my love. Then didst thou utter,
> "I am yours for ever."
>
> (1.2.103–7)

This is one of the most extended marital conversations that Shakespeare ever wrote, and despite its slight air of formality—husband and wife are speaking, after all, in the presence of their close friend and others—it is powerfully convincing in its suggestion of entangled love, tightly coiled tension, and playfulness. Leontes and Hermione can look back with amusement at their shared past. They are not afraid to tease one another; they care what each other thinks and feels; they still experience sexual desire even as they go about forming a family and entertaining guests. But it is precisely at this moment of slightly edgy intimacy that Leontes is seized by a paranoid fear of his wife's infidelity. At the end of the catastrophic events brought on by this paranoia, there is a moving reconciliation scene, but Hermione's words then are focused entirely on the recovery of her lost daughter. To Leontes, whom she embraces, Hermione says precisely nothing.

The Winter's Tale suggests that the marriage of Leontes and Hermione could not sustain—and could certainly not recover—the emotional, sexual, and psychological intimacy, at once so gratifying and so disturbing, that it once possessed. So too in *Othello*, a tragedy with strong affinities to *The Winter's Tale*, Desdemona's full, bold presence in the marriage—

> That I did love the Moor to live with him,
> My downright violence and storm of fortunes
> May trumpet to the world
>
> (1.3.247–49)

—seems to trigger her husband's homicidal jealousy. But perhaps it is wrong even to speak of that particular relationship as a marriage: it seems to last something like a day and a half before it falls apart.

At least these *are* couples. Many of the significant married pairs in Shakespeare have been divorced by death long before the play begins. For the most part it is the women who have vanished: no Mrs. Bolingbroke, Mrs. Shylock, Mrs. Leonato, Mrs. Brabanzio, Mrs. Lear, Mrs. Prospero. Very infrequently there is a faint trace: Shylock's wife was named Leah, and she gave her husband a turquoise ring that their daughter Jessica heartlessly trades for a monkey. Even less frequently, there is a tiny hint, such as this one from *A Midsummer Night's Dream*, of what has taken a missing woman from the world: "But she, being mortal, of that boy did die" (2.1.135). But for the most part Shakespeare doesn't bother.

Demographers have shown that the risks of childbirth in Elizabethan England were high, but not nearly high enough to explain the wholesale absence of spouses from the plays. (Shakespeare's mother outlived his father by seven years, and despite their age difference, his own wife would also outlive him by seven years.) Clearly Shakespeare did not want a *Taming of the Shrew* in which Mrs. Minola would have her own ideas on her daughters' suitors or a *King Lear* in which the old king's wife would dispute his plans for retirement.

There are few happy marriages in all of literature, just as there are rather few representations of goodness. But most eighteenth- and nineteenth-century novels have an important stake in persuading the reader that the romantic young couple, with whose wedding the work ends, will find their deepest fulfillment in each other, even if most of the marriages actually depicted in the course of the narrative are humdrum or desperate. In Jane Austen's *Pride and Prejudice*, Mr. and Mrs. Bennett have a miserable relationship, as do Charlotte Lucas and the asinine Mr.

Collins, but Elizabeth Bennett and Darcy will, the reader is assured, beat the odds. Shakespeare, even in his sunniest comedies, had no stake in persuading his audience of any such thing.

"Men are April when they woo, December when they wed," says Rosalind in *As You Like It*. "Maids are May when they are maids, but the sky changes when they are wives" (4.1.124–27). Rosalind may not herself believe what she says—disguised as a young boy, she is playfully testing Orlando's love for her—but she articulates the cynical wisdom of the everyday world. In *The Merry Wives of Windsor*, there are the same hard-edged sentiments tumbling inadvertently from the mouth of the simpleton Slender: "if there be no great love in the beginning, yet heaven may decrease it upon better acquaintance, when we are married and have more occasion to know one another. I hope upon familiarity will grow more contempt" (1.1.206–10). What is envisaged is an almost inevitable sequence summed up in Beatrice's succinct formula, from *Much Ado About Nothing*: "wooing, wedding, and repenting" (2.1.60).

The tone in which these views are uttered is not so much gloomy as humorous and jauntily realistic, a realism that does not actually get in the way of anyone's wedding. At the play's end Beatrice and Benedick too will embark on marriage, as do all the other lovers in Shakespearean comedy, despite the clear-eyed calculation of the likely consequences. Part of the magic of these plays is to register this calculation without inhibiting the joy and optimism of each of the couples. Shakespeare expended little or no effort to persuade the audience that these particular pairs will be an exception to the rule; on the contrary, they themselves give voice to the rule. The spectators are invited to enter into the charmed circle of love, knowing that it is probably a transitory illusion but, for the moment at least—the moment of the play—not caring.

Shakespeare's imagination did not easily conjure up a couple with long-term prospects for happiness. In *A Midsummer Night's Dream*, the love between Lysander and Hermia vanishes in a second, while Demetrius and Helena will cherish each other as long as the love juice sprinkled in their eyes holds out. In *The Taming of the Shrew*, a pair of good actors can persuade audiences that there is a powerful sexual attraction half-hidden in the quarreling of Petruccio and Kate, but the end of the play goes out of its way to offer two almost equally disagreeable visions of marriage, one in which the couple is constantly quarreling, the other in which the wife's will has been broken. The end of *As You Like It* succeeds only because no one is forced to contemplate the future home life of Rosalind and Orlando or of the rest of the "country copulatives," as Touchstone calls them (5.4.53). Since Viola keeps on the male attire with which she has disguised herself, *Twelfth Night* relieves the audience of the burden of seeing her dressed as a demure young woman; even at the end of the play Orsino seems betrothed to his effeminate boyfriend. Nothing about their relationship in the course of the play suggests that they are well matched or that great happiness lies ahead of them. In *The Merchant of Venice*, Jessica and Lorenzo may take pleasure together in spending the money they have stolen from her father, Shylock, but their playful banter has a distinctly uneasy tone:

> LORENZO: In such a night
>   Did Jessica steal from the wealthy Jew,
>   And with an unthrift love did run from Venice
>   As far as Belmont.
> JESSICA: In such a night
>   Did young Lorenzo swear he loved her well,
>   Stealing her soul with many vows of faith,
>   And ne'er a true one.
>   (5.1.14–19)

The currents of uneasiness here—mingling together fears of fortune hunting, bad faith, and betrayal—extend to Portia and Bassanio and even to their comic sidekicks Nerissa and Graziano. And these are newlyweds with blissful prospects compared to Hero and the callow, cruel Claudio in *Much Ado About Nothing*. Only Beatrice and Benedick, in that play and indeed among all the couples of the principal comedies, seem to hold out the possibility of a sustained intimacy, and then only if the audience discounts their many insults, forgets that they have been tricked into wooing, and assumes, against their own mutual assertions, that they genuinely love each other.

It is worth pausing and trying to get it all in focus: in the great succession of comedies that Shakespeare wrote in the latter half of the

1590s, romantic masterpieces with their marvelous depictions of desire and their cheerfully relentless drive toward marriage, there is scarcely a single pair of lovers who seem deeply, inwardly suited for one another. There is no end of longing, flirtation, and pursuit, but strikingly little long-term promise of mutual understanding. How could earnest, decent, slightly dim Orlando ever truly take in Rosalind? How could the fatuous, self-absorbed Orsino ever come to understand Viola? And these are couples joyously embarking on what officially promise to be good marriages. There is a striking sign that Shakespeare was himself aware of the problem he was posing in the romantic comedies: a few years after these plays, sometime between 1602 and 1606, he wrote two comedies that bring the latent tensions in virtually all these happy pairings right up to the surface.

At the close of *Measure for Measure*, Mariana insists on marrying the repellent Angelo, who has continued to lie, connive, and slander until the moment he has been exposed. In the same strange climax, Duke Vincentio proposes marriage with Isabella, who has made it abundantly clear that her real desire is to enter a strict nunnery. As if this were not uncomfortable enough, the duke punishes the scoundrel Lucio by ordering him to marry a woman he has made pregnant. "I beseech your highness, do not marry me to a whore," Lucio pleads, but the duke is implacable, insisting on what is explicitly understood as a form of punishment, the equivalent of "pressing to death, whipping, and hanging" (5.1.508, 515–16). *All's Well That Ends Well* is, if anything, still more uncomfortable: the beautiful, accomplished Helen has unaccountably fixed her heart on the loutish Count Bertram, and in the end, despite his fierce resistance to the match, she gets her nasty bargain. There cannot be even the pretence of a rosy future for the mismatched pair.

In both *Measure for Measure* and *All's Well That Ends Well*, virtually all the marriages appear to be forced upon one party or another, and the pattern of celestial peace seems infinitely remote. The sourness at the end of these famously uncomfortable plays—often labeled "problem comedies"—is not the result of carelessness; it seems to be the expression of a deep skepticism about the long-term prospects for happiness in marriage, even though the plays continue to insist upon marriage as the only legitimate and satisfactory resolution to human desire.

There are two significant exceptions to Shakespeare's unwillingness or inability to imagine a married couple in a relationship of sustained intimacy, but they are unnervingly strange: Gertrude and Claudius in *Hamlet* and the Macbeths. These marriages are powerful, in their distinct ways, but they are also upsetting, even terrifying, in their glimpses of genuine intimacy. The villainous Claudius, fraudulent in almost everything he utters, speaks with oddly convincing tenderness about his feelings for his wife: "She's so conjunctive to my life and soul," he tells Laertes, "That, as the star moves not but in his sphere, / I could not but by her" (4.7.14–16). And Gertrude, for her part, seems equally devoted. Not only does she ratify Claudius's attempt to adopt Hamlet as his own son—"Hamlet, thou hast thy father much offended," she chides him after he has staged the play-within-the-play to catch his uncle's conscience (3.4.9)—but, more telling still, she heroically defends her husband at the risk of her own life, when Laertes storms the palace. Bent on avenging the murdered Polonius, Laertes is out for blood, and Shakespeare here provided, as he often did at crucial moments, an indication within the text of how he wanted the scene staged. Gertrude apparently throws herself between her husband and the would-be avenger; indeed, she must physically restrain the enraged Laertes, since Claudius twice says, "Let him go, Gertrude." To Laertes' demand, "Where is my father?" Claudius forthrightly answers, "Dead," whereupon Gertrude immediately adds, "But not by him" (4.5.119, 123–25).

In a play heavily freighted with commentary, those four simple words have received little attention. Gertrude is directing the murderous Laertes' rage away from her husband and toward someone else: Polonius's actual murderer, Prince Hamlet. She is not directly contriving to have her beloved son killed, but her overmastering impulse is to save her husband. This does not mean that she is a co-conspirator—the play never settles the question of whether she knew that Claudius murdered old Hamlet. When Claudius confesses the crime, he does not do so to his wife but speaks to himself alone, in his closet, in a failed attempt to clear his conscience in prayer.

The deep bond between Gertrude and Claudius, as Hamlet perceives to his horror and disgust, is based upon not shared secrets but an intense mutual sexual attraction. "You cannot call it love," declares the son, sickened by the very thought of his middle-aged mother's sexuality, "for at your age / The heyday in the blood is tame." But he knows that the heyday in Gertrude's blood is not tame, and his imagination dwells on the image of his mother and uncle "In the rank sweat of an enseamèd bed, / Stewed in corruption, honeying and making love." The dirty-minded obsession with the greasy or semen-stained ("enseamèd") sheets calls up a hallucinatory vision of his father—or is it an actual haunting?—that provides a momentary distraction. Yet as soon as the ghost vanishes, the son is at it again, pleading with his mother to "Refrain tonight" (3.4.67–68, 82–83, 152).

If spousal intimacy in *Hamlet* is vaguely nauseating, in *Macbeth* it is terrifying. Here, almost uniquely in Shakespeare, husband and wife speak to each other playfully, as if they were a genuine couple. "Dearest chuck," Macbeth affectionately calls his wife, as he withholds from her an account of what he has been doing—as it happens, arranging the murder of his friend Banquo—so that she can better applaud the deed when it is done. When they host a dinner party that goes horribly awry, the loyal wife tries to cover for her husband: "Sit, worthy friends," she tells the guests, startled when Macbeth starts screaming at the apparition, which he alone sees, of the murdered Banquo sitting in his chair.

> My lord is often thus,
> And hath been from his youth. Pray you, keep seat.
> The fit is momentary. Upon a thought
> He will again be well.
>
> (3.4.52–55)

Then, under her breath, she tries to make him get a grip on himself: "Are you a man?" (3.4.57).

The sexual taunt half-hidden in these words is the crucial note that Lady Macbeth strikes again and again. It is the principal means by which she gets her wavering husband to kill the king:

> When you durst do it, then you were a man;
> And to be more than what you were, you would
> Be so much more the man.
>
> (1.7.49–51)

If these taunts work on Macbeth, it is because husband and wife know and play upon each other's innermost fears and desires. They meet on the ground of a shared, willed, murderous ferocity:

> I have given suck, and know
> How tender 'tis to love the babe that milks me.
> I would, while it was smiling in my face,
> Have plucked my nipple from his boneless gums
> And dashed the brains out, had I so sworn
> As you have done to this.
>
> (1.7.54–59)

Macbeth is weirdly aroused by this fantasy:

> Bring forth men-children only,
> For thy undaunted mettle should compose
> Nothing but males.
>
> (1.7.72–74)

The exchange takes the audience deep inside this particular marriage. Whatever has led Lady Macbeth to imagine the bloody scene she describes and whatever Macbeth feels in response to her fantasy—terror, sexual excitement, envy, soul sickness, companionship in evil—lie at the heart of what it means to be the principal married couple conjured up by Shakespeare's imagination.

What is startling about this scene, and about the whole relationship between Macbeth and his wife, is the extent to which they inhabit each other's minds. When Lady Macbeth first appears, she is reading a letter from her husband that describes his encounter with the witches who have prophesied that he will be king: "'This have I thought good to deliver thee, my dearest partner of greatness, that thou mightst not lose the dues of rejoicing by being ignorant of what greatness is promised thee.'" He cannot wait until he gets home to tell her; he needs her to share the fantasy with him at once. And she, for her part, not only plunges into it immediately but also begins almost in the same breath to reflect with studied insight upon her husband's nature:

> It is too full o'th' milk of human kindness
> To catch the nearest way. Thou wouldst be great,
> Art not without ambition, but without
> The illness should attend it. What thou wouldst highly,
> That wouldst thou holily; wouldst not play false,
> And yet wouldst wrongly win. Thou'dst have, great Glamis,
> That which cries 'Thus thou must do' if thou have it,
> And that which rather thou dost fear to do
> Than wishest should be undone.
>
> (1.5.9–11, 15–23)

The richness of this account, the way it opens up from the first simple observation to something almost queasily complicated, is vivid evidence of the wife's ability to follow the twists and turns of her husband's innermost character, to take her spouse in. And her intimate understanding leads her to desire to enter into him: "Hie thee hither, / That I may pour my spirits in thine ear" (1.5.23–24).

Shakespeare's plays then combine, on the one hand, an overall diffidence in depicting marriages and, on the other hand, the image of a kind of nightmare in the two marriages they do depict with some care. It is difficult *not* to read his works in the context of his decision to live for most of a long marriage away from his wife. Perhaps, for whatever reason, Shakespeare feared to be taken in fully by his spouse or by anyone else; perhaps he could not let anyone so completely in; or perhaps he simply made a disastrous mistake, when he was eighteen, and had to live with the consequences as a husband and as a writer. Most couples, he may have told himself, are mismatched, even couples marrying for love; you should never marry in haste; a young man should not marry an older woman; a marriage under compulsion—"wedlock forcèd"—is a hell. And perhaps, beyond these, he told himself, in imagining *Hamlet* and *Macbeth, Othello* and *The Winter's Tale*, that marital intimacy is dangerous, that the very dream is a threat.

Shakespeare may have told himself too that his marriage to Anne was doomed from the beginning. Certainly he told his audience repeatedly that it was crucially important to preserve virginity until marriage. Though she calls the vows she has exchanged in the darkness with Romeo a "contract," Juliet makes it clear that this contract is not in her eyes the equivalent of a marriage (as some Elizabethans would have held) and that she must therefore on that night leave Romeo "unsatisfied" (2.1.159, 167). Once protected by the wedding performed by the friar— not a social ritual in *Romeo and Juliet* but a sacrament hidden from the feuding families—Juliet can throw off the retiring coyness expected of girls. The young lovers are splendidly frank, confident, and unembarrassed about their desires—they are able, as Juliet puts it, to "Think true love acted simple modesty" (3.2.16)—but their frankness depends upon their shared commitment to marrying before enacting these desires. That commitment confers upon their love, rash and secret though it is, a certain sublime innocence. It is as if the formal ceremony of marriage, performed as the condition of sexual consummation, had an almost magical efficacy, a power to make desire and fulfillment, which would otherwise be tainted and shameful, perfectly modest.

In *Measure for Measure*, written some eight years after *Romeo and Juliet*, Shakespeare came closer to depicting the situation in which he may have found himself as an adolescent. Claudio and Juliet have privately made solemn vows to one another—"a true contract," Claudio calls it—and have consummated their marriage without a public ceremony. His wife is now visibly pregnant—"The stealth of our most mutual entertainment / With character too gross is writ on Juliet" (1.2.122, 131–32). When the state embarks on a ruthless campaign against "fornication," Claudio is arrested and condemned to die. What is startling is that he seems ready to concede the point. Without the public ceremony, his "true contract" appears worthless, and in lines saturated with self-revulsion, he speaks of the fate that looms over him as the result of unrestrained sexual appetite:

> Our natures do pursue,
> Like rats that raven down their proper bane,

> A thirsty evil; and when we drink, we die.
>
> (1.2.108–10)

The natural desire that can be so frankly and comfortably acknowledged within the bounds of marriage becomes a poison outside of it.

The intensity of the dire visions of premarital sex and its consequences may have had much to do with the fact that Shakespeare was the father of two growing daughters. His most explicit warnings about the dangers of premarital sex take the form, in *The Tempest*, of a father's stern words to the young man who is courting his daughter. Yet in Prospero's lines from this play, written late in his career, there is a sense that Shakespeare was looking back at his own unhappy marriage and linking that unhappiness to the way in which it all began, so many years before. "Take my daughter," Prospero says to Ferdinand, and then adds something halfway between a curse and a prediction:

> If thou dost break her virgin-knot before
> All sanctimonious ceremonies may
> With full and holy rite be ministered,
> No sweet aspersion shall the heavens let fall
> To make this contract grow; but barren hate,
> Sour-eyed disdain, and discord, shall bestrew
> The union of your bed with weeds so loathly
> That you shall hate it both.
>
> (4.1.14–22)

These lines—so much more intense and vivid than the play calls for—seem to draw upon a deep pool of bitterness about a miserable marriage. Instead of a shower of grace ("sweet aspersion"), the union will inevitably be plagued, Prospero warns, if sexual consummation precedes the "sanctimonious ceremonies." That was precisely the circumstance of the marriage of Will and Anne.

Even if these bleak lines were a summary reflection on his own marriage, Shakespeare was not necessarily doomed to a life without love. He certainly knew bitterness, sourness, and cynicism, but he did not retreat into them, nor did he attempt to escape from them by renouncing desire. Desire is everywhere in his work. But his imagination of love and in all likelihood his experiences of love flourished outside of the marriage bond. The greatest lovers in Shakespeare are Antony and Cleopatra, the supreme emblems of adultery. And when he wrote love poems—among the most complex and intense in the English language, before or since— he constructed a sequence of sonnets not about his wife and not about courtship of anyone who could be his wife but about his tangled relationships with a fair young man and a sexually sophisticated dark lady.

Anne Hathaway was excluded completely from the sonnets' story of same-sex love and adultery—or at least almost completely. It is possible, as several critics have suggested, that sonnet 145—"Those lips that love's own hand did make"—alludes to her in its closing couplet. The speaker of the poem recalls that his love once spoke to him the terrible words "I hate," but then gave him a reprieve from the doom that the words seemed to announce:

> "I hate" from hate away she threw,
> And saved my life, saying "not you."

If "hate away" is a pun on Hathaway, as has been proposed, then this might be a very early poem by Shakespeare, perhaps the earliest that survives, conceivably written at the time of his courtship and then casually incorporated into the sequence. Such an origin might help to explain its anomalous meter—it is the only sonnet in the sequence written in eight-syllable, rather than ten-syllable, lines—and, still more, its ineptitude.

He could not get out of it. That is the overwhelming sense of the bond that rushed the marriage through. But he contrived, after three years' time, not to live with his wife. Two days' hard ride from Stratford, at a safe distance from Henley Street and later from New Place, he made his astonishing works and his fortune. In his rented rooms in London, he contrived to have a private life—that too, perhaps, is the meaning of Aubrey's report that he was not a "company keeper," that he refused invitations to be "debauched." Not the regular denizen of taverns, not the familiar companion of his cronies, he found intimacy and lust and love with people whose names he managed to keep to himself. "Women he won to him," says Stephen Daedalus, James Joyce's alter ego in *Ulysses*, in one of the greatest meditations on Shakespeare's marriage, "tender people, a whore of Babylon, ladies of justices, bully tapsters' wives. Fox and geese. And in New Place a slack dishonoured body that once was comely, once as sweet, as fresh as cinnamon, now her leaves falling, all, bare, frighted of the narrow grave and unforgiven."

Sometime around 1610, Shakespeare, a wealthy man with many investments, retired from London and returned to Stratford, to his neglected wife in New Place. Does this mean that he had finally achieved some loving intimacy with her? *The Winter's Tale*, written at about this time, ends with the moving reconciliation of a husband and wife who had seemed lost to one another forever. Perhaps this was indeed Shakespeare's fantasy for his own life, but if so the fantasy does not seem to correspond to what actually happened. When Shakespeare, evidently gravely ill, came to draw up his will, in January 1616, he took care to leave virtually everything, including New Place and all his "barns, stables, orchards, gardens, lands, tenements" and lands in and around Stratford, to his elder daughter, Susanna. Provisions were made for his other daughter, Judith; for his only surviving sibling, Joan; and for several other friends and relatives, and a modest donation was made to the town's poor, but the great bulk of the estate went to Susanna and her husband, Dr. John Hall, who were clearly the principal objects of the dying Shakespeare's love and trust. As he left the world, he did not want to think of his wealth going to his wife; he wanted to imagine it descending to his eldest daughter and thence to her eldest son, yet unborn, and thence to the son of that son and on and on through the generations. And he did not want to brook any interference or hindrance in this design: Susanna and her husband were named as the executors. They would enact the design—so overwhelmingly in their interest—that he had devised.

To his wife of thirty-four years, Anne, he left nothing, nothing at all. Some have argued in mitigation of this conspicuous omission that a widow would in any case have been entitled to a life interest in a one-third share of her deceased husband's estate. Others have countered that thoughtful husbands in this period often spelled out this entitlement in their wills, since it was not in fact always guaranteed. But as a document charged with the remembering of friends and family in the final disposition of the goods so carefully accumulated during a lifetime, Shakespeare's will—the last trace of his network of relationships—remains startling in its absolute silence in regard to his wife. The issue is not simply that there are none of the terms of endearment—"my beloved wife," "my loving Anne," or whatever—that conventionally signaled an enduring bond between husband and wife. The will contains no such term for any of those named as heirs, so perhaps Shakespeare or the lawyer who penned the words simply chose to write a relatively cool, impersonal document. The problem is that in the will Shakespeare initially drafted, Anne Shakespeare was not mentioned at all; it is as if she had been completely erased.

Someone—his daughter Susanna, perhaps, or his lawyer—may have called this erasure, this total absence of acknowledgment, to his attention. Or perhaps as he lay in his bed, his strength ebbing away, Shakespeare himself brooded on his relationship to Anne—on the sexual excitement that once drew him to her, on the failure of the marriage to give him what he wanted, on his own infidelities and perhaps on hers, on the intimacies he had forged elsewhere, on the son they had buried, on the strange, ineradicable distaste for her that he felt deep within him. For on March 25, in a series of additions to the will—mostly focused on keeping his daughter Judith's husband from getting his hands on the money Shakespeare was leaving her—he finally acknowledged his wife's existence. On the last of the three pages, interlined between the careful specification of the line of descent, so as to ensure that the property would go if at all possible to the eldest male heir of his daughter Susanna, and the bestowal of the "broad silver-gilt bowl" on Judith and all the rest of the "goods, chattel, leases, plate, jewels, and household stuff" on Susanna, there is a new provision: "Item I gyve vnto my wife my second best bed with the furniture."

Scholars and other writers have made a strenuous effort to give these words a positive spin: other wills in this period can be found in which the best bed is left to someone other than the wife; the bequest to Anne could have been their marriage bed (the best bed possibly being reserved for important guests); "the furniture"—that is, the bed furnishings, such as coverlets and curtains—might have been valuable; and even, as Joseph Quincy Adams hoped, "the second-best bed, though less expensive, was probably the more comfortable." In short, as one biographer in 1940 cheerfully persuaded himself, "It was a husband's tender remembrance."

If this is an instance of Shakespeare's tender remembrance, one shudders to think of what one of his insults would have looked like. But the notion of tenderness is surely absurd wishful thinking: this is a person who had spent a lifetime imagining exquisitely precise shadings of love and injury. It is for legal historians to debate whether by specifying a single object, the testator was in effect attempting to wipe out the widow's customary one-third life interest—that is, to disinherit her. But what the eloquently hostile gesture seems to say emotionally is that Shakespeare had found his trust, his happiness, his capacity for intimacy, his best bed elsewhere.

"Shine here to us," John Donne addressed the rising sun, "and thou art every where; / This bed thy center is, these walls, thy sphere." Donne may have been the great Renaissance exception to the rule: he seems to have written many of his most passionate love poems to his wife. In "The Funeral," he imagines being buried with some precious bodily token of the woman he has loved:

> Who ever comes to shroud me, do not harm
>   Nor question much
> That subtle wreath of hair, which crowns my arm.

And in "The Relic" he returns to this fantasy—"A bracelet of bright hair about the bone"—and imagines that whoever might open his grave to add another corpse will let the remains alone, thinking "that there a loving couple lies." For Donne, the dream is to make it possible for his soul and that of his beloved "at the last busy day" to "Meet at this grave, and make a little stay."

Shakespeare's greatest lovers—Romeo and Juliet, in the sweet frenzy of adolescent passion, and Antony and Cleopatra, in the sophisticated, lightly ironic intensity of middle-aged adultery—share something of the same fantasy. "Ah, dear Juliet," poor, deluded Romeo muses in the Capulet tomb,

> Why art thou yet so fair? Shall I believe
> That unsubstantial death is amorous,
> And that the lean abhorrèd monster keeps
> Thee here in dark to be his paramour?
> For fear of that I still will stay with thee,
> And never from this pallet of dim night
> Depart again.
>
> (5.3.101–8)

When Juliet awakes and finds Romeo dead, she in turn hastens to join him forever. So too, feeling "Immortal longings" in her, Cleopatra dresses to meet and to marry Antony in the afterlife— "Husband, I come" (5.2.272, 278)—and victorious Caesar understands what should be done:

> Take up her bed,
> And bear her women from the monument.
> She shall be buried by her Antony.
> No grave upon the earth shall clip in it
> A pair so famous.
>
> (5.2.346–50)

So much for the dream of love. When Shakespeare lay dying, he tried to forget his wife and then remembered her with the second-best bed. And when he thought of the afterlife, the last thing he wanted was to be mingled with the woman he married. There are four lines carved in his gravestone in the chancel of Stratford Church:

> GOOD FRIEND FOR JESUS SAKE FORBEARE,
> TO DIGG THE DUST ENCLOASED HEARE:
> BLESTE BE YE MAN YT SPARES THES STONES,
> AND CURST BE HE YT MOVES MY BONES.

In 1693 a visitor to the grave was told that the epitaph was "made by himself a little before his death." If so, these are probably the last lines that Shakespeare wrote. Perhaps he simply feared that his bones would be dug up and thrown in the nearby charnel house—he seems to have regarded that fate with horror—but he may have feared still more that one day his grave would be opened to let in the body of Anne Shakespeare.

CHAPTER 5

Crossing the Bridge

I N THE SUMMER of 1583 the nineteen-year-old William Shakespeare was settling into the life of a married man with a newborn
daughter, living all together with his parents and his sister, Joan, and
his brothers, Gilbert, Richard, and Edmund, and however many
servants they could afford in the spacious house on Henley Street. He may
have been working in the glover's shop, perhaps, or making a bit of money
as a teacher's or lawyer's assistant. In his spare time he must have continued
to write poetry, practice the lute, hone his skills as a fencer—that is, work
on his ability to impersonate the lifestyle of a gentleman. His northern
sojourn, assuming he had one, was behind him. If in Lancashire he had
begun a career as a professional player, he must, for the moment at least,
have put it aside. And if he had had a brush with the dark world of
Catholic conspiracy, sainthood, and martyrdom—the world that took
Campion to the scaffold—he must still more decisively have turned away
from it with a shudder. He had embraced ordinariness, or ordinariness had
embraced him.

Then sometime in the mid-1580s (the precise date is not known), he
tore himself away from his family, left Stratford-upon-Avon, and made

his way to London. How or why he took this momentous step is unclear, though until recently biographers were generally content with a story first recorded in the late seventeenth century by the clergyman Richard Davies. Davies wrote that Shakespeare was "much given to all unluckiness in stealing venison and rabbits, particularly from Sir ——— Lucy, who had him oft whipped and sometimes imprisoned and at last made him fly his native country to his great advancement." The early-eighteenth-century biographer and editor Nicholas Rowe printed a similar account of the "Extravagance" that forced Shakespeare "both out of his country and that way of living which he had taken up." Will had, in Rowe's account, fallen into bad company: he began to consort with youths who made a practice of deer poaching; in their company, he went more than once to rob Sir Thomas Lucy's park at Charlecote, about four miles from Stratford.

> For this he was prosecuted by that gentleman, as he thought, somewhat too severely; and in order to revenge that ill usage, he made a ballad upon him. And though this, probably the first essay of his poetry, be lost, yet it is said to have been so very bit-ter, that it redoubled the prosecution against him to that degree, that he was obliged to leave his business and family in Warwick-shire, for some time, and shelter himself in London.

By the mid-eighteenth century this story had acquired a sequel related by Dr. Johnson: having fled his home "from the terror of a crimi-nal prosecution," Will found himself alone in London, without money or friends. He picked up enough to live on by standing at the playhouse door and holding the horses of those that had no servants. "In this office he became so conspicuous for his care and readiness," Johnson writes, "that in a short time every man as he alighted called for *Will. Shakespear*, and scarcely any other waiter was trusted with a horse while *Will. Shake-spear* could be had. This was the first dawn of better fortune." There is something appealing about Shakespeare as the patron saint of parking lot attendants, but few biographers of the last two centuries have taken this story seriously. The problem in part is that archival scholars began to recognize that Shakespeare's family, even in the period of his father's decline, remained part of a network of kin and friends; that his father never lost everything; and that therefore the vision of the uprooted young man holding horses at the playhouse door, in penury and isolation, is unlikely.

As for the deer-poaching story itself, though four independent versions were in circulation by the later seventeenth century, recent biographers have treated it too with comparable skepticism. For one thing, Sir Thomas Lucy did not have a deer park at Charlecote at the time in question; for another, whipping was not a legal punishment for poaching in this period. But these arguments are not decisive. While Lucy did not keep an enclosed park at the time that Shakespeare would have been caught poaching, he did maintain a warren, an enclosed area where rabbits and other game, possibly including deer, could breed. And he was evidently not indifferent to his property rights: he hired keepers to protect the game and watch for poachers, and he introduced a bill in Parliament in 1584 against poaching. As for whipping, it may not have been a legal punishment, but the justice of the peace may have been inclined to teach the young offender a lesson, particularly if he suspected that the poacher and his parents might be recusants. No doubt it would have been improper for Sir Thomas Lucy, as justice of the peace, to sit in judgment on a case in which he himself was the alleged victim, but it would be naive to imagine that local magnates always stayed within the letter of the law or carefully avoided conflicts of interest. After all, the story refers to Shakespeare's sense of ill-usage—that is, to his being treated worse than he felt he deserved to be treated for what he was caught doing.

The question, then, is not the degree of evidence but rather the imaginative life that the incident has, the access it gives to something important in Shakespeare's life and work. The particular act with which he was charged has by now ceased to have much meaning, and the story correspondingly has begun to drop away from biographies. But in Shakespeare's time and into the eighteenth century the idea of deer poaching had a special resonance; it was good to think with, a powerful tool for reconstructing the sequence of events that led the young man to leave Stratford.

For Elizabethans deer poaching was not understood principally as having to do with hunger; it was a story not about desperation but about risk. Oxford students were famous for this escapade. It was, for a start, a daring game: it took impressive skill and cool nerves to trespass on a powerful person's land, kill a large animal, and drag it away, without getting caught by those who patrolled the area. "What, hast not thou full often struck a doe," someone asks in one of Shakespeare's early plays, "And borne her cleanly by the keeper's nose?" (*Titus Andronicus*, 2.1.93-94). It was a skillful assault upon property, a symbolic violation of the social order, a coded challenge to authority. That challenge was supposed to be kept within bounds: the game involved cunning and an awareness of limits. After all, one was not supposed to beat up the keeper—then misdemeanor turns into felony—and one was not supposed to get caught. Deer poaching was about the pleasures of hunting and killing but also about the pleasures of stealth and trickery, about knowing how far to go, about contriving to get away with something.

Throughout Shakespeare's career as a playwright he was a brilliant poacher—deftly entering into territory marked out by others, taking for himself what he wanted, and walking away with his prize under the keeper's nose. He was particularly good at seizing and making his own the property of the elite, the music, the gestures, the language. This is only a metaphor, of course; it is not evidence that young Will engaged in actual poaching. What we know, and what those who originally circulated the legend knew, is that he had a complex attitude toward authority, at once sly, genially submissive, and subtly challenging. He was capable of devastating criticism; he saw through lies, hypocrisies, and distortions; he undermined virtually all of the claims that those in power made for themselves. And yet he was easygoing, humorous, pleasantly indirect, almost apologetic. If this relation to authority was not simply implanted in him, if it was more likely something he learned, then his formative learning experience may well have been a nasty encounter with one of the principal authorities in his district.

For in all the versions of the story something went wrong: Shakespeare was caught and then treated more harshly than he felt was appropriate (and indeed than the law allowed). He responded, it is said, with a bitter ballad. Versions of the ballad have predictably surfaced—none of them interesting as poetry or believable as Shakespeare's actual verses. "If lowsie is Lucy, as some volke miscalle it, / Then Lucy is lowsie whatever befall it," etc. More interesting is the idea that Shakespeare must have responded to harsh treatment with an insulting piece of writing, presumably an attack on Lucy's character or the honor of his wife.

Modern biographers are skeptical largely because they believe that Shakespeare was not that kind of person and that Lucy was both too powerful and too respectable to be slandered. "In public feared and respected, Sir Thomas in his domestic affairs appears to have been not unamiable," observes one of Shakespeare's most amiable and brilliant biographers, Samuel Schoenbaum. "He wrote testimonial letters for an honest gentlewoman and an ailing servant." But the late-seventeenth-century gossips who circulated the story may have had a better understanding of that world. They grasped that a man like Lucy could combine geniality and public-spiritedness—entertaining the queen at Charlecote, keeping a company of players, acting boldly and decisively in times of plague—with ruthless violence. They knew that it was dangerous to write anything against a person in authority—you could be charged with "scandalium magnatum," slandering an official—and at the same time that such writing was the prime weapon of the powerless. Above all, they believed that something serious must have driven Shakespeare out of Stratford, something more than his own poetic dreams and theatrical skill, something more than dissatisfaction with his marriage, and something more than the limited economic opportunities in the immediate area.

They doubted, in other words, that Shakespeare simply wandered off to London in search of new opportunities. Whether he was helping in his father's failing business, or working as a poor scrivener (a noverint, as it was sometimes called) in a lawyer's office, or teaching the rudiments of Latin grammar to schoolboys, they believed that without some shock Shakespeare would have continued in the rut that life had prepared for him. With the family's lands mortgaged, his education finished, no profession, a wife and three children to support, he had already begun to deepen that rut for himself. Rumormongers heard something that led them to believe that trouble with authority drove him out and that the

authority in question was Sir Thomas Lucy. They thought too that something Shakespeare wrote was involved in the trouble.

Early biographers not only went in search of the missing satiric
poem but also carefully scanned Shakespeare's printed works for traces of
his early encounter with the angry justice of the peace. Centuries ago
both Rowe and Davies pointed to the opening scene in *The Merry Wives
of Windsor*, in which Shakespeare depicts pompous Justice Shallow complaining that Falstaff has killed his deer and threatening a Star Chamber
suit. Shallow stands on his dignity; he is, as his nephew Slender says, "a
gentleman born," one who "writes himself 'Armigero' in any bill, warrant,
quittance, or obligation: 'Armigero.'" "Ay, that I do, and have done any
time these three hundred years" (1.1.7–11). Laughter is directed at the
self-importance that is crystallized in the lovingly reiterated Latinism
"Armigero," one who bears a coat of arms. The mockery ripples across a
whole class of gentry inordinately proud of their birth and eager to maintain a distinction between their inherited status and that of mere
upstarts. (Some argued in this period that a family must have had a coat
of arms for at least three generations before it could be securely identified
as authentically armigerous.) But Rowe and Davies suggest that Shallow
was intended specifically as a dig at Sir Thomas Lucy, Will's persecutor
for the crime of deer poaching.

This suggestion is apparently borne out by the ensuing flurry of
jokes on the heraldic symbol of the Lucy family, a freshwater fish called
a luce. It is not only Shallow who writes himself "Armigero," adds Slender: "All his successors gone before him hath done't, and all his ancestors
that come after him may. They may give the dozen white luces in their
coat" (1.1.12–14). There follows an exchange that is by now almost
entirely obscure—it is cut in most modern performances—and that even
in Shakespeare's time would have been difficult to follow. It depends
upon a series of puns unintentionally generated by Sir Hugh Evans, the
Welsh parson who pronounces "luces" as "louses" and "coat" as "cod"—
Elizabethan slang for "scrotum." As in the schoolroom scene from the
same play, obscenities are scribbled in the margins of respect. The dialogue manages, with a perfect miming of innocence, to deface the Lucy
coat of arms.

But if this is the case—if Shakespeare was taking symbolic revenge on the proud man who had humiliated him and persecuted him over some infraction or other—then it was a muted, delayed, and half-hidden revenge. *The Merry Wives of Windsor* was written in 1597–98, at least a decade after events that might have driven Shakespeare out of Stratford. Closer to those events, as if to placate his persecutor, the playwright had gone out of his way in one of his earliest plays, *1 Henry VI,* to present an admirable portrait of a Lucy ancestor, Sir William Lucy.

The "Armigero" satire was hardly violent or bitter—it was the quietly mocking laughter of someone whose wounds were no longer raw. And it was a laughter that did not insist on identifying its object outside the charmed circle of the play. Very few of the members of the audience could have picked up on the specific allusion to a Warwickshire notable: it was there—if it was there at all—principally for the playwright himself and a small group of his friends. And in laughing at a person who is proud of his coat of arms, the playwright was also quietly turning the laughter back upon himself. For *The Merry Wives of Windsor* was written immediately in the wake of Shakespeare's own successful attempt to write himself "Armigero" by renewing his father's application for gentle-manly status. Perhaps it was only the achievement of the coat of arms that enabled him to make fun of Lucy and at the same time to distance himself from his own social desire.

Shakespeare was a master of double consciousness. He was a man who spent his money on a coat of arms but who mocked the pretentious-ness of such a claim; a man who invested in real estate but who ridiculed in *Hamlet* precisely such an entrepreneur as he himself was; a man who spent his life and his deepest energies on the theater but who laughed at the theater and regretted making himself a show. Though Shakespeare seems to have recycled every word he ever encountered, every person he ever met, every experience he ever had—it is difficult otherwise to explain the enormous richness of his work—he contrived at the same time to hide himself from view, to ward off vulnerability, to forswear inti-macy. And in the case of his encounter with Thomas Lucy, he may, by the late 1590s, have buried inside light public laughter the traces of an intense fear that had once gripped him.

Even after he had moved to London and established himself as an actor and playwright, Shakespeare might not have been able to conceal entirely that as a young man he had fallen afoul of a Warwickshire magnate. But he had ample reason to recast and to sanitize whatever it was that had sent him packing. Hidden within the legend of Thomas Lucy's deer park may have been a more serious trouble, which the poaching episode, whether or not it actually occurred, at once represented and concealed. Long before he floated the hints in *The Merry Wives of Windsor*, Shakespeare may in his private conversation have told the story of a slightly comical misadventure to account for his departure from Stratford. The story might have served as a convenient cover, all the more convenient if it had at least some basis in fact: it acknowledged that Lucy played a role, but a role that could be parodied in no more disturbing a figure than Justice Shallow. It acknowledged too that Shakespeare was in trouble, but trouble of the kind, more winked at than prosecuted, for which Oxford students were famous. The far more serious threat that Lucy would have posed—his role not as defender of his game but as relentless persecutor of recusancy—was effaced, and Stratford took on the tranquil glow of a sleepy country town.

But in the 1580s ordinary life in Stratford, as elsewhere, had not been tranquil. The capture, trial, and execution of Campion and the other Jesuit missionaries had by no means settled the religious struggles in England. It was not only a matter of international plots and the ambitions of the great. Even if he was altogether untouched by fantasies of martyrdom, even if he had plunged into the everyday concerns of a family man in a provincial town, Shakespeare could not have lived his life as if there were no questions about belief. No one with any capacity for thought at this moment could have done so.

Many men and women in England—more radical Protestants as well as Catholics—were dissatisfied with the religious settlement and felt that they could not worship as they wished. Shakespeare unquestionably knew such people; members of his own family may have been among them. For the more pious, the experience must have been anguishing: they believed that their eternal salvation, and the salvation of their kin and fellow countrymen, depended upon their form of worship and upon the faith that this worship expressed. This is why, for example, a young Warwickshire gentleman, John Somerville of Edstone, began in the summer of 1583 to spend a great deal of time in intense conversation with a gardener on the estate of his father-in-law. The conversation was not about the flowers; the man dressed as a gardener was Hugh Hall, a Catholic priest, whom his father-in-law secretly harbored.

Will Shakespeare was at this point a virtual nobody, the knockabout son of a failing glover; John Somerville, educated at Oxford, was wealthy, wellborn, and well connected. But there could have been a distant family link between these two young men from Warwickshire: Somerville had married the daughter of Edward Arden of Park Hall, the head of the family probably distantly related to Mary Arden, Shakespeare's mother. And these possible cousins may both have had implanted in them from childhood the same longing to restore England to the old faith.

But if Will was moving away from this longing, John Somerville was being drawn more and more dangerously into its power. The priest Hugh Hall—according to the prosecutor's account, at the trial of Hall and Somerville—had talked to him about the plight of the Catholic Church in England; the hopes that lay in the beautiful, shamefully mistreated Mary, Queen of Scots; and the moral corruption of Henry VIII's bastard daughter, the excommunicated Queen Elizabeth. He rehearsed some of the scabrous gossip about the queen's favorite, Robert Dudley; reminded the young man that the pope had explicitly freed Englishmen from any obligation to obey her; and approvingly recounted a Spanish Catholic's recent attempt to assassinate the Protestant Prince of Orange.

At the same time, probably by coincidence, Somerville's sister gave him a translation of a book by the Spanish friar Luis de Granada, *Of Prayer and Meditation.* Printed in Paris in 1582, the book opened with a letter by the translator, Richard Harris, lamenting the rise of Schism, Heresy, Infidelity, and Atheism in England. These evils were dark signs that the world was nearing its end, Harris argued, and that Satan was frantically struggling to make a last demonic triumph. It behooved young noblemen and gentlemen in particular, he wrote, to "remember what great inclination ye have unto virtue more than others of obscure parentage, and base estate."

Somerville was deeply moved. The book seems to have pushed the young man toward a desperate determination: he would single-handedly rid the country of the viper on its throne. On October 24, 1583, attended by a single servant whom he soon dismissed, he slipped away from his wife and two small daughters and set out for London. He did not make it very far. At an inn about four miles distant, where he stopped for the night, he was overheard shouting to himself that he was going to shoot the queen with his pistol. He was immediately arrested, and a few days later found himself under interrogation in the Tower of London.

The authorities clearly understood that the young man was deranged, but, taking his wild threats seriously or simply using them as an excuse to settle old scores, they immediately moved to arrest his wife, his sister, his father-in-law and mother-in-law, the priest Hugh Hall, and others. Convicted of treason, Somerville and his father-in-law were condemned to be executed. The young man managed to hang himself in his cell the night before the sentence was to be carried out, but that did not prevent the authorities from cutting off his head to display as a warning. Edward Arden, who was probably not guilty of more than overt Catholic piety and the choice of a mad son-in-law, met the full, grisly fate of a traitor. Their severed heads, impaled on pikes, were set up on London Bridge.

In Stratford-upon-Avon Will would at the very least have heard endless talk of these events, and if the distant family link meant something to him—and the fact that he eventually attempted to "impale" the Shakespeare coat of arms with that of the Ardens implies that it did—then he would clearly have been interested in them. He may simply have felt relief that he had distanced himself from whatever Catholic intrigues he may have encountered, but there are several odd clues that suggest a more complex attitude.

Shakespeare had evidently read and absorbed the Catholic book that had fatally influenced Somerville. Behind Hamlet's melancholy brooding in the graveyard—"Dost thou think Alexander looked o' this fashion i'th' earth? . . . And smelt so? Pah!" (5.1.182–85)—probably lies Luis de Granada's meditation on the horror of the grave: "What thing is more esteemed than the body of a prince whiles he is alive? And what thing is more contemptible, and more vile, than the very same body when it is dead? Then do they make a hole in the earth of seven or eight foot long, (and no longer though it be for Alexander the Great, whom the whole world could not hold) and with that small room only must his body be content." This and many other echoes may only show that the two young Warwickshire men, so different in their character and fate, shared some of the same cultural points of reference.

A more intriguing link between Somerville and Shakespeare is not a shared book but a shared persecutor. The principal local agent in the sweep of the neighborhood after Somerville's arrest—the justice of the peace who busied himself with the arrests, the searches of suspected Catholic houses, the examination of servants, and the like—was Sir Thomas Lucy.

Lucy, born in 1532, had long wielded considerable influence in the area. Married at the age of fourteen to a wealthy heiress, he had built a great house at Charlecote, where Queen Elizabeth herself had visited in 1572 and presented his daughter (as noted in the careful list of gifts that the Crown compiled) with an enameled butterfly between two daisies. Lucy's account books show that he employed about forty servants, including a troupe of actors, referred to in the Coventry records as "Sir Thomas Lucy's Players."

Lucy had strong Protestant credentials. As a boy he had been tutored for a period by John Foxe, who subsequently wrote a Reformation classic. *Acts and Monuments*, better known as Foxe's *Book of Martyrs*, is a history of those who sacrificed their lives in the service of the true, Reformed religion. The book, which all English churches were required to purchase, includes near contemporaries who had been burned at the stake during the reign of Mary Tudor and also their precursors, famous proto-Reformers like Sir John Oldcastle, Lord Cobham, who had been executed in 1417.

In the months when Foxe lived as a tutor at Charlecote, his hugely influential history was not yet written and perhaps not even conceived, but the deep conviction behind it—the belief that England was God's chosen agent in the apocalyptic struggle against the Antichrist and his demonic agent, the Roman Catholic Church—was already strong within him and seems to have influenced his young charge. Thomas Lucy became an energetic agent of the most militant Protestant faction in the state. Knighted by the Earl of Leicester, he served in Parliament, where he distinguished himself for his work on a bill against priests disguising themselves as servingmen and, more generally, for his vehement support of the cause of the Reformation.

At the time of Somerville's arrest, Lucy was a principal figure in the commission empowered, in the wake of the Jesuit mission, to ferret out Catholic conspirators. He was a dangerous man, not treacherous or malicious perhaps, but tough, fiercely determined, and ruthless in the pursuit of what he regarded as God's own cause. He was specifically interested in the kin of Edward Arden—the government seemed to regard this as a family conspiracy—and he could have heard rumors that John Shakespeare's wife Mary was related to Edward Arden's wife Mary. John Shakespeare, from the time that he was bailiff of Stratford, would have known Lucy and understood what he was capable of. If the Shakespeares harbored Catholic sympathies, they would have had cause for alarm.

The local Catholic community was frightened and hastened to hide any incriminating papers or religious objects. "Unless you can make Somerville, Arden, Hall the Priest, Somerville's wife and his sister to speak directly to those things which you desire to have discovered," wrote the secretary of the Privy Council to his superiors in London, "it will not be possible for us here to find out more than is found already, for that the Papists in this county greatly do work upon the advantage of clearing their houses of all shows of suspicion." The remark provides a glimpse of something rarely reported in detail, though it must have been a frequent enough occurrence: Catholic families scurrying to burn or bury incriminating evidence—a rosary, a family crucifix, a picture of a favorite saint—while the government agents hammer at the doors, impatient to begin their search. On Henley Street in Stratford, the Shakespeare family may have been busy hiding their "shows of suspicion."

Their fear would not have ended with the deaths of Somerville and Arden. In 1585 Sir Thomas Lucy returned to Warwickshire from a year in Parliament with a new achievement to boast of: he had helped to promote a bill "against Jesuits, seminary priests, and other such-like disobedient persons." The bill met with unanimous approval, but on its third reading a solitary member of Parliament, William Parry, arose and denounced it as "a measure savoring of treasons, full of blood, danger, and despair to English subjects, and pregnant with fines and forfeitures which would go to enrich not the queen, but private individuals." He was immediately arrested and examined. When it came out that Parry was ambiguously implicated in a tangle of Catholic conspiracies against the queen, Lucy was at the forefront in petitioning for his execution as a traitor. Parry was hanged and disemboweled on March 2, 1585. All the ministers in the land were instructed to deliver sermons condemning attempts to assassinate God's chosen ruler, Queen Elizabeth, and celebrating her escape from the wicked traitor.

The triumphant Lucy must have been more militant and more vigilant than ever. And, after all, in the mid-1580s, with constant talk of conspiracies to kill the queen and put her imprisoned cousin, the Catholic Mary, Queen of Scots, on the throne, it made sense to be vigilant. Members of the Privy Council and hundreds of Protestants throughout the country took an oath to kill any Catholic pretender to the throne, in the event that Elizabeth was assassinated. There were dark rumors that Spain's Philip II was assembling a fleet large enough to carry an army across the English Channel in an invasion that would be abetted by treasonous English Catholics. It was in this time of extreme tension that Shakespeare may have run afoul of Lucy and decided that he had to get out.

Judging from the birth of his twins in February 1585, it seems likely that Shakespeare remained in Stratford at least until the summer of 1586, but at some point shortly after he turned his back on his wife and children and made his way to London. A piece of personal good fortune may have come his way, making the escape possible. Perhaps he had encountered Lord Strange's Men during his sojourn in the north and had renewed contact with them, perhaps he learned of another troupe of touring players that happened to be in need of an extra actor. The Earl of Leicester's Men were at nearby Coventry and Leicester in 1584–85 and in Stratford-upon-Avon in 1586–87, as were the Earl of Essex's Men. The Lord Admiral's Men were at Coventry and Leicester in 1585–86 and again in Leicester in 1586–87, and the Earl of Sussex's Men followed a similar itinerary.

The most intriguing possibility that scholars have explored in recent years concerns the Queen's Men, at the time the leading touring company in the country. The Queen's Men were in Stratford in 1587, and they were shorthanded. For in the nearby town of Thame, on June 13 between 9 and 10 P.M., one of their leading actors, William Knell, had been killed in a drunken fight with a fellow actor, John Towne. The inexperienced Shakespeare was not likely to have stood in for the celebrated Knell, but in the sudden shifting of the parts, the Queen's Men may have had a place for a novice. And if this were the company in which Shakespeare got his start, he would have had particular reason to be cautious about disclosing any residual Catholic loyalties or any trouble, aside from deer poaching, with Thomas Lucy. For the Queen's Men, scholars have argued, had been established in 1583 to spread Protestant propaganda and royalist enthusiasm through the troubled kingdom.

If any of these companies offered to take him on as a hired man, however modest the salary, Shakespeare would have had the happy occasion to leave Stratford. Of course, to his wife and three very small children, the departure might not have seemed such a piece of good fortune: even if he promised to send them money and to return home as soon or as often as possible, his leaving would inevitably have seemed an abandonment. The meaning of that abandonment—its justification, if there was any—could not at this moment have been at all clear. From an ethical point of view, if he cared to reflect about what he was doing, he might have been hoping for what a modern philosopher, thinking about Paul Gauguin's abandonment of his family in order to pursue his art, has termed "moral luck." That is, if Shakespeare felt he had something important within him that he could only realize by turning away from his domestic obligations, he could only hope to justify his actions if he actually succeeded. He stood in need of moral as well as financial luck.

Assuming that Shakespeare attached himself as a hired man to a playing company, it is not likely that this company headed immediately for London. If in June 1587 he was taken on by the Queen's Men, for example, the company would have continued to tour the towns and hospitable noblemen's houses of the Midlands. By August of that summer, the company, or part of it—for the Queen's Men often divided into touring branches—had gone to the southeast, perhaps providing the young man his first glimpse of the chalk cliffs at Dover (which later figure so powerfully in *King Lear*). The company then worked its way through towns like Hythe and Canterbury toward the capital. Such a route would have given Shakespeare the chance in a comfortingly familiar provincial setting to hone his skills: to learn some of the dance steps, figure out how to change his costume quickly, convincingly swell out a crowd scene or a battle, and begin to grasp the repertoire. He had to be a quick study—no one who did not possess an exceptional memory and a remarkable gift for improvisation could have survived in the competitive world of the Elizabethan theater. His work suggests that he had an almost unique gift for plunging into unfamiliar worlds, mastering their complexities, and making himself almost immediately at home. Still, the most seasoned actor, let alone a neophyte, must have felt a rush of nervous energy on approaching London.

LONDON WAS A CITY of newcomers, flooded every year with fresh arrivals from the country, mostly men and women in their late teens and early twenties, drawn by the promise of work, the spectacle of wealth and power, the dream of some extraordinary destiny. For many their destiny was an early death: rat-infested, overcrowded, polluted, prone to fire and on occasion to riot, London was a startlingly unsafe and unhealthy place. To the ordinary degree of hazard—appallingly high by our own standards—was conjoined the ravages of epidemic diseases. The worst of these, bubonic plague, swept through the city again and again, spreading panic, wiping out whole families, decimating neighborhoods. Even in years spared by the plague, the number of deaths recorded in London's parish records always exceeded the live births. And yet the city kept growing, a seemingly irresistible lure.

The bulk of the burgeoning populace lived and worked within the small area bounded to the south by the Thames and on the other sides by a high crenellated stone wall originally built by the Romans some fourteen hundred years earlier. The wall was pierced by a series of gates some of whose names—Ludgate, Aldgate, Cripplegate, Moorgate—still resonate for Londoners today, long after the structures themselves have vanished. Even in Shakespeare's time, when the wall was more or less intact, it was becoming less visible: the old, wide moat, still deep enough earlier in the century to drown unwary horses and men, was being filled up, and the new land was leased out for carpenters' yards, garden plots, and tenements "whereby," as one contemporary observer noted, "the city wall is hidden."

The eastern edge of the walled city was marked by the massive, grim Tower of London, begun by William the Conqueror; the west, by old St. Paul's Cathedral, which boasted the longest nave in Europe. Further to the west, along the north bank of the Thames, was a succession of mansions, formerly the London residences of the princes of the church and now, in the wake of the Reformation, the seats of powerful aristocrats and royal favorites. The glittering upstart Sir Walter Ralegh, for example, entertained his guests where the bishops of Durham had once held court, and the Earl of Southampton lived in the grand house of the bishops of Bath and Wells. Each of these residences had its own riverside mooring from which the wealthy owners with their liveried attendants could be rowed further upriver to the royal palace at Whitehall for an audience with the queen or to a session of Parliament close by. If they were less fortunate, they could also be rowed downriver to the Tower of London, where they would enter, heartsick and trembling, by Traitor's Gate.

With its crush of small factories, dockyards, and warehouses; its huge food markets, breweries, print shops, hospitals, orphanages, law schools, and guildhalls; its cloth makers, glassmakers, basket makers, brick makers, shipwrights, carpenters, tinsmiths, armorers, haberdashers, furriers, dyers, goldsmiths, fishmongers, booksellers, chandlers, drapers, grocers, and their crowds of unruly apprentices; not to mention its government officials, courtiers, lawyers, merchants, ministers, teachers, soldiers, sailors, porters, carters, watermen, innkeepers, cooks, servants, peddlers, minstrels, acrobats, cardsharps, pimps, whores, and beggars, London overflowed all boundaries. It was a city in ceaseless motion, transforming itself at an unprecedented rate. In his old age, the great London-born antiquary, John Stow, wrote at the end of the sixteenth century a remarkable survey of his city, carefully noting the thousands of changes he had witnessed in his own lifetime. A single example: when he was a boy, Stow recalled, there was an abbey of nuns of the order of St. Clare, known as the Minories, where he went to fetch "many a halfpenny of milk . . . always hot from the kine" from the abbey farm. The abbey was demolished—a casualty of the Reformation—and in its place, Stow wrote, there were now "fair and large storehouses for armour and habiliments of war." As for the farm, its new owner first used it for the grazing of horses and then subdivided it into garden plots that produced enough revenue so that the farmer's son and heir now lived "like a gentleman."

The oligarchy of aldermen, with the sheriffs and mayor, struggled to keep some control of the city through an elaborate system of regulations, but enforcement was complicated by the sheer pressure of numbers and by the existence of numerous precincts, known as liberties, that were exempt from their jurisdiction. Decades earlier, these precincts—the Black Friars, the Austin Friars, the priory of Holy Trinity, Aldgate, or the Minories where Stow went for his halfpenny of milk—had been large monasteries, with outbuildings, spacious gardens, and farms, and as such had enjoyed ecclesiastical exemptions from city codes. After the Reformation, the monks and nuns were all gone, and the buildings and land had passed into private hands. But the exemptions remained, enabling the owners to flout any attempt by the city fathers to stop activities—such as performing plays—that they regarded as nuisances or scandals.

Moreover, ringing the city were sprawling suburbs that were virtually without regulation of any kind. Within living memory, these precincts were still quite open and uncrowded. Stow recalled that near Bishopsgate, when he was a young man, there were "pleasant fields, very commodious for citizens therein to walk, shoot, and otherwise to recreate and refresh their dull spirits in the sweet and wholesome air." Now, he complained, this area, like others, had been turned into "a continual building throughout" of filthy cottages, small tenements, kitchen gardens, workshops, refuse heaps, and the like, "from Houndsditch in the west as far as Whitechapel and further towards the east." Not only had the once-beautiful approaches to the city been sullied, but the traffic had become horrendous: "The coachman rides behind the horse tails, lasheth them, and looketh not behind him; the drayman sitteth and sleepeth on his dray, and letteth his horse lead him home." And what made it worse, Stow wrote, was that young people seemed to have forgotten how to walk: "The world runs on wheels with many whose parents were glad to go on foot."

There were other bustling cities in England, and, if he had traveled, the young Shakespeare could conceivably have seen one or two or them, but none was like London. With a population nearing two hundred thousand, it was some fifteen times larger than the next most populous cities in England and Wales; in all of Europe only Naples and Paris exceeded it in size. Its commercial vitality was intense: London, as one contemporary put it, was "the Fair that lasts all year." This meant that it was fast escaping the seasonal rhythms by which the rest of the country lived; and it was escaping too the deep sense of the local that governed identity elsewhere. It was one of the only places in England where you were not surrounded by people who knew you, your family, and many of the most intimate details of your life, one of the only places in which your clothes and food and furniture were not produced by people you knew personally. It was in consequence the preeminent site not only of relative anonymity but also of fantasy: a place where you could dream of escaping your origins and turning into someone else.

That Shakespeare had this dream is virtually certain: it lies at the heart of what it means to be an actor, it is essential to the craft of the playwright, and it fuels the willingness of audiences to part with their pennies in order to see a play. He may also have had more private motives, a desire to escape whatever had led him into difficulties with Thomas Lucy, a desire to escape his wife and his three children, a desire to escape the glove and illegal wool trade of his improvident father. In his plays, he repeatedly staged scenes of characters separated from their familial bonds, stripped of their identities, stumbling into unfamiliar territory: Rosalind and Celia in the Forest of Arden; Viola on the seacoast of Illyria; Lear, Gloucester, and Edgar on the heath; Pericles in Tarsus; the infant Perdita in Sicily; Innogen (or Imogen) in the mountains of Wales; and all the humans on the spirit-haunted island in *The Tempest*.

Few of these scenes, however, depend upon the idea of the city. London may have been the principal staging ground for fantasies of meta-morphosis, and it was certainly the site where Shakespeare remade him-self, but it did not in an immediately obvious way shape his own theatrical imagination. In *The Alchemist* and *Bartholomew Fair*, his colleague Ben Jonson showed himself passionately interested in the city in which he grew up, the stepson of a master bricklayer living in Hartshorn Lane, near Charing Cross. Other contemporary London-born playwrights, such as Thomas Dekker and Thomas Middleton, similarly interested themselves in the lives of ordinary citizens: shoemakers, whores, shopkeepers, and watermen. But what principally excited Shakespeare's imagination about London were its more sinister or disturbing aspects.

In his very early history play *2 Henry VI*, Shakespeare depicted a band of lower-class Kentish rebels, led by the clothworker Jack Cade, descending on London to overthrow the social order. Cade promises a kind of primitive economic reform: "There shall be in England seven halfpenny loaves sold for a penny, the three-hooped pot shall have ten hoops, and I will make it felony to drink small beer" (4.2.58–60). The rebels—"a ragged multitude / Of hinds and peasants, rude and merciless" (4.4.31–32)—want to burn the records of the realm, abolish literacy, break into prisons and free the prisoners, make the fountains run with wine, execute the gentry. "The first thing we do," famously says one of Cade's followers, "let's kill all the lawyers" (4.2.68).

In a sequence of wild scenes, poised between grotesque comedy and nightmare, the young Shakespeare imagined—and invited his audience to imagine—what it would be like to have London controlled by a half-mad, belligerently illiterate rabble from the country. Something about the fantasy seems to have released a current of personal energy in the neophyte playwright, himself only recently arrived in the capital. While the upper-class characters in this early history play are for the most part stiff and unconvincing—the king in particular is almost completely a cipher—the lower-class rebels are startlingly vital. It is as if Shakespeare had grasped something crucial for the writing of plays: he could split apart elements of himself and his background, mold each of them into vivid form, and then at once laugh, shudder, and destroy them.

He emphasized the destruction, as if to insist that these illiterate, rebellious yokels, these loudmouthed butchers and weavers, had absolutely nothing to do with the playwright himself. "Die, damnèd wretch, the curse of her that bore thee!" exclaims the prosperous country squire who eventually kills Cade (5.1.74), and then, as if killing were not enough, thrusts his sword into the dead man's body. What is being destroyed with such gleeful vehemence is not only an enemy of property but an enemy of the kind of person that Shakespeare understood himself to be. It is possible to detect a disguised self-portrait in Cade's first victim. "Dost thou use to write thy name?" Cade asks an unfortunate clerk seized by the mob. "Or hast thou a mark to thyself like an honest plain-dealing man?"

> CLERK: Sir, I thank God I have been so well brought up that I can write my name.
> ALL CADE'S FOLLOWERS: He hath confessed—away with him! He's a villain and a traitor.
> CADE: Away with him, I say, hang him with his pen and inkhorn about his neck.
>
> (4.2.89–97)

These are lines written by a playwright whose parents signed with a mark and who was probably the first in his family to learn to write his name.

At the same time it is possible to detect Shakespeare on the other side as well, in the rebels swarming toward London with their fantasies of wealth and their intimate knowledge of humble trades.

> SECOND REBEL: I see them! I see them! There's Best's son, the tanner of Wingham—
> FIRST REBEL: He shall have the skins of our enemies to make dog's leather of.
>
> (4.2.18–21)

Tanning was Shakespeare's father's trade—and, in all likelihood, his own too: "dog's leather" was what they called inferior leather used in glove making. He was oddly close, then, to these grotesques, startlingly close even to their leader, Jack Cade, with his claim to be "of an honourable house" (4.2.43), his inveterate pretending, his dream of high station.

Shakespeare was dramatizing something from the chronicles—he characteristically mined these books, particularly Edward Hall's *The Union of the Two Noble and Illustre Families of Lancaster and* York and Raphael Holinshed's *The Chronicles of England, Scotland, and Ireland*, for the materials of his history plays. And he pushed Cade, the fifteenth-century rebel, still further back into the past by adding details drawn from the Peasants' Revolt of 1381. But just as Ephesus in *The Comedy of Errors* is far more a portrait of Shakespeare's contemporary London than of ancient Asia Minor, so too the medieval England in *2 Henry VI* is suffused less with the otherness of the past than with the familiar coordinates of Shakespeare's own present.

And it is the London crowd—the unprecedented concentration of bodies jostling through the narrow streets, crossing and recrossing the great bridge, pressing into taverns and churches and theaters—that is the key to the whole spectacle. The sight of all those people—along with their noise, the smell of their breath, their rowdiness and potential for violence—seems to have been Shakespeare's first and most enduring impression of the great city. In *Julius Caesar*, he returned to the spectacle of the bloodthirsty mob, roaming the streets in search of the conspirators who have killed their hero Caesar:

> THIRD PLEBEIAN: Your name, sir, truly.
> CINNA: Truly, my name is Cinna.
> FIRST PLEBEIAN: Tear him to pieces! He's a conspirator.
> CINNA: I am Cinna the poet, I am Cinna the poet.
> FOURTH PLEBEIAN: Tear him for his bad verses, tear him for his
> bad verses.
> CINNA: I am not Cinna the conspirator.
> FOURTH PLEBEIAN: It is no matter, his name's Cinna. Pluck but his
> name out of his heart, and turn him going.
> THIRD PLEBEIAN: Tear him, tear him!
>
> (3.3.25–34)

This urban mob, rioting for bread and threatening to overturn the social order, figures as well in *Coriolanus*. And it is this same mob—"Mechanic slaves / With greasy aprons, rules, and hammers"—that Cleopatra imagines watching her being led captive through the streets of the great city. The very thought of smelling their "thick breaths," as they cheer the triumph of Rome, is enough to confirm her in her determination to commit suicide (*Antony and Cleopatra*, 5.205–7).

Even when his scene is Rome, Ephesus, Vienna, or Venice, Shakespeare's fixed point of urban reference was London. Ancient Romans may have worn togas and gone hatless, but when the rioting plebeians in *Coriolanus* get what they want, they throw their caps in the air, just as Elizabethan Londoners did. Only in his very early history play, however, did Shakespeare place this London crowd firmly in the city in which he lived and worked, without disguise. "Here sitting upon London Stone," says the megalomaniac Cade, referring to a famous landmark on Cannon Street, "I charge and command that, of the city's cost, the Pissing Conduit run nothing but claret wine this first year of our reign" (4.6.1–4). "So, sirs, now go some and pull down the Savoy," he tells his followers; "others to th' Inns of Court—down with them all" (4.7.1–2). As in a poor man's utopian dream, the law courts will be destroyed and the fountains will run with wine. Small wonder that the middle-class citizens flee in panic and the urban lower classes—"The rascal people" (4.4.50)—rise up in support of the rebels.

When the insurgents get their hands on one of their most hated enemies, Lord Saye, Cade lays out the charges against him:

> Thou hast most traitorously corrupted the youth of the realm in erecting a grammar school; and, whereas before, our forefathers had no other books but the score and the tally, thou hast caused printing to be used and, contrary to the King his crown and dignity, thou hast built a paper-mill. It will be proved to thy face that thou hast men about thee that usually talk of a noun and a verb and such abominable words as no Christian ear can endure to hear. (4.7.27–34)

The paper mill and the printing press are anachronisms—neither existed in England at the time of Cade's rebellion—but that does not matter: Shakespeare was interested in the sources of his own consciousness, the grammar school that took him away from the world of the score and tally (the stick on which people reckoned their small debts) and into the world of the printed book.

Shakespeare was fascinated by the crazed ranting of those who hate modernity, despise learning, and celebrate the virtue of ignorance. And it is characteristic of him even here—when he was imagining those who would have attacked his own identity—that he heard not only the grotesque stupidity but also the grievance:

> Thou hast appointed justices of peace to call poor men before them about matters they were not able to answer. Moreover, thou hast put them in prison, and, because they could not read, thou hast hanged them when indeed only for that cause they have been most worthy to live. (4.7.34–39)

It is mad to think that felons should be spared because they are illiterate, but Cade is lodging a protest against an actual feature of English law at the time that seems equally mad: if an accused felon could demonstrate that he was literate—usually by reading a verse from the Psalms—he could claim "benefit of clergy"; that is, he could, for legal purposes, be classified by virtue of literacy as a clergyman and therefore officially be subject to the jurisdiction of the ecclesiastical courts, which did not have the death penalty. The result in most cases was that the literate thief or murderer went scot-free, though only once: the perpetrator who successfully claimed benefit of clergy was branded with a T for thief or an M for Murderer, and a second offense was fatal. Hence Cade's otherwise incomprehensible charge makes perfect sense: "thou hast put them in prison, and, because they could not read, thou hast hanged them." And hence some of the otherwise incomprehensible rage against nouns and verbs and grammar schools: Cade commands that Lord Saye, along with his son-in-law, Sir James Cromer, be beheaded. "Let them kiss one another," he orders, when their heads are returned to him on poles, "for they loved well when they were alive." Pleased with the spectacle, he proposes parading through London: "with these borne before us instead of maces will we ride through the streets, and at every corner have them kiss." The grisly sight is meant to excite further bloodshed. "Up Fish Street!" he shouts. "Down Saint Magnus' Corner! Kill and knock down! Throw them into Thames!" (4.7.138–39, 142–44, 145–46).

Saint Magnus' Corner was at the northern end of London Bridge, the place where Shakespeare himself may have first set foot in the city. He would, in all likelihood, have been traveling with the troupe of actors he had joined. Perhaps, as they approached the capital, they joked about the rebellious butchers and weavers who long ago had marched on London. The playing company, in any case, would have wanted to attract attention to themselves, to let the populace know that they were back in the city and that they were performing at a particular place and time. In their gaudiest clothes, beating drums and waving flags, they would have timed their arrival and sought the busiest route; if they were approaching from the south, they would have marched up Southwark High Street and across London Bridge.

This, then, might well have been Shakespeare's initial glimpse of London: an architectural marvel, some eight hundred feet in length, that a French visitor, Etienne Perlin, called "the most beautiful bridge in the world." The congested roadway, supported on twenty piers of stone sixty feet high and thirty broad, was lined with tall houses and shops extending out over the water on struts. Many of the shops sold luxury goods— fine silks, hosiery, velvet caps—and some of the buildings themselves commanded attention: you could buy groceries in a two-story thirteenth-century stone building that had formerly been a chantry dedicated to St. Thomas à Becket where Masses were once sung for the souls of the dead. From the breaks between the buildings there were splendid views up and down the great river, especially to the west; overhead there were scavenging birds, wheeling in the air; and in the river hundreds of swans, plucked once a year for the queen's bedding and upholstery.

But one sight in particular would certainly have arrested Shakespeare's attention; it was a major tourist attraction, always pointed out to new arrivals. Stuck on poles on the Great Stone Gate, two arches from the Southwark side, were severed heads, some completely reduced to skulls, others parboiled and tanned, still identifiable. These were not the remains of common thieves, rapists, and murderers. Ordinary criminals were strung up by the hundreds on gibbets located around the margins of the city. The heads on the bridge, visitors were duly informed, were those of gentlemen and nobles who suffered the fate of traitors. A foreign visitor to London in 1592 counted thirty-four of them; another in 1598 said he counted more than thirty. When he first walked across the bridge, or very soon after, Shakespeare must have realized that among the heads were those of John Somerville and the man who bore his own mother's name and may have been his distant kinsman, Edward Arden.

A father and his son-in-law, their severed heads grinning on poles across from one another. "Let them kiss one another, for they loved well when they were alive." The severed heads he saw on the bridge must have made an impact upon his imagination, and not only as demonstrated in the Cade scenes of *2 Henry VI*. If he had spent some dangerous months in Lancashire, Shakespeare would already have imbibed powerful lessons about danger and the need for discretion, concealment, and fiction. These lessons would have been reinforced in Stratford, as tensions rose and rumors of conspiracy, assassination, and invasion spread. But the sight on the bridge was the most compelling instruction yet: keep control of yourself; do not fall into the hands of your enemies; be smart, tough, and realistic; master strategies of concealment and evasion; keep your head on your shoulders.

Hard lessons for a poet and an actor aspiring to be heard and seen by the world. But some such lessons may have caused Shakespeare to reach a decision that has since made it difficult to understand who he was. Where are his personal letters? Why have scholars, ferreting for centuries, failed to find the books he must have owned—or rather, why did he choose not to write his name in those books, the way that Jonson or Donne or many of his contemporaries did? Why, in the huge, glorious body of his writing, is there no direct access to his thoughts about politics or religion or art? Why is everything he wrote—even in the sonnets—couched in a way that enables him to hide his face and his innermost thoughts? Scholars have long thought that the answer must lie in indifference and accident: no contemporary thought that this play-wright's personal views were sufficiently important to record, no one bothered to save his casual letters, and the boxes of papers that may have been left to his daughter Susanna were eventually sold off and used to wrap fish or stiffen the spines of new books or were simply burned. Pos-sibly. But the heads on the pikes may have spoken to him on the day he entered London—and he may well have heeded their warning.

CHAPTER 6

Life in the Suburbs

H E HAD GROWN UP in a world where the fields began just at the end of the street, or at most within a few minutes' walk. Now all around him, extending for miles beyond London's crumbling city walls, were tenements, warehouses, small vegetable gardens, workshops, gun foundries, brick kilns, and windmills, along with stinking ditches and refuse heaps. Shakespeare made his acquaintance for the first time with the suburbs. He discovered what it was to pine for open country.

Londoners too liked to walk out into the fields to take some fresh air—the familiar joy of the countryside was intensified by a widespread belief that the plague was airborne, carried by foul smells. City dwellers passed through the crowded, reeking streets sniffing nosegays or stuffing their nostrils with cloves. In their rooms they burned scented candles and fuming pots to keep the city's pestilential stench at bay. The sweet country air was regarded as literally lifesaving—hence the rush out of the city, during times of plague, by those who could afford to leave and hence too the ordinary craving for a stroll in the fields.

Setting out from the center of the city, an energetic walker could still fairly quickly reach hedged pastures where cows peacefully grazed or ground where laundresses pegged their washing and dyers stretched cloth tautly on what were known as tenter frames or tenterhooks (from whence our phrase "to be on tenterhooks"). And though in Shakespeare's time the open spaces to which Londoners had once had easy access had already begun to disappear, other attractions drew people through the gates or across the river to the suburbs. Many taverns and inns, some of them quite venerable—the famous Tabard Inn, where Chaucer's pilgrims started their journey to Canterbury, was located in Southwark, on the south bank of the Thames—offered food and drink and private rooms in a world that had almost no privacy. In Finsbury Field, to the north of the city, archers could stroll about shooting at painted stakes and trying to avoid passersby. (In 1557 a pregnant woman out for a walk with her husband was struck in the neck by a stray arrow and killed.) Other places of amusement included firing ranges (for practicing pistol shooting), cockfighting pits, wrestling rings, bowling alleys, places for music and dancing, platforms upon which criminals were mutilated or hanged, and an impressive array of "houses of resort," that is, whorehouses. Moralists denounced the latter with particular fierceness, of course, and demanded that they be closed, but the moves against them by city authorities always fell short. In *Measure for Measure*, a play set in a Vienna that looks and sounds like London, the ruler, embarking on a campaign of moral reform, gives an order to pull down the "houses of resort in the suburbs" (1.2.82–83). The order is not carried out.

The congested city, then, was effectively surrounded by an all-purpose entertainment zone, the place where Shakespeare spent much of his professional life. His imagination took it all in, even things that at this distance seem quite negligible. He was forcefully struck, for example, by the game of bowls, particularly by the way the ball with the off-center weight swerved, so that you hit your target only by seeming to aim elsewhere. The image came to him repeatedly as a way of figuring the surprising twists of his cunningly devised plots. So too with archery, wrestling, tilting at posts called quintains, and the whole range of Elizabethan sports and contests: when he did not actually depict them (like in the wrestling scene in *As You Like It*), he used them again and again as images.

Shakespeare's imagination was excited as well by the less innocuous amusements of the suburbs. Henry VIII bequeathed to his royal children a love of seeing bulls and bears "baited," that is, penned up in a ring or chained to a stake and set upon by fierce dogs. The bulls—on occasion "wearied to death" for sport—seem to have been more or less anonymous, but the bears acquired names and personalities: Sackerson, Ned Whiting, George Stone, and Harry Hunks (the latter blinded to increase the fun). The game was something of an English specialty—in their travel journals foreign tourists frequently noted that they took in the sight, and Queen Elizabeth treated visiting ambassadors to it. The cost of keeping the animals was defrayed by making it an entertainment available to the public: large crowds paid admission to the great circular wooden arenas to see the spectacle. In a popular variation, an ape was tied to the back of a pony, which was then attacked by the dogs: "To see the animal kicking amongst the dogs, with the screams of the ape," wrote one observer, "beholding the curs hanging from the ears and neck of the pony, is very laughable."

"Be there bears i'th' town?" asks the asinine Slender, in *The Merry Wives of Windsor*, "I love the sport well" (1.1.241, 243). Shakespeare clearly visited the bear garden in person—he had professional reasons to be interested in what crowds were excited by—but evidently he was less wholeheartedly enamored. The sport, he saw wryly, served to make the Slenders of the world feel more like real men. "I have seen Sackerson loose twenty times, and have taken him by the chain," Slender boasts. "But I warrant you, the women have so cried and shrieked at it that it passed. But women, indeed, cannot abide 'em. They are very ill-favoured, rough things" (1.1.247–51).

Elizabethans perceived bears as supremely ugly, embodiments of everything coarse and violent, and Shakespeare repeatedly echoed this view, but he also grasped something else: "They have tied me to a stake. I cannot fly," says Macbeth, his enemies closing in around him, "But bear-like I must fight the course" (5.7.1–2). This was hardly a sentimental account of either bearbaiting or murder—Macbeth is a traitor who deserves what he gets in the end—but it suspended the coarse laughter of the arena and got at something almost unendurable about the spectacle.

Why did Elizabethan and Jacobean people, including, notably, the Tudor and Stuart monarchs who were its special patrons, enjoy something so brutal and nasty? (Though there was an attempt to revive the "royal sport" at the end of the seventeenth century, it never really recovered from the blow it suffered when seven bears were shot to death in 1655 by Puritan soldiers.) The answer is as difficult to determine as it is to explain why we love our own cruel spectacles. But one key is found in a remark by Shakespeare's contemporary Thomas Dekker: "At length a blind bear was tied to the stake, and instead of baiting him with dogs, a company of creatures that had the shapes of men and faces of Christians (being either colliers, carters, or watermen) took the office of beadles upon them, and whipped Monsieur Hunks till the blood ran down his old shoulders." What the crowds saw in this instance, at least, was a grotesque—and therefore amusing—version of the disciplinary whippings that were routinely inflicted throughout society: parents frequently whipped children, teachers whipped students, masters whipped servants, beadles whipped whores, sheriffs whipped vagrants and "sturdy beggars." The spectacle in the arena had an odd double effect that Shakespeare would immeasurably intensify. It confirmed the order of things—this is what we do—and at the same time it called that order into question— what we do is grotesque.

London was a nonstop theater of punishments. Shakespeare had certainly witnessed corporal discipline before he came to London—Stratford had whipping posts, pillories, and stocks—but the frequency and ferocity of sentences meted out on public scaffolds at Tower Hill, Tyburn, and Smithfield; at Bridewell and the Marshalsea prisons; and at many other sites both within and outside the city walls would have been new. Almost daily he could have watched the state brand, cut, and kill those it deemed offenders. London's many established punishment grounds did not exhaust the locations of these spectacles: in some cases of murder the offender's right hand was cut off at or near the place where the crime was committed and the bleeding malefactor was then paraded through the streets to the execution site. Such spectacles were virtually inescapable for anyone who lived in the great city.

What was it like to walk through these streets? To see such sights every few days? To live in a city where popular entertainments mirrored these constant torments in the whipping of blind bears or, for that matter, in the performance of tragedies? Whether or not Shakespeare went out of his way to witness the gory rituals of law and order (there were other playwrights who were more interested in competing with the public torturer and hangman), they figure repeatedly in his plays. Lavinia's ghastly fate in *Titus Andronicus*—her hands lopped off, her tongue cut out—would have been easy for Elizabethan actors to represent in graphic, realistic detail, for they had seen such things performed in the flesh on scaffolds in the suburbs, near the playhouse. And when Shakespeare's characters displayed the bloody heads of Richard III or Macbeth, members of the audience could easily have compared the simulation with the real thing.

Shakespeare was not simply giving the vulgar crowd what they craved; he himself was manifestly fascinated by the penal spectacles all around him. His fascination was not the same as endorsement; indeed it included a strong current of revulsion. The most terrible scene of torture in his works—the blinding of the Earl of Gloucester in *King Lear*—is, the playwright makes clear, unequivocally the act of moral monsters. But the horror with which this particular wicked act is depicted is not the same as a blanket repudiation of his society's savage judicial punishments. When at the end of *Othello* the wicked Iago refuses to explain why he has woven his vicious plot—"Demand me nothing. What you know, you know. / From this time forth I never will speak word"—the agents of the Venetian state are confident that they will get some answer from him: "Torments will ope your lips" (5.2.309–10, 312). And even if they do not succeed—Iago remains silent for the remainder of the play, and nothing encourages us to believe that torments will lead him to alter his resolution—the Venetians are determined to exact some vengeance on the villain for what he has done. Indeed they will, as the official of the state explains, use all of their ingenuity in order to intensify and prolong his agony:

> If there be any cunning cruelty
> That can torment him much and hold him long,
> It shall be his.
>
> (5.2.342–44)

Though torturing Iago cannot revive Desdemona or restore Othello's ruined life, *Othello* encourages the audience to accept the legitimacy of this proposed course of action: it is a gesture, however inadequate, toward repairing the damaged moral order. State torture is part of the world as Shakespeare and his audience experienced and thus imagined it, and not only from the special perspective of tragedy. In the glow at the end of one of Shakespeare's happiest comedies, *Much Ado About Nothing,* when all the dark suspicions have been vanquished and the bitter misunderstandings have been resolved, there is still time to think ahead to the rack and the thumbscrew. The schemes of Don John the Bastard—a kind of inept Iago—have been exposed, and the villain has fled. Claudio and Hero have been reconciled and are about to join that most delicious couple, Beatrice and Benedick, in marrying. The merry Benedick calls for music—"let's have a dance ere we are married"—when word is brought that Don John has been captured. "Think not on him till tomorrow," Benedick says, speaking the play's closing words, "I'll devise thee brave punishments for him. Strike up, pipers" (5.4.112–13, 121–22).

This then is the answer, or at least part of the answer, to the question of what it was like to live in such a city as London, amidst the endless, grim spectacles of penal justice. The spectacles were part of the structure of life and were accepted as such; the trick was to know when to look and when to look away, when to punish and when to dance. In close proximity to the sites of pain and death were sites of pleasure—the punishment scaffolds of the Bankside were close to the brothels—and these too seized Shakespeare's imagination. Whorehouses ("stews") figure frequently in his plays—Doll Tearsheet, Mistress Overdone, and their fellow workers in the sex industry are quickly but indelibly sketched, along with assorted panders, doorkeepers, tapsters, and servants. He depicted brothels as places of disease, vice, and disorder, but also as places that satisfy ineradicable human needs, bringing together men and women, gentlemen and common people, old and young, the educated and the illiterate, in a camaraderie rarely found elsewhere in the highly stratified society. Above all, he depicted them as small businesses that struggle against high odds—stiff competition, rowdy or indifferent clients, hostile civic authorities—to make a modest profit.

These qualities closely linked whorehouses in Shakespeare's imagination, and probably in that of most of his contemporaries, with another
suburban institution, one that had only recently come into its own and
that was the center of his professional life. The theater, which did not
exist as a freestanding structure anywhere in England when Shakespeare
was born, at once conjoined and played with almost everything that the
"entertainment zone" had to offer: dancing, music, games of skill, blood
sports, punishment, sex. Indeed, the boundaries between theatrical imitation and reality, between one form of amusement and another, were
often blurred. Whores worked the playhouse crowd and, at least in the
fantasies of the theater's enemies, conducted their trade in small rooms
on-site.

A foreign visitor to London in 1584 described the elaborate spectacle he had witnessed in Southwark one August afternoon:

There is a round building three stories high, in which are kept
about a hundred large English dogs, with separate wooden ken-
nels for each of them. These dogs were made to fight singly with
three bears, the second bear being larger than the first and the
third larger than the second. After this a horse was brought in
and chased by the dogs, and at last a bull, who defended himself
bravely. The next was that a number of men and women came
forward from a separate compartment, dancing, conversing and
fighting with each other: also a man who threw some white
bread among the crowd, that scrambled for it. Right over the
middle of the place a rose was fixed, this rose being set on fire by
a rocket: suddenly lots of apples and pears fell out of it down
upon the people standing below. Whilst the people were scrambling for the apples, some rockets were made to fall down upon
them out of the rose, which caused a great fright but amused the
spectators. After this, rockets and other fireworks came flying
out of all corners, and that was the end of the play.

"That was the end of the play": few today would classify this gory,
gaudy spectacle as theater, but in Elizabethan London the baiting of ani-

mals and the performing of plays were curiously intertwined. They both aroused the ire of the city authorities, fretting about traffic congestion, idleness, disorder, and public health—hence the location of performances in places like Southwark, outside the jurisdiction of the aldermen and mayor. They were attacked in similar terms by moralists and preachers, threatening divine vengeance upon all who took pleasure in filthy, godless shows. They attracted crowds of common people and at the same time were patronized and protected by aristocrats. They even took place in strikingly similar buildings. Indeed, one of these buildings—the Hope playhouse—served for both bearbaiting and playacting: in Ben Jonson's *Bartholomew Fair*, performed there in 1614, one of the characters refers to the stench that still lingered from the previous day's sport. The Hope was owned by the pawnbroker, moneylender, and theatrical impresario Philip Henslowe, who also owned whorehouses. London entertainments—and the money they generated—all, in some sense, flowed into one another.

At the same time, the theater, which had (with the exception of the Hope) genuinely differentiated itself from all other types of arenas, was a remarkably important innovation. Playacting in purpose-built playhouses (as opposed to candlelit private halls, innyards, and the backs of wagons) had only recently come to London, significantly later than blood sports. A map of Southwark from 1542 already shows a bullring on High Street, but it was not until 1567 that a prosperous London grocer, John Brayne, put up the city's first freestanding public playhouse, the Red Lion, in Stepney. The enterprise was a bold one—nothing of the kind had been built in England since the decline and fall of the Roman Empire. Very little is known about the Red Lion—it may have been pulled down or transformed to other uses very quickly—but to the intrepid Brayne it must have seemed a promising speculation, for nine years later he was at it again, in a far more important venture. This time he took a business partner, his brother-in-law James Burbage, a joiner by trade who had turned actor under the patronage of the Earl of Leicester. Burbage's carpentry skills were probably at least as important as his playacting, for he played a major role in constructing the complex polygonal timber building that the entrepreneurs called simply the Theater.

The name befits the notion of the Renaissance, in the literal sense of a rebirth of classical antiquity: in 1576 the relatively unfamiliar word "theater" self-consciously conjured up ancient amphitheaters. Not surprisingly, then, the Theater was almost immediately attacked from the pulpit for being made "after the manner of the old heathenish Theatre at Rome." Burbage and Brayne were wise to build it on land they had leased in the liberty of Holywell in the suburb of Shoreditch, outside the Bishopsgate entrance to the city. Here, on the site of what had been a priory of Benedictine nuns, the enterprise was subject to the queen's Privy Council rather than the city. The preachers could fulminate and the city fathers could threaten, but the show would go on.

When Shakespeare came to London, he had seen and acted in plays, but he had never before seen a freestanding playhouse. Probably it had already been described to him in detail, perhaps carefully sketched by a family member who had been to London or by a friend, but there was a moment when he set foot in one for the first time. He saw a rectangular elevated platform, jutting out into the middle of a large yard surrounded by tiered galleries. The yard, for the "groundlings" to stand and watch the play, was open to the elements, but the stage was covered by a painted canopy—known as "the heavens"—supported by two columns. The stage, five feet above the ground, had no protective railings—an actor in the midst of a sword fight had to keep a sharp sense of where he was. Set into the stage was a trapdoor that led to a storage space known as "hell," which could be used to powerful theatrical effect. At the back of the stage was a wooden wall with two doors, for entrances and exits, and between them, in some theaters, a central curtained space that could be opened for formal entrances or for more intimate scenes. Above these doors on the back wall ran a gallery partitioned into rooms for the highest-paying spectators. The central part of this gallery could be used for staging scenes: if not at once then very soon after, Shakespeare began to imagine the ways he might use that space, say, as a balcony or the high parapet of a castle wall.

With no lighting and nothing more than minimal scenery, there would have been little scope for creating the types of illusions routinely used by modern theaters, but audiences have proved again and again that they do not need to be plunged into darkness in order to imagine the night or to see papier-mâché trees in order to conjure up a forest. What Elizabethan audiences did take seriously was the illusionistic effect of clothes; behind the back wall of the stage was a "tiring house," where the actors could don their elaborate costumes, costumes that were carefully protected from the rain by the overhanging canopy. The whole design was wonderfully functional and flexible. The handsome guildhalls and the private halls of the nobility and gentry in which the touring companies performed had their advantages, but the actors had constantly to rethink the show, altering the blocking to fit each different space and working around features that were never intended to accommodate performances. Any young actor or aspiring playwright up from the provinces must have felt on entering a London playhouse that he had died and gone to theatrical heaven.

That heaven had the agreeable quality of looking at least in certain respects reassuringly familiar. An open space, surrounded by galleries, was reminiscent of the innyards in London and throughout the country where plays were occasionally performed in the open air. (More often they were performed in large rooms.) The innkeepers—or housekeepers, as they were called in this period—rented space, along with costumes and props, to itinerant players who would, at the end of the performance, pass the hat among the crowd. By the time he reached London young Will may have collected the pennies himself more than once, though the companies in the 1580s had also begun to experiment with charging for admission at the inn door. The new Theater and the other public theaters that were built in its wake were run on different principles, but the proprietors similarly called themselves housekeepers, as if they simply owned an inn (presumably, this is why we still speak of dimming the "houselights" or of playing to a "full house").

Burbage and Brayne's investment, in fact, included an inn, the Cross Keys on Gracechurch Street (near what is now Liverpool Street Station), where players on occasion also performed, but their principal theater was a separate structure, enabling the entrepreneurs fully to implement the new idea: the spectators would have to pay at the door, before they saw the show. At the end of the play the actors would only beg for applause and urge return visits. Thus was the box office—originally a locked cash-box—born. The innovation—significantly changing the relationship between the entertainers and their customers—must have been an immediate commercial success, since another theater, the Curtain, soon went up in the same neighborhood, and other theaters soon followed. One penny would get you into the yard where you could stand for the two or three hours with the crowd, milling about, buying apples, oranges, nuts, and bottled ale, or pushing in as close as you could get to the edge of the stage. Another penny would get you out of the rain (or on occasion the hot sun) and onto a seat in one of the covered galleries that ringed the playhouse; a third penny would get you a cushioned seat in one of the "gentlemen's rooms" on the lower level of the galleries, "the pleasantest place," as a theatergoer of the time put it, "where [one] not only sees everything well but can also be seen."

The system of payment was meant in part to ensure some financial transparency: the first penny was supposed to go to the players; the second and third pennies in whole or in part to the "housekeepers." But the partners soon fell out—Burbage, Brayne alleged, had been filching money from the cashbox to which he had a secret key—and they did what Elizabethans with any money at stake constantly did: they went to court. Even after Brayne's death in 1586, the charges and countercharges had not been settled. On the contrary, they grew more tangled and bitter, culminating in a pitched battle on November 16, 1590, when Brayne's widow came with her allies to the Theater to attempt to collect a share of the receipts. Leaning out of a window, James Burbage and his wife shouted that their sister-in-law was a whore and the collectors knaves. Their youngest son, Richard, then about sixteen years old, lay about him with a broomstick and assaulted one of the collectors, "scornfully and disdainfully," as the deposition puts it, "playing with this deponent's nose." This rowdy boy with the broomstick is the first recorded glimpse of the celebrated actor who subsequently played Hamlet and most of the other great Shakespearean heroes.

The theatrical world Shakespeare found his way into was volatile, speculative, competitive, and precarious. The stage had vociferous enemies: the theaters, preachers and moralists charged, were temples to

Venus and other devilish pagan deities; respectable matrons who went innocently enough to watch the plays were quickly lured into lives of licentiousness; men were sexually aroused by seductive boy actors; the Word of God was mocked and piety held up to ridicule; grave authorities were brought into contempt; seditious ideas were planted in the minds of the multitude. Go to plays, thundered one irate minister, John Northbrooke, "if you will learn how to be false and deceive your husbands, or husbands their wives, how to play the harlots to obtain one's love, how to ravish, how to beguile, how to betray, to flatter, lie, swear, forswear, how to allure to whoredom, how to murder, how to poison, how to disobey and rebel against princes, to consume treasures prodigally, to move to lusts, to ransack and spoil cities and towns, to be idle, to blaspheme, to sing filthy songs of love, to speak filthily, to be proud. . . ." The catalog of vicious lessons continues breathlessly, to be augmented over the years by many other preachers. And as if this were not enough, the wickedness on stage, the theater's enemies complained, was matched by the wickedness of the audience. At our playhouses, wrote Stephen Gosson in 1579, "you shall see such heaving and shoving, such itching and shouldering to sit by the women; such care for their garments, that they be not trod on; such eyes to their laps, that no chips light in them; such pillows to their backs, that they take no hurt; such masking in their ears, I know not what; such giving them pippins, to pass the time; such playing at foot saunt [i.e., footsie] . . . ; such ticking, such toying, such smiling, such winking, and such manning them home, when the sports are ended." It is a terrible thing, moralists sourly observed, that many who sit happily for two hours to watch a play cannot bear to sit for an hour to hear a sermon.

These charges were leveled in the name of closing down the theaters, but apart from leading to a ban on Sunday performances, they principally served, not surprisingly, to intensify the public's interest. "Where shall we go?" wrote John Florio, in an English-Italian phrase book that he published in 1578. "To a play at the Bull, or else to some other place." Florio was born and brought up in London, the son of refugee Italian Protestants. His little language lesson—revealing, as those in modern textbooks are, precisely because it was attempting to be so ordinary and everyday—continued:

Do comedies like you well?

Yea sir, on holy days.

They please me also well, but the preachers will not allow them.

Wherefore? Know you it?

They say, they are not good.

And wherefore are they used?

Because every man delights in them.

"Because every man delights in them": defenders of the stage marshaled many arguments—plays showed virtue rewarded and vice punished, taught good manners, kept minds that might otherwise be plotting mischief occupied with harmless things, and so forth—but the theaters survived and flourished simply because people ranging from lowly apprentices to the queen enjoyed what they saw.

Powerful aristocrats, key government officials, and the queen herself protected the public theaters and the playing companies. If there was a dangerous, subversive force in the realm, they thought, it was not the theaters but the theaters' enemies, the discontented, tirelessly meddlesome Protestant radicals who wanted to sweep away all profane pleasures. But the protection that the queen and her advisers afforded the stage was by no means unconditional; they too were nervous about public assemblies. They behaved, whether from paranoia or from bitter practical experience, as if crowds were inherently dangerous, as if they could easily turn violent, as if, given the chance, they would attack their social superiors and strike at the fundamental institutions of the society. Though official documents always stressed the queen's serene confidence in her loving subjects, many of her less guarded remarks suggest a strong current of suspicion. When Sir Philip Sidney had a shoving match with his social superior, the Earl of Oxford, over a tennis court, Elizabeth gave Sidney a lecture on the difference between an earl and a mere knight, along with a warning: Can you imagine, she asked, what would happen if common people learned that you yourself did not respect rank and title?

Elizabethan officials worried about any public spectacle that they could not control. Even the gathering together of a handful of people could alarm the authorities. Spies were assigned to taverns and inns to listen into conversations and report anything suspicious. Proclamations were issued asking people to be on the watch for anyone speaking "undutiful words." The government issued warnings against people who "lie privily in corners and bad houses, listening after news and stirs, and spreading rumors and tales." Vagabonds lurking in London were subject to harsh punishments. Small wonder that the position of the theaters, even with its powerful friends, was precarious.

Arriving in London in the late 1580s, probably as a hired actor in a troupe of players, Shakespeare entered a relatively new scene, not so new that its basic outlines were unformed but new enough that it was still open and evolving. The playing companies had been accustomed to a nomadic life of almost perpetual touring, with their membership frequently shifting, temporarily splitting apart, and recombining. The rise of the public theaters in a city with a rapidly expanding population hungry for amusement gave at least some of these companies the opportunity to have a lucrative home base where they would do most of their performing. They would still go out on the road from time to time, but the wagon with the costumes and props, the scrambling to find a place to perform, the fraught negotiations with the local authorities would no longer occupy the center of their professional lives.

But even for the most successful companies the transition to a more settled London-centered existence was not easy. Touring was no doubt tiring—after a handful of performances, the troupe would have to pack up and move on—but the actors could get by with a modest repertory. Not so in London. The open amphitheaters were large—they could hold two thousand or more—and the city, though populous by sixteenth-century standards, was only two hundred thousand. This meant that to survive economically it was not enough to mount one or two successful plays a season and keep them up for reasonable runs. The companies had to induce people, large numbers of people, to get in the habit of coming to the theater again and again, and this meant a constantly changing repertoire, as many as five or six plays per week. The sheer magnitude of the enterprise is astonishing: for each company, approximately twenty new plays per year in addition to some twenty plays carried over from previous seasons.

Shakespeare seems to have grasped quickly the special opportunity that the burgeoning public theaters had created. The companies that performed in them had an enormous appetite for new plays. He could help to satisfy this appetite, either on his own or in collaboration with others. His timing could not have been better. There was no writers' guild, no special credentials that he needed to possess, no prerequisites for venturing forth. London would enable him to realize the embryonic ambition to write as well as to act that he may have brought with him from Stratford.

Later in his life it was said that Shakespeare wrote with astonishing facility. "The Players have often mentioned it as an honor to Shakespeare," his friend and rival Ben Jonson wrote, "that in his writing, whatsoever he penned, he never blotted out line." "My answer hath been," Jonson tartly added, "would he had blotted a thousand." Judging from the multiple versions that exist of many of his plays and poems, Shakespeare in fact must have quietly blotted thousands of lines. There is powerful evidence that he extensively revised his work. Yet the impression of a great ease in writing remains and may have extended back even to his early efforts. Words came easily to him, he was a quick study, and he had already absorbed several richly suggestive theatrical models. Though young and untried, he was poised to begin writing for the stage at once. Nonetheless, there are signs that it took a startling aesthetic shock to set Shakespeare's career as a writer fully in motion.

London, the chronicler Stow wrote, "was a mighty arm and instrument to bring any great desire to effect." The great public theaters that went up from the 1570s onward—the Theater, the Curtain, the Rose, the Swan, the Globe, the Red Bull, the Fortune, and the Hope—were in the business of fostering and catering to such great desires. Shakespeare encountered this central principle in its purest form almost immediately upon his arrival, for in 1587, just at the time he was finding his feet in London, crowds were flocking to the Rose to see the Lord Admiral's Men perform Christopher Marlowe's *Tamburlaine*. Shakespeare almost certainly saw the play (along with the sequel that shortly followed), and he probably went back again and again. It may indeed have been one of the first performances he ever saw in a playhouse—perhaps *the* first— and, from its effect upon his early work, it appears to have had upon him an intense, visceral, indeed life-transforming impact.

The dream that Marlowe's startlingly cruel play aroused and brilliantly gratified was the dream of domination. His hero is a poor Scythian shepherd who rises by determination, charismatic energy, and utter ruthlessness to conquer much of the known world. The play, conceived on an epic scale, is full of noise, exotic pageantry, and rivers of stage blood—flags fly, chariots are dragged across the stage, cannons are fired—but the core of its appeal is its incantatory celebration of the will to power:

> Nature, that framed us of four elements,
> Warring within our breasts for regiment,
> Doth teach us all to have aspiring minds.
> Our souls, whose faculties can comprehend
> The wondrous architecture of the world
> And measure every wand'ring planet's course,
> Still climbing after knowledge infinite
> And always moving as the restless spheres,
> Wills us to wear ourselves and never rest
> Until we reach the ripest fruit of all:
> That perfect bliss and sole felicity,
> The sweet fruition of an earthly crown.
>   (2.7.18–29)

For the space of this play, all of the moral rules inculcated in schools and churches, in homilies and proclamations and sober-minded tracts, are suspended. The highest good—"That perfect bliss and sole felicity"—is not the contemplation of God but the possession of a crown. There is no hierarchy of blood, no divinely sanctioned legitimate authority, no inherited obligation to obey, no moral restraint. Instead, there is a restless, violent striving that can be fully appeased only by grasping (or dreaming of grasping) supreme power.

The part of Tamburlaine was created by an astonishingly gifted young actor in the Lord Admiral's Men, Edward Alleyn, at the time only twenty-one years old. At the sight of the performance, Shakespeare, two years his senior, may have grasped, if he had not already begun to do so, that he was not likely to become one of the leading actors on the London stage. Alleyn was the real thing: a majestic physical presence, with a "well-tuned," clear voice capable of seizing and holding the attention of enormous audiences. Achieving instant and enduring fame for his "stalking and roaring" in the part, Alleyn went on to play Faustus, Barabas, and many other great roles; to marry Henslowe's step-daughter; to become immensely rich from the business side of entertainment; and to found a distinguished educational institution, Dulwich College.

The actor in Shakespeare would have perceived what was powerful in Alleyn's interpretation of Tamburlaine, but the poet in him understood something else: the magic that was drawing audiences did not reside entirely in the actor's fine voice, nor even in the hero's daring vision of the blissful object at which he lunges, the earthy crown. The hushed crowd was already tasting Tamburlaine's power in the unprecedented energy and commanding eloquence of the play's blank verse—the dynamic flow of unrhymed five-stress, ten-syllable lines—that the author, Christopher Marlowe, had mastered for the stage. This verse, like the dream of what ordinary speech would be like were human beings something greater than they are, was by no means only bombast and bragging. Its appeal lay in its own "wondrous architecture": its subtle rhythms, the way in which a succession of monosyllables suddenly flowers into the word "aspiring," the pleasure of hearing "fruit" become "fruition."

Shakespeare had never heard anything quite like this before—certainly not in the morality plays or mystery cycles he had watched back in Warwickshire. He must have said to himself something like, "You are not in Stratford anymore." To someone raised on a diet of moralities and mysteries, it must have seemed as if the figure of Riot had somehow seized control of the stage, and with it an unparalleled power of language. Perhaps, at one of those early performances—before the full extent of Marlowe's recklessness became known—Shakespeare waited, with others in the audience, for the tyrant, soaked with the blood of innocents, to be brought low. That, after all, is what always happened to Riot or to Herod in the religious drama. But what he saw instead was one insanely cruel victory follow another, the rhetoric of triumph becoming ever more intoxicating. "Millions of souls sit on the banks of Styx," exults the murderous conqueror at the play's close,

> Waiting the back return of Charon's boat.
> Hell and Elysium swarm with ghosts of men
> That I have sent. . . .
>
> (5.1.463–66)

Nothing holds Tamburlaine back, no fear, no deference, no respect for the established order of things: "Emperors and kings lie breathless at my feet" (5.1.469). With these words and with the slaughter of the innocent virgins of Damascus, he takes his beautiful bride, the divine Zenocrate, daughter of the conquered sultan of Egypt. Then, shockingly, outrageously, the play was over, and the crowd applauded, cheering the trampling of everything that they had been instructed with numbing repetition to hold dear.

This was a crucial experience for Shakespeare, a challenge to all of his aesthetic and moral and professional assumptions. The challenge must have been intensified when he learned that Marlowe was in effect his double: born in the same year, 1564, in a provincial town; the son not of a wealthy gentleman but of a common artisan, a shoemaker. Had Marlowe not existed, Shakespeare would no doubt have written plays, but those plays would have been decisively different. As it is, he gives the impression that he made the key move in his career—the decision not to make his living as an actor alone but to try also to write for the stage on which he performed—under Marlowe's influence. The fingerprints of *Tamburlaine* (both the initial play and the sequel that soon followed) are all over the plays that are among Shakespeare's earliest known ventures as a playwright, the three parts of *Henry VI*—so much so that earlier textual scholars thought that the *Henry VI* plays must have been collaborative enterprises undertaken with Marlowe himself. The decided unevenness in the style of the plays suggests that Shakespeare may well have been working with others, though few scholars any longer believe that Marlowe was among them. Rather, the neophyte Shakespeare and his collaborators seem to have been looking over their shoulders at Marlowe's achievement.

Marlowe had put together the two parts of *Tamburlaine* out of his strange personal history—spy, double agent, counterfeiter, atheist—but also and as important, out of his voraciously wide reading. Some of the details of the life of the Scythian conqueror he could have culled from popular English books, but scholars have shown that Marlowe must have followed the leads in these books back to other, less readily available sources in Latin. Some of the details in *Tamburlaine* suggest that Marlowe even picked up information found in Turkish sources not yet translated during the playwright's lifetime into any Western European languages. And crucially, for these plays full of exotic geographical locations, he had access to the recent and very expensive *Theatrum orbis terrarum* by the great Flemish geographer Ortelius. Where could a shoemaker's son find access to this and all the rest? The explanation must lie in the bibliographical and human resources of Cambridge University, where Marlowe enrolled as a student in 1581. In July of that year, for example, a copy of Ortelius's atlas was presented to the university library, and Marlowe's own college, Corpus Christi, already owned a copy.

Shakespeare had no comparable resources upon which he could draw. But he did have a friend in London who probably played a crucial role at this point in his career. Richard Field had come to London in 1578 from Stratford-upon-Avon, where his father and Shakespeare's father were associates, to serve as an apprentice to the printer Thomas Vautrollier, a Protestant refugee from Paris. Vautrollier had a good business: he published schoolbooks, an edition of Calvin's *Institutes of the Christian Religion*, a Latin Book of Common Prayer, works in French, and editions of important classics. Thus described, the list sounds rather dull, but Vautrollier also allowed himself to take certain risks, such as bringing out important works by the heretical theologian and radical Italian philosopher Giordano Bruno (who was later burned at the stake in Naples). And among his best-known publications was a book that turned out to be one of Shakespeare's favorites: Sir Thomas North's translation of Plutarch's *Lives*, a principal source for *Julius Caesar, Timon of Athens, Coriolanus*, and, above all, *Antony and Cleopatra*.

Richard Field did well for himself in his new calling: after serving for six years as Vautrollier's apprentice and for a seventh year as the apprentice of another printer, in 1587 he obtained admission to the printers' guild, the Stationer's Company. When, in that same year, Vautrollier died, Field married his widow, Jacqueline, and took over the business. By 1589, then, he was established as a master printer, with a busy workshop and an impressive, wide-ranging, and intellectually challenging list of authors. He must also have owned books by his competitors and would have had access to others. He was a hugely valuable resource for his young playwright friend from Stratford.

Even though as a poet Shakespeare dreamed of eternal fame, he does not seem to have associated that fame with the phenomenon of the printed book. And even when he was well established as a playwright, with his plays for sale in the bookstalls in St. Paul's Churchyard, he showed little or no personal interest in seeing his plays on the printed page, let alone assuring the accuracy of the editions. He never, it seems, anticipated what turned out to be the case: that he would live as much on the page as on the stage and that his destiny as a writer was deeply bound up with the technology he must have glimpsed the first time he visited his friend's printing shop in Blackfriars.

When the door opened, Shakespeare would have seen firsthand the beating heart of the London book trade: the compositor bending over the manuscripts, reaching into the trays, pulling out the bits of type and setting them in the rows; the printer inking the completed "formes," or frames in which the printing type was secured, and turning the great screws that pressed the inked formes down onto the mechanical bed on which large sheets of paper were laid; the printing press casting off the sheets which were then folded to make the pages; the proofreader correcting the sheets and going back to the compositor for changes before the pages were taken to the binders to be stitched together. All of this would have been interesting enough in itself as a spectacle (there are many images in Shakespeare's work of the imprinting of marks or signs), but the real excitement for him would have been access to books. Books were expensive, far too expensive for a young actor and untried playwright to buy out of his own pocket, and yet the ambitious Shakespeare needed them if he was to rise to the challenge posed by Marlowe's stupendous work.

How Shakespeare came to the idea of writing his counterthrust to *Tamburlaine*—the three plays about the troubled fifteenth-century reign of Henry VI—is not known. Perhaps the idea was not originally his: there is evidence that the Queen's Men, with which he may have been affiliated at the time, was troubled by Marlowe's success and determined to counter it. Shakespeare may have been invited to join in a project already under way that had bogged down. Plays were often written collaboratively, and the more established writers may have welcomed another hand. Perhaps he began by making a few small suggestions and then found himself increasingly involved and responsible. Alternatively, he may have been in charge from the beginning. But whatever the case, he and any collaborators he had needed books, as Marlowe had needed books. The key books—English chronicles such as Edward Hall's *The Union of the Two Noble and Illustre Families of Lancaster and York*, Geoffrey of Monmouth's *Historia regum Britanniae*, *A Mirror for Magistrates* by Willam Baldwin and others, and, above all, Raphael Holinshed's indispensable and just-published *Chronicles*—were not published by Field or his former master Vautrollier, but it is quite possible that Shakespeare's friend may have owned copies or been able to put him in touch with those who did.

Shakespeare had determined to write a historical epic, like Marlowe's, but to make it an English epic, an account of the bloody time of troubles that preceded the order brought by the Tudors. He wanted to resurrect a whole world, as Marlowe had done, bringing forth astonishing larger-than-life figures engaged in struggles to the death, but it was now not the exotic realms of the East that would be brought to the stage but England's own past. The great idea of the history play—taking the audience back into a time that had dropped away from living memory but that was still eerily familiar and crucially important—was not absolutely new, but Shakespeare gave it an energy, power, and conviction that it had never before possessed. The *Henry VI* plays are still crude, especially in comparison with Shakespeare's later triumphs in the same genre, but they convey a striking picture of the playwright poring over Holinshed's *Chronicles* in search of materials that would enable him to imitate *Tamburlaine*.

The imitation, though real enough, is not exactly an expression of homage; it is a skeptical reply. Marlowe's play concentrated all of the world's driving ambition in a single charismatic superhero; Shakespeare's trilogy is full of Tamburlaine-like grotesques, including one already encountered, the peasant Jack Cade. Cade turns out to be the unwitting puppet of the power-crazed Duke of York, who echoes Tamburlaine's boast:

> I will stir up in England some black storm
> Shall blow ten thousand souls to heaven or hell,
> And this fell tempest shall not cease to rage
> Until the golden circuit on my head
> Like to the glorious sun's transparent beams
> Do calm the fury of this mad-bred flaw.
> (2 Henry VI, 3.1.349–54)

The Marlovian accents are still clearer in the speeches of York's evil son, Richard:

> How sweet a thing it is to wear a crown,
> Within whose circuit is Elysium
> And all that poets feign of bliss and joy.
> (3 Henry VI, 1.2.29–31)

And the sadistic pleasure is no longer limited to the male world; it extends to the formidable Queen Margaret, triumphing over her enemy York:

> Why art thou patient, man? Thou shouldst be mad,
> And I, to make thee mad, do mock thee thus.
> Stamp, rave, and fret, that I may sing and dance.
> (3 Henry VI, 1.4.90–92)

This savage cruelty in a woman astonishes even the fierce York: "O tiger's heart wrapped in a woman's hide!" he exclaims (1.4.138). When order breaks down, everyone wants to be a Tamburlaine.

In Marlowe's vision of the exotic East, vaunting ambition, stopping at nothing, leads to the establishment of a grand world order, cruel but magnificent. That order, as part two of *Tamburlaine* shows, crumbles, but only because everything eventually crumbles: there is no moral other than the brute fact of mortality. In Shakespeare's vision of English history, vaunting ambition leads to chaos, an ungovernable, murderous factionalism and the consequent loss of power at home and abroad. Despite or even because of his ruthlessness, Marlowe's hero bestrides the world like a god, doing whatever it pleases him to do—"This is my mind, and I will have it so" (4.2.91). By contrast, Shakespeare's petty Tamburlaines, even though they are queens and dukes, are like mentally unbalanced small-town criminals: they are capable of incredible nastiness but cannot achieve a hint of grandeur.

In part, this limitation was a consequence of poetic inexperience: Shakespeare was not able, at least at this point in his life, to match the unstoppable, monomaniacal grandiloquence Marlowe commanded. But in part it was a clear choice: Shakespeare refused to give any of his characters, even his stalwart English military hero Talbot, the limitless power Marlowe gleefully conferred on Tamburlaine. Simply to look at Tamburlaine is to see the embodiment of Herculean power; to look on Talbot, by contrast, is to be disappointed. "I see report is fabulous and false," says the Countess of Auvergne, who has lured Talbot to her castle.

> It cannot be this weak and writhled shrimp
> Should strike such terror to his enemies.
>
> (*1 Henry VI*, 2.3.17, 22–3)

Talbot is an ordinary mortal. When the English forces are routed, he is killed, along with his son, by a French army led by the demonic Joan of Arc. No one in this world is invincible: abandoned by her devils, Joan is soon afterward captured by the resurgent English army, tried for sorcery, and burned at the stake.

Crowds flocked in the late 1580s to see the *Henry VI* plays—this was Shakespeare's first great theatrical success, establishing him as a viable playwright—but they did not come to fantasize about possessing absolute power. On the contrary, they came to shudder at the horrors of popular uprising and civil war. The crowds came too, it seems, to savor heroic sacrifice and to mourn loss. "How it would have joyed brave Talbot," wrote a contemporary playwright, Thomas Nashe, "to think that after he had lain two hundred years in his Tomb, he should triumph again on the Stage, and have his bones new embalmed with the tears of ten thousand spectators at least (at several times) who, in the Tragedian that represents his person, imagine they behold him fresh bleeding." Nashe, who may have been one of Shakespeare's collaborators on *1 Henry VI*, was not an objective witness. But even if he was exaggerating, he was pointing to a major commercial triumph. Edward Alleyn had found a rival in the "Tragedian" who played Talbot—in all likelihood, Richard Burbage; and the visionary poetic genius of Christopher Marlowe had been challenged from a hitherto unknown talent, a minor actor from Stratford-upon-Avon.

CHAPTER 7

Shakescene

I F BEFORE HIS SUCCESS with the *Henry VI* plays Shakespeare had not already met Marlowe, he would certainly have met him soon afterward, and along with Marlowe he would have met many of the other playwrights—poets, as they were then called—who were writing for the London stage. They were an extraordinary group, of the kind that emerges all at once in charmed moments, as when a dozen or more brilliant painters all seemed to converge at the same time on Florence or when for years at a time New Orleans or Chicago seemed to have a seemingly limitless supply of stupendous jazz and blues musicians. In all such moments, of course, sheer genetic accident is at work, but there are always institutional and cultural circumstances that help the accident make sense. In late-sixteenth-century London those circumstances included the phenomenal growth of the urban population, the emergence of the public theaters, and the existence of a competitive market for new plays. They included too an impressive, widespread growth in literacy; an educational system that trained its students to be highly sensitive to rhetorical effects; a social and political taste for elaborate display; a religious culture that compelled parishioners to listen to long, complex sermons; and a vibrant, restless intellectual culture. There were very few options for promising intellectuals: the educational system had surged ahead of the existing social system, so that highly educated men who did not want to pursue a career in the church or law had to cast about for something to do with themselves. Disreputable though it was, the theater beckoned.

At some moment in the late 1580s, Shakespeare walked into a room—most likely, in an inn in Shoreditch, Southwark, or the Bankside—and quite possibly found many of the leading writers drinking and eating together: Christopher Marlowe, Thomas Watson, Thomas Lodge, George Peele, Thomas Nashe, and Robert Greene. Other playwrights might have been there as well—Thomas Kyd, for example, or John Lyly, but Lyly, born in 1554, was substantially older than the rest, and Kyd, though he subsequently shared a room with Marlowe, seems to have been held at a distance by the group as a whole. For despite his success as a playwright, Kyd made enough to live on by plodding away as a mere scrivener, a professional penman who copied out texts, and the most stylish writers held such humble occupations in disdain. The group shared a combination of extreme marginality and arrogant snobbishness.

For Marlowe, at least, the marginality of the playhouse may have been part of the pleasure. He led a notoriously risk-taking life. But he had only an extreme case of a restless, risk-taking streak present in many of those who responded to the lure of the theater. One of Marlowe's closest friends, London-born Thomas Watson, had studied at Oxford but left without a degree, at the age of thirteen or fourteen, to travel and study on the Continent, learning, as he put it, "to utter words of diverse sound." He returned to London ostensibly to study law, though he also seems to have been engaged in duplicitous, high-stakes games, somewhere between espionage and extortion. At the same time he threw himself into the literary scene, where he quickly emerged as one of its most learned figures, publishing by the time he was twenty-four years old a Latin translation of Sophocles' *Antigone*, composing original Latin poetry, translating Petrarch and Tasso into Latin hexameters, and experimenting in English for the first time since Wyatt and Surrey with the fashionable Continental form, the sonnet.

Somehow in this hectic life Watson also found time to write plays in

English for the popular stage. Surveying the theater in the late 1590s, Francis Meres ranked Watson with Peele, Marlowe, and Shakespeare as "the best for tragedy"; more sourly, an antagonist, accusing him of fraud, declared that he "could devise twenty fictions and knaveries in a play which was his daily practice and his living." None of these plays survives, and Watson is now best known as the friend who intervened in a street brawl between Marlowe and an innkeeper's son named William Bradley. The brawl, on Hog Lane, near the Theater and the Curtain, ended with Watson's sword stuck six inches into Bradley's chest. Watson and Marlowe were both arrested on suspicion of murder but were eventually released, on grounds of self-defense.

Watson's disturbing combination of impressive learning, literary ambition, duplicity, violence, and rootlessness is a clue to understanding his deep kinship—his blood brotherhood—with Marlowe. It serves as well as an introduction to the group of writers, the so-called university wits, whom the young Shakespeare would have encountered at the outset of his career. Not all of them were quite as sinister as Marlowe and Watson. Thomas Lodge, about six years older than Shakespeare, graduated from Oxford and began to study law. The second son of London's lord mayor, Lodge had a course of respectable prosperity laid out for him, his dying mother having left a bequest to support his studies and to launch him in his legal career. But the prospect of this career evidently disagreed with him, for he forfeited this bequest and his father's goodwill by dropping out and plunging into the literary scene. At about the time Shakespeare was writing or collaborating on the *Henry VI* trilogy, Lodge penned his own play about a country destroyed by factional conflict, *The Wounds of Civil War,* performed by the Lord Admiral's Men. Neither this nor the other plays in which Lodge had a hand showed much talent, and he seems in any case not to have staked all his hopes on a career as a playwright, for in 1588 he embarked on an adventurous voyage to the Canary Islands. He returned with a new literary composition to show for himself, a fine prose romance he titled *Rosalind*: "the fruits of his labors," he wrote of himself, "that he wrought in the ocean when every line was wet with a surge." Like Marlowe and Watson, then, Lodge was a bold risk-taker— in 1591 he sailed with Thomas Cavendish to Brazil and the Straits of

Magellan and returned to tell the tale. But he was a less turbulent spirit: it would have been easier to have a drink with him without fearing for your purse or your life.

Another member of the circle of writers, George Peele, the son of a London salt merchant and accountant, had already as a student at Oxford begun to earn a reputation for wild pranks and riotous living—a book was published chronicling his supposed adventures—but he was also early noted for his gifts as a poet and a translator of Euripides. He seems to have been a sometime actor as well as an energetic writer of lyric poems, pastorals, pageants, and plays for the popular stage. At the time Shakespeare would have first met him, Peele had published verses in praise of his friend Thomas Watson, scripted the lord mayor's pageant, and had a play, *The Arraignment of Paris*, successfully presented to the queen. He was probably at work on *The Battle of Alcazar*, his own response to the immense popularity of Marlowe's *Tamburlaine*. None of this feverish activity brought in much money, and Peele was rapidly running through the dowry brought to him by his wife. But he must have been amusing company: his friend Thomas Nashe called him "the chief supporter of pleasance now living."

Nashe was not normally one to give compliments. Of the university wits, he was the most bitingly satiric, and in the late 1580s, newly arrived in London, he was demonstrating his gift for mockery in a succession of anti-Puritan pamphlets. Three years younger than Shakespeare, the son of the curate of a small Herefordshire parish, Nashe had gone to Cambridge as a "sizar," a scholarship student, and had continued his studies there for a year or more after he took the B.A. degree that enabled him to write "gentleman" by his name. His first publication, an epistle addressed to "the Gentleman Students of both universities," was a harsh review of recent literary efforts—the cruel judgments of a brash young man, leavened with some flattering remarks about his best friends.

Nashe praised Peele, Watson, and a few others for their "deep-witted scholarship," but he had particularly acerbic things to say about upstarts "who (mounted on the stage of arrogance) think to out-brave better pens with the swelling bombast of a bragging blank verse." Nashe's florid style delighted in its own obscurity: "Indeed it may be the engrafted overflow of some kill-cow conceit, that overcloyeth their imagination with a more than drunken resolution, being not extemporal in the invention of any other means to vent their manhood, commits the digestion of their choleric encumbrances to the spacious volubility of a drumming decasyllabon." But through the haze of verbal self-display, the point is sharply clear: certain men with only a grammar school education have had the audacity to write plays in blank verse for the public stage. This type of impudent rustic—a man with little or no Latin, French, or Italian, born to be a servant or small-town lawyer's clerk—busies himself with "the endeavors of Art," imitates the poetic style and favorite meter of his university-trained betters, and thinks he can leap into a new occupation: "if you entreat him fair in a frosty morning, he will afford you whole *Hamlets*, I should say handfuls of tragical speeches." These words were written well before Shakespeare wrote *Hamlet*. Presumably, the specific object of nastiness here was Thomas Kyd, who had no university degree, had served as a lawyer's clerk and a servingman, and had written a play, now lost, about Hamlet. But the general terms of the withering attack also applied perfectly to Shakespeare, as Shakespeare would have understood.

Nashe's epistle was prefixed to a lurid romance, *Menaphon*, penned by the central figure in this circle of writers, Robert Greene. Though he turned out to play an important role in Shakespeare's life, Greene was by no means the most accomplished; Marlowe towered above him, and he would never write anything as good as Nashe's wild picaresque novel, *The Unfortunate Traveler*; Peele's charming play *The Old Wives' Tale*; or even Lodge's elegant Ovidian poem, *Scylla's Metamorphosis*. But Greene was larger than life, a hugely talented, learned, narcissistic, self-dramatizing, self-promoting, shameless, and undisciplined scoundrel. Four years older than Shakespeare, the son of poor parents from Norwich, he managed, like Marlowe and Nashe, to get a scholarship to Cambridge, where he took his M.A. in 1583. He went on to receive another degree from Oxford. With these impressive qualifications and with a marriage to "a gentleman's daughter of good account," Greene seemed set for a prosperous life (he briefly thought he might study medicine), but his desires led him in a different direction. Having squandered his wife's marriage portion, he abandoned her and their small child and headed off to London, uncertain how he would support himself.

Greene, who constantly fictionalized his life, wrote a story of how he was recruited to write for the stage. Since he was an inveterate liar, there is no reason to believe a word of his account, but it must have struck contemporaries as at least plausible, and it served as a kind of literary initiation myth. "Roberto"—for so he calls himself—was sitting by a hedge at the side of the road, complaining about his lot, when he was approached by a man who recognized that he was a gentleman down on his luck. "I suppose you are a scholar," the stranger said, "and pity it is men of learning should live in lack."

Greene then recounted a revelatory moment of social misrecognition. How, he asked the affable stranger, could a scholar possibly be profitably employed? The stranger replied that men of his profession get their whole living by employing scholars.

> "What is your profession?" said Roberto.
> "Truly sir," said he, "I am a player."
> "A player!" quoth Roberto. "I took you rather for a gentleman of great living, for if by outward habit men should be censured [i.e., judged], I tell you, you would be taken for a substantial man."

Here in strikingly pure form is the convincing performance of status, the miming of the "outward habit" of a gentleman, that served to draw Will to the profession of acting. For Greene, however, the performance was a fraud: the actor could pretend to be a substantial man, but in himself he was a thing of nothing.

To succeed in creating his illusion, the actor needed not only expensive costumes but also persuasive words, poetry that he, a mere sham gentleman, could not generate. Hence his need to find a real gentleman like Roberto—educated, cultivated, and in need of cash—whom he could hire. Roberto signs on, in Greene's account, follows the actor to town, and finds himself lodged in "a house of retail," that is, a whorehouse. He is no longer in danger of starving—"Roberto now famozed [*sic*] for an Arch-playmaking poet, his purse like the sea sometime swelled, anon the like the same sea fell to a low ebb; yet seldom he wanted, his labors were so well esteemed"—but he has prostituted his learning and his talent; his ordinary companions become cardsharps, forgers, and pickpockets; his bones are ravaged by syphilis; and his belly is so puffed up by "immeasurable drinking" that he becomes "the perfect image of the dropsy." He experiences brief bursts of repentance, accompanied by noisy resolutions to change his life, but the resolutions give way at the slightest provocation to renewed dissipation. When the "gentlewoman his wife" begs him to return to her, he ridicules her. With his mistress and their bastard son, he moves from place to place, cheating the innkeepers, running up unpaid tavern scores, eluding his creditors. "So cunning he was in all crafts, as nothing rested in him almost but craftiness."

Such was Greene's self-portrait—"Hereafter suppose me the said Roberto," he wrote halfway through his account, throwing away the thin fictional mask—and for such a notorious liar, it seems surprisingly accurate. He was famous for a life that combined drunken idleness and gluttony with energetic bursts of writing, famous too for his impecuniousness, his duplicity, his intimate knowledge of the underworld, his fleeting attempts at moral reform, and his inevitable backsliding. Back in Norwich once, he wrote, he heard a sermon that moved him to a firm resolution to amend his life, but his profligate friends all laughed at him, and his resolution collapsed. His mistress, Em Ball—with whom he had a short-lived son whom he named Fortunatus—was the sister of the leader of a gang of thieves, one Cutting Ball, who was eventually hanged at Tyburn. Aided no doubt by this accomplished native informant, Greene, setting himself up as a kind of ethnographer, made money turning out pamphlets introducing respectable English readers to London's dense society of cheats, swindlers, and pickpockets: "cozeners," "nips," "foists," "crossbiters," "shifters." Despite his university degrees and his snobbery, he himself had the morals and the manners of a thief: he was particularly proud of the fact that he had sold the same play, *Orlando Furioso*, to two different companies of players, the Queen's Men and the Admiral's Men. His friend Nashe called him "the Monarch of Crossbiters and the very Emperor of shifters." Evidently, Greene regarded actors—by whom he saw himself and other gentleman poets exploited—as particularly appropriate targets for his chicanery. Where the actor's dream was to pass himself off as a gentleman, Greene's dream, realized with perfect success, was to transform himself into a cynical, swaggering London bully.

"Who in London hath not heard of his dissolute and licentious living?" asked one of Greene's bitter enemies, the Cambridge pedagogue Gabriel Harvey. This is a master of arts, Harvey wrote, an educated man, who has chosen to deck himself out "with ruffianly hair, unseemly apparel, and more unseemly company." He has become notorious for his vainglorious boasting, his vulgar clowning, and his trashy imitating of every new fashion. But it is important not to underestimate him: he is sly enough to cheat professional gamesters at their own dirty tricks. An oath breaker and a foulmouthed blasphemer, Greene is a man with no moral compass, and his life is a shambles. Harvey rehearsed as many of the scabrous details as he could muster: Greene's monstrous overeating, his constant shifting of his lodgings, his feasting his friends and then skipping out before paying the bill, his abandonment of his virtuous wife, his pawning of his sword and cloak, his prostitute-mistress and their bastard son Infortunatus, his employment of the mistress's thuggish brother-in-law as a bodyguard, the brother-in-law's execution, his insolence to his superiors, and, when money is short, "his impudent pamphleting, phantastical interluding, and desperate libeling." "Phantastical interluding," Harvey's term for Greene's playwriting, is linked to yet another item in the litany of scandals: "his infamous resorting to the Bankside, Shoreditch, Southwark, and other filthy haunts." Greene could always be found in his true element: the neighborhood of the theaters.

This was the neighborhood to which Shakespeare came in the late 1580s, and this was the figure at the center of the group of playwrights, all in their twenties or very early thirties, whom he encountered. Shakespeare would have had no difficulty recognizing that Marlowe was the great talent, but it was the flamboyant Greene, with his two M.A. degrees, sharp peak of red hair, enormous appetites, and volcanic energy, who was the most striking figure in the fraternity of restless, hungry writers.

Shakespeare's relations to Greene and company might at first have been cordial. The newcomer clearly found much to interest, even fascinate, him in this grotesque figure and his remarkable friends; indeed, he might have sensed immediately what would turn out in fact to be the case: these were people with whom he could get his start as a writer and whom he would remember and imaginatively exploit for the rest of his life. The electrifying effect of *Tamburlaine* upon him was only one facet of this fascination. Shakespeare studied Watson's sonnets and Lodge's *Scylla's Metamorphosis* (whose stanza he borrowed for *Venus and Adonis*); he probably collaborated with Peele in the bloody revenge tragedy *Titus Andronicus*; he repeatedly mined Nashe's satiric wit and probably used him as the model for Mote in *Love's Labour's Lost*; at the height of his powers he took Lodge's prose romance *Rosalind* and turned it into *As You Like It*; and near the end of his career, when he wanted to stage an old-fashioned piece, a "winter's tale," he dramatized Greene's by-now-forgotten story of irrational jealousy, *Pandosto*. In Shakespeare's work there are relatively few signs of the influence of Spenser, Donne, Bacon, or Ralegh, to name a few of his great contemporaries; the living writers who meant the most to him were those he encountered in the seedy inns near the theaters soon after he arrived in London.

For their part, the group of reckless young writers and their leader, Greene, may initially have found Shakespeare an agreeable fellow. He was, by all accounts, pleasant company, affable and witty; and his writing, even at that very early point, doubtless showed that he had real talent. It is possible that he had initially been hired to assist Nashe or Peele in the writing of a play about Henry VI and then displayed his mettle. Alternatively, he undertook to write the history play on his own. In either case, his surprising success as a playwright commanded respect. Not only did Nashe acknowledge in print that something extraordinary had happened—thousands of people wept for the death of an English hero who had been dead for two hundred years—but Marlowe offered the still more impressive tribute of imitation: he sat down to write his own English history play, chronicling the tragic life and death of a king, Edward II, brought down by his consuming love for his handsome favorite. Several of the others also began to mine the chronicles and scribble English history plays, though only Marlowe came close to what Shakespeare had achieved. There are, in any case, enough signs of serious attention to Shakespeare's early work to suggest that the group of writers may at first have actively wanted to cultivate his acquaintance.

The group would probably have been sorely disappointed. First and foremost, of course, Shakespeare lacked the principal qualification of belonging to their charmed circle; he had not attended either Oxford or Cambridge. The little society of writers was, by Tudor standards, quite democratic. Birth and wealth did not greatly matter: Nashe, whose family, as he put it, boasted "longer pedigrees than patrimonies" rubbed shoulders with Marlowe, the cobbler's son; Lodge, the son of the former lord mayor of London, drank with Greene, whose parents in Norwich lived sober, modest lives at a far remove from the glittering guildhall. What mattered was attendance at one or the other of the universities. Even the acerbic Nashe found warm words for his Cambridge college, St. John's, writing years later that he "loved it still, for it ever was and is the sweetest nurse of knowledge in all that university." And long after he had left the university, Greene signed one of his dedicatory epistles "From my Study in Clare Hall."

University education carried a significant social cachet, which these writers were only too happy to vaunt. But, to be fair, it was valued as well for the learning that it signified. Nashe pored over Aretino and Rabelais and gleefully coined words out of Greek, Latin, Spanish, and Italian. Peele joined Nashe in ridiculing an inept hexameter written by Gabriel Harvey. Watson's youthful translation of *Antigone* ended with allegorical exercises in different kinds of Latin verse: iambics, sapphics, anapestic dimeters, and choriambic asclepiadean meter. Shakespeare was by no means without learning—*The Comedy of Errors,* written early in his career, shows how elegantly and lightly he carried his knowledge of Latin comedy—but he was neither capable of nor interested in Watson's type of academic self-display.

Moreover, Shakespeare was by origin a provincial, and, more to the point, he had not completely left the provinces behind. If he had turned away from his father's occupation and left his parents, he had not, like Lodge, incurred a parental curse; if he had left his wife and three small children, he had not, like Greene, burned his bridges. He had none of the dark glamour of the prodigal son. Indeed, even his imagination remained bound up with the local details of country living. And if the young bohemian writers recognized with surprise that the man they deemed a country bumpkin had thought hard about many things; if they grasped that his imagination was far less constrained by convention than theirs; if they were startled by the quickness of his intellect, the breadth of his vocabulary, and his astonishing power to absorb everything he encountered and make it his own, perhaps they also were nettled by something morally conservative in him. The conservatism was already visible in the *Henvy VI* trilogy, with its reaffirmation of the traditional cautionary precepts that Marlowe in *Tamburlaine* had boldly called into question. But it was visible as well in Shakespeare's refusal to throw himself fully into a chaotic, disorderly life. Aubrey did not specify what particular social situation he was referring to when he wrote that Shakespeare "wouldn't be debauched," but a strong candidate would be any invitation from Robert Greene.

Shakespeare may have sensed a snobbish assumption of superiority on the part of the university wits; it would be surprising if they did not look down upon him and surprising if he did not perceive it. He did not contribute commendatory verses to any of the books that they published in the late 1580s and early '90s. No doubt he was not asked to do so. He, in turn, did not likely solicit for himself any commendations of the kind they routinely wrote for one another. None in any case appeared. He did not enter into their literary controversies, just as he seems to have been kept—or kept himself—outside their raucous social circle. This is, after all, a man who soon went on to manage the affairs of his playing company, to write steadily (not to mention brilliantly) for more than two decades, to accumulate and keep a great deal of money, to stay out of prison and to avoid ruinous lawsuits, to invest in agricultural land and in London property, to purchase one of the finest houses in the town where he was born, and to retire to that town in his late forties. This pattern of behavior did not suddenly and belatedly emerge; it established itself early, probably quite soon after the turbulent, confused, painful years that led up to his escape from Stratford and his arrival in London.

Shakespeare looked around at the gentleman poets who were supplying the playing companies with plays. He took in what was exciting about their writing. He made their acquaintance and savored what was startling or amusing about their reckless lives. In the light of his subsequent career, it is possible to imagine his response more fully. He saw that they were proud of their university degrees, their fine Latin and Greek, their scoffing and mockery and carelessness. He saw that they drank for days and nights at a time and then, still half-drunk, threw something together for the printer or the players. He grasped, in all likelihood, that no matter what he wrote, he would remain in their eyes a player, not a poet. Though they may occasionally have exhibited signs of nervousness about the young man from Stratford—they were impressed and troubled, after all, by the success of the *Henry VI* plays—they probably thought that he was rather naive and guileless and that they could easily take advantage of him. Greene in particular, making everyone laugh with his zany stories of coney catching, was confident, in all likelihood, that Shakespeare was a coney to be caught.

One part of this at least is indubitably true: Shakespeare wrote for the theater not as a poet, in the sense that Greene and company understood themselves, but as a player. He was not alone in writing for the stage on which he also performed, but he was the one who was best at it, and the players were quick to recognize how valuable he was. He must also have seemed exceptionally canny and trustworthy about money— the very opposite of the university wits—for a treasury document that mentions him in December 1594, in the company of Burbage and Kempe, suggests that he was already one of those fiscally responsible for the troupe. He knew how to put money in his purse and to keep it there.

Greene's purse, by contrast, was evidently empty when, in August 1592, he fell ill after a dinner, at which Nashe was present, of pickled her- ring and Rhenish wine. Abandoned by all of his friends, he would have died like a homeless beggar had a poor shoemaker named Isam and his kindly wife not taken him in and cared for him through his final days. Digging for dirt, Greene's inveterate enemy, Gabriel Harvey, went in person to talk with Mrs. Isam. Much of the scene Harvey depicts—the shameless scoundrel, "attended by lice" and begging for a "penny-pot of malmsey," seized by the grip of a terrible fear—may be discounted as the expression of bilious hatred, but some of the melancholy details ring true. The woman told me, Harvey writes, how the dying man "was fain, poor soul, to borrow her husband's shirt, whiles his own was a-washing: and

how his doublet and hose and sword were sold for three shillings: and
beside the charges of his winding sheet, which was four shillings; and the
charges of his burial yesterday, in the New-churchyard near Bedlam,
which was six shillings, and four pence, how deeply he was indebted to
her poor husband, as appeared by his own bond of ten pounds, which the
good woman kindly showed me." She showed him as well a letter Greene
left for the wife he had abandoned: "Doll, I charge thee by the love of our
youth, and by my soul's rest, that thou wilt see this man paid: for if he and
his wife had not succored me, I had died in the streets."

Greene had another dying wish. He asked Mrs. Isam to place "a gar-
land of bayes"—a laurel wreath—on his head: he would go to the grave a
poet laureate, even if he had to be crowned by a shoemaker's wife. Harvey takes a predictably sour view of this leave-taking —"vermin to vermin must repair at last"—but he also provides a fuller epitaph:

> Lo, a wild head, full of mad brain and a thousand crotchets: A
> Scholar, a Discourser, a Courtier, a Ruffian, a Gamester, a Lover,
> a Soldier, a Traveler, a Merchant, a Broker, an Artificer, a Botcher,
> a Pettifogger, a Player, a Cozener, a Railer, a Beggar, an Omni-
> gatherum [i.e., miscellaneous assemblage], a Gay Nothing: a
> Storehouse of bald and baggage stuff, unworth the answering or
> reading: a trivial and triobular [i.e., worthless] Author for knaves
> and fools: an Image of Idleness; an Epitome of Fantasticality; a
> Mirror of Vanity.

Though this catalog suggests a remarkably full life of vice, and though
Greene himself often adopted the melancholy voice of an old man looking back upon his prodigal youth, at his death he was only thirty-two
years old.

The others in the group quickly followed their leader to the grave. In
the same month, September 1592, Thomas Watson, aged about thirty-
five, was buried, cause of death unknown—or perhaps in that terrible
year of plague, it was not necessary to specify it. Two volumes of his
poems were printed posthumously—his friends had no doubt read them
already in manuscript—and his name remained for some time in circula-

tion for a less honorable reason: he was invoked in the courts as a scoundrel in two particularly nasty swindles. The following May, Watson's friend Marlowe, who had not yet reached his thirtieth birthday, was killed in a tavern fight, allegedly over the "reckoning," that is, the bill.

George Peele, the great reveler, published a moving verse tribute to his dead friends Watson and Marlowe. Then a few years later, probably in 1596, Peele too was gone. Not quite forty years old, he died, it was said, of a "loathsome disease," possibly syphilis. And in 1601, at thirty-three, the youngest of the original group, Thomas Nashe, died, leaving his grieving father, the minister, to bury him in the country churchyard.

Of the six young university-trained playwrights whom Shakespeare encountered in the late 1580s, only one, Thomas Lodge, managed to survive his thirties and to live what the age would have considered a long life. But not a literary life: abandoning poetry and fiction, Lodge took a degree in medicine and became one of the leading physicians of his day. He died in 1625, at the ripe age of sixty-seven.

After 1593, with Greene, Watson, and Marlowe all dead, Shakespeare, not yet thirty years old, had no serious rivals. He followed up on his major success with the *Henry VI* plays by writing the brilliant *Richard III*. He had experimented, crudely but energetically, with tragedy in the bloody *Titus Andronicus*, and had demonstrated his great strengths as a comic playwright, with *The Two Gentlemen of Verona*, *The Taming of the Shrew*, and *The Comedy of Errors*. He had triumphed. But there was a bitter aftertaste. Greene kept scribbling, or so it was said, even on his deathbed. The claim is not implausible: he was the kind of writer who turned his entire existence into a lurid penny pamphlet. He had left behind him enough material to enable a hack printer and sometime playwright, Henry Chettle, to bring out a posthumous book. *Greene's Groatsworth of Wit, Bought with a Million of Repentance*, rushed into print before the corpse was fully cold, was probably mostly written by Chettle or by someone collaborating with Chettle—perhaps, as some rumors had it, Nashe. But it carried the marks of Greene's own seething resentments. He noisily berated himself. He dangerously accused Marlowe—"thou famous gracer of Tragedians"—of atheism. And then he turned his anger on Shakespeare.

Rehearsing the old rivalry between poets and players, Greene warned his gentlemen friends Marlowe, Nashe, and Peele not to trust those "puppets," the actors, that "speak from our mouths." Actors were mere burrs that cleave to the garments of writers. They would be virtually invisible were they not "garnished in our colors," and yet the ingrates have forsaken him, in his hour of need. Thus far Greene's words might apply to actors like Burbage or Alleyn, but they could hardly fit a player who had also proved himself a successful playwright. To make them fit, Greene (or his ghostwriter) famously shifted ground: "Yes trust them not: for there is an upstart Crow, beautified with our feathers, that with his *Tiger's heart wrapped in a Player's hide*, supposes he is as well able to bombast out a blank verse as the best of you: and being an absolute *Johannes Factotum*, is in his own conceit the only Shakescene in a country." "O tiger's heart wrapped in a woman's hide!" York cries in the third part of *Henry VI*, to describe the ghastly, ruthless woman who waves in his face a handkerchief that she has steeped in the blood of his murdered child.

When he read the line twisted to describe him, Shakespeare might have thought that Greene was accusing him of ruthlessness. Alternatively, he was being charged with poetic excess, the bombastic exaggeration of the style of his betters. The insult is ambiguous, but it would have been clear to Shakespeare that there was an issue of status: an "upstart" is someone who pushes himself in where he does not belong, who dresses himself up as a nightingale though he caws like a crow, who imagines that he is a Johannes Factotum— a "Johnny-do-everything"—when in fact he is merely a second-rate drudge, a "rude groom," who thinks he is an accomplished poet when he is only an "ape" imitating the inventions of others.

These were painful words, particularly in the mouth—as they were said to be—of a dying man; they had something of the finality of a curse, in a world that took such curses with deadly seriousness. And *Greene's Groatsworth* ended with a coda, a retelling of Aesop's fable of the grasshopper and the ant, in which at least one modern interpreter, Ernst Honigmann, detects a further insult. Greene was, of course, himself the wanton grasshopper, carelessly skipping through the meadows in pursuit of pleasure. If Honigmann is right, the miserly ant, a "waspish little worm" who refused to help his "foodless, helpless, and strengthless" acquaintance, was Shakespeare. Greene, in this account, must have asked Shakespeare—who may at this point have already been handling some of the players' finances—for assistance and been refused. The refusal would help to explain the bitterness of the satiric portrait: upstart crow, rude groom, ape, worm.

How Shakespeare responded to the attack tells us a great deal about him. He did not directly answer the charges or, like Harvey, launch a polemical counteroffensive. But he must have quietly done something unusually effective. For, less than three months after publication of the pamphlet, Henry Chettle flatly denied in print having any hand in it: it "was all Greene's." As for himself, Chettle averred, it is well known that he always "in printing hindered the bitter inveighing against scholars." "Scholars"—so Shakespeare was now being treated as if he had, after all, attended university.

There was more: he was not, Chettle wrote, personally acquainted with either of the two playwrights who took offense at Greene's attack, "and with one of them I care not if I never be." This playwright, unnamed, was unquestionably Marlowe, who in December 1592 was evidently not a person whom the hack, his ear to the ground, thought it safe to know. But the other was a different matter. Chettle now understood, as he explained in a twisted and unctuous apology, that he should have blocked the printing of Greene's unwarranted remarks about this second playwright: "That I did not, I am as sorry as if the original fault had been my fault, because myself have seen his demeanor no less civil than he excellent in the quality he professes." This offended figure was also unnamed, but the likeliest candidate is the "upstart Crow." At some point in the past three months, then, Chettle had a "civil" conversation with Shakespeare, or at the very least he had the occasion to observe him in person. He had also, it seems, suddenly acquainted himself with Shakespeare's excellence "in the quality he professes"—an oily periphrasis for writing and acting in plays. And then comes a further motive for this recantation: "Besides, diverse of worship have reported his uprightness of dealing, which argues his honesty, and his facetious grace in writing, that approves his art." "Diverse of worship," that is, socially prominent people, people who have it in their power to make my life miserable, have spoken to me both about the honorableness of Shakespeare's character and about the "facetious grace," the facility and polish, of his writing.

From Shakespeare himself, not a word about Chettle, in the immediate wake of Greene's attack or subsequently, but he got an apology of the kind that poor, impotently sputtering Gabriel Harvey could only dream. Indeed, in the years that followed, relations between Shakespeare and Chettle may well have been cordial. They collaborated, with several other playwrights, on a play, apparently never performed, about Sir Thomas More.

The account was almost settled, but not quite. Greene's phrase "beautified with our feathers" must have stung. For in 1601, when the *Groatsworth of Wit* and the fat scoundrel who penned it had long vanished from view, Shakespeare allowed himself an unusual self-indulgence. Polonius—whose literary pretensions go back to the time when he was "accounted a good actor" "i'th' university" (*Hamlet*, 3.2.91, 90) where, as he tells us, he played Julius Caesar—has put his hands on one of the love letters that Hamlet has sent to his daughter. "Now gather and surmise," he says to Claudius and Gertrude, starting to read: "'To the celestial and my soul's idol, the most beautified Ophelia.'" Then abruptly the old councillor comes to a halt for a piece of literary criticism: "that's an ill phrase, a vile phrase, 'beautified' is a vile phrase" (2.2.109–12).

"Thus," as the clown Feste says in *Twelfth Night*, "the whirligig of time brings in his revenges" (5.1.364). Shakespeare's plays from the 1590s are sprinkled with sly parodies of the words of his erstwhile rivals. Falstaff's overheated sexual excitement in *The Merry Wives of Windsor*— "Let the sky rain potatoes, let it thunder to the tune of 'Greensleeves,' hail kissing-comfits, and snow eringoes" (5.5.16–18)—ridicules Lodge's *Wit's Misery and the World's Madness*. The Moorish king's plaintive words to his starving mother in Peele's *Battle of Alcazar*—"Hold thee, Calipolis. . . . Feed and be fat that we may meet the foe" —returns as a piece of tavern swaggering in *2 Henry IV*: "Then feed and be fat, my fair Calipolis" (2.4.155). And a moment earlier the same drunken swaggerer, Ensign

Pistol, has taken Tamburlaine's famously sadistic taunting of the kings he
has yoked to his chariot—"Holla, ye pampered jades of Asia! / What, can
ye draw but twenty miles a day?"—and turned it into fustian nonsense:

> Shall pack-horses
> And hollow pampered jades of Asia,
> Which cannot go but thirty mile a day,
> Compare with Caesars and with cannibals,
> And Trojan Greeks?
>
> (2.4.140–44)

There is much more in the same vein, and if all the plays by the university wits had survived, scholars would no doubt have identified still other
instances.

These parodies only suggest that Shakespeare was, after all, a
human being, who could take some pleasure in returning literary insults
and mocking rivals, even dead ones. But something far more remarkable
and unpredictable happened in his work with the grotesque figure of
Robert Greene. "Thou whoreson little tidy Bartholomew boar-pig,"
Falstaff's whore, Doll Tearsheet, pouts endearingly, "when wilt thou
leave fighting o'days, and foining o'nights, and begin to patch up thine
old body for heaven?" To which the fat knight replies, "Peace, good Doll,
do not speak like a death's-head, do not bid me remember mine end" (2
Henry IV, 2.4.206–10). The deeper we plunge into the tavern world of
Falstaff—gross, drunken, irresponsible, self-dramatizing, and astonishingly witty Falstaff—the closer we come to the world of Greene; his
wife, Doll; his mistress, Em; her thuggish brother, Cutting Ball; and the
whole crew.

Falstaff and his friends have the raffish appeal that the wild crowd of
London writers must have exercised on the young Shakespeare. In Falstaff's seedy haunts in Eastcheap, not far from London Bridge, Prince
Hal gains access to an urban cast of characters far removed from anything
he has known before, and he takes particular delight in having learned
their language: "They call drinking deep 'dyeing scarlet,' and when you
breathe in your watering they cry 'Hem!' and bid you 'Play it off!' To con-

clude, I am so good a proficient in one quarter of an hour that I can drink with any tinker in his own language during my life" (*1 Henry IV*, 2.5.13–17). There is, the play suggests, a politics to this language lesson—"when I am King of England I shall command all the good lads in Eastcheap"—but at the same time it seems a thinly disguised depiction of Shakespeare's own linguistic apprenticeship in taverns.

So too the relationship between Falstaff and Hal centers on fantastically inventive, aggressive language games of the kind that several of the university wits specialized in:

> PRINCE HARRY: . . . This sanguine coward, this bed-presser, this horse-back-breaker, this huge hill of flesh—
> FALSTAFF: 'Sblood, you starveling, you elf-skin, you dried neat's tongue, you bull's pizzle, you stock-fish—O, for breath to utter what is like thee!—you tailor's yard, you sheath, you bow-case, you vile standing tuck—
>
> (*1 Henry IV*, 2.5.223–29)

This is precisely the trading of comic insults, the public flyting, the madcap linguistic excess for which Greene and Nashe in particular were famous. Perhaps Shakespeare had participated in the games; in any case, he had absorbed the lesson and could outdo their best efforts.

Above all, the prince and his grotesque friend—"that trunk of humours, that bolting-hutch of beastliness, that swollen parcel of dropsies, that huge bombard of sack, that stuffed cloak-bag of guts, that roasted Manningtree ox with the pudding in his belly" (2.5.409–13)— spend their time inventing and playing theatrical games, acting out scenes, and parodying styles of playwriting that had gone out of fashion. The theatrical games make visible other dark thoughts as well: kingship is a theatrical performance by a gifted scoundrel; Hal's father, King Henry IV, has no more legitimacy than Falstaff; Falstaff has taken the place of Hal's father, but the position is precarious; Falstaff, fearing that he will be turned away by Hal, is willing to betray his friends; Hal is planning to throw them all off. "No, my good lord," pleads Falstaff, ostensibly in the role of the prince speaking to his father,

banish Peto, banish Bardolph, banish Poins, but for sweet Jack
Falstaff, kind Jack Falstaff, true Jack Falstaff, valiant Jack Fal-
staff, and therefore more valiant being, as he is, old Jack Falstaff,
Banish not him thy Harry's company,
Banish not him thy Harry's company.
Banish plump Jack, and banish all the world.

(2.5.431–38)

To which Hal, ostensibly in the role of his father, quietly, chillingly
replies, "I do; I will."

While probing the relationships at the center of the plays, the brilliant scenes of improvisatory playacting also probe deeply Shakespeare's
relationship with Greene and company. Or rather, they provide a glimpse
of how Shakespeare looked back upon that relationship years later, when
most of the doomed lot were dead and his own position as England's
reigning playwright was secure. "I know you all," Shakespeare has Hal say
early in *1 Henry IV*, after a scene of jesting and genial wit,

> and will a while uphold
> The unyoked humour of your idleness.
> Yet herein will I imitate the sun,
> Who doth permit the base contagious clouds
> To smother up his beauty from the world,
> That when he please again to be himself,
> Being wanted he may be more wondered at
> By breaking through the foul and ugly mists
> Of vapours that did seem to strangle him.

(1.2.173–81)

To recognize this proximity between Greene and Falstaff is not only
to see how "foul and ugly" were the origins of Shakespeare's golden, capacious, and endlessly fascinating character. To be sure, Greene was tawdry
enough—a drunk, a cheat, and a liar whose actual horizons were pathetically narrow compared to his grandiose projections. That tawdriness is
precisely one of Falstaff's characteristics, quite literally itemized in the

"tavern reckonings, memorandums of bawdy-houses, and one poor pen-nyworth of sugar-candy to make thee long-winded" that Hal finds when he searches his pockets (3.3.146–48). It takes no great detective work on Hal's part to discover how empty Falstaff's claims are—only a fool would take him at his word, and clear-eyed Hal is anything but a fool. It also takes no special gift to see how nasty and common were the actual cir-cumstances of Robert Greene's life. The more demanding and interesting task is to savor the power of the illusions without simply submitting to the cheating and the lies. What Falstaff helps to reveal is that for Shake-speare, Greene was a sleazy parasite, but he was also a grotesque titan, a real-life version of the drunken Silenus in Greek mythology or of Rabelais' irrepressible trickster, Panurge.

Shakespeare seized upon the central paradox of Greene's life—that this graduate of Oxford and Cambridge hung out in low taverns in the company of ruffians—and turned it into Falstaff's supremely ambiguous social position, the knight who is intimate with both the Prince of Wales and a pack of thieves. Falstaff captured Greene's bingeing and whoring, his "dropsical" belly, his prodigal wasting of his impressive talents, his cynical exploitation of friends, his brazenness, his seedy charm. He cap-tured too the noisy, short-lived fits of repentance for which Greene was famous, along with the solemn moralizing that swerved effortlessly into irreverent laughter. "Before I knew thee, Hal, I knew nothing," Falstaff says, adopting the role of the corrupted innocent: "and now am I, if a man should speak truly, little better than one of the wicked. I must give over this life, and I will give it over. By the Lord, an I do not, I am a villain. I'll be damned for never a king's son in Christendom." To which Hal—like the friends who mocked Greene out of his pious resolutions—replies with a simple question: "Where shall we take a purse tomorrow, Jack?" "Zounds, where thou wilt, lad! I'll make one; an I do not, call me villain" (1.2.82–89). So much for moral reform.

Falstaff was not a straightforward portrait of Robert Greene (who was neither a knight nor an old man), any more than the whore Doll Tearsheet was a faithful portrait of the virtuous country wife named Doll whom Greene abandoned or the tavern hostess Mistress Quickly was a portrait of the Mistress Isam from whom he borrowed money and who nursed him through his final illness. Here as elsewhere, Shakespeare's actual world gets into his work, but most often in a distorted, inverted, disguised, or reimagined form. The point is not to strip away the reimaginings, as if the life sources were somehow more interesting than the metamorphoses, but rather to enhance a sense of the wonder of Shakespeare's creation— the immensely bold, generous imaginative work that took elements from the wasted life of Robert Greene and used them to fashion the greatest comic character in English literature.

Greene was by no means the sole source. Like many of Shakespeare's most memorable creations, Falstaff is made out of multiple materials, much of it not from life but from literature. Shakespeare understood his world in the ways that we understand our world—his experiences, like ours, were mediated by whatever stories and images were available to him. When he was in a tavern and encountered a loudmouthed soldier who bragged about his daring adventures, Shakespeare saw that soldier through the lens of characters he had read in fiction, and at that same time he adjusted his image of those fictional characters by means of the actual person standing before him.

In inventing Falstaff, Shakespeare started, as he so often did, from a character in a play by someone else, *The Famous Victories of Henry the Fifth,* which had been performed by the Queen's Men in London and on tour. This crude anonymous play, which chronicled the near-miraculous transformation of Prince Hal from wastrel youth to heroic king, included a dissolute knight, Sir John Oldcastle, as part of the crew of thieves and ruffians in which Hal had become enmeshed. Shakespeare took over this figure (he originally used the same name, only changing it to Falstaff after the descendants of Oldcastle objected) and built upon its spare frame his vast creation. He took the stock figure of the braggart soldier, the blowhard who is always going on about his martial accomplishments but who plays dead when danger comes too close, and combined him with another venerable comic type, the parasite, always hungry and thirsty and always conniving to get his wealthy patron to pick up the tab. To these he added features of the Vice in the morality play—shameless irreverence, the exuberant pursuit of pleasures, and a seductive ability to draw naive youth away from the austere paths of virtue. And he conjoined with these some elements of a newer cultural stereotype, the hypocritical Puritan who noisily trumpets his commitment to virtue while secretly indulging his every sensual vice. But to contemplate these pieces of literary flotsam and jetsam is already to see how complete and unexpected was Shakespeare's transformation of them.

He himself must have been surprised by what began to emerge when he sat down to write *Henry IV*. What would have been predictable, what he may initially have intended, was some version of the lively but largely conventional figure whom in fact he created some years later in *All's Well That Ends Well*. That character, Paroles, has all the appropriately obnoxious traits of the loudmouthed, bragging corrupter of the young, and the audience is invited to delight in his discomfiture. But even here, when his imagination was not operating at the very pinnacle of its power, Shakespeare did something odd, something that casts light back on the infinitely greater Falstaff. Paroles has been utterly humiliated, exposed and disgraced before his friends and fellow officers so devastatingly that the suicide proposed to him is the only honorable course of action. But he is anything but honorable, and, rejecting any thought of putting an end to himself, he takes his leave. "Captain I'll be no more," Paroles ruefully acknowledges, and then his mood shifts:

> But I will eat and drink and sleep as soft
> As captain shall. Simply the thing I am
> Shall make me live.
>
> (4.3.308–11)

This is the life force itself.

This life force is at work to an unparalleled degree in Falstaff. In him too it burns brightest when everything that goes by the word "honor"— name, reputation, dignity, vocation, trustworthiness, truthfulness—is stripped away. "Can honour set-to a leg?" Falstaff asks, at the brink of battle.

No. Or an arm? No. Or take away the grief of a wound? No. Honour hath not skill in surgery, then? No. What is honour? A word. What is in that word "honour"? What is that "honour"? Air. A trim reckoning! Who hath it? He that died o'Wednesday. Doth he feel it? No. Doth he hear it? No. 'Tis insensible then? Yea, to the dead. But will it not live with the living? No. Why? Detraction will not suffer it. Therefore I'll none of it. (*1 Henry IV*, 5.1.130–38)

A few moments later, standing over the corpse of Sir Walter Blunt (killed fighting bravely for the king), Falstaff sharpens the stark opposition between empty words and the only thing that actually matters, at least to him: "I like not such grinning honour as Sir Walter hath. Give me life" (5.3.57–58).

To a degree unparalleled in Shakespeare's work and perhaps in all of English literature, Falstaff seems actually to possess a mysterious inner principle of vitality, as if he could float free not only of Shakespeare's sources in life and in art but also of the play in which he appears. If a theatrical tradition, first recorded in 1702, is correct, Queen Elizabeth herself not only admired Shakespeare's great comic character but also sensed this inner principle: she commanded the author to write a play showing Falstaff in love. In two weeks' time, or so it is said, *The Merry Wives of Windsor* was written, to be first performed on April 23, 1597, at the annual feast to commemorate the founding of the Order of the Garter. Famous already in Shakespeare's lifetime, constantly alluded to throughout the seventeenth century, and the subject of a distinguished book-length study as early as the eighteenth century, the fat knight has for centuries provoked admirers to attempt to pluck out the heart of his mystery: great wit and the ability to provoke wit in others; spectacular resilience; fierce, subversive intelligence; carnivalesque exuberance. Each of these qualities seems true, and yet there is always something else, something elusive that remains to be accounted for, as if the scoundrel had the power in himself to resist all efforts to explain or contain him.

Shakespeare himself evidently struggled to keep his own creation within bounds. The climax of the second of the great history plays in which Falstaff appears is a scene in which Hal, newly crowned as Henry V, brutally dashes his friend's wild expectations of plunder: "I know thee not, old man" (*2 Henry IV*, 5.5.45). It is the most decisive of repudiations. Falstaff is banished from the royal presence on pain of death, and the king's coldly ironic words to the onetime "tutor and feeder of my riots" conjure up the final, literal containment of all that corpulent energy: "know the grave doth gape / For thee thrice wider than for other men" (5.5.60, 51–2). Yet a moment later Falstaff seems already to be slipping free from this noose—"Go with me to dinner. Come, Lieutenant Pistol; come, Bardolph. I shall be sent for soon at night" (5.5.83–85)—and at the play's close Shakespeare announces that he will bring him back once again. "One word more, I beseech you," says the actor who speaks the epilogue. "If you be not too much cloyed with fat meat, our humble author will continue the story with Sir John in it" (lines 22–24). It is as if Falstaff himself refuses to accept the symbolic structure of the play that has just ended.

Yet when he actually sat down to continue the story, by writing a play about Henry V's great triumph over the French at Agincourt, Shakespeare had second thoughts. Falstaff's cynical, antiheroic stance—his ruthless, comic deflation of the idealizing claims of those in power and his steadfast insistence on the primacy of the flesh—proved impossible to incorporate into a celebration of charismatic leadership and martial heroism. That celebration was not without Shakespeare's characteristic skeptical intelligence, but for the play to succeed—for Hal to be something more than a mock king—skepticism had to stop short of the relentless mockery that in two consecutive plays Falstaff so brilliantly articulated. Hence Shakespeare decided to break his promise to the audience and to keep his comic masterpiece out of *Henry V*. Indeed, he decided to get rid of him permanently by providing a detailed narrative of death: "A parted ev'n just between twelve and one, ev'n at the turning o'th' tide," Mistress Quickly memorably recounts,

for after I saw him fumble with the sheets, and play with flowers, and smile upon his finger's end, I knew there was but one

way. For his nose was as sharp as a pen, and a babbled of green
fields. "How now, Sir John?" quoth I. "What, man! Be o' good
cheer." So a cried out, "God, God, God," three or four times.
Now I, to comfort him, bid him a should not think of God; I
hoped there was no need to trouble himself with any such
thoughts yet. So a bade me lay more clothes on his feet. I put my
hand into the bed and felt them, and they were as cold as any
stone. Then I felt to his knees, and so up'ard and up'ard, and all
was as cold as any stone. (*Henry V*, 2.3.11–23)

The drama here is not the death scene itself, which is carefully kept off-
stage; the drama, as Shakespeare and his audience understood, is the
spectacle of a great playwright killing off the greatest of his comic characters. Of course, given Falstaff's manner of life, the official cause of
death must be overindulgence—the equivalent of Greene's fatal feast of
pickled herring and Rhenish wine—but the play makes clear that it has
staged a symbolic murder: "The King has killed his heart" (2.1.79).

"An upstart Crow, beautified with our feathers": Greene and his
crowd, despite their drunken recklessness and bohemian snobbery, saw
something frightening in Shakespeare, a usurper's knack for displaying as
his own what he had plucked from others, an alarming ability to plunder,
appropriate, and absorb. Shakespeare, for his part, understood that he did
not belong with these grasshoppers, and he may, as Greene himself seems
to imply, have turned down some request for help from the indigent,
desperate scoundrel.

In Prince Hal, the author of the *Henry IV* plays saw himself, projecting onto his character a blend of experimental participation and careful,
self-protective distance; recognizing the functional utility of his tavern
lessons in language games and in role-playing; and unsentimentally
accepting the charge of calculated self-interest. Reflecting on the scene
he entered into in the late 1580s, Shakespeare acknowledged what he
had had to do in order to survive. But the coldness that he attributed to
himself—or rather to Hal—was only one aspect of his relationship with
Greene, and perhaps not the most important aspect. For if Shakespeare
took what he could from Greene—if, as an artist, he took what he could

from everyone he encountered—he also performed a miraculous act of imaginative generosity, utterly unsentimental and, if the truth be told, not entirely human. Human generosity would have involved actually giving money to the desperate Greene; it would have been foolish, quixotic, and easily abused. Shakespeare's generosity was aesthetic, rather than pecuniary. He conferred upon Greene an incalculable gift, the gift of transforming him into Falstaff.

CHAPTER 8

Master-Mistress

THE HACK PRINTER Henry Chettle was not the only one to be squirming in the wake of the attack on Shakespeare as an "upstart Crow." There were rumors that Thomas Nashe also had his hand in the attack, that perhaps he had even ghostwritten the farewell words of his friend Robert Greene. The rumors make perfect sense: after all, the Cambridge-educated satirist had earlier heaped comparable scorn in print on poorly educated players, whom he described as a "rabble of counterfeits" who rashly attempt to imitate their betters in the writing of blank verse. Nashe might ordinarily have been pleased thus to be the object of suspicion: in the business of giving offense, he cultivated the reputation of a reckless wit. But he too must have had an unusually alarming conversation with someone, for, though he was not given to backing away from a squabble, he rushed into print to disclaim any connection to *Greene's Groatsworth of Wit*, which he called a "trivial lying pamphlet." Nashe did everything he could to ensure that his vehement disclaimer would be taken seriously: "God never have care of my soul, but utterly renounce me, if the least word or syllable in it

proceeded from my pen, or if I were any way privy to the writing or printing of it." That seems to be the sound of abject panic.

The question is who put Nashe into such a sweat. The answer is not
the upstart Shakespeare himself; it must have been someone much more
powerful and intimidating. But who? The likeliest candidate by far is
someone connected to Henry Wriothesley, third Earl of Southampton.
The nineteen-year-old earl is highly unlikely to have gone himself on
such a lowly errand, but, like Duke Orsino in *Twelfth Night*, he had many
dependent gentlemen eager to do his bidding and serve as his go-
between. (A few years later, Southampton mentioned being accompanied
somewhere by "only ten or twelve" of his usual attendants.) One candidate for this particular errand would have been his French and Italian
tutor, John Florio. Born in London, the son of Protestant refugees from
Italy, Florio had already published several language manuals, along with
a compendium of six thousand Italian proverbs; he would go on to produce an important Italian-English dictionary and a vigorous translation,
much used by Shakespeare, of Montaigne's *Essays*. Florio became a
friend of Ben Jonson, and there is evidence that already in the early 1590s
he was a man highly familiar with the theater.

But if Southampton, far too grand to meddle in person with a backstage squabble, would have sent someone like Florio to do his bidding,
how would an earl—at the very pinnacle of the status hierarchy—have
come to know Shakespeare in the first place? Here, as usual, the precise
link is missing, probably irretrievably, but the social ambiguity of the theater would certainly have helped to make a meeting possible. Players
belonged to an entirely different social universe from noblemen, but
playhouses decidedly did not: while whores, pickpockets, and shabby
apprentices crowded into the pit, aristocrats, smoking their pipes or sniffing pomanders, sat on cushions in the expensive "lords' rooms" to watch
the performances and be watched in turn.

Southampton, described in the early 1590s as "young and fantastical"
and easily "carried away," was evidently one of these theater lovers. As a
contemporary observer once wrote, the young earl and his friend the Earl
of Rutland "pass the time in London merely in going to plays every day."

On one of these occasions, struck by Shakespeare's acting in a play or by his gifts as a writer or by his lively good looks, Southampton could easily have gone backstage after the performance to make his acquaintance, or asked a mutual acquaintance to introduce them, or simply and imperiously summoned him to a rendezvous. The likeliest time for their first encounter would have been in 1591 or early 1592, when the earl, having graduated from Cambridge, was attending upon the queen at court and studying law at Gray's Inn.

Courtiers and law students were among the playhouses' most enthusiastic patrons, but Southampton may have taken special pleasure in imaginative escape at this particular moment in his life: he was under enormous pressure to marry. The stakes were not sentimental; they were financial, and they were huge. When Southampton was a young child, his parents had a spectacular breakup. His father accused his mother of adultery, and in the wake of their bitter separation, his mother was forbidden ever to see her son again. Then, just shy of Southampton's eighth birthday, his father died, and the wealthy young heir became the ward of the most powerful man in England, Elizabeth's lord treasurer, Lord Burghley. The elderly Burghley was reasonably attentive to his ward's upbringing—he took the boy into his house, hired distinguished tutors to educate him, and then sent him off to Cambridge University at the tender age of twelve—but the whole wardship system was rotten to the core. Its most sinister feature was the guardian's legal right to negotiate a marriage for his ward. If, upon turning twenty-one, the ward declined the match, he could be liable for substantial damages, to be paid to the family of the rejected party. As it just so happened, Burghley arranged for Southampton to marry his own granddaughter. As it just so happened too, Burghley held the position of Master of the Wards, which meant that he could virtually dictate the fine that would be assessed should Southampton be rash enough to decline. In the event, the young earl did decline, and when he came of age, he was fined the truly staggering sum of five thousand pounds.

Sixteen or seventeen years old when the match was first proposed to him, Southampton refused, declaring that he was averse not to this particular girl but to marriage itself. When it became clear that this was not a passing mood but a fixed resolution, the alarmed kin, foreseeing very clearly the blow to the family fortune, began to increase the pressure. The problem was that the young earl was so enormously rich, and so habitually reckless with his money and land, that the prospect of a substantial loss did not frighten him. He was unaffected too by the displeasure of his guardian and by the urgent pleas of a mother and other more distant relations with whom he had had little or no contact.

In these circumstances, the family, along with Lord Burghley, turned to other tactics. They had to address not Southampton's material interests—that had failed miserably—but his psyche. That is, the task was somehow to enter Southampton's innermost spirit, the hidden place from which his aversion to marriage arose, and refashion it. One of the means they chose was poetry.

The strategy was not entirely foolish: the stubborn, self-willed young nobleman, who had received a fine humanistic education, was steeped in poetry and had been brought up to expect that he would in time be a significant patron of the arts. If he would not take counsel from his sober elders, he might conceivably be reached by more indirect, more artful means. In 1591 he was presented with an elegant Latin poem dedicated to him—the first such dedication that he had received. The poem, *Narcissus,* rehearsed the story of the handsome youth who falls in love with his own reflection in the water and, in a vain attempt to embrace this reflection, drowns. The poem's author, John Clapham, was one of Burghley's secretaries, and the application of the monitory lesson to Southampton seems clear enough.

Clapham may have taken it upon himself to warn his master's ward about the dangers of self-love, but it is more likely that he was charged to do so. The clock was ticking: Southampton was going to turn twenty-one on October 6, 1594. Clapham's poem suggests that already in 1591 the looming deadline was provoking a search for effective methods of persuasion. And this leads us back to Shakespeare. It is possible that someone, either in the circle of Burghley or in the circle of Southampton's mother, had taken note of the fact that the young earl was excited by the talents or by the person of an actor who was also a promising poet. Whoever noticed this excitement—and a wealthy nobleman's slightest inclinations would have been carefully watched—might well have had the clever idea of commissioning the poet to try his hand at persuading the narcissistic, effeminate young earl to marry. Such a commission would help to account for the first 17 of the extraordinary sequence of 154 sonnets that were eventually printed—presumably, though not certainly, with Shakespeare's approval—many years later.

The opening group of Shakespeare's sonnets clearly has a specific person in mind: an exceptionally beautiful, "self-willed" (6.13) young man, who has refused to marry and is thus consuming himself "in single life" (9.2). The poet is careful not to press the specificity too far; a direct, identifiable address to the earl would have been presumptuous and indiscreet. Each of the poems has in effect a built-in principle of deniability. That is, if confronted by an irate reader, the poet could always say, "You have misunderstood me and jumped to a false conclusion. I wasn't referring to *him* at all." But if these poems were in fact written for Southampton, as many believe they were, then Shakespeare fully embraced the analysis of the problem articulated in Clapham's *Narcissus*: the young man is in love with himself, "contracted," as the first sonnet tells him plainly, "to thine own bright eyes" (1.5).

Shakespeare's psychological strategy, however, is the opposite of Clapham's. He does not tell the fair youth that he should tear himself away from his own reflection and beware of self-love. Rather, he tells him that he is insufficiently self-loving:

> Look in thy glass, and tell the face thou viewest
> Now is the time that face should form another.
> (3.1–2)

By looking longingly at his reflection, in contemplation of his own beauty, the young man will resolve to do in the flesh what he has done by standing in front of the mirror: produce an image of himself. It is through reproduction—"fresh repair"—that a person can truly love himself by projecting himself into the future; only a fool would "be the tomb / Of his self-love to stop posterity" (3.3, 7–8).

As a subject for sonnets, this procreation theme is wildly unusual, perhaps unprecedented. A sonneteer characteristically woos his beloved or laments her coldness or analyzes his own intense passion. He does not tell a young man that in order to make a precise copy of his own exquisite face, he should resolve to reproduce. Had he written sonnets in praise of the young man's prospective bride, Shakespeare could have held onto at least a semblance of conventionality. He would, in that case, have functioned like one of the painters hired in long-distance marriage negotiations to produce an image of the proposed spouse. But he did nothing of the kind. Though he is urging the youth to eschew mastur-bation and have sex with a woman—do not "spend / Upon thyself," he writes with striking explicitness, do not have "traffic with thyself alone" (4.1–2, 9)—the identity of the woman, the prospective mother of his child, is apparently a matter of indifference. No woman, he writes, will refuse: "where is she so fair whose uneared womb / Disdains the tillage of thy husbandry?" (3.5–16).

The vision of reproduction Shakespeare is offering his young man is not absolutely female-free, but, within the limits of the flesh, it reduces the role of the woman to the barest minimum: a piece of untilled ground that has not yet brought forth ripe ears of corn. The whole project will be spoiled if the child bears any resemblance to its mother, for the goal is to produce a mirror image of the father alone. In the fertile soil of a name-less, faceless breeder—and, if nameless and faceless, why not simply accept the choice that his guardian has already made for him?—the young man will plant the seed of his own perfect beauty. That beauty itself possesses whatever one might hope to find in a woman's face: "Thou art thy mother's glass," the poet tells the young man, "and she in thee / Calls back the lovely April of her prime" (3.9–10).

A painting has recently been discovered that is thought to be a por-trait of Southampton at the time that Shakespeare's procreation sonnets were probably written. The image is a startling one because it transforms what had always seemed hyperbolic in the language of the sonnets into something quite literal. The long ringlets, the rosebud mouth, the con-sciousness of being "the world's fresh ornament" (1.9), the palpable air of a young man in love with himself, and, above all, the sexual ambiguity make the painting—which had long been mistaken as the image of a woman—serve as a vivid illustration of the qualities Shakespeare was addressing in these exceptionally strange opening sonnets.

The first edition of the entire sequence—a quarto volume bearing the title *Shake-speares Sonnets*—did not appear until 1609. Shakespeare's name, appearing in very large type, clearly was expected to sell copies. But while most printed books in this period eagerly trumpeted, through a dedication, an author's epistle, or some other means, a connection to a powerful patron, this book claimed no clear link and offered no identification of the persons to whom the poems were originally addressed. The publisher's famous dedication in the first edition—"To the only begetter of these ensuing sonnets, Mr. W. H., all happiness and that eternity promised by our ever-living poet, wisheth the well-wishing adventurer in setting forth. T. T."—does not help. It is not clear whether these words reveal something crucial about Shakespeare or merely about the publisher, Thomas Thorpe, whose initials seem to lay claim to the dedication as his own. And if it were somehow established that Shakespeare, rather than Thorpe, wrote the dedication, it would still not be known whether "W. H.," the initials of the "only begetter," slyly reverse those of Henry Wriothesley, the Earl of Southampton, or refer to someone else—perhaps to William Herbert, the Earl of Pembroke, who subsequently showed favor to Shakespeare and to whom (along with his brother Philip) the 1623 folio edition of Shakespeare's works was dedicated. As it happens, in 1597 this wealthy aristocrat, part of a family celebrated for its literary interests, was also being urged to marry. If the opening poems in the sequence seem suited in style to the earlier 1590s, a time for which Southampton is the likeliest candidate, most of the later poems seem on stylistic grounds to date from the late 1590s and the early years of the new century, when Herbert's case is stronger. Could Shakespeare have, as some scholars have proposed, been addressing both young men in succession, cleverly recycling the love tokens? Could some of those same love tokens have originated as poems addressed to other young men or women whom the poet was wooing? There is no way of achieving any certainty. After generations of feverish research, no one has been able to offer more than guesses, careful or wild, which are immediately countered (often with accompanying snorts of derision) by other guesses.

The 154 sonnets are ordered in such a way as to suggest at least the vague outlines of a story, in which the players include, besides the amorous poet and the beautiful young man, one or more rival poets and a dark lady. The reader is positively encouraged to identify Shakespeare with the speaker. Many love poets of the period used a witty alias as a mask: Philip Sidney called himself "Astrophil"; Spenser was the shepherd "Colin Clout"; Walter Ralegh (whose first name was pronounced "water"), "Ocean." But there is no mask here; these are, as the title announces, *Shake-speare's Sonnets*, and the poet puns repeatedly on his own first name:

> Whoever hath her wish, thou hast thy Will,
> And Will to boot, and Will in overplus."
>
> (135.1–2)

One of the startling effects of the best of these poems—a prime reason they have drawn madly fluttering biographical speculations like moths to a flame—is an almost painful intimacy. They seem to offer access to Shakespeare's most private retreat. But the other figures are carefully shrouded. The reader is clearly not meant to grasp, with any assurance, their actual identities.

Enormous effort has been expended to identify the principal rival poet and the "dark lady." Was the rival poet Marlowe or Chapman? Was the dark lady the poet Emilia Lanier, former mistress of the lord chamberlain, or the courtier Mary Fitton, or the prostitute known as Lucy Negro? If even to identify the young man of the first seventeen sonnets as Southampton is rash, to attempt to name these other figures is beyond rashness. In part, the problem is an inability, at this distance in time, to answer key questions: Who constituted Shakespeare's intimate circle in London? Over how long a period of time were these poems written? Did Shakespeare place them in the order in which they were printed? Did he approve their publication? To what degree are the poems directly confessional?

But it is not simply the passage of time that has made the details of the relationship murky. The whole enterprise of writing a sonnet sequence precisely involved drawing a translucent curtain—of one of those gauzy fabrics Elizabethans loved—over the scene, so that only shadowy figures are visible to the public. At the very center of the original title page, beneath *Shake-speare's Sonnets*, there are the words "Never before Imprinted." This prominent announcement (accurate, with two small exceptions, described below) implies that the public has long heard of the existence of these poems but has not until now been able to purchase them. For the writing of sonnets, as contemporary readers well understood, was not normally about getting them into print, where they would simply fall into the hands of anyone who had the money and the interest to buy the book. What mattered was getting the poems at the right moment into the right hands—most obviously, of course, the object of the poet's passion, but also the intimate (and, in the case of Shakespeare and the aristocratic young man, quite distinct) social circles surrounding both the poet and his beloved.

Sonnet writing was in its most prestigious and defining form the sophisticated game of courtiers. Sir Thomas Wyatt and the Earl of Surrey had made it fashionable in the reign of Henry VIII; Sir Philip Sidney had brought it to perfection in the reign of Elizabeth. The challenge of the game was to sound as intimate, self-revealing, and emotionally vulnerable as possible, without actually disclosing anything compromising to anyone outside the innermost circle. In Henry VIII's court the stakes were particularly high—rumors of adultery swirled around the royal household and could lead to the Tower and the scaffold —but even in less alarming social settings sonnets always carried an air of risk. Sonnets that were too cautious were insipid and would only show the poet to be a bore; sonnets that were too transparent could give mortal offense.

There were circles within circles. Presumably, if the first seventeen of Shakespeare's sonnets—the sonnets urging the young man to marry and father a child—were written to Southampton, then Southampton constituted the innermost circle: he was the reader who was privileged to know almost everything. But their closest friends would have known something; those in their wider social circles considerably less; those outside this orbit but still within social range something less again; and so on. The poet's true mastery is most fully displayed if those on the outermost edges still find the poems thrilling and revealing, even though they know absolutely nothing about any of the key players, not so much as their names.

By keeping his poems at some remove from the actual, Shakespeare was able both to share them intimately with the young man, who would have been able easily to fill in the missing personal details, and to circulate them safely among readers who could savor their beauty and admire their maker. "The sweet, witty soul of Ovid lives in mellifluous and honey-tongued Shakespeare," wrote one informed observer of the literary scene in 1598, praising "his sugared Sonnets among his private friends, etc."

Soon the poems started to float free of the group of private friends and take on a life of their own, independent of their immediate circumstances, whatever those circumstances might have been. Versions of two of the sonnets appeared in print in 1599 in an unauthorized collection, *The Passionate Pilgrim. By W. Shakespeare*, whose publisher, William Jaggard, was clearly trying to profit from the poet's celebrity. (Of the twenty poems in the collection, only five are actually by Shakespeare.) It is not only a modern misapprehension to think of such poems as "Shall I compare thee to a summer's day?" as having been written not to a young man but to a woman; already by the 1620s and '30s the sonnets were being copied out as heterosexual rather than homosexual. And this fluidity, this ability to be imaginatively transformed, seems part of the poet's own design, a manifestation of his supreme skill at playing this special game.

Sonnets, then, were at once private and social; that is, they characteristically took the form of a personal, intimate address, and at the same time they circulated within a small group whose values and desires they reflected, articulated, and reinforced. They could eventually reach a wider world—Sir Philip Sidney's sequence of 108 sonnets and eleven songs, *Astrophil and Stella*, written in the early 1580s, came to define courtly elegance for a whole generation of readers—but only a tiny number of readers would know the actual individuals and precise situations to which these intricate poems cunningly allude. Those outside the charmed coterie—and all are now in this category—had to content themselves with admiration for the poet's craft and with groping in the darkness of biographical speculation.

There were reasons in the summer of 1592 why Shakespeare would have been particularly eager to take on a commission to write poems urging a wealthy young man to marry. One of his principal sources of income—the income that supported him and the wife and children he had left behind in Stratford—had vanished. On June 12, 1592, London's lord mayor, Sir William Webbe, had written to Burghley about a riot that had taken place, the night before, in Southwark. A group of felt makers' servants, along with a crowd of "loose and masterless men," had tried to rescue a companion who had been arrested. The unruly mob had assembled, the lord mayor ominously noted, "at a play, which, besides the breach of the Sabbath day, giveth opportunity of committing these and such like disorders." Evidently, Burghley took the threat of further unrest seriously, for on June 23 the Privy Council issued an order suspending all performances in the London theaters. The suspension might not have lasted through the whole summer season—the theater companies, along with other people adversely affected (such as the "poor Watermen of the Bankside," that is, the boatmen who provided transportation across the river), vigorously petitioned for relief—but a far worse disaster struck some six weeks later.

The theater's most dreadful adversary, far worse than puritanical preachers or hostile magistrates, was bubonic plague. Public health regulation in Elizabethan England was haphazard at best, and nothing, or at least nothing accurate, was known about the actual causes of plague. Indeed, one of the official measures routinely taken when plague deaths began to rise—the killing of dogs and cats—undoubtedly made matters worse by destroying the enemies of the rats that in fact, as we now know, carried the fleas that carried the dread bacillus. But people had grasped, through bitter experience, that the isolation of plague victims slowed the spread of the disease—hence the terrible nailing shut of the quarantined houses—and they grasped too that there was a relation between the progress of epidemics and large crowds. Authorities did not cancel church services, but when plague deaths began to rise, they looked askance at any other public assemblies, and when such deaths reached a certain number (above thirty a week in London), they shut the theaters down.

Shakespeare and his fellow actors must have watched nervously as the mortality figures inched up in the warm summer weather and become more and more alarmed as they increased. No doubt the voices of the theater's enemies became more strident, shouting that God had sent the plague to punish London for its sins, above all for whoredom, sodomy, and playacting. Playhouses, bearbaiting arenas, and other places of public assembly—the churches excepted—were ordered to close until further notice. If the playing companies were lucky, the patrons would give them small sums to tide them over. Some of the actors would have packed up some props and costumes in wagons and gone on tour, garnering what income they could, however meager, in the provinces. But that life was a decidedly difficult one, and Shakespeare would doubtless have welcomed an alternative, if one came his way. A proposal to write sonnets to a fabulously wealthy, spoiled young man reluctant to marry would have seemed like a gift from the gods.

Yet even within the first seventeen sonnets, written as if to order, there are signs that the poet's task was complicated by thoughts and feelings that were difficult to reconcile perfectly with the assignment. Perhaps the very relationship that made it plausible for someone to suggest that Shakespeare write these poems stood in the way of their satisfactory accomplishment. "Make thee another self for love of me," the poet urges (10.13), as if he expected his emotional claims to count. But how exactly could they count? And if they did, how exactly could they bear on the plea that the youth father a child? What stake does the poet have in his friend's child? The answer nominally lies in the child's ability to counterbalance the malevolent power of time: when the passing years have irreparably destroyed the exquisite beauty the youth currently possesses, his son will carry that beauty forward into the next generation. But even as he presents this argument, the poet brings forth another, one that manifestly means far more to him and that fulfills the fantasy of perfect, female-free reproduction:

> And all in war with time for love of you,
> As he takes from you, I engraft you new.
>   (15.13–14)

"I engraft you new"—the reproductive power in question here is the power of poetry. For a lingering moment the birth of a child still matters: Without a living image of the fair youth to verify all of the poet's claims,

"Who will believe my verse in time to come" (17.1)? But the imagined child here has been reduced to a piece of corroborating evidence, and he soon disappears entirely:

> Shall I compare thee to a summer's day?
> Thou art more lovely and more temperate.
> Rough winds do shake the darling buds of May,
> And summer's lease hath all too short a date.
> Sometime too hot the eye of heaven shines,
> And often is his gold complexion dimmed,
> And every fair from fair sometime declines,
> By chance or nature's changing course untrimmed;
> But thy eternal summer shall not fade
> Nor lose possession of that fair thou ow'st.
> Nor shall death brag thou wander'st in his shade
> When in eternal lines to time thou grow'st.
>> So long as men can breathe or eyes can see,
>> So long lives this, and this gives life to thee.
>>> (sonnet 18)

The dream of the child as mirror image, projected into the future, has been shouldered aside by "this"—*this* love poem, this exquisite mirror made of language, this far more secure way of preserving perfect beauty intact and carrying it forward to succeeding generations. Shakespeare has in effect displaced the woman he was urging the young man to impregnate; the poet's labor, not the woman's, will bring forth the young man's enduring image.

It is, as Shakespeare supremely understood, the stuff of romantic comedy: the go-between becomes romantically entangled. This is the central plot device of *Twelfth Night*. Viola, disguised as a boy and serving Duke Orsino, is assigned the task of helping him woo the countess Olivia: "I'll do my best / To woo your lady," Viola tells her master, adding, in an aside, that her assignment is a painful one: "Whoe'er I woo, myself would be his wife" (1.4.39–41). There is, of course, a striking difference between this situation and the one sketched in the sonnets. Though Viola is dressed like a boy when she sighs longingly for her master, her desire is a woman's desire for a man and thus can be consummated in marriage (as soon as she changes her clothes). But *Twelfth Night* goes out of its way to suggest that gender is not, after all, the crucial issue: Orsino is clearly attracted to the servant he believes to be a sexually ambiguous boy, and Olivia falls madly in love with this same ambiguous go-between. In something of the same spirit, though without the explicit narrative, Shakespeare's sonnets stage the triumph of the poet's own overwhelming love over the initial project of persuading the young man to marry.

Is it the truth or a piece of flattering rhetoric? Impossible to say. But for the vain young recipient of these poems, Shakespeare's narrative—never explicit, but never completely out of view—must have been very gratifying. Something happened to the poet, the sonnets imply, when he undertook to persuade the beautiful youth to marry: he became aware that he was longing for the youth himself. The poet can no longer understand how it will all work out. He knows that the young man regards him as little more than a servant—an aging one at that. But he craves his company, and he feels in his presence something that he never felt with any woman. He wants to charm him, he wants to be with him, he wants to be him; he is his vision of youth, of nobility, of perfect beauty. He is in love with him.

The sonnets express this love in impassioned and extravagant praise: the image of the young man is "like a jewel hung in ghastly night" (27.11); his loveliness exceeds the most idealized accounts of Adonis or Helen (53); he is "as fair in knowledge as in hue" (82.5); his hand is whiter than a lily, and the tint on his cheeks is more delicate than a rose (98); whatever "antique pens" expressed "In praise of ladies dead and lovely knights"—"Of hand, of foot, of lip, of eye, of brow"—was a prophecy of his own beauty (106.4–7). He is the poet's sun, his rose, his dear heart, his "best of dearest" (48.7), his fair flower, his sweet love, his lovely boy.

At the same time, and in comparably impassioned terms, the sonnets elaborate the claims of poetry: "My love shall in my verse ever live young" (19.4); "Not marble nor the gilded monuments / Of princes shall outlive this powerful rhyme" (55.1–2); time's scythe mows everything down and yet "my verse shall stand" (60.13); the remorseless hours will drain the young man's blood and carve wrinkles on his brow, but "His beauty shall in these black lines be seen" (63.13); age's cruel knife may cut "my lover's life" but "never cut from memory / My sweet love's beauty" (63.11–12); "when I in earth am rotten" and you are in your tomb, "Your monument shall be my gentle verse" (81.3, 9). This last phrase casually incorporates the social status that Shakespeare constantly dreamed of, but the dream here is far more ambitious, laying claim to a godlike power: "Your name from hence"—that is, from my gentle verse—"immortal life shall have" (81.5).

The irony, of course, is that the sonnets themselves do not confer any life at all on the *name* of the beloved, for the simple reason that he is never actually named. Shakespeare, it seems, has deliberately kept the beloved's name out of poems that claim to confer upon that name an immortal life.

If it is not unreasonable to speculate that the young man of the opening suite of sonnets is the Earl of Southampton, it is because the earl's personal circumstances perfectly fit the situation that is sketched, because his family had already tried literary persuasion, and, above all, because Shakespeare in the 1590s dedicated to Southampton two long, elaborate nondramatic poems: *Venus and Adonis* and *The Rape of Lucrece*. The dedicatory letters to these long poems are the only such documents from Shakespeare's hand, and, along with the poems they introduce, they tell us a great deal about the man who wrote them—or at least about the side that he wished to present to the earl.

The language of the first of these dedications, to *Venus and Adonis*, is formal, emotionally cautious, and socially defensive: "I know not how I shall offend in dedicating my unpolished lines to your lordship, nor how the world will censure me for choosing so strong a prop to support so weak a burden." Probably written in late 1592, very close to the time he may have written the procreation sonnets, the elegant narrative poem, anything but "unpolished," was clearly a bid for patronage—that is, for protection against renewed "censure" and for any more tangible rewards that the free-spending nobleman might care to offer.

The poet's display of diffidence and anxiety in the dedication may well have been sincere. Published in 1593, *Venus and Adonis* was the first of Shakespeare's works to appear in print. Apparently indifferent to the printing house through most of his career, here for once he showed clear signs of caring. He chose for the printer someone he could trust, his fellow Stratford-upon-Avon native Richard Field. The choice was a good one: Field produced an unusually handsome small book, suitable for presentation. Shakespeare was attempting, probably for the first and only time in his career, to find a patron, and with the theaters shut down and the plague continuing to rage, he may have thought that a great deal was riding on whether he was successful. Even if Southampton had already manifested his favor, in the wake of *Greene's Groatworth of Wit*, and even if the exalted aristocrat and the lowly player had already had some encouraging personal contact with one another—and, of course, these are merely speculations—Shakespeare could well have been uncertain about the reception of *Venus and Adonis*.

It was as if, in his late twenties, Shakespeare had decided to start afresh in a new profession, as if he had not written anything before. He was attempting to establish himself now not as a popular playwright but as a cultivated poet, someone who could gracefully conjure up the mythological world to which his university-educated rival poets claimed virtually exclusive access. And he was attempting also to address Southampton's particular situation: the poem takes up the theme of the beautiful young man, scarcely more than a boy, who resists the blandishments of the goddess of love. If the poem's "godfather"—the eighteen-year-old nobleman—is pleased with it, Shakespeare writes, then he will attempt "some graver labour. But if the first heir of my invention prove deformed"—like the sonnets, the dedicatory letter metamorphoses poems into children—then the poet will "never after ear so barren a land." Perhaps Shakespeare meant it, for there would be no point in making another effort if Southampton rejected this one out of hand.

The plot of *Venus and Adonis* echoes the sonnets' warning: a beautiful boy's rejection of love—Love herself, in the person of Venus—enables death to triumph over him. For three-quarters of the poem's nearly twelve hundred lines, Venus, feverish with desire, pleads, caresses, lures, harangues, and all but assaults Adonis. Accusing the young man of self-love, she begs him to produce an heir. But all is in vain. Breaking away from the goddess's embrace, Adonis goes off to hunt and is promptly killed by a "foul, grim, and urchin-snouted boar" (line 1105). From the blood that spills from his wound springs a purple flower, the anemone, which grief-stricken Venus plucks and cradles in her bosom.

Taken in the abstract, the argument of *Venus and Adonis* could have appealed to the sober, calculating guardian Burghley. But the experience of the poem is anything but sober. Here too, as in the sonnets, prudential warning cedes place to something else, something seductive that this particular poet, William Shakespeare, is offering the young man. *Venus and Adonis* is a spectacular display of Shakespeare's signature characteristic, his astonishing capacity to be everywhere and nowhere, to assume all positions and to slip free of all constraints. The capacity depends upon a simultaneous, deeply paradoxical achievement of proximity and distance, intimacy and detachment. How otherwise would it be possible to be in so many places at once? Shakespeare offers here in a weirdly concentrated form the sensibility that enabled him to write his plays.

The effect is a tangle of erotic arousal, pain, and cool laughter. At moments, the love goddess seems enormous, a dominatrix towering over her diminutive, unwilling lover:

> Over one arm, the lusty courser's rein;
> Under her other was the tender boy,
> Who blushed and pouted in a dull disdain
> With leaden appetite, unapt to toy.
> (lines 31–34)

At other moments, she is the fragile heroine of a romance, fainting at a mere disapproving glance, and then, when the remorseful boy tries to revive her, suddenly reduced to a farcical rag doll:

> He wrings her nose, he strikes her on the cheeks,
> He bends her fingers, holds her pulses hard;
> He chafes her lips; a thousand ways he seeks
> To mend the hurt that his unkindness marred.
> (lines 475–78)

In such passages we seem to be at a great distance from the figures, watching their frantic movements the way the audience of *A Midsummer Night's Dream* watches the crazed lovers in the Athenian woods. But then

without warning—and without ever completely losing the comic detachment—we are unnervingly close. Venus not only sighs for Adonis; she
"locks her lily fingers one in one" (line 228) around the struggling boy
and proposes that he "graze" (line 233) on her body:

> "Within this limit is relief enough,
> Sweet bottom-grass, and high delightful plain,
> Round rising hillocks, brakes obscure and rough,
> To shelter thee from tempest and from rain."
>
> (lines 235–38)

Adonis attempts to pull back from her frantic kisses only to submit pas-
sively for a few moments out of sheer exhaustion:

> Hot, faint, and weary with her hard embracing,
> Like a wild bird being tamed with too much handling.
>
> (lines 559–60)

Metaphors frequently function in poetry as a way of distancing the reader
from a character or situation, but not here. Here they are ways of intensifying physical and emotional proximity, so that we view everything in a
sustained close-up. The dimples in Adonis's cheeks are "round enchant-
ing pits" that "Opened their mouths to swallow Venus' liking" (lines
247–48). The goddess's face "doth reek and smoke" (line 555) with erotic
arousal. And when the two recline—or rather when Venus pulls Adonis
down to the ground—they lie not simply on a bed of flowers, but on
"blue-veined violets" (line 125).

Without once making an appearance in his own person—for, after
all, this is a mythological fantasy—Shakespeare is constantly, inescapably
present in *Venus and Adonis*, as if he wanted Southampton (and perhaps
"the world," at which he glances in his dedication) fully to understand his
extraordinary powers of playful identification. He is manifestly in Venus,
in her physical urgency and her rhetorical inventiveness, and he is in Adonis too, in his impatience and his misogynistic distaste. But he is in
everything else as well. If a mare could write a love poem to a stallion

(and, more precisely, the ecstatic inventory of the beloved's features, known as a blazon), she might write this:

> Round-hoofed, short-jointed, fetlocks shag and long,
> Broad breast, full eye, small head, and nostril wide,
> High crest, short ears, straight legs, and passing strong;
> Thin mane, thick tail, broad buttock, tender hide.
> (lines 295–98)

If a hare could write a poem about the misery of being hunted, he might write this:

> Then shalt thou see the dew-bedabbled wretch
> Turn, and return, indenting with the way.
> Each envious brier his weary legs do scratch;
> Each shadow makes him stop, each murmur stay.
> (lines 703–6)

The point is not that horses or hares are central to the poem—they are not. The point is that Shakespeare effortlessly enters into their existence.

What do you offer a beautiful, spoiled young aristocrat who has everything? You present him with a universe where everything has an erotic charge, a charge whose urgency confounds the roles of mother and lover. Here is Venus hearing the sound of the hunt and running in panic toward the scene:

> And as she runs, the bushes in the way
> Some catch her by the neck, some kiss her face,
> Some twine about her thigh to make her stay.
> She wildly breaketh from their strict embrace,
>   Like a milch doe whose swelling dugs do ache,
>   Hasting to feed her fawn hid in some brake.
> (lines 871–76)

How do you awaken and hold a jaded young man's attention? You introduce him to a world of heightened sensitivity to pleasure and to pain. Here is Venus shutting her eyes at the sight of Adonis's fatal wound:

> Or as the snail, whose tender horns being hit
> Shrinks backward in his shelly cave with pain,
> And there, all smothered up, in shade doth sit,
> Long after fearing to creep forth again;
> So at his bloody view her eyes are fled
> Into the deep dark cabins of her head.
>
> (lines 1033–38)

And if you are begging for the generosity of a noble patron, what stupendous gift can you possibly give in return? You propose symbolically to turn death itself into orgasm. Here is Venus telling herself that the boar intended not to kill Adonis but to kiss him:

> "And, nuzzling in his flank, the loving swine
> Sheathed unaware the tusk in his soft groin."
>
> (lines 1115–16)

The "loving swine" has only done what she herself has all along been proposing to do:

> "Had I been toothed like him, I must confess
> With kissing him I should have killed him first."
>
> (lines 1117–18)

This is what Shakespeare had to offer.

Evidently, *Venus and Adonis* pleased the earl: judging from the rush of imitations, admiring comments, and reprintings—ten times by 1602!—the poem pleased virtually everyone. (It was particularly popular, it seems, with young men.) Flush with his success, Shakespeare was as good as his word, bringing forth within a year's time the much graver

Lucrece. But this time the tone of the dedicatory letter to Southampton was no longer diffident, tentative, or anxious: "The love I dedicate to your lordship is without end. . . . What I have done is yours; what I have to do is yours, being part in all I have, devoted yours." Elizabethan dedicatory letters were often quite florid, but what Shakespeare wrote here is not at all typical. This was not, as might have been expected, an exercise in praise or the desire to please or a plea for patronage; this was a public declaration of fervent, boundless love.

Something happened in the course of the year between *Venus and Adonis* and *The Rape of Lucrece*, something led Shakespeare to shift from "I know not how I shall offend" to "love . . . without end." There is no direct access to whatever it was, but it is possible that hints may lie in the sonnets. For the sonnets—assuming that most of the first 126 of them were written to the same person—do not merely praise the young man and affirm the power of poetry; they sketch a relationship unfolding over time, in all probability over years. Admiration ripens into adoration; periods of joyful intimacy are followed by absence and desperate longing; the poet finds it tormenting to endure separation from his beloved; he feels in many ways unworthy of so precious a love, but he is also aware that he is able by his art to confer eternity upon the mortal beauty of the young man; he knows that a time will come, perhaps soon, when the young man will see him as decrepit and no longer care for him; he struggles to accept the inevitable loss of a love that has sustained his life; exuberant praise gives way to reproach and self-doubt; the poet is at once excited and tormented by his social inferiority; his passionate devotion slides toward abject subservience, and then this subservience slowly modulates back into a partial critical independence; he insists that the young man is perfect, even as he recognizes deep flaws in his character.

In the midst of this tangle of shifting, obsessive emotions, there are glimpses of what seem to be specific events. The young man succumbs to temptation and sleeps with the poet's mistress. The betrayal is painful less because of her infidelity—"And yet it may be said I loved her dearly" (42.2)—than because of his, for his is the love that truly matters. The poet himself is in some unspecified way unfaithful to the young man but ventures to hope that he will be forgiven for his "transgression" (120.3), just as in comparable circumstances he earlier forgave the young man. The poet has given away a keepsake—a small notebook or writing tablet—that the young man has presented to him, but it does not matter, for the gift is inalienably lodged in his brain and heart. Several rivals—one of them, at least, a writer of considerable distinction—are competing, apparently successfully, for the young man's attention and favor. And the culminating "event": from sonnet 127 onward the poet shifts his obsessive attention away from the fair young man and focuses instead on his feelings—a tangle of desire and revulsion—toward his black-eyed, black-haired, sexually voracious mistress.

Biographers have often succumbed to the temptation to turn these intimations of events into a full-blown romantic plot, but to do so requires pulling against the strong gravitational force of the individual poems. Shakespeare, who had an effortless genius at narrative, made certain that his sonnets would not yield an entirely coherent story. Each of the great poems in the sequence—and there are many—is its own distinct world, a compressed, often fantastically complex fourteen-line rehearsal of an emotional scenario that the playwright could, if he chose, have developed into a scene or an entire play. An example is the justly celebrated sonnet 138, a poem already removed from any narrative context and anthologized during Shakespeare's own lifetime:

> When my love swears that she is made of truth
> I do believe her though I know she lies,
> That she might think me some untutored youth
> Unlearnèd in the world's false subtleties.
> Thus vainly thinking that she thinks me young,
> Although she knows my days are past the best,
> Simply I credit her false-speaking tongue;
> On both sides thus is simple truth suppressed.
> But wherefore says she not she is unjust,
> And wherefore say not I that I am old?
> O, love's best habit is in seeming trust,
> And age in love loves not to have years told.
>> Therefore I lie with her, and she with me,
>> And in our faults by lies we flattered be.

"I do believe her though I know she lies." Since the poet makes clear he knows perfectly well that his mistress is unfaithful, "I do believe her" seems to be short for "I pretend to believe her." The plot, it seems, is one of those cuckoldry stories that fascinated Shakespeare and his contemporaries; the opening lines give voice to the shadowy suspicion that pulls toward farce in *Much Ado About Nothing*, or toward murder in *The Winter's Tale*. The suspicion here has a May-December twist, the anxiety that preys on the mind of Othello, excruciatingly aware that, compared with Desdemona, he is "declined / Into the vale of years—yet that's not much" (3.3.269–70).

The poet goes on, however, to acknowledge that his strategy—pretending to be gullible so as to seem younger than his years—does not actually fool his mistress for a moment, any more than he is fooled by her "false-speaking tongue": "On both sides thus is simple truth suppressed." By now a different plot is in place, neither familiarly farcical nor tragic, something more like the strategic game of mutual lying in which Shakespeare's Antony and Cleopatra (along with almost every other character in that play) indulge. "Simple truth"—the truth of the dark lady's infidelity and the poet's aging—is suppressed by his "simply" crediting her lies, that is, by a deliberate indulgence in a fiction. A way to characterize this indulgence might be Coleridge's phrase for what one does when watching a play: a "willing suspension of disbelief." But the poet is describing his relationship to his lying mistress, not to a work of art.

The game could well lead to an explosion of moral disapproval or self-reproach, conventional ways to banish the deceit and to restore moral order. Indeed, Shakespeare seems to be building toward such an explosion, as he calls the whole pattern of their lives into question:

> But wherefore says she not she is unjust,
> And wherefore say not I that I am old?

But the close of the poem—sliding from "old" to a sighing "O"—surprises us by frankly suspending the impulse to strip away the veil of deception: "O, love's best habit is in seeming trust." Love's "habit," both its habitual behavior and its finest clothing, is a tissue of lies. Instead of moral judgment, there is a candid acceptance of the erotic virtue of mendacity. As the final couplet makes clear, the man and woman who lie to each other lie with each other.

Sonnet writing was a courtly and aristocratic performance, and Shakespeare was decidedly not a courtier or an aristocrat. Yet the challenge of this form proved agreeable to him. To be a very public man—an actor onstage, a successful playwright, a celebrated poet; and at the same time to be a very private man—a man who can be trusted with secrets, a writer who keeps his intimate affairs to himself and subtly encodes all references to others: this was the double life Shakespeare had chosen for himself. If his astonishing verbal skills and his compulsive habit of imaginative identification, coupled with deep ambition, drove him to public performance, his family secrets and his wary intelligence—perhaps reinforced by the sight of the severed heads on London Bridge—counseled absolute discretion.

Such a deliberately chosen double existence helps to explain the paradox that has tantalized centuries of readers: the sonnets are a thrilling, deeply convincing staging of the poet's inner life, an intimate performance of Shakespeare's response to his tangled emotional relationships with a young man, a rival poet, and a dark lady; and the sonnets are a cunning sequence of beautiful locked boxes to which there are no keys, an exquisitely constructed screen behind which it is virtually impossible to venture with any confidence.

A code of discretion and the practice of concealment shape the sonnets, but so do certain shared excitements, recurrent preoccupations, and seductive strategies. It would be folly to take these as a kind of confidential diary, a straightforward record of what actually went on in the relationship between Shakespeare and his deceitful dark lady, whoever she was in real life, or between Shakespeare and the aristocratic young man, whether he was Southampton or someone else, or perhaps an amalgam of multiple lovers. But even a record of fantasies, in part adapted from other poets, in part spun out of the threads of actual relationships, may reveal something about Shakespeare's emotional life.

The sonnets represent the poet and the young man as excited by the immense class and status difference between them. Even while slyly criticizing his beloved—or perhaps because he is slyly criticizing him—Shakespeare plays at utter subservience:

> Being your slave, what should I do but tend
> Upon the hours and times of your desire?
>
> (571–2)

And he stages too his intense awareness of the social stigma that attaches to his profession:

> Alas, 'tis true, I have gone here and there
> And made myself a motley to the view.
>
> (110.1–2)

Perhaps this shame, the shame of dressing up like a fool in motley and putting on a show before the gaping public, was something that Shakespeare actually felt, quite apart from the relationship depicted in the sonnets. But here it is part of the erotic dance between himself and the beautiful boy:

> O, for my sake do you with fortune chide,
> The guilty goddess of my harmful deeds,
> That did not better for my life provide
> Than public means which public manners breeds.
> Thence comes it that my name receives a brand,
> And almost thence my nature is subdued
> To what it works in, like the dyer's hand.
> Pity me. . . .
>
> (111.1–8)

The permanent stain that Shakespeare the performer bears and that indelibly marks his social distance from his aristocratic beloved becomes quite literally part of the appeal: "Pity me."

The age difference between the poet and the young man functions in a similar way, not, that is, as an impediment to desire, but rather as a paradoxical source of excitement, something to be noted, highlighted, and exaggerated:

As a decrepit father takes delight
To see his active child do deeds of youth,
So I, made lame by fortune's dearest spite,
Take all my comfort of thy worth and truth.
                              (37.1–4)

Where could the seductive pleasure possibly lie here? Perhaps in a
patriarchal society where the young were accustomed to domineering
fathers or tyrannical guardians, a weak father figure was thrilling. The
excitement of the role reversal must have been intense, intense enough
to lead Shakespeare to stage himself as a kind of parasite on the
younger man. The poet's performance does not preclude vanity. "Sin of
self-love possesseth all mine eye," Shakespeare writes, "And all my soul,
and all my every part." But this frank admission of narcissism—
"Methinks no face so gracious is as mine"—is only a way of intensifying the beloved's triumph. When he looks into the mirror, Shakespeare
writes, he sees that in reality his face is "Beated and chapped with
tanned antiquity" (62.1–2, 5, 10) and that whatever pleasure he takes in
himself is borrowed from the man he loves: "Painting my age with
beauty of thy days" (10.14).

The emotions at play here have something of the blend of adoration
and appetite that Shakespeare depicted in Falstaff's feelings toward his
sweet boy, Prince Hal. But the roles are reversed: where Shakespeare
imagined himself as the young prince in relation to Robert Greene's calculating older man, now he plays the older man to the sweet boy. Perhaps
this was one of the inner currents that enabled Shakespeare to transform
the character he based on Greene from a mere braggart into the complex,
poignant figure of Falstaff, self-loving, calculating, cynical, adoring,
abject, and doomed. As Hal sweeps away his memories of Falstaff—"I
know thee not, old man"—so the poet urges the young man simply to
forget him: "Nay, if you read this line, remember not / The hand that writ
it." But the difference is that the poet's request to be forgotten is in reality a declaration of abject love and a thinly disguised appeal to be remembered and loved:

Nay, if you read this line, remember not
The hand that writ it; for I love you so
That I in your sweet thoughts would be forgot
If thinking on me then should make you woe.

                              (71.5–8)

Again and again, the young man is invited to embrace the father he will displace and bury and eventually forget. And the oblivion that lies in the future only serves to intensify the appeal.

One of the most famous of the sonnets (73) sums up the emotional claim that Shakespeare is making on the young man by exaggerating their age difference:

That time of year thou mayst in me behold
When yellow leaves, or none, or few, do hang
Upon those boughs which shake against the cold,
Bare ruined choirs where late the sweet birds sang.
In me thou seest the twilight of such day
As after sunset fadeth in the west,
Which by and by black night doth take away,
Death's second self, that seals up all in rest.
In me thou seest the glowing of such fire
That on the ashes of his youth doth lie
As the death-bed whereon it must expire,
Consumed with that which it was nourished by.
    This thou perceiv'st, which makes thy love more strong,
    To love that well which thou must leave ere long.

Elsewhere in the sonnet sequence there is an emphasis on eternity—the timelessness of the poet's lines, the endless replication of the young man's beauty—but not here. Each of the images—the yellow leaves, the twilight, and the embers—exquisitely conveys transience. It is only a matter of time before it will be irrevocably over: naked branches, darkness, cold ashes lie just ahead. And the transience, the coming-to-an-end that

Shakespeare sees even in the moment of love's flourishing, confers a painful intensity upon the relationship.

For whatever actually happened between Shakespeare and the young man—whether they only stared longingly at one another or embraced, kissed passionately, went to bed together—was almost certainly shaped by an overwhelming sense of transience. This sense did not only, or even principally, derive from the age and class differences that intensified their desires; it derived from the period's understanding of male homosexual love. Elizabethans acknowledged the existence of same-sex desire; indeed, it was in a certain sense easier for them to justify than heterosexual desire. That men were inherently superior to women was widely preached; why then wouldn't men naturally be drawn to love other men? Sodomy was strictly prohibited by religious teaching and the law, but that prohibition aside, it was perfectly understandable that men would love and desire men.

Shakespeare's contemporary Edmund Spenser, a poet celebrated for his moral seriousness, wrote a pastoral poem in which a shepherd declares his passionate love for a youth. Attached to the poem is a commentary by Spenser himself or someone very close to him that notes uneasily that the relationship has some savor of the "disorderly love" that the Greeks called "paederastice." But after all, the commentary continues, from the right perspective "paederastice" is "much to be preferred before gynerastice, that is, the love which enflameth men with lust toward womankind." And then, as if alarmed by what he has just said, the commentator adds a final disclaimer: let no man think that he is defending the "execrable and horrible sins of forbidden and execrable fleshliness."

It is in the context of this seesaw game of acknowledgment and denial that Shakespeare stages his sexual desire for the young man: it is explicitly accepted and ardently expressed as if it were the most natural thing in the world, and at the same time it is deflected, disavowed, or defeated, as if it could never be fully realized. The young man, in sonnet 20, has a woman's face and a woman's gentle heart, but he is better, truer, and more steadfast than any woman. He is, the poet writes, "the master-mistress of my passion." Nature indeed intended to create a woman when she made the young man, but, doting on her own creation, she added something—"she pricked thee out" (20.2, 13)—and therefore defeated the poet of his long-term sexual fulfillment. Shakespeare does not adopt the outraged moralizing tone of Spenser's commentator, but he plays with the same materials—misogyny, intense homosexual desire, disavowal—to which he adds a sense of transience. For even if in the actual relationship half-hidden in the sonnets Shakespeare fulfilled his erotic longings, he knew that this love would never be allowed to stand in the way of the social imperative to marry and produce heirs, precisely that imperative to which Shakespeare gave voice in the opening sonnets.

It was possible for the adolescent Southampton to declare that he was not ready to marry, provided he was prepared to accept the huge financial sacrifice that his refusal entailed. It was possible too for him to have an affair with one or more of the men—and there must have been many—who courted him. It would have been quite another thing for him to abjure marriage altogether. A few men of high rank (though not as high as Southampton's) did indeed refuse to marry—Francis Bacon is a notable example—but quite apart from sexual orientation, most were committed to passing along their name, title, and wealth. In 1598, shortly before his twenty-fifth birthday, Southampton secretly wed one of the queen's maids of honor, Elizabeth Vernon, who was pregnant with his child. The queen was enraged: her maids of honor were meant actually to be maids, and she hated clandestine marriages among her followers. Still, this marriage seems to have been a happy one, sustaining the earl through a long, turbulent, and on occasion extremely dangerous career.

As for the poet, if there is one thing that the sonnets, taken as biographical documents, strongly suggest, it is that he could not find what he craved, emotionally or sexually, within his marriage. Part of the problem may have been the evident mismatch with Anne Hathaway; but perhaps the sonnets suggest too that no single person could ever have satisfied Shakespeare's longings or made him happy. It is not as if he found, outside of his marriage, someone who fulfilled him completely. He focused, it seems, his capacity for ecstatic idealization largely on the young man and his capacity for desire largely on his mistress. And in both cases, there is an obstacle to fulfillment. The poet adores a man whom he cannot possess and desires a woman whom he cannot admire. The beautiful young man, the sonnets ruefully acknowledge, cannot ultimately be his, while the dark lady, even if he could securely possess her, is everything that should arouse revulsion in him. Dishonest, unchaste, and faithless, she has, according to the last sonnets in the sequence, given him something more than revulsion; she has infected him with venereal disease. But still he cannot give her up: "My love is as a fever, longing still / For that which longer nurseth the disease" (147.1–2). That he cannot do so has everything to do with the compulsions of "lust in action" (129.2), the rhythm of tumescence and detumescence that defines for him what it means to be with her: "I call / Her 'love' for whose dear love I rise and fall" (151.13–14). This sexual rhythm, yoking vitality and death, pleasure and disgust, longing and loathing, is not a mere recreation or an escape. As the sonnets insist again and again, the poet's witty, anxious, self-conscious embrace of his own desires defines what it means to be "Will."

There is no room, in the way in which Shakespeare represents himself in the sonnets, for his wife or his children. It does not matter, in this regard, whether the poems were written in the mid-1590s or a decade later: since no one thinks that they were written before Shakespeare married and became a father, all of the sonnets are in effect acts of erasure. There are perhaps a few small exceptions: the possible glimpse of the bygone courtship of his wife in a pun on "hate away" and "Hathaway" in sonnet 145; a very indirect acknowledgment of his infidelity in the opening line of sonnet 152—"In loving thee thou know'st I am forsworn." The sonnet characteristically goes on to berate his mistress for breaking her "bed-vow," but at least for a moment he recognizes that he too has broken his vow. For the most part, he seems to forget. Or rather, the figures of the young man and the dark lady seem to displace and absorb emotions that we might have conventionally expected Shakespeare to feel in and for his family. About Anne Shakespeare he is silent; it is to his beautiful male friend that he writes his most celebrated words about love: "Let me not to the marriage of true minds / Admit impediments" (116.1–2).

CHAPTER 9

Laughter at the Scaffold

H OWEVER GENEROUSLY he may have been rewarded for the sonnets, *Venus and Adonis,* and *The Rape of Lucrece,* Shakespeare did not choose to stake his fortunes, financial or artistic, on his relation to a patron. He chose instead, when the plague abated, to return to the theater, where he rose to preeminence as a playwright remarkably quickly. The playing companies needed to please many different tastes, and they had a huge appetite for new scripts. Hardworking hacks could make good money grinding out dozens of plays: *Three Ladies of London, Peddler's Prophecy, Fair Em, A Sackful of News, The Tragical History of the Tartarian Cripple, Emperor of Constantinople.* But until the impressive, boisterous arrival on the scene of Ben Jonson in 1597, Shakespeare had only one serious rival, Christopher Marlowe. The two immensely talented young poets, exactly the same age, were evidently locked in mutual emulation and contest. They circled warily, watching with intense attention, imitating, and then attempting to surpass each other. The contest extended beyond the momentous early works, *Tamburlaine* and *Henry VI,* to a brilliant pair of strikingly similar history plays, Shakespeare's *Richard II* and Marlowe's *Edward II,* and an equally brilliant pair of long erotic poems, Shakespeare's *Venus and Adonis* and Marlowe's *Hero and Leander*. Marlowe would not have made the mistake of underestimating Shakespeare. He would have immediately understood that in the words of the hunchback duke of Gloucester, in the third part of *Henry VI* —"I'll make my heaven to dream upon the crown" (3.2.168)—Shakespeare was at once invoking and slyly mocking Tamburlaine's dream of "The sweet fruition of an earthly crown" (2.7.29). Shakespeare, for his part, was in no danger of underestimating Marlowe. Marlowe was the only one of the university wits whose talent Shakespeare might have seriously envied, whose aesthetic judgment he might have feared, whose admiration he might have earnestly wanted to win, and whose achievements he certainly attempted to equal and outdo.

One of Marlowe's achievements might have seemed to Shakespeare, at this early point in his career, beyond his grasp. *Doctor Faustus*, the powerful tragedy of the scholar who sells his soul to the devil, drew deeply on Marlowe's theological education at Cambridge. Though years later, in *Hamlet*, Shakespeare depicted a bookish prince who has been abruptly pulled away from his university studies, and in *The Tempest* he explored the fate of a prince who becomes rapt in his occult reading, he never attempted, early or late, to make the scholar's study the center of the theatrical scene. His fullest answer to Marlowe came on neutral ground, that is, in the depiction of a person whom neither of them is likely ever to have encountered, a Jew.

But how did Marlowe and Shakespeare come to write two of their most memorable plays, *The Jew of Malta* and *The Merchant of Venice*, about Jews? Or rather, in the case of Shakespeare, why did the character of Shylock the Jew take over the comedy in which he appears? For almost everyone thinks that the merchant of Venice of the play's title is Shylock. Even when you realize that the merchant is not the Jew, even when you know that the title is referring to the Christian Antonio, you still instinctively make the mistake. And it is not exactly a mistake: the Jew is at the play's center. *The Merchant of Venice* has a host of characters who compete for the audience's attention: a handsome, impecunious young man in search of a wealthy wife; a melancholy, rich merchant who is hopelessly in love with the young man; women—three of them, no less—who dress

themselves as men; a mischievous clown; an irrepressible sidekick; an
exotic Moroccan; an absurd Spaniard. The list could be extended. But it
is the Jewish villain everyone remembers, and not simply as villain. Shylock seems to have a stronger claim to attention, quite simply more life,
than anyone else. The same can be said for Marlowe's Jewish villain,
Barabas. Why were the imaginations of Shakespeare and Marlowe set on
fire by the figure of the Jew?

The fire glowed against the darkness of almost complete erasure: in
1290, two hundred years before the momentous expulsion from Spain,
the entire Jewish community of England had been expelled and forbidden on pain of death to return. The act of expulsion, in the reign of
Edward I, was unprecedented; England was the first nation in medieval
Christendom to rid itself by law of its entire Jewish population. There
was no precipitating crisis, as far as is known, no state of emergency, not
even any public explanation. No jurist seems to have thought it necessary
to justify the deportations; no chronicler bothered to record the official
reasons. Perhaps no one, Jew or Christian, thought reasons needed to be
given. For decades the Jewish population in England had been in desperate trouble: accused of Host desecration and the ritual murder of Christian children, hated as moneylenders, reviled as Christ killers, beaten and
lynched by mobs whipped into anti-Jewish frenzy by the incendiary sermons of itinerant friars.

By the time of Marlowe and Shakespeare, three centuries later, the
Jewish population of England was ancient history. London had a small
population of Spanish and Portuguese converts from Judaism, and some
of these may have been Marranos, secretly maintaining Jewish practices.
But the Jewish community in England had long vanished, and there were
no Jews who openly practiced their religion. Yet in fact the Jews left traces
far more difficult to eradicate than people, and the English brooded on
these traces—stories circulated, reiterated, and elaborated—continually
and virtually obsessively. There were Jewish fables and Jewish jokes and
Jewish nightmares: Jews lured little children into their clutches, murdered them, and took their blood to make bread for Passover. Jews were
immensely wealthy—even when they looked like paupers—and covertly
pulled the strings of an enormous international network of capital and

goods. Jews poisoned wells and were responsible for spreading the bubonic plague. Jews secretly plotted an apocalyptic war against the Christians. Jews had a peculiar stink. Jewish men menstruated.

Even though almost no one had actually laid eyes on one for generations, the Jews, like wolves in modern children's stories, played a powerful symbolic role in the country's imaginative economy. Not surprisingly, they found their way into the ordinary language that theatrical characters, including Shakespeare's, speak. "If I do not take pity of her I am a villain," says Benedick in *Much Ado About Nothing*, tricked by his friends into declaring a passion for Beatrice. "If I do not love her, I am a Jew" (2.3.231–32). Everyone knew what that meant: Jews were by nature villainous, unnatural, coldhearted. England's royal kings, says the dying John of Gaunt, are renowned for their deeds as far from home "As is the sepulchre, in stubborn Jewry, / Of the world's ransom, blessèd Mary's son" (*Richard II*, 2.1.55–56). Everyone knew what that meant: even in the wake of the Messiah's presence in their midst, Jews stubbornly and perversely clung to their old beliefs, beliefs that could not cleanse and hence ransom them from sin. "No, no, they were not bound," says Peto, contradicting Gadshill's brazen lie that they had bound the men with whom Falstaff says he had fought. "You rogue," rejoins Falstaff, "they were bound every man of them, or I am a Jew else, an Hebrew Jew" (*1 Henry IV*, 2.5.163–65). Everyone knew what that meant: a Jew—here, in Falstaff's comic turn, a Jew squared—was a person without valor and without honor, the very antithesis of what the fat braggart is claiming to be.

Shakespeare and his contemporaries found Jews, along with Ethopians, Turks, witches, hunchbacks, and others, useful conceptual tools. These feared and despised figures provided quick, easy orientation, clear boundaries, limit cases. "I think Crab, my dog, be the sourest-natured dog that lives," says the clown Lance in *The Two Gentlemen of Verona*. Everyone in his household weeps at Lance's departure, but the "cruel-hearted cur" does not shed a tear: "He is a stone, a very pebble-stone, and has no more pity in him than a dog. A Jew would have wept to have seen our parting" (2.3.4–5, 8–10). The Jew was a measuring device—here of degrees of heartlessness. He was also an identity marker, as another remark by the merry Lance makes clear: "If thou wilt, go with me to the alehouse. If not, thou art an Hebrew, a Jew, and not worth the name of a Christian" (2.5.44–45). The dog is real, at least in the special sense in which stage animals are real; Lance is real, at least in the special sense in which theatrical characters are real; but the Jew has no comparable reality. Perhaps the most casually devastating sign of the disappearance of real Jews is a quiet joke, rather than an insult: "Signor Costard, adieu," says the diminutive page Mote in *Love's Labour's Lost*, and the clownish Costard replies, "My sweet ounce of man's flesh, my incony Jew!" (3.1.123–24). "Incony," meaning "fine," was a piece of Elizabethan slang. But what is "Jew" doing here? The answer: nothing. Perhaps Costard has simply misheard "adieu" (presumably pronounced "a-Jew"); perhaps in a slangy way he is calling Mote a "jewel" or a "juvenile." Whatever he is saying, he is not referring to actual Jews; Shakespeare calculated, probably correctly, that the accidental reference would make his audience chuckle.

So, some three hundred years after their expulsion from England, the Jews were in circulation as despised figures in stories and in everyday speech, and Shakespeare, particularly early in his career, reflected and furthered this circulation, apparently without moral reservation. For though the audience is meant to feel various degrees of detachment from Benedick, Falstaff, Lance, and Costard, it is not distanced from a casual anti-Semitism that is simply an incidental feature of their comic energy. Jews do not actually appear in these plays, nor do they occupy a significant place in the language the characters speak; on the contrary, they are all but invisible, even in those few minor instances when they are invoked. Shakespeare was being a man of his times. Jews in England in the late sixteenth century had virtually no claim on reality; they had been subject to what the German language so eloquently calls *Vernichtung*, being made nothing.

Yet that is not quite right, for Jews were also constantly and more substantially present to all Christians as "the People of the Book." Without the Hebrew Bible, whose prophesies he fulfills, no Christ. It is possible to be unclear or evasive about whether Jesus was a Jew, but, conceptually at least, it is not possible for Christianity to do without Jews. Every Sunday, in a society in which weekly church attendance was obligatory for everyone, ministers edified their parishioners with passages, in translation, from the sacred Scriptures of the ancient Israelites. A people utterly despised and degraded, a people who had been deported en masse from England in the late thirteenth century and had never been allowed to return, an invisible people who functioned as symbolic tokens of all that was heartless, vicious, rapacious, and unnatural also functioned as the source of the most exalted spiritual poetry in the English language and as the necessary conduit through which the Redeemer came to all Christians.

This conceptual necessity—this historical interlacing of the destiny of Jews and Christians—had, of course, nothing to do with toleration for actual Jews. Certain cities—Venice among them—permitted Jews to reside relatively unmolested for extended periods of time, forbidding them, to be sure, to own land or practice most "honest" trades but allowing, even encouraging, them to lend money at interest. Such fiscal liquidity was highly useful in a society where canon law prohibited Christians from taking interest, but it made the Jews predictable objects of popular loathing and upper-class exploitation. Medieval popes periodically voiced a wish to protect Jews against those more radical Christian voices that called for their complete extinction, man, woman, and child, but the protection was only for the purposes of preserving an object lesson in misery. The papal argument was that an unhappy, impoverished, weak, and insecure remnant was a useful reminder of the consequences of rejecting Christ. Protestants had a somewhat greater interest in exploring the historical reality of ancient Judaism. The drive to return to the practices and beliefs of early Christianity led to a scholarly investigation of Hebrew prayer, the Passover, atonement, general confession, funeral customs, and the like. For a brief time Luther even felt kindly disposed toward contemporary Jews, who had, he thought, refused to convert to a corrupt and magical Catholicism. But when they stubbornly refused to convert to the purified, reformed Christianity he was championing, Luther's muted respect turned to rage, and in terms rivaling those of the most bigoted medieval friar, he called upon Christians to burn the Jews to death in their synagogues.

Luther's *On the Jews and Their Lies* probably had little currency in Elizabethan England. There were, after all, no synagogues left in England to burn, no Jewish community to hate or to protect. Marlowe and

Shakespeare encountered "strangers," vulnerable to attack, but these were men and women belonging to the small communities of Flemish, Dutch, French, and Italian artisans, mostly Protestant exiles, who lived in London. In economic hard times, these aliens were the victims of resentment, targeted by gangs of drunken, loudmouthed, club-wielding idlers baying for blood.

The evidence that Marlowe and Shakespeare personally concerned themselves with this xenophobic violence is, in both cases, suggestive but ambiguous. In 1593 someone nailed up, on the Dutch Church wall in London, an incendiary placard against the resident aliens, one of a series of attacks that the authorities feared would incite violence. The authorities, launching a sweep against the troublemakers, apparently suspected that the author of the placard was Marlowe. Informed that Marlowe had been living with Thomas Kyd, officers went to Kyd's rooms. They did not find Marlowe there, but they searched the rooms and found heretical and blasphemous papers. Kyd, subjected to a brutal interrogation, said that the papers were all Marlowe's. Marlowe was called before the Privy Council, questioned, and released only under orders to report daily in person to the Palace of Westminster.

The suspicion that Marlowe wrote the Dutch Church libel was probably baseless, but it was not motivated by idle paranoia. The author or authors of the toxic words that worried the authorities complained that "like the Jews" the aliens "eat us up as bread"—the image may well have been drawn from a popular play like *The Jew of Malta*—and the nasty placard not only alluded to Marlowe's play *The Massacre at Paris* but was also signed "Tamburlaine." The allusions show that Marlowe's fantasies were current in the minds of some aggrieved people, that his plays had excited them, that his famous eloquence had helped them give their feelings a voice.

Shakespeare's very different response to the xenophobia was signaled in a play that he apparently collaborated in writing with several other playwrights, including Anthony Munday (the probable originator), Henry Chettle, Thomas Heywood, and Thomas Dekker. Before its first performance, the script, *Sir Thomas More,* ran afoul of the censor, Edmund Tilney, Master of the Revels. Tilney did not reject the play outright, but he demanded substantial revisions in several scenes depicting the hatred of "strangers," and he called for the complete elimination of a scene showing the 1517 riots against their presence in England. The reason for this demand seems clear: intensifying tensions culminated in periodic outbursts of rioting. There were particularly ugly episodes in 1592–93 and again in 1595. The authors of *Sir Thomas More* obviously wanted to capitalize on the tensions—everyone in the audience would understand that the scenes from the past were a thinly disguised representation of the world just outside the playhouse walls. The censor evidently was afraid that the play, even if it formally disapproved of the riots it staged, could stir up more trouble.

Though alterations were made and new scenes were written, possibly in response to the censor's demands, the script does not seem to have received official approval, and the play was apparently never performed. But the manuscript, written in multiple hands, somehow survived (it is now in the British Library) and has been pored over for more than a century with extraordinary attention. For though many puzzles about it remain unsolved, including the year the play was first drafted and the year or years when the revisions were made, the manuscript contains what most scholars agree are passages Shakespeare himself penned, the only such autograph manuscript to have been discovered.

One of the passages in Shakespeare's hand—Hand D, as it is more cautiously called—depicts Thomas More, as sheriff of London, successfully persuading the antialien rioters to abandon their rebellious violence and submit themselves to the king. Shakespeare wrote lines that seem exceptionally alert to the human misery and political dangers of forced expulsions. "Grant them removed," Shakespeare's More tells the mob that is demanding that the strangers be driven out of the kingdom,

> and grant that this your noise
> Hath chid down all the majesty of England.
> Imagine that you see the wretched strangers,
> Their babies at their backs, with their poor luggage
> Plodding to th' ports and coasts for transportation,
> And that you sit as kings in your desires,

Authority quite silenced by your brawl
And you in ruff of your opinions clothed:
What had you got? I'll tell you. You had taught
How insolence and strong hand should prevail,
How order should be quelled—and by this pattern
Not one of you should live an agèd man,
For other ruffians as their fancies wrought
With selfsame hand, self reasons, and self right
Would shark on you, and men like ravenous fishes
Would feed on one another.

The overarching point here is a traditional argument for obedience to higher authority, an argument Shakespeare had Ulysses make with even greater eloquence in *Troilus and Cressida*. Once the rabble take matters into their own hands, the warning goes, once the chain of due deference is broken, all civil protections immediately vanish, and the world is given over to the whims of the strong. But it is striking that the point was made through an exercise of sympathetic imagination, and that the scene most vividly conjured up was the moment of collective exile:

Imagine that you see the wretched strangers,
Their babies at their backs, with their poor luggage
Plodding to th' ports and coasts for transportation.

Shakespeare was not writing about the deported Jews of England; it is overwhelmingly unlikely that he was even thinking about Jews. But his lines convey a glimpse of scenes that must have occurred centuries earlier when, as the documentary record shows, at least 1,335 of the Jews expelled from England plodded to the ports and paid for passage to France.

Here is a certain capacity to conjure up the lives of others, an ability to identify even with despised and degraded humanity that sits uncomfortably in Shakespeare's work with "If I do not love her I am a Jew," and other moments of impulsive, unself-conscious Jew-baiting. These latter obviously cannot be taken as the expression of the playwright's considered

"opinion" about Jews or other strangers, nor are they sufficiently individu-
ated or detailed to tell us much about the characters in whose mouths they
appear. They are simply instances of lively or amusing speech, rhetorically
enhanced no doubt, but close enough to ordinary usage to count as realistic representation. Such realism was the medium in which Shakespeare
frequently worked, particularly in the comedies and histories. He seemed
quite comfortable with it; that is, there was little or no sense of strain, no
signal that he wished to rise above and judge the language of the crowd,
no moral revulsion. But there was a different principle at work in the lines
he gave More, a current of feeling that Shakespeare attributed to the
capacity of the imagination. The effect is like a quick sketch by Dürer or
Rembrandt: a few black lines on a blank page and suddenly a whole scene,
charged with pain and loss, surges up. Since the "wretched strangers" in
Sir Thomas More are not Jews, there was no inherent reason for the two
impulses—mockery and identification—to come into tension or to con-
tradict one another. They could have just sat there side by side. But they
did in fact come into conflict for Shakespeare, and the remarkable record
of the conflict is *The Merchant of Venice*.

To understand how this conflict came about, we must return to the
play that Christopher Marlowe had written about a Jew. A black comedy,
brilliant but exceptionally cynical and cruel, *The Jew of Malta* was probably first performed in 1589, near the beginning of Shakespeare's career as
a playwright, and it was an immediate success. Marlowe's antihero, the
Jew Barabas, with his Muslim slave Ithamore, exposes the rottenness of
Malta's Christian world, but in the course of the gleeful exposure, the
play gives voice to a full range of the worst anti-Jewish fantasies. "I walk
abroad a-nights," Barabas declares,

> And kill sick people groaning under walls.
> Sometimes I go about and poison wells;
> And now and then, to cherish Christian thieves,
> I am content to lose some of my crowns,
> That I may, walking in my gallery,
> See 'em go pinioned along by my door.
>
> (2.3.178–84)

Barabas's love of money is surpassed by his hatred of Christians, his pleasure in contriving and savoring as many of their deaths as he can possibly bring about. The Jew may speak cordially to his Christian neighbors, he may seem to allow his daughter to convert to Christianity, he may even imply his own interest in conversion, but in his heart he is always hatching murder. His homicidal career began, he explains, in the practice of medicine, and he then turned to other professions, always with the same malevolent motive:

> Being young, I studied physic, and began
> To practice first upon the Italian;
> There I enriched the priests with burials,
> And always kept the sexton's arms in ure
> With digging graves and ringing dead men's knells.
> And after that was I an engineer,
> And in the wars 'twixt France and Germany,
> Under pretense of helping Charles the Fifth,
> Slew friend and enemy with my stratagems.
> Then after that was I an usurer,
> And with extorting, cozening, forfeiting,
> And tricks belonging unto brokery,
> I filled the jails with bankrupts in a year,
> And with young orphans planted hospitals,
> And every moon made some or other mad,
> And now and then one hang himself for grief,
> Pinning upon his breast a long great scroll
> How I with interest tormented him.
>   (2.3.185–202)

Where was Marlowe in all of this? Where was his audience? The spectators were invited to share imaginatively in the homicidal reverie, a reverie built out of the recycled religious hatreds of centuries, but then what? What happened to the poison after it had been vented on the public stage? Perhaps it evaporated; perhaps precisely by venting it, by giving the grotesque libel a full airing, it was exposed as the murderous daydream that it was. No one was ever like Barbaras or Ithamore; no one ever could be, and staging the impossible would have made clear to the audience the absurdity of its fantasy.

The Jew of Malta may indeed have produced such a liberating effect, but probably only among those in the audience already disposed to be liberated. In any case, successful playwrights were in the business of exciting their audiences—the point was to bring crowds of paying customers into the theater—and whatever playing company had the rights to the script must have been pleased to have, in The Jew of Malta, a licensed play they could repeatedly dust off and revive profitably at moments of popular agitation. The group of playwrights who wrote Sir Thomas More also hoped to profit from the excitement of the crowd— the censor who struck the depiction of the popular riot saw very clearly what was going on. But the lines Shakespeare gave to More, in facing down the antialien rioters, pull so sharply against the work of the irresponsible, bloody-minded, cynical Marlowe as to constitute a deliberate reproach. "Imagine that you see the wretched strangers, / Their babies at their backs."

Current scholarly consensus holds that Shakespeare probably wrote his contribution to Sir Thomas More sometime between 1600 and 1605. Like his response to Greene's insults, his response to Marlowe, then, probably came many years after his rival's death. For on May 30, 1593, a few weeks after the posting of the placard on the Dutch Church wall, Marlowe, not yet thirty years old, had gone to Deptford, down by the shipyards east of London, to meet with three men, Ingram Frizer, Nicholas Skeres, and Robert Poley. They spent the day quietly, eating, drinking, and smoking at the house of Eleanor Bull, a bailiff's widow. In the evening after supper, there was a fight, allegedly over the "reckoning," that is, the bill. Frizer claimed that an enraged Marlowe had snatched Frizer's own weapon—a dagger, as the inquest carefully put it, "of the value of twelve pence"—and attacked him. In the ensuing struggle, Marlowe was killed, stabbed through the right eye. Frizer's account was corroborated by the other two men in the room, and the inquest concurred in its report. A month later the queen formally pardoned Frizer, on the grounds of self-defense. Only in the twentieth century did scholarly detective work disclose that the widow Bull's house was not an ordinary tavern but a place with links to the government's spy network, and that Frizer, Skeres, and Poley all had sinister connections to that network, as did Marlowe himself, connections not mentioned, of course, in the inquest. The murder, then, was quite possibly an assassination, though the precise motive has remained obscure.

Already before he left Cambridge, Marlowe had demonstrated not only his power as a poet but also his penchant for risk-taking. Spectacularly ill suited for the life of a country parson or a sober academic, he early became involved in the murky world of conspiracy and spying, the world that Shakespeare may have briefly glimpsed and fled from in Lancashire. The precise circumstances would have been strictly secret at the time and are still more obscure after four hundred years, but it seems that Marlowe was recruited, while still a student, into the intelligence service run by Elizabeth's spymaster, her secretary of state Sir Francis Walsingham. Marlowe was apparently sent to Reims, where he mingled with the English Catholics living in France. Such information as he could ferret out— or provoke—about plots to mount a foreign invasion or assassinate the heretic queen he would have passed along to his superiors. He must have been reasonably good at his nasty work, since the Privy Council wrote to the Cambridge authorities instructing them to award Marlowe his M.A. degree, despite his unexplained absences during term time.

When he came to London to try his hand at playwriting, Marlowe had already begun a move from the artisan class to which his father belonged to the status of a gentleman—he had his university degree in hand—but he was hardly following a conventional life course. His overt sexual interest in men made that course still less conventional, while his opinions—according to the report of the intelligence agent who was assigned to spy on him and the testimony of his roommate Kyd—pushed him to the most dangerous frontiers of freethinking. He used to declare (or so the spy claimed) that Jesus was a bastard and his mother a whore; that Moses was a "juggler," that is, a trickster, who had deceived the ignorant Jews; that the existence of the American Indians disproved Old Testament chronology; that the New Testament was "filthily written" and that he, Marlowe, could do better; that Jesus and St. John were homosexual lovers; and so on. If Marlowe said even a fraction of what was attributed to him, then he could only have survived—and that not for very long—in a social and professional sphere that winked at views that would elsewhere have been instantly and ferociously punished.

At the time of the death, at the age of twenty-nine, of his greatest professional rival, Shakespeare had already shown considerable promise, but his actual achievements could not begin to match the astonishing succession of plays and poems written by Marlowe. They must have known each other personally; the world they inhabited was far too small for anonymity. They may have liked each other, but there were as many grounds for suspicion and dislike as for affection and admiration. Some five years after Marlowe's death, in *As You Like It*, Shakespeare obliquely paid tribute to his rival by quoting one of his most famous lines. A lovesick character, invoking Marlowe as a "dead shepherd," says she now finds his "saw of might" (that is, she finds that his saying is powerful):

> Dead shepherd, now I find thy saw of might:
> "Who ever loved that loved not at first sight?"
> (3.5.82–83)

But elsewhere in the same play there may be a less generous glance at Marlowe. "When a man's verses cannot be understood," complains the clown Touchstone, "nor a man's good wit seconded with the forward child, understanding, it strikes a man more dead than a great reckoning in a little room" (3.3.9–12). These words were not exactly an attack on Marlowe, but insofar as they may have alluded to his murder over a "reckoning," they did so with a complete absence of sentimental feeling.

Beyond the trace of personal competitiveness that had outlasted even the rival's death and beyond the commercial competitiveness of rival playing companies vying for the same audience, there was a disagreement about the nature of the theater, which was also a disagreement about human imagination and human values. Shakespeare saw what was marvelous in Marlowe (there is much more evidence than the passing tribute in *As You Like It*), but he also seems to have disliked quite deeply something in Marlowe's language and imagination. Shakespeare left no programmatic statement of this difference, only his responses in the play-house. And the most sustained of these responses involved the represen-tation of Jews, the marked difference, that is, between Barbaras in *The Jew of Malta* and Shylock in *The Merchant of Venice*.

Marlowe was already dead when Shakespeare began, some time after 1594 and before 1598, to write *The Merchant of Venice*. Though a suc-cessful revival of *The Jew of Malta* probably prompted him to try his hand at a play about Jews, Shakespeare was not only glancing over his shoulder at his erstwhile rival. He did not even need Marlowe's play to give him his subject; he may, for example, have seen and remembered an old play entitled *The Jew* that was in vogue when he was still a boy and could well have been performed in the provinces. The play is now lost, but in 1579 a man who generally hated and attacked the theater, Stephen Gosson, went out of his way to praise *The Jew* for exposing "the greediness of worldly choosers" and the "bloody minds of usurers."

But something other than this old play or even Marlowe's newer one must serve to explain why Shakespeare's play turned out to be the pecu-liarly disturbing achievement that it is. The explanation does not lie in the plot, which is not original to Shakespeare and is highly conventional. At some point in his restless, voluminous reading, Shakespeare came across an Italian story about a Jewish usurer, Ser Giovanni's *Il Pecarone*, which must have struck him as good material for a comedy. (It is worth noting, in passing, that Shakespeare's reading, and indeed the entire Eliz-abethan book trade, was conspicuously international. The reading public, by modern standards, may have been fairly small, but its interests were strikingly cosmopolitan.) As he often did with texts he liked, Shake-speare lifted the plot wholesale from *Il Pecarone*: the merchant of Venice who borrows money for someone (here, not his friend but his "godson") from a Jewish moneylender; the terrible bond with its forfeit of a pound of the merchant's flesh; the successful wooing of a lady of "Belmonte" who comes to Venice disguised as a lawyer; her clever solution to the threat of the bond by pointing out that the legal right to take a pound of flesh does not include the legal right to take a drop of blood; the slightly nervous comic business of the rings. There was nothing original, then, in the shape of Shakespeare's play; even the Belmont plot of the caskets and the suitors, which did not come from Ser Giovanni, was lifted from else-where and thoroughly shopworn. There is exquisite poetry in the scene of Bassanio's successful wooing and, still more so, in the throwaway scene near the end of the play between Jessica and Lorenzo, sitting on the moonlit bank; there is a memorable depiction in Antonio of a state of depression, an unshakable melancholy that seems linked to his frustrated love for Bassanio. But the play would not count for much—it would seem roughly comparable to, say, *The Two Gentlemen of Verona* and other lesser efforts—were it not for the stupendous power of Shylock.

Shakespeare may have long had it in mind that he would write a play about a usurer. He may not have known any Jews, but he would certainly have known usurers, beginning with his own father, who had twice been accused of violating the law by charging usurious interest. The regula-tions against moneylending had been eased in 1591, and after he grew wealthy from the theater, Shakespeare himself seems to have been involved in at least one such transaction, either on his own or as a mid-dleman. A letter has survived by chance, in the archives of the Stratford Corporation, to Shakespeare from Richard Quiney, a prominent Stratford tradesman. Quiney's letter, dated October 25, 1598, was written from his inn in London, where he had evidently come in the hope of borrowing money for himself and another Stratford citizen, Abraham Sturley, from their "Loveing good ffrend & contreymann m^r w^m Shackespere." On the same day, Quiney wrote to Sturley with the terms of the proposed loan—a rate of thirty or forty shillings on a loan of thrity or forty pounds—and ten days later Sturley replied. He was pleased to hear "that our country-man Mr. Wm. Shak. would procure us money."

It is only the fact that Shakespeare wrote *The Merchant of Venice* that makes these transactions surprising. For though officially the English declared by statute that usury was illegal under the law of God and had driven out the only people who were exempt, by reason of being Jews, from this prohibition, the realm's mercantile economy could not function without the possibility of moneylending. In the absence of a banking sys-tem, in our sense of the term, the English tried at least to hold lending rates down to 10 percent, and many individuals devised clever means, legal and illegal, to get around the official constraints. Even John Shakespeare's robustly illegal dealings—interest rates of 20 and 25 percent—were fairly standard.

Christian usurers, even when they were not directly called by that name, occupied a position roughly comparable to the one held by the Jews: officially, they were despised, harassed, condemned from the pulpit and the stage, but they also played a key role, a role that could not be conveniently eliminated. It was possible for usurers to live more or less respectable lives, as Shakespeare's father did, but the deep contradiction between stigma and esteem, contempt and centrality, was probably always there in the shadows, ready to emerge. Shakespeare loved contradictions of this kind; his art greedily pounced upon them and played with them. But there is still the question of how he got to Shylock.

Something set Shakespeare's imagination on fire, something enabled him to discover in his stock villain a certain music—the sounds of a tense psychological inwardness, a soul under siege—that no one, not even Marlowe, had been able to call forth from the despised figure of the Jew. Very little is understood about the life experiences, either then or now, that make such creative leaps possible, but one can at least imagine a set of plausible triggering events in the everyday world Shakespeare inhabited.

Shakespeare was in London for at least part of 1594. In that year the bubonic plague, which had caused the theaters to be shut down for much of the season, abated enough to allow the players to perform once again in the city. The closing of the theaters had taken a severe toll on the playing companies. The Queen's Men were tottering; the Earl of Hertford's Men called it quits; the Earl of Pembroke's Men went bankrupt and had to sell their costumes; the Earl of Sussex's Men were forced to disband when their patron died; and the same fate befell the Earl of Derby's Men upon the mysterious death—by poison, it was rumored—of their patron, Ferdinando, Lord Strange. Out of this ruinous situation, two companies, absorbing the best talent, emerged to dominate the London theater scene: the Lord Admiral's Men, under the protection of Charles Howard, Lord Howard of Effingham, and the Lord Chamberlain's Men, under the protection of Howard's father-in-law, Henry Carey, Lord Hunsdon. The Lord Admiral's Men had, above all, the celebrated actor

Edward Alleyn and the great impresario Philip Henslowe; they performed south of the river, in the handsome Rose playhouse. The Lord Chamberlain's Men performed at Shoreditch, in Burbage's Theater. Their leading actor was Richard Burbage, and they picked up, from the ruins of the Earl of Derby's Men, the celebrated clown Will Kempe, along with John Heminges, Augustine Phillips, George Bryan, and Thomas Pope. All of these men, and one more besides, were "sharers"— that is, shareholders in the enterprise, managing affairs, bearing the costs, and splitting the profits. The additional sharer was William Shakespeare.

Shakespeare's company was poised to take advantage of the renewed opportunities, provided that the plague deaths did not once again soar. Mercifully, the death rates remained relatively low, and the populace could once again begin to look for amusements. London, however, was by no means completely calm: though the famous "Protestant wind" had scuttled the Spanish Armada in 1588, there were recurrent fears of invasion and constant rumors of plots against the life of Queen Elizabeth. The threat was real enough to be taken seriously by sober people; government spies, penetrating swirling, murky intrigues in embassies and at court, found ample reason to be jittery. One group, the fiercely anti-Spanish, militantly Protestant faction around the queen's ambitious favorite, the Earl of Essex, was particularly exercised about actual or potential plots. On January 21, 1594, the Essex faction got what it wanted: the queen's personal physician, Portuguese-born Roderigo (or Ruy) Lopez, was arrested on the charge that he was intriguing with the king of Spain, who had, according to intercepted letters, agreed to send him an enormous sum of money—50,000 crowns, equal to 18,800 pounds—to do some important service.

Essex had tried some years before to recruit Lopez as a secret agent. Lopez's refusal—he chose instead directly to inform the queen—may have been prudent, but it created in the powerful earl a very dangerous enemy. After his arrest, he was initially imprisoned at Essex House and interrogated by the earl himself. But Lopez had powerful allies in the rival faction of the queen's senior adviser William Cecil, Lord Burghley, and his son, Robert Cecil, who also participated in the interrogation and reported to the queen that the charges against her physician were baseless. According to court observers, Elizabeth gave Essex a tongue-lashing, "calling him *rash and temerarious youth*, to enter into a matter against the poor man, which he could not prove, and whose innocence she knew well enough; but malice against him, and no other, hatch'd all this matter, which displeas'd her much, and the more, for that, she said, her honor was interested herein." Now, of course, Essex's own honor was at stake, and he and his allies moved quickly to find evidence to substantiate their charges. The complex tangle of spies and sleazy informers and the laborious sifting of documents—what the rival Cecils grudgingly describe as "all the Confessions, Examinations, Depositions, Declarations, Messages, Letters, Tickets, Tokens, Conferences, Plots and Practices"—need not detain us. Suffice it to say that at the trial that took place in London on February 28, 1594, Dr. Ruy Lopez was charged and promptly convicted of conspiring to poison his royal patient. According to informers, Lopez had agreed to undertake the poisoning in exchange for 50,000 crowns to be paid by Philip II of Spain. Strangely enough, the supposed agent of this Catholic conspiracy, Lopez, was not a secret Catholic. He was—or rather, since he now professed to be a good Protestant, he had once been—a Jew. Many suspected, as Essex's ally Francis Bacon wrote, that he was still "in sect secretly a Jew (though here he conformed himself to the rites of Christian religion)."

It is difficult to say whether Lopez was actually guilty of high treason. Once the case came to trial, the result was almost a foregone conclusion, so there is no certainty to be drawn from the conviction. That it came to trial is testimony to the power of Essex, whose prestige was on the line, but it is also testimony to Lopez's taste for international and domestic intrigue, to his unsavory acquaintances, and to his venality—he was evidently taking bribes from many different sources. These qualities, however, only bear witness to the fact that the royal physician was a man of the court, with privileged access to the queen herself and therefore in a position to profit. He may have gone still further: after maintaining his innocence, he confessed, perhaps in earnest or perhaps only to avoid being tortured, that he had indeed entered into a treasonous-sounding negotiation with the king of Spain, but he insisted that he had done so only in order to cozen the king out of his money. Whatever else he was—scoundrel, confidence man, or traitor—Lopez was a pawn in tense factional rivalries of the kind that Elizabeth manipulated adroitly. As long as the Cecils saw fit to support him, in the hope that Essex would be embarrassed, the physician was safe; as soon as that support vanished—as soon as his dubious associations made him a liability—he was as good as dead.

In the prosecutor's summary, Roderigo Lopez was not only a greedy villain; he was, like the sly Jesuits he so much resembled, the sinister agent of wicked Catholic powers determined to destroy the Protestant queen. At the same time, he was a Jewish villain:

> Lopez, a perjured murdering traitor, and Jewish doctor, worse than Judas himself, undertook to poison her, which was a plot more wicked, dangerous, and detestable than all the former. He was Her Majesty's sworn servant, graced and advanced with many princely favors, used in special places of credit, permitted often access to her person, and so not suspected, especially by her, who never fears her enemies nor suspects her servants. The bargain was made, and the price agreed upon, and the fact only deferred until payment of the money was assured; the letters of credit for his assurance were sent, but before they came into his hands, God most wonderfully and miraculously revealed and prevented it.

Lopez was, by all accounts, a practicing Christian, an observant Protestant, thoroughly assimilated into high society, and the English generally contented themselves with outward religious conformity. But the particular profile of his wickedness—the greed, perfidiousness, secret malice, ingratitude, and murderousness—seemed to call for a special explanation, one that would also reinforce the sense that the queen had been miraculously saved by divine intervention. Traditional hatred of Jews and the particular topicality of Marlowe's *Jew of Malta* (whose antihero, one might recall, began his career as a doctor who poisoned his patients) gave Lopez's Jewish origins an important place in the narrative of his conspiracy.

Lopez and the two Portuguese agents who allegedly were his inter-mediaries were quickly convicted, but the queen unaccountably delayed the approval needed to carry out the death sentence, a delay that pro-voked what government officials described as "the general discontent of the people, who much expected this execution." Finally, on June 7, 1594, the people—or, in any case, the factions who were pressing for execu-tion—got what they wanted. Lopez and the others were taken from the Tower of London, where they had been held. Asked if he could declare any reason why the sentence should not be carried out, Lopez replied that he appealed to the queen's own knowledge and goodness. After legal formalities were concluded, the three prisoners were carried on a hurdle past jeering spectators to the execution ground at Tyburn, where a crowd was awaiting them.

Was William Shakespeare in this crowd? The trial of Lopez, with its factional infighting and lurid charges, had generated intense interest. Shakespeare, in any case, was interested in executions: his early farce, *The Comedy of Errors*, is structured around the countdown to an execution, and the executioner's ax casts a grim shadow across *Richard III* and other histories. He was fascinated professionally by the behavior of mobs and fascinated too by the comportment of men and women facing the end. His most famous lines on the subject come in *Macbeth*, in the description of the last moments in the life of a thane who had betrayed the king:

> Nothing in his life
> Became him like the leaving it. He died
> As one that had been studied in his death
> To throw away the dearest thing he owed
> As 'twere a careless trifle.
>
> (1.4.7–11)

It is reasonable to suppose that the dramatist who wrote those lines had wit-nessed executions for himself, events that occurred in the capital city with horrifying frequency. Indeed, the lines betray a certain connoisseurship.

The execution of Dr. Lopez was a public event. If Shakespeare did personally witness it, he would have seen and heard something beyond the ordinary, ghastly display of fear and ferocious cruelty. In the wake of his conviction, Lopez evidently had sunk into a deep depression, but on the scaffold he roused himself and declared, according to the Elizabethan historian William Camden, that "he loved the Queen as well as he loved Jesus Christ." "Which coming from a man of the Jewish profession," Camden adds, "moved no small Laughter in the Standers-by."

This laughter, welling up from the crowd at the foot of the scaffold, could well have triggered Shakespeare's achievement in *The Merchant of Venice*. It was, for a start, exceptionally cruel: in a matter of moments, a living man would be hanged and his body torn into pieces. The crowd's laughter denied the solemnity of the event and treated violent death as an occasion for amusement. More specifically, it denied Lopez the end he was attempting to make, an end in which he hoped to reassert his faith as the queen's loyal subject and as a Christian soul. The last words a person spoke were ordinarily charged with the presumption of absolute honesty: there was no longer any room for equivocation, no longer any hope of deferral, no longer any distance between the self and whatever judgment lies beyond the grave. This was, in the most literal sense, the moment of truth. Those who stood and laughed made it clear—clear to one another and clear to Lopez himself—that they did not believe him. "Coming from a man of the Jewish profession": Lopez did *not* profess Judaism; he publicly adhered to Protestantism and invoked Jesus Christ. The laughter turned Lopez's last words from a profession of faith into a sly joke, a carefully crafted double entendre: "he loved the Queen as well as he loved Jesus Christ." Precisely: since, in the eyes of the crowd, Lopez was a Jew and a Jew does not in fact love Jesus Christ, his real meaning was that he tried to do to the queen what his accursed race did to Jesus. His words took the form of a declaration of innocence, but the crowd's response turned them into an ambiguous admission of guilt. Some in the crowd could have thought that the admission was inadvertent, a hypocritical overreaching that had toppled unwittingly into confession. Others, still more amused, could have concluded that the ambiguity was deliberate. Lopez the Jew was practicing an art perfected, it was said, by the Jesuits: equivocation. He was trying to protect his family and reputation by fraudulently insisting on his innocence while at the same time subtly telling the truth.

These laughing spectators, in other words, thought they were watching a real-life version of *The Jew of Malta*.

Early in Marlowe's play, the villainous Jew persuades his daughter to pretend that she wishes to convert to Christianity and enter a nunnery. He tells her that "A counterfeit profession," that is, a falsely pretended belief, a mendacious performance, "is better / Than unseen hypocrisy" (1.2.292–93). On this dubious moral principle—that it is better deliberately to dissemble than to be an unconscious hypocrite—Barabas fashions his own performance, crafting a string of double entendres delivered with a wink or a sly aside to the audience. Plotting murder, he lures the governor's lovesick son Lodowick to his house by offering him a precious "diamond"—his daughter Abigail. When Lodowick, continuing the metaphor, asks, "And what's the price?" Barabas mutters as an aside, "Your life." "Come to my house," he adds aloud, "And I will giv't Your Honor"; then again, the murderous aside, "with a vengeance." To reassure his intended Christian victim, Barabas speaks of his "burning zeal" for the nunnery, and then adds, for the audience's amusement, "Hoping ere long to set the house afire!" (2.3.65–68, 88–89). That is precisely the kind of joke that the crowd thought it heard when Lopez made his last speech.

Lopez's execution was the last act of a comedy, or so the crowd's laughter, conditioned by *The Jew of Malta*, suggested. If it was cruel, it was also perfectly reasonable to laugh. A wicked plot to murder the queen—a plot that combined the hated figure of the Catholic king of Spain and the hated figure of the Jew—had been providentially thwarted. Was Shakespeare attracted or repelled by what went on at the foot of the scaffold? Did he admire the way Marlowe's dark comedy had helped to shape the crowd's response, or was he sickened by it? The only evidence is the play that Shakespeare wrote in the wake of Lopez's death, and the answer it suggests is that he was both intrigued and nauseated. He borrowed heavily from Marlowe—Shakespeare was always a great borrower—but he created a set of characters and a range of emotions utterly alien to Marlowe's art. He wanted, it seems, to excite laughter at a wicked Jew's discomfiture—not, to be sure, in a play about international intrigue, but in a play about money and love—and he wanted at the same time to call the laughter into question, to make the amusement excruciatingly uncomfortable.

The Merchant of Venice is full of amused mockery: "I never heard a passion so confused," chuckles one of the Venetian Christians, Solanio,

> So strange, outrageous, and so variable
> As the dog Jew did utter in the streets.
> "My daughter! O, my ducats! O, my daughter!
> Fled with a Christian! O, my Christian ducats!"
>   (2.8.12–16)

"Why, all the boys in Venice follow him," laughs his friend Salerio, giving us a glimpse of the crowd's raucous amusement, "Crying, 'His stones, his daughter, and his ducats!'" (2.8.23–24). And when Shylock's fiendish plot to avenge himself by cutting out a pound of good Antonio's flesh is defeated in court, the Jew's discomfiture, as he is forced to convert, is accompanied by a chorus of triumphant mockery from Graziano:

> Beg that thou mayst have leave to hang thyself—
>
> .   .   .   .
>
> A halter, gratis. Nothing else, for God's sake.
>
> .   .   .   .
>
> In christ'ning shalt thou have two godfathers.
> Had I been judge thou should have had ten more,
> To bring thee to the gallows, not the font.
>   (4.1.359–96)

Shakespeare chose not to bring his Jew to the gallows—in all of his comedies, he carefully avoided killing off his villains, at least onstage—but the mocking voices of Salerio, Solanio, and Graziano are very close to what the playwright would have heard at the foot of the scaffold on which Lopez was hanged. *The Merchant of Venice* found a way to give the spectators something of what the crowd at the execution enjoyed, but without the blood and gore. Shylock is the traditional killjoy of romantic comedy: deaf to music, the enemy of pleasure, he stands in the way of young love. But he is something worse than the conventional tyrannical, possessive father who must be defeated by budding youth. "Shylock the

Jew" is, as the title page of the first quarto puts it, a figure of "extreme cruelty," the rigid, inflexible representative of the Old Law, an unforgiving, remorseless, embittered, and murderous alien who threatens the happiness of the entire community. Defeated in court—not as a Jew but as a non-Venetian, an "alien"—Shylock is forcibly drawn into that community, but Graziano's mockery makes it clear that the newly christened convert will always be, as Camden said of the convert Lopez, "a man of the Jewish profession"; that is, Shylock's conversion is just comedy's kinder, gentler way of killing him off.

Yet the fact is that the mockers Salerio, Solanio, and Graziano are probably the least likable characters in *The Merchant of Venice*. They are not depicted as villainous, and their laughter echoes through the play, but their grating words are repeatedly registered as embarrassing, coarse, and unpleasant. "Thou art," as Bassanio tells Graziano, "too wild, too rude and bold of voice" (2.2.162). Shakespeare did not repudiate their raucous voices—the voices that he may have heard laughing at the Jew Lopez; on the contrary, he wanted his comedy to draw them into the celebration of Shylock's undoing. But the spirit of the play is not their spirit.

A comic playwright thrives on laughter, but it is as if Shakespeare had looked too closely at the faces of the crowd, as if he were repelled as well as fascinated by the mockery of the vanquished alien, as if he understood the mass appeal of the ancient game he was playing but suddenly felt queasy about the rules. "Imagine that you see the wretched strangers": When he had such strangers—Lopez or Shylock—fixed in his imagination, Shakespeare was uneasy with what he saw. Shylock's forced conversion—a plot device not found in Shakespeare's source—is an attempt to evade the nastier historical alternatives: the grisly execution Shakespeare may have personally witnessed; the mass expulsion of the Jews he could have read about in the chronicles of England. But as the laughter in the courtroom plainly demonstrates, conversion does not actually work to settle the issue of the stranger. Even Shylock's daughter Jessica, who has eloped and become a Christian of her own volition, is not exempt: the clown Lancelot grumbles that as a Jew's daughter she is damned, and, besides, "This making of Christians will raise the price of hogs" (3.5.19).

But rising pork prices are the least of the problems that the play explores. Shakespeare chose not to do to Shylock what the Elizabethan state did to Lopez, but he opted for anatomy of a different kind. Unsettling the whole comic structure that he borrowed from his Italian source, he took the risk of dissecting the interior of his villain and probing more deeply than he had ever done before. To be sure, Shylock at moments is something of a puppet, but, even jerked upon his strings, he reveals what Shakespeare has achieved. In one of the more rigidly mechanistic moments in the play, Shylock is pulled in radically different directions: he tries to track down his daughter Jessica, who has robbed him and eloped with the Christian Lorenzo; at the same time Shylock learns that the merchant Antonio, whom he hates and would like to destroy, is suffering serious business reverses. Salerio and Solanio have already mocked the Jew's frantic outcries—"'My daughter! O, my ducats! O, my daughter!'"—and now the comic spectacle itself takes place. Shylock impatiently asks for news—of all Shakespeare's characters, he is the most obsessed with news—from the fellow Jew he has sent to find his daughter.

> SHYLOCK: How now, Tubal? What news from Genoa? Hast thou found my daughter?
> TUBAL: I often came where I did hear of her, but cannot find her.
> SHYLOCK: Why, there, there, there, there.
>
> (3.1.67–71)

Repetition is one of the keys to Shylock's music. In sound and sense both, "there" seems to spring from Tubal's "where," yet it is not really about place, Genoa or anywhere else. It is the register of Shylock's disappointment, and it is an attempt at consolation, the "there, there" spoken by a friend. But a friend does not speak the words; they are spoken by Shylock himself, and their numb repetition moves beyond frustrated hope and failed consolation to something else. Repeated words of this kind are drained of whatever meaning they may have started with; they become instead placeholders for silent thinking.

How do characters in a play—who are, after all, only jumbles of words upon a page—convey that they have something going on inside them? How do spectators get the impression of depths comparable to those they can barely fathom and understand within themselves? Shakespeare, unrivaled at conveying this impression, in the course of his career developed many means for doing so, including most famously the soliloquy. But his mastery of the soliloquy was gradual, and, along the way, he explored other devices, including repetition. Shylock does not articulate a coherent response to the news that his daughter has not been found; he only mumbles the same, meaningless word. But some emotional and thought process is occurring beneath the surface—the repeated word functions precisely to create such a surface—and we begin to glimpse whatever it is in his next words: "A diamond gone." The diamond seems for an instant to refer to Jessica (Barabas refers to his daughter Abigail as a diamond), but the completion of the sentence wrenches us in a different direction: "A diamond gone cost me two thousand ducats in Frankfurt" (3.1.71–72).

At such a moment the audience has in effect seen something invisible: the grieving mind's queasy, unconscious shift from emotional to monetary loss. Or rather, it has glimpsed the secret passage that links the Jew's daughter and the Jew's ducats. For as the next lines make clear, Shakespeare implies that there is something Jewish, something specific to the Jewish "nation," in this confounding of the familial and the financial: "The curse never fell upon our nation till now—I never felt it till now. Two thousand ducats in that and other precious, precious jewels." What curse? For a moment, Shylock seems to accede fully to the Christian belief that the Jews are accursed, a terrible fate he has now for the first time directly experienced. And in his pain and rage he attempts to turn the curse upon his daughter:

> I would my daughter were dead at my foot and the jewels in her ear! I would she were hearsed at my foot and the ducats in her coffin! No news of them? Why, so. And I know not what's spent in the search. Why thou, loss upon loss: the thief gone with so much, and so much to find the thief, and no satisfaction, no revenge, nor

no ill luck stirring but what lights o' my shoulders, no sighs but o' my breathing, no tears but o' my shedding. (3.1.72–81)

Did Shakespeare know that Orthodox Jews customarily mourn, as if dead, children who have abandoned the faith? Perhaps. He surely believed that moneylenders, Jewish or not, treated money as if it were alive and could breed, and hence could treat lost money as if it were dead. Perhaps Shylock means to say that he would wish his daughter dead if only he could recover his money; perhaps that he wishes both the death of his daughter and the recovery of his money. But his words also express a morbid fantasy of giving daughter and money together a proper burial, "loss upon loss."

When Tubal contradicts Shylock's claim that he alone is suffering— "Yes, other men have ill luck too. Antonio, as I heard in Genoa"—Shylock interrupts excitedly, his manic, repetitive phrases now signaling not secret thoughts but excitement, surprise, and stabs of pain:

SHYLOCK: What, what, what? Ill luck, ill luck?
TUBAL: Hath an argosy cast away coming from Tripolis.
SHYLOCK: I thank God, I thank God! Is it true, is it true?
TUBAL: I spoke with some of the sailors that escaped the wreck.
SHYLOCK: I thank thee, good Tubal. Good news, good news! Ha, ha—heard in Genoa?
TUBAL: Your daughter spent in Genoa, as I heard, one night fourscore ducats.
SHYLOCK: Thou stick'st a dagger in me. I shall never see my gold again. Fourscore ducats at a sitting? Fourscore ducats?
TUBAL: There came divers of Antonio's creditors in my company to Venice that swear he cannot choose but break.
SHYLOCK: I am very glad of it. I'll plague him, I'll torture him. I am glad of it.

(3.1.82–97)

This is the stuff of comedy, and it is certainly possible to play the scene for laughs, but the rising tide of anguish stifles the laughter, even as it forms. The audience is brought in too close for psychological comfort to the suffering figure. Spattered by Shylock's exclamations, it cannot get to the distance appropriate for detached amusement.

It is possible that Shakespeare lost control of his own imagination here. Apart from "Hand D" of *Sir Thomas More,* no manuscript record of his writing process survives, but in an anecdote that circulated in the seventeenth century, he is said to have remarked of *Romeo and Juliet* that he had in the third act to kill Mercutio—the wildly anarchic mocker of romantic love—before Mercutio killed him. Perhaps something of the same kind began to happen with *The Merchant of Venice;* perhaps Shylock refused to keep his place in the imaginative scheme that had consigned him to the role of comic villain. But Shylock is more central than Mercutio, and there is too much evidence of authorial craft to be comfortable with the notion that the character simply escaped the playwright's control. Shakespeare could easily have ended the scene between Shylock and Tubal at the point at which the comic spirit makes a strong bid to reassert itself. But instead Tubal continues his report:

> TUBAL: One of them showed me a ring that he had of your daughter
> for a monkey.
> SHYLOCK: Out upon her! Thou torturest me, Tubal. It was my
> turquoise. I had it of Leah when I was a bachelor. I would not
> have given it for a wilderness of monkeys.
> TUBAL: But Antonio is certainly undone.
> SHYLOCK: Nay, that's true, that's very true. Go, Tubal, fee me an
> officer. Bespeak him a fortnight before. I will have the heart of
> him if he forfeit, for were he out of Venice I can make what mer-
> chandise I will. Go, Tubal, and meet me at our synagogue. Go,
> good Tubal; at our synagogue, Tubal.
>
> (3.1.98–108)

The words about Jessica's extravagance seem for a moment simply to continue Shylock's fretting about his lost jewels, but suddenly the pain deepens and the laughter dries up. It is as if the ring were something more than a piece of the Jew's wealth, as if it were a piece of his heart.

The Merchant of Venice is a play in which material objects are strangely charged or animated. There is the "Jewish gaberdine" on which Antonio spits (1.3.108); the "vile squealing of the wry-necked fife" that Shylock cannot abide and against which he hopes to "stop my house's ears—I mean my casements" (2.5.29, 33); the "merry bond" whose physical existence directly threatens Antonio's life (1.3.169). At first glance this animation might seem solely the malign effect of the Jewish moneylender, who makes barren metal "breed" (1.3.92, 129), but the Christians turn out to be equally involved. Salerio and Solanio imagine

> dangerous rocks
> Which, touching but my gentle vessel's side,
> Would scatter all her spices on the stream.
> (1.1.31–33)

The suitors who seek Portia's hand in marriage discover their fate by unlocking one of three metal "caskets" that contain emblematic pictures, while the whole last act plays with the symbolic power of rings. But no object has greater power than that turquoise, linked to the name of Shylock's dead wife and glimpsed for a brief moment of anguish. Shylock immediately turns to plotting against Antonio—"I will have the heart of him if he forfeit, for were he out of Venice I can make what merchandise I will"—but what he has just said about the ring anticipates what the courtroom scene definitively discloses: revenge, not money, is what Shylock is after.

Does this mean that Shakespeare thought that Dr. Lopez—who received a valuable ring, sent to him by the king of Spain, that figured in his trial and that the queen kept after his execution—was after something other than money when he allegedly plotted to kill the queen for 50,000 crowns? There is no way to know. *The Merchant of Venice* is not a commentary on a case of treason; it is a romantic comedy with a villainous usurer whose principal resemblances to Lopez are his alien status and the

Jewishness that Lopez himself denied. The key link, apart from a general public excitement that may have helped box-office receipts, is the crowd's laughter, laughter that Shakespeare at once sought to capture and to unsettle. The crowd laughed because it thought it was in on a sly, Marlovian joke: "he loved the Queen as well as he loved Jesus Christ." This was, or so they understood, the confession of a would-be murderer, a man for whom the word "love" actually meant "hate."

Though he was in the business of amusing a popular audience, Shakespeare was clearly not altogether comfortable with this laughter. The play that he wrote at once borrows from *The Jew of Malta* and repudiates its corrosive, merciless irony. Whatever else I am, the playwright seems to be saying, I am not laughing at the foot of the scaffold, and I am not Marlowe. What sprang up in place of Marlovian irony was not tolerance—the play, after all, stages a forced conversion as the price of a pardon—but rather shoots of a strange, irrepressible imaginative generosity. This generosity makes theatrical trouble; it prevents any straightforward amusement at Shylock's confusion of his daughter and his ducats, and, what is more disturbing, it undermines the climactic trial scene. That scene is the comedy's equivalent of the real-world execution: it is meant to reach satisfying legal and moral closure, to punish villainy, and to affirm central values of the dominant culture. All of the elements seem to be in place: a wise duke, an implacable Jewish villain sharpening his knife for slaughter, a supremely eloquent appeal for mercy, a thrilling resolution. Yet this scene, as the experience of both the page and the stage repeatedly demonstrates, is deeply unsettled and unsettling. The resolution depends upon the manipulation of a legal technicality, the appeal for mercy gives way to the staccato imposition of punishments, and the affirmation of values is swamped by a flood of mingled self-righteousness and vindictiveness. Above all, without mitigating Shylock's vicious nature, without denying the need to thwart his murderous intentions, the play has given us too much insight into his inner life, too much of a stake in his identity and his fate, to enable us to laugh freely and without pain. For Shakespeare did something that Marlowe never chose to do and that the mocking crowd at Lopez's execution could not do; he wrote out what he imagined such a twisted man, about to be destroyed, would inwardly say:

I am a Jew. Hath not a Jew eyes? Hath not a Jew hands, organs, dimensions, senses, affections, passions; fed with the same food, hurt with the same weapons, subject to the same diseases, healed by the same means, warmed and cooled by the same winter and summer as a Christian is? If you prick us do we not bleed? If you tickle us do we not laugh? If you poison us do we not die? And if you wrong us shall we not revenge? (3.1.49–56)

CHAPTER 10

Speaking with the Dead

S OMETIME IN THE SPRING or summer of 1596 Shakespeare may have received word that his only son, Hamnet, eleven years old, was ill. It is possible he understood and responded at once, or he may have been distracted by affairs in London. There was much to preoccupy him. On July 22 the lord chamberlain, Henry Carey, the queen's powerful cousin and the patron of Shakespeare's company, died. The lord chamberlainship went to Lord Cobham, but the players were kept by Carey's son George, Lord Hunsdon. (When Cobham died within less than a year, the post of lord chamberlain went to George Carey, so that the company, after only a brief interval of being known as the Lord Hunsdon's Men, once again became the Lord Chamberlain's Men.) The death of their patron and the flurry of uncertainty must have been disconcerting for the players, and their disquiet was no doubt intensified by renewed calls by preachers and civic officials for the closing of the theaters in order to protect London's moral and physical health. Performances were banned in all city inns, and it is possible that during the summer of 1596 the city authorities managed to obtain an order temporarily closing down all the playhouses. Such a closure—known as an inhibition—would help to explain why some members of Shakespeare's company were on the road that summer, performing at Faversham (in Kent) and other places.

Shakespeare may have accompanied his fellow actors on tour, or he may well have stayed back in London to work on one or another of the plays he must have been writing for the company at this time: *King John*, *1 Henry IV*, or *The Merchant of Venice*. Whether in London or on tour he would at best have only been able to receive news intermittently from Stratford, but at some point in the summer he must have learned that Hamnet's condition had worsened and that it was necessary to drop everything and hurry home. By the time he reached Stratford the eleven-year-old boy—whom, apart from brief returns, Shakespeare had in effect abandoned in his infancy—may already have died. On August 11, the father presumably saw his son buried at Holy Trinity Church: the clerk duly noted in the burial register, "Hamnet filius William Shakspere."

Unlike Ben Jonson and others who wrote grief-stricken poems about the loss of beloved children, Shakespeare published no elegies and left no direct record of his paternal feelings. The whole enterprise of acquiring the coat of arms must at one point have had something to do with his expectations for his son and heir, and Shakespeare's last will and testament displays a strong interest in passing along his property to his male descendants; but these are signs too formal and conventional perhaps to tell us about his inward state. It is sometimes said that parents in Shakespeare's time could not afford to invest too much love and hope in any one child. One out of three children died by the age of ten, and overall mortality rates were by our standards exceedingly high.

Death was a familiar spectacle; it took place at home, not out of sight. When Shakespeare was fifteen, his nine-year-old sister Anne died, and there must have been many other occasions for him to witness the death of children. But did familiarity breed detachment? The private diary of a contemporary doctor, recently deciphered, shows that desperate spouses and parents, inconsolable with grief, were constantly coming to him for treatment. Human emotions are not rationally coordinated with actuarial figures. Some Elizabethan parents may have learned to withhold affection or to protect themselves from misery, but by no means all did.

In the four years following Hamnet's death, the playwright, as many have pointed out, wrote some of his sunniest comedies: *The Merry Wives of Windsor, Much Ado About Nothing, As You Like It.* But the plays of these years were by no means uniformly cheerful, and at moments they seem to reflect an experience of deep personal loss. In *King John,* probably written in 1596, just after the boy was laid to rest, Shakespeare depicted a mother so frantic at the loss of her son that she is driven to thoughts of suicide. Observing her, a clerical bystander remarks that she is mad, but she insists that she is perfectly sane: "I am not mad; I would to God I were" (3.4.48). Reason, she says, and not madness, has put the thoughts of suicide in her head, for it is her reason that tenaciously keeps hold of the image of her child. When she is accused of perversely insisting on her grief, she replies with an eloquent simplicity that breaks free from the tangled plot:

> Grief fills the room up of my absent child,
> Lies in his bed, walks up and down with me,
> Puts on his pretty looks, repeats his words,
> Remembers me of all his gracious parts,
> Stuffs out his vacant garments with his form.
>   (3.4.93–97)

If there is no secure link between these lines and the death of Hamnet, there is, at the very least, no reason to think that Shakespeare simply buried his son and moved on unscathed. He might have brooded inwardly and obsessively, even as he was making audiences laugh at Falstaff in love or at the wit contests of Beatrice and Benedick. Nor is it implausible that it took years for the trauma of his son's death fully to erupt in Shakespeare's work.

In a very late play, there may be a trace of Shakespeare's periodic visits to Stratford at the time when his son was still alive. "Are you so fond of your young prince as we / Do seem to be of ours?" one friend asks another. "If at home, sir," is the reply,

> He's all my exercise, my mirth, my matter;
> Now my sword friend, and then mine enemy;
> My parasite, my soldier, statesman, all.

He makes a July's day short as December,
And with his varying childness cures in me
Thoughts that would thick my blood.
                                        (1.2.165–72)

"If at home, sir": the words fit the play, but they also fit the playwright. Perhaps, reflecting upon what might have kept thick blood, that
is, melancholy, at bay, Shakespeare found himself thinking back to his
son. The play in which these lines appear, *The Winter's Tale*, features a
precocious little boy who languishes and dies when his madly jealous
father turns against his mother.

Whether in the wake of Hamnet's death Shakespeare was suicidal or
serene, he threw himself into his work. The later 1590s was an amazingly
busy and productive period in his life, with a succession of brilliant plays,
frequent performances at court and in the public theaters, and growing
celebrity and wealth. As a sharer in his company, Shakespeare was probably directly involved in all aspects of its daily affairs, including the
increasingly acrimonious conflict with Giles Allen, the owner of the land
in Shoreditch on which the Theater, where the Lord Chamberlain's Men
chiefly performed, had been built. The lease that James Burbage and his
partner had taken back in 1576 was about to expire, and Allen refused to
renew it, at least on terms that Burbage's sons, who had taken over the
protracted negotiation upon the death of their father, could accept.

Finally, the talks broke off, and the Theater was closed. In some desperation, the company began to perform at the nearby Curtain, but the
venue was not nearly so successful, and revenues evidently began to fall
off. To raise money, they did something that playing companies generally
resisted: they sold off four of their most popular playbooks, *Richard III,
Richard II, 1 Henry IV,* and *Love's Labour's Lost,* to an enterprising publisher who brought them out in quarto editions. No doubt the ready cash
was of some help, but it must have seemed less like a solution than an
ominous step in a direction that would eventually lead to selling off their
costumes and disbanding altogether.

The real solution was a daring one. On the snowy night of December 28, 1598, in a season cold enough to make the Thames freeze over,

the players came together in Shoreditch. They carried lanterns and bore arms—in the words of one deposition, "swords, daggers, bills, axes and such like." The small company, aided perhaps by a few hired thugs, may not immediately strike one as a formidable force, but as actors were all trained in wielding weapons and as London had no regular police force, they were adequate for the enterprise. They posted guards around the perimeter, and then together with a dozen workmen, they proceeded to dismantle the Theater. In the morning light they loaded the heavy timbers on wagons and began the work of carting them across the river to a site they had secured not far from the Rose Theatre, in Southwark. The landlord, Allen, was apoplectic and sued for trespass, but the legal situation was a complex one, for the Burbages' lease stipulated a right to retrieve any structures they had built on Allen's land. The deed, in any event, was done, though it is difficult to understand how it was accomplished in a single night in the darkness.

Over the next months the gifted carpenter Peter Streete cleverly recycled the pieces of the old playhouse and fashioned a splendid new theater. A many-sided wooden polygon, roughly one hundred feet across, with a huge platform stage jutting into the pit and three galleries, it could hold over three thousand spectators, an astonishing figure for a city London's size and a tribute to the actors' immense power to project complex words and emotions. (Today's Globe, on the Bankside, has about half the capacity.) A small group of investors, Shakespeare among them, had financed the ambitious enterprise. For their motto they chose the phrase *Totus mundus agit histroniem,* roughly, "The whole world plays the actor," and for their sign they apparently had an image of Hercules bearing the world on his shoulders. They called their new playhouse the Globe.

By virtue of his investment, Shakespeare was now more than a sharer in the playing company. By the terms of the contract signed on February 21, 1599, he owned a tenth of the Globe, as did four of his fellow actors, John Heminges, Thomas Pope, Augustine Phillips, and Will Kempe. Kempe, the company's popular clown, famous for his antic dancing and his obscene songs, had an immediate falling-out with his partners; he sold his share and went off, making a sour joke about those he called

"Shakerags." The company was temporarily without a clown—it took some time to find the subtle, dwarfish Robert Armin—and Shakespeare's next play, *Julius Caesar,* was notably without a juicy part for a fool.

Shakespeare moved to Southwark, to be near the Globe, which was ready by June, a stunningly rapid turnaround. One might have expected them to open with a light crowd-pleaser, but the Lord Chamberlain's Men chose to inaugurate their new theater with *Julius Caesar,* a tragedy apt for a public still intensely anxious about the threat of an assassination attempt against their queen. A Swiss tourist to London, Thomas Platter, went to see it and wrote home one of the few contemporary eyewitness accounts of a Shakespeare performance: "On the 21st of September after lunch, about two o'clock, I crossed the water with my party, and we saw the tragedy of the first emperor Julius Caesar acted very prettily in the house with the thatched roof, with about fifteen characters." At the play's end, Platter notes, "according to their custom, they danced with exceeding elegance, two each in men's and two in women's clothes, wonderfully together." With *Julius Caesar* and the other strong plays in the company's repertoire, the Globe was launched, so successfully indeed that in six months' time their rivals at the nearby Rose Theatre packed up and headed across the river, to a new theater in Cripplegate, called the Fortune.

Driving the competition out of the immediate neighborhood did not mean an end to commercial competition altogether. On the contrary, by the end of 1599, the Lord Chamberlain's Men were engaged in an increasingly intense theatrical struggle with a newly revived private company, the Children of Paul's, followed the next year by another repertory company, the Children of the Chapel at Blackfriars. The fact that the players were boys did not lessen the seriousness of their challenge: these were sophisticated, sharp-witted, highly accomplished companies with a very strong audience appeal. In his next play Shakespeare provided a glimpse of the competition. Why has the company of players come all the way to Elsinore, Hamlet asks; surely their reputation and profit were both greater in the city. Rosencrantz explains that their audience has drastically fallen off: "there is, sir, an eyrie of children, little eyases," that is, young hawks; "These are now the fashion" (2.2.326, 328). When he sat down to write *Hamlet*, Shakespeare was looking over his shoulder at the children's companies and pretending to worry—not altogether comically—that they would put his troupe out of business.

Writing a play about Hamlet, in or around 1600, may not have been Shakespeare's own idea. At least one play, now lost, about the Danish prince who avenges his father's murder had already been performed on the English stage, successfully enough to be casually alluded to by contemporary writers, as if everyone had seen it or at least knew about it. Back in 1589 it was a play on Hamlet that figured in Nashe's ridicule of the rude upstart (probably Thomas Kyd) who never attended university but still had the impudence to set himself up as a playwright: "if you entreat him fair in a frosty morning, he will afford you whole *Hamlets*, I should say handfuls of tragical speeches." And seven years later another one of the university wits, Thomas Lodge, echoed the mocking tone when he referred to a devil who looked "as pale as the Vizard of the ghost which cried so miserably at the Theatre, like an oyster-wife, 'Hamlet, revenge!'" Either the play was still onstage—an exceptionally long run in the Elizabethan theater—or it had been recently revived, or it had simply become proverbial for somewhat vulgar theatrical intensity. Lodge and Nashe thought that their readers would effortlessly conjure up the story.

Someone in the Lord Chamberlain's Men, with an eye on revenues, may simply have suggested to Shakespeare that the time might be ripe for a new, improved version of Hamlet. For that matter, with his high stakes in the company's profits, Shakespeare was singularly alert to whatever attracted London crowds, and he had by now long experience in dusting off old plays and making them startlingly new. The likely author of the earlier play, Thomas Kyd, was no obstacle: possibly broken by the torture inflicted upon him when he was interrogated about his roommate Marlowe, he had died back in 1594, at the age of thirty-six. In any case, neither Shakespeare nor his contemporaries were squeamish about stealing from one another.

Shakespeare had certainly seen the earlier Hamlet play, probably on several occasions. He may well have acted in it, in which case he would have had in his possession the roll of paper strips, glued together, on which his part and the cues for his entries and exits were written. Elizabethan actors generally had access only to their particular roll—from whence we get the term "role"—and not to the script as a whole; it was too expensive to copy it out in its entirety, and the playing companies were wary about allowing their scripts to circulate widely. They might on special occasions make copies for favored patrons, and in times of financial necessity they would sometimes sell plays to printers. But they wanted the public principally to encounter plays in the playhouse, not in the study. (Of course, keeping the scripts out of print greatly increased the likelihood that they would eventually be lost—as the early version of Hamlet and many others were—but that was no concern of the companies.)

Whether or not he had access to the script of the Hamlet play, Shakespeare had to an astounding degree something that virtually every actor at the time had to possess: an acute memory. Everything he encountered, even tangentially and in passing, seems to have stayed with him and remained available to him years later. Scraps of conversation, official proclamations, long-winded sermons, remarks overheard in the tavern or on the street, insults exchanged by carters and fishwives, a few pages that he could only have glanced at idly in a bookseller's shop—all was somehow stored away in his brain, in files that his imagination could open up at will. His memory was not perfect—he made mistakes, confused one place for another, transposed names, and the like—but the imperfections only demonstrate that there was nothing compulsive or mechanical about his remarkable gift. His memory was an immense creative resource.

When he set to work on his new tragedy, then, Shakespeare likely had the old play about Hamlet by heart, or as much of it as he chose to remember. It is impossible to determine, in this case, whether he sat down with books open before him—as he clearly did, for example, when writing *Antony and Cleopatra*—or relied on his memory, but he had also certainly read one and probably more than one version of the old Danish tale of murder and revenge. At the very least, judging from the play he wrote, he carefully read the story as narrated in French by François de Belleforest, whose collection of tragic tales was a publishing phenomenon in the late sixteenth century. (It went through at least ten editions.) Belleforest had taken the Hamlet story from a chronicle of Denmark compiled in Latin in the late twelfth century by a Dane known as Saxo the Grammarian. And Saxo in turn was recycling written and oral legends that reached back for centuries before him. Here then, as so often throughout his career, Shakespeare was working with known materials— a well-established story, a familiar cast of characters, a set of predictable excitements.

Shakespeare was himself a known quantity. It would have been reasonable for anyone who had followed his career to conclude by 1600 that he had already fully mapped the capacious boundaries of his imaginative kingdom. It must have seemed likely that he would continue as a professional playwright to repeat in imaginative ways what he had already brilliantly accomplished, but it would have seemed scarcely probable that he could find new continents to explore. No one, probably not Shakespeare himself, could have predicted that something astonishing was about to happen.

Though he was still young (only thirty-six years old), he had in the course of a decade achieved extraordinary things in three major genres— comedy, history, and tragedy—with plays that are each in their way so perfect that it would have been difficult to imagine going beyond them. Indeed, in the years that followed he made no attempt to surpass the two parts of *Henry IV* and *Henry V*, as if he understood that he had done what he was capable of doing in the history play. And though he shortly was to write the stupendous *Twelfth Night*, he did not in the genre of comedy actually go beyond what he had created in *A Midsummer Night's Dream*, *Much Ado About Nothing*, and *As You Like It*. *Hamlet* turned out to inaugurate a creative frenzy that also brought forth *Othello, King Lear, Macbeth, Antony and Cleopatra*, and *Coriolanus*, but a well-informed contemporary theatergoer in 1600 had no reason to expect that Shakespeare had not already demonstrated what he could do in tragedy as well. Among the more than twenty plays he had written were *Titus Andronicus, Romeo and Juliet,* and *Julius Caesar*. Indeed, these were not his only tragedies; three of the plays that modern editors (following the editors of the first folio) now classify as histories—the third part of *Henry VI, Richard III,* and *Richard II*—were published during his lifetime as tragedies.

The distinction between tragedy and history was not an important one for Shakespeare, or indeed for many of his playwriting contemporaries: the underlying structure of most of human history, with its endless pattern of rise and fall, seemed to him tragic, and conversely tragedy as he conceived it was rooted in history. For that matter, as *The Merchant of Venice* amply shows, his sense of comedy was laced through with pain, loss, and the threat of death, and his sense of tragedy had room for clowning and laughter. Literary theorists of the time urged strict adherence to the rules of decorum that derived from Aristotle: they vehemently opposed what Sir Philip Sidney called the mingling of kings and clowns. Writing in 1579, when Shakespeare was still a schoolboy, Sidney wrote a mocking description of a typical English play, with its loose, wildly free-form plot. The description, meant to make readers groan, turns out to anticipate precisely what Shakespeare would do brilliantly throughout his career. At one moment, Sidney snorted in derision, three ladies walk across the stage, and you are supposed to imagine them gathering flowers; by and by four actors appear with swords and bucklers, and you are expected to see the clash of two great armies; then comes news of a shipwreck, and you are to blame if you do not take the stage for a perilous rock. "You shall have Asia of one side, and Afric of the other, and so many other under-kingdoms, that the player, when he cometh in, must ever begin with telling where he is, or else the tale will not be conceived."

What Sidney and others wanted was something altogether more orderly. The stage, they argued, should always represent but one place; the time represented should at most be a single day; and exalted emotions aroused by tragedy should never be tainted with the "scornful tickling" and lewd laughter of comedy. These are strictures, derived from Aristotle, that Shakespeare, along with his fellow professional playwrights, routinely violated.

The indifference to the boundaries that obsessed learned critics in England and on the Continent helps to explain something baffling about Shakespeare's whole career, and particularly about its first decade: the absence of any clear or logical pattern of artistic development. Editions of the collected works that organize them neatly into groups—first the comedies one after another, followed by the histories, the tragedies, and finally the romances—completely misrepresent what actually happened. Attempts to organize the works according to an orderly progression of Shakespeare's soul—from lighthearted youth to a serious engagement with power to a melancholy brooding about mortality and finally to the wise serenity of old age—are similarly misleading. This is someone who had *A Midsummer Night's Dream* and *Romeo and Juliet* on his desk (and in his imagination) at the same moment, and who perceived that the joyous laughter of the one could be almost effortlessly transformed into the tears of the other. This is someone who climaxes his witty, lighthearted comedy of upper-class courtship, *Love's Labour's Lost*, with news that the princess's father has suddenly died, so that all the impending marriages must be put on hold. This is someone who gets his audience to laugh at the ghastly Richard III assessing the team of murderers he has hired to kill his brother:

> Your eyes drop millstones when fools' eyes fall tears.
> I like you, lads.
>
> (1.3.351–2)

And finally, this is someone who in successive plays written in the years directly before *Hamlet* shifted ground from the civil wars of late medieval England to the Sicilian courtship of Beatrice and Benedick to the battle of Agincourt to the assassination of Julius Caesar to a pastoral romance in the Forest of Arden. Each of these plays has its own distinct vision, and yet, strangely, each also has room for what it would at first glance seem to exclude.

IF SHAKESPEARE HAD DIED in 1600, it would have been difficult to think that anything was missing from his achievement and still more difficult to think that anything yet unrealized was brewing in his work. But *Hamlet* makes clear that Shakespeare had been quietly, steadily developing a special technical skill. This development may have been entirely deliberate, the consequence of a clear, ongoing professional design, or it may have been more haphazard and opportunistic. The achievement was, in any case, gradual: not a sudden, definitive discovery or a grandiose invention, but the subtle refinement of a particular set of representational techniques. By the turn of the century Shakespeare was poised to make an epochal breakthrough. He had perfected the means to represent inwardness.

What the audience sees and hears is always in some sense or other public utterance—the words that the characters say to one another or, in occasional asides and soliloquies, directly to the onlookers. Playwrights can pretend, of course, that the audience is overhearing a kind of internal monologue, but it is difficult to keep such monologues from sounding stagy. *Richard III*, written around 1592, is hugely energetic and powerful, with a marvelous, unforgettable main character, but when that character, alone at night, reveals what is going on inside of him, he sounds oddly wooden and artificial:

> It is now dead midnight.
> Cold fearful drops stand on my trembling flesh.
> What do I fear? Myself? There's none else by.
> Richard loves Richard; that is, I am I.
> Is there a murderer here? No. Yes, I am.
> Then fly! What, from myself? Great reason. Why?
> Lest I revenge. Myself upon myself?
> Alack, I love myself. Wherefore? For any good
> That I myself have done unto myself?
> O no, alas, I rather hate myself
> For hateful deeds committed by myself.
> I am a villain. Yet I lie: I am not.
>
> (5.5.134–45)

Shakespeare is following his chronicle source, which states that Richard could not sleep on the eve of his death, because he felt unwonted pricks of conscience. But though it has a staccato vigor, the soliloquy, as a way of sketching inner conflict, is schematic and mechanical, as if within the character onstage there was simply another tiny stage on which puppets were performing a Punch-and-Judy show.

In *Richard II,* written some three years later, there is a comparable moment that marks Shakespeare's burgeoning skills. Deposed and imprisoned by his cousin Bolingbroke, the ruined king, shortly before his murder, looks within himself:

> I have been studying how I may compare
> This prison where I live unto the world;
> And for because the world is populous,
> And here is not a creature but myself,
> I cannot do it. Yet I'll hammer it out.
> My brain I'll prove the female to my soul,
> My soul the father, and these two beget
> A generation of still-breeding thoughts.
>   (5.5.1–8)

Much of the difference between the two passages has to do with the very different characters: the one a murderous tyrant full of manic energy, the other a spoiled, narcissistic, self-destructive poet. But the turn from one character to the other is itself significant; it signals Shakespeare's growing interest in the hidden processes of interiority. Locked in a window-less room, Richard II watches himself think, struggling to forge a metaphoric link between his prison and the world, reaching a dead end, and then forcing his imagination to renew the effort: "Yet I'll hammer it out." The world, crowded with people, is not, as he himself recognizes, remotely comparable to the solitude of his prison cell, but Richard wills himself to generate—out of what he pictures as the intercourse of his brain and soul—an imaginary populace. What he hammers out is a kind of inner theater, akin to that already found in Richard III's soliloquy but with a vastly increased complexity, subtlety, and, above all, self-consciousness. Now the character himself is fully aware that he has constructed such a theater, and he teases out the bleak implications of the imaginary world he has struggled to create:

> Thus play I in one person many people,
> And none contented. Sometimes am I king;

Then treason makes me wish myself a beggar,
And so I am. Then crushing penury
Persuades me I was better when a king.
Then am I kinged again, and by and by
Think that I am unkinged by Bolingbroke,
And straight am nothing. But whate'er I be,
Nor I, nor any man that but man is,
With nothing shall be pleased till he be eased
With being nothing.

                                    (5.5.31–41)

Richard II characteristically rehearses the drama of his fall from kingship as a fall into nothingness and then fashions his experience of lost identity—"whate'er I be"—into an intricate poem of despair.

Written in 1595, *Richard II* marked a major advance in the playwright's ability to represent inwardness, but *Julius Caesar*, written four years later, shows that, not content with what he had mastered, Shakespeare subtly experimented with new techniques. Alone, pacing in his orchard in the middle of night, Brutus begins to speak:

It must be by his death. And for my part
I know no personal cause to spurn at him,
But for the general. He would be crowned.
How that might change his nature, there's the question.
It is the bright day that brings forth the adder,
And that craves wary walking. Crown him: that!

                                    (2.1.10–15)

This soliloquy is far less fluid, less an elegant and self-conscious poetic meditation, than the prison soliloquy of Richard II. But it has something new: the unmistakable marks of actual thinking. Richard speaks of hammering it out, but the words he utters are already highly polished. Brutus's words by contrast seem to flow immediately from the still inchoate to-ing and fro-ing of his wavering mind, as he grapples with a set of momentous questions: How should he respond to the crowd's desire to crown the ambitious Caesar? How can he balance his own personal friendship with Caesar against what he construes to be the general good? How might Caesar, who has thus far served that general good, change his nature and turn dangerous if he is crowned? "It must be by his death"— without prelude, the audience is launched into the midst of Brutus's obsessive brooding. It is impossible to know if he is weighing a proposition, trying out a decision, reiterating words that someone else has spoken. He does not need to mention whose death he is contemplating, nor does he need to make clear—for it is already part of his thought—that it will be by assassination.

Brutus is speaking to himself, and his words have the peculiar shorthand of the brain at work. "Crown him: that!"—the exclamation is barely comprehensible, except as a burst of anger provoked by a phantasmic image passing at that instant through the speaker's mind. The spectators are pulled in eerily close, watching firsthand the forming of a fatal resolution—a determination to assassinate Caesar—that will change the world. A few moments later, Brutus, intensely self-aware, describes for himself the molten state of consciousness in which he finds himself:

> Between the acting of a dreadful thing
> And the first motion, all the interim is
> Like a phantasma or a hideous dream.
> The genius and the mortal instruments
> Are then in counsel, and the state of man,
> Like to a little kingdom, suffers then
> The nature of an insurrection.
> (2.1.63–69)

Was it at this moment, in 1599, that Shakespeare first conceived of the possibility of writing about a character suspended, for virtually the whole length of a play, in this strange interim? Brutus himself is not such a character; by the middle of *Julius Caesar*, he has done the dreadful thing, the killing of his mentor and friend—possibly his own father— and the remainder of the play teases out the fatal consequences of his act.

If Shakespeare did not grasp it at once, then certainly by the follow-

ing year he understood perfectly that there was a character, already popular on the Elizabethan stage, whose life he could depict as one long
phantasma or hideous dream. That character, the prince of the inward
insurrection, was Hamlet.

Even in its earliest known medieval telling, Hamlet's saga was the
story of the long interval between the first motion—the initial impulse or
design—and the acting of the dreadful thing. In Saxo the Grammarian's
account, King Horwendil (the equivalent of Shakespeare's old King
Hamlet) is killed by his envious brother Feng (the equivalent of
Claudius) not secretly but in plain view. The brother has a thin cover
story—he says that Horwendil had been brutally abusing his gentle wife,
Gerutha—but the reality is that the ruthless Feng is powerful enough to
seize his brother's crown, his realm, and his wife and get away with it.
The only potential obstacle is Horwendil's young son Amleth, for everyone in this pre-Christian world of treachery and vengeance understood
that a son must avenge his father's murder. Amleth is still a child and no
danger to anyone, but when he grows up, his obligation will be clear. The
murderous Feng understands this strict social code as well, of course, and,
if the boy does not quickly come up with a stratagem, his life is worth
nothing. In order to survive long enough to take his just revenge, Amleth
feigns madness, persuading his uncle that he cannot ever pose a threat.
Flinging dirt and slime on himself, he sits by the fire, listlessly whittling
away at small sticks and turning them into barbed hooks. Though the
wary Feng repeatedly sets traps to try to discern some hidden sparks of
intelligence behind his nephew's apparent idiocy, Amleth cunningly
avoids detection. He bides his time and makes plans. Mocked as a fool,
treated with contempt and derision, he eventually succeeds in burning to
death Feng's entire retinue and in running his uncle through with a
sword. He summons an assembly of nobles, explains why he has done
what he has done, and is enthusiastically acclaimed as the new king.
"Many could have been seen marvelling how he had concealed so subtle
a plan over so long a space of time."

Amleth thus spends years in the interim state that Brutus can barely
endure for a few days. Shakespeare had developed the means to represent
the psychological reality of such a condition—something that neither

Saxo nor his followers even dreamed of being able to do. He saw that the Hamlet story, ripe for revision, would enable him to make a play about what it is like to live inwardly in the queasy interval between a murderous design and its fulfillment. The problem, however, is that the theater is not particularly tolerant of long gestation periods: to represent the child Hamlet feigning idiocy for years in order to reach the age at which he could act would be exceedingly difficult to render dramatically compelling. The obvious solution, probably already reached in the lost play, is to start the action at the point at which Hamlet has come of age and is ready to undertake his act of revenge.

Thomas Lodge's allusion to the ghost that cried so miserably, like an oyster-wife, "Hamlet, revenge!" suggests that this lost play also added a key character to the story: the spirit of Hamlet's murdered father. Perhaps that ghost only appeared to give the audience a shiver of fear—that is how Thomas Kyd had used a ghost in his greatest success, *The Spanish Tragedy*—but it is equally possible that Kyd (or whoever wrote the lost *Hamlet*), rather than Shakespeare, first introduced a crucial change in the plot that made the ghost's appearance much more than decorative. In Saxo the Grammarian's Hamlet story, as in the popular tale by Belleforest, no ghost appears. There is no need for a ghost, for the murder is public knowledge, as is the son's obligation to take revenge. But when he set out to write his version of the Hamlet story, either following Kyd's lead or on his own, Shakespeare made the murder a secret. Everyone in Denmark believes that old Hamlet was fatally stung by a serpent. The ghost appears in order to tell the terrible truth:

> The serpent that did sting thy father's life
> Now wears his crown.
>
> (1.5.39–40)

Shakespeare's play begins just before the ghost reveals the murder to Hamlet and ends just after Hamlet exacts his revenge. Hence the decisive change in the plot—from a public killing known to everyone to a secret murder revealed to Hamlet alone by the ghost of the murdered man—enabled the playwright to focus almost the entire tragedy on the con-

This *"Long View" of London from Bankside,* etched in 1647 by Wenceslaus Hollar (1607–1677), provides a strikingly detailed glimpse of a neighborhood with which Shakespeare was intimately familiar. The labels for the bearbaiting arena (also known as the Hope Theater) and the Globe Theater were inadvertently reversed. *By courtesy of the Guildhall Library, London.*

The attack on Shakespeare as an "upstart Crow" in *Greene's Groatsworth of Wit* (1592). Note that the words parodying a line from Shakespeare's Henry VI—"Tygers hart wrapt in a Players hyde"—are marked as a quotation by a different typeface. *By courtesy of the Folger Shakespeare Library.*

pendeſt on ſo meane a ſtay. Baſe minded men all three of you, if by my miſerie you be not warnd:for vnto none of you (like mee) ſought thoſe burres to cleaue : thoſe Puppets (I meane) that ſpake from our mouths, thoſe Anticks garniſht in our colours. Is it not ſtrange, that I, to whom they all haue beene beholding: is it not like that you, to whom they all haue beene beholding, ſhall (were yee in that caſe as I am now) bee both at once of them forſaken: Yes truſt them not : for there is an vp=ſtart Crow, beautified with our feathers, that with his *Tygers hart wrapt in a Players hyde*, ſuppoſes he is as well able to bombaſt out a blanke verſe as the beſt of you : and beeing an abſolute Iohannes fac totum, is in his owne conceit the onely Shake-ſcene in a countrey. O that I might intreat your rare wits to be imploied in more profitable courſes : & let thoſe Apes imitate your paſt excellence, and neuer more acquaint them with your admired inuentions. I knowe the beſt huſband of you

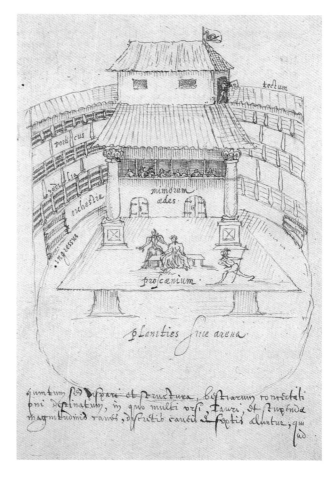

The Dutch traveler Johannes de Witt sketched the Swan Theater in 1596. His lost drawing, preserved in a friend's copy, shows a raised stage on which two women characters (presumably played by boys) are addressed by a chamberlain. *By kind permission of the Univeriteitsbibliotheek, Utrecht.*

"H and D" in the manuscript of *The Book of Sir Thomas More* (above) is widely believed to be Shakespeare's. As this sample suggests, the claim that he rarely changed or corrected what he wrote down was probably an exaggeration. *By courtesy of the British Library.*

The earliest image of Falstaff and Mistress Quickly, in the frontis-
piece to *The Wits, or Sport upon Sport* (1662), a collection of short
dramatic pieces, one of which featured Falstaff and his exploits.
By courtesy of the Huntington Library.

This engraving, by the Flemish artist Jan van der Straet (1523–1605), of a sixteenth-century printing shop shows two presses, with compositors and proofreaders. *By courtesy of the Folger Shakespeare Library.*

The dedicatory epistle of *The Rape of Lucrece* (1594). *By courtesy of the Folger Shakespeare Library.*

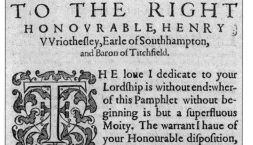

TO THE RIGHT
HONOVRABLE, HENRY
VVriothefley, Earle of Southhampton,
and Baron of Titchfield.

THE loue I dedicate to your Lordfhip is without end:wherof this Pamphlet without beginning is but a fuperfluous Moity. The warrant I haue of your Honourable difpofition, not the worth of my vntutord Lines makes it affured of acceptance. VVhat I haue done is yours, what I haue to doe is yours, being part in all I haue, deuoted yours. VVere my worth greater, my duety would fhew greater, meane time, as it is, it is bound to your Lordfhip; To whom I wifh long life ftill lengthned with all happineffe.

Your Lordfhips in all duety.

William Shakefpeare.

A 2

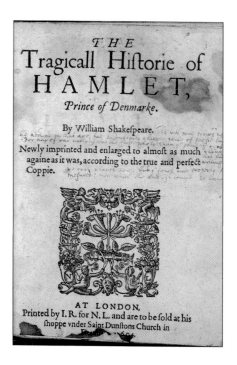

Hamlet exists in three distinct early texts. The second quarto (1604) makes good on the claim, on the title page reproduced here, that it is almost twice as long as the first edition of 1603. The text in the First Folio (1623) is shorter, possibly reflecting cuts made for performance. *By courtesy of the Folger Shakespeare Library.*

In times of plague, as this woodcut suggests, death had dominion over London. *By courtesy of the British Library.*

This portrait, widely identified as Shakespeare, was said to have been owned by Sir William Davenant, who claimed to be Shakespeare's godson and hinted that he was his illegitimate child. The simplicity of the dress is set off by the gold earring. *By courtesy of the National Portrait Gallery, England.*

Shakespeare's funeral monument, in Holy Trinity Church, Stratford-upon-Avon, depicts him as he evidently wished in his last years to be seen: the poet as a dignified burgher. *By permission of the Bridgeman Art Library.*

Interior of the new Globe, showing the general dimensions of the yard and the surrounding galleries. *By courtesy of the International Shakespeare Globe Center, Ltd.*

sciousness of the hero suspended between his "first motion" and "the acting of a dreadful thing." But something in the plot has to account for this
suspension. After all, Hamlet is no longer, in this revised version, a child
who needs to play for time, and the murderer has no reason to suspect that
Hamlet has or can ever acquire any inkling of his crime. Far from keeping
his distance from his nephew (or setting subtle tests for him), Claudius
refuses to let Hamlet return to university, calls him "Our chiefest courtier,
cousin, and son" (1.2.117), and declares that he is next in succession to the
throne. Once the ghost of his father has disclosed the actual cause of
death—"Murder most foul, as in the best it is, / But this most foul,
strange, and unnatural"—Hamlet, who has full access to the unguarded
Claudius, is in the perfect position to act immediately. And such an
instantaneous response is precisely what Hamlet himself anticipates:

> Haste, haste me to know it, that with wings as swift
> As meditation or the thoughts of love
> May sweep to my revenge.
>
> (1.5.27–31)

The play should be over by the end of the first act. But Hamlet
emphatically does not sweep to his revenge. As soon as the ghost vanishes, he tells the sentries and his friend Horatio that he intends "To put
an antic disposition on" (1.5.173), that is, to pretend to be mad. The
behavior makes perfect sense in the old version of the story, where it is a
ruse to deflect suspicion and to buy time. The emblem of that time, and
the proof of the avenger's brilliant, long-term planning, are the wooden
hooks that the boy Amleth, apparently deranged, endlessly whittles away
on with his little knife. These are the means that, at the tale's climax,
Amleth uses to secure a net over the sleeping courtiers, before he sets the
hall on fire. What had looked like mere distraction turns out to be brilliantly strategic. But in Shakespeare's version, Hamlet's feigned madness
is no longer coherently tactical. Shakespeare in effect wrecked the compelling and coherent plot with which his sources conveniently provided
him. And out of the wreckage he constructed what most modern audiences would regard as the best play he had ever written.

Far from offering a cover, the antic disposition leads the murderer to set close watch upon Hamlet, to turn to his counselor Polonius for advice, to discuss the problem with Gertrude, to observe Ophelia carefully, to send for Rosencrantz and Guildenstern to spy upon their friend. Instead of leading the court to ignore him, Hamlet's madness becomes the object of everyone's endless speculation. And strangely enough, the speculation sweeps Hamlet along with it:

> I have of late—but wherefore I know not—lost all my mirth, forgone all custom of exercise; and indeed it goes so heavily with my disposition that this goodly frame, the earth, seems to me a sterile promontory. This most excellent canopy the air, look you, this brave o'erhanging, this majestical roof fretted with golden fire— why, it appears no other thing to me than a foul and pestilent congregation of vapours. What a piece of work is a man! How noble in reason, how infinite in faculty, in form and moving how express and admirable, in action how like an angel, in apprehension how like a god—the beauty of the world, the paragon of animals! And yet to me what is this quintessence of dust? (2.2.287–98)

"But wherefore I know not"—Hamlet, entirely aware that he is speaking to court spies, does not breathe a word of his father's ghost, but then it is not at all clear that the ghost is actually responsible for his profound depression. Already in the first scene in which he appears, before he has encountered the ghost, he is voicing to himself, as the innermost secret of his heart, virtually the identical disillusionment he discloses to the oily Rosencrantz and Guildenstern:

> O God, O God,
> How weary, stale, flat, and unprofitable
> Seem to me all the uses of this world!
> Fie on't, ah fie, fie! 'Tis an unweeded garden
> That grows to seed; things rank and gross in nature
> Possess it merely.
>
> (1.2.132–37)

His father's death and his mother's hasty remarriage, public events and not secret revelations, have driven him to thoughts of "self-slaughter."

Hamlet's show of madness, then, seems a cover for something like madness. Indeed, he never seems more genuinely insane than at the moment, in his mother's closet, in which he insists that he is perfectly sane and warns his mother not to disclose his strategy. "What shall I do?" cries the frightened queen. "Not this, by no means, that I bid you do," answers Hamlet, jumbling together his injunction with his obsessive fantasies:

> Let the bloat King tempt you again to bed,
> Pinch wanton on your cheek, call you his mouse,
> And let him for a pair of reechy kisses,
> Or paddling in your neck with his damned fingers,
> Make you to ravel all this matter out,
> That I essentially am not in madness,
> But mad in craft.
>
> (3.4.164–72)

Gertrude may be saying exactly what she believes when she tells Claudius a few moments later that Hamlet is "Mad as the sea and wind when both contend / Which is the mightier" (4.1.6–7).

By excising the rationale for Hamlet's madness, Shakespeare made it the central focus of the entire tragedy. The play's key moment of psychological revelation—the moment that virtually everyone remembers—is not the hero's plotting of revenge, not even his repeated, passionate self-reproach for inaction, but rather his contemplation of suicide: "To be, or not to be; that is the question." This suicidal urge has nothing to do with the ghost—indeed, Hamlet has so far forgotten the apparition as to speak of death as "The undiscovered country from whose bourn / No traveller returns" (3.1.58, 81–82)—but rather has to do with a soul sickness brought on by one of "the thousand natural shocks / That flesh is heir to."

Hamlet marks a sufficient enough break in Shakespeare's career as to suggest some more personal cause for his daring transformation both of his sources and of his whole way of writing. A simple index of this transformation is the astonishing rush of new words, words that he had never used before in some twenty-one plays and in two long poems. There are, scholars have calculated, more than six hundred of these words, many of them not only new to Shakespeare but also new to the written record of the English language. This linguistic explosion seems to come not from a broadened vision of the world but from some shock or series of shocks to his whole life. If *Hamlet* was written not in 1600 but in early 1601, then, as some scholars believe, one shock might have been the insurrection—to use Brutus's word, in *Julius Caesar*—that led to the execution of the Earl of Essex and, more important, to the imprisonment of Shakespeare's patron, friend, and possible lover, the Earl of Southampton. Accompanied by Southampton, Essex, who had long been the queen's cosseted favorite, had gone off to Ireland in 1599 as the general of an expeditionary force designed to crush a rebellion led by the Earl of Tyrone. The enterprise, like so many others in Ireland, had failed miserably in the face of staunch Irish resistance, and late that year, suddenly and without the queen's permission, Essex returned to London. Placed under house arrest and enraged by the queen's refusal to readmit him to favor, the proud and impetuous earl assembled his friends and attempted to stage an armed putsch—the official purpose was to defend his life and save the queen from her evil counselors, Cecil and Ralegh. The London crowd refused to back the rising, and it was quickly over. The outcome of the trial was a foregone conclusion. On February 25, 1601, three strokes of the ax separated Essex's head from his shoulders. The execution of several of his principal supporters and friends followed in short order.

Shakespeare had every reason to be shaken by the upheaval. It was not only a matter of the possible loss of Southampton, who, though ultimately spared, seemed in early 1601 likely to be executed along with Essex. For the playwright personally and for his company, a set of decisions that they had made in the years leading up to the insurrection could have led to disaster. In late 1596 or early 1597, Shakespeare had elected, by using the name Oldcastle for the fat knight in *Henry IV*, whom he eventually and under pressure renamed Falstaff, to risk offending William Brook, the seventh Lord Cobham, who traced his descent from the historical Oldcastle. Brook was not the wisest choice of an antagonist, for at the time or very soon after, he was appointed lord chamberlain, the post ultimately responsible for overseeing the licensing of plays. But he was the known enemy of Essex and Southampton, and it was presumably for this reason that Shakespeare felt licensed, like the fool in one of his plays, to take a jibe at him.

Then in 1599, quite uncharacteristically, Shakespeare introduced a direct topical reference into one of his plays. Near the close of *Henry V*, the Chorus, conjuring up the scene of the king's triumphal return to London after the battle of Agincourt, abruptly turns to contemporary events. "How London doth pour out her citizens," the Chorus exclaims.

> As, by a lower but high-loving likelihood,
> Were now the General of our gracious Empress—
> Bringing rebellion broachèd on his sword,
> How many would the peaceful city quit
> To welcome him!
>
> (5.0.24, 29–34)

"A lower but high-loving likelihood": even with the note of prudential caution and calculation, the Chorus's lines were a gesture of support for Essex, a gesture soon followed by something much more dangerous. Several days before the rising, a few of the conspirators called on Shakespeare's company, the Lord Chamberlain's Men, and asked to "have the play of the deposing and killing of King Richard II to be played the Saturday next." The representatives of the company—and it seems likely that Shakespeare, along with Augustine Phillips and a few other veteran players, was among them—protested that the play was too old to make a profit. The conspirators offered to subsidize the performance with an extra payment of forty shillings, a substantial sum, and the play was accordingly performed.

The strategy, it seems, was to plant the idea of a successful rebellion in the minds of the London crowd and perhaps also to shore up the plotters' own courage. This at least is how, in the wake of the arrests, the authorities regarded the special performance, and this is how the queen herself seems to have understood it. "I am Richard II," she fumed. "Know ye not that?" The Lord Chamberlain's Men had ventured onto exceedingly dangerous ground—two of the key conspirators were questioned about the performance, as if it might have been an integral part of the plot—but somehow Augustine Phillips, who spoke on behalf of the company, managed to persuade the magistrates that the players knew nothing about the intended rising. "They had their forty shillings more than their ordinary for it," he testified, "and so played it accordingly."

These events, which took place in February 1601, would certainly have alarmed Shakespeare. The brush with disaster might have led a more timid playwright to be cautious: he could have set aside the tragedy and quickly turned to another, more innocuous project. Instead, with the same eye for box-office receipts that governed the negotiation over *Richard II*, his company performed *Hamlet,* a highly political play about betrayal and assassination, a play that includes a remarkable scene of an armed popular insurrection breaking into the royal sanctuary past the guards and threatening the life of the king. Of course, the insurrection, led by Laertes, does not succeed, and Claudius's exquisite piece of hypocrisy eerily mimes the official line about Queen Elizabeth:

> There's such a divinity doth hedge a king
> That treason can but peep to what it would,
> Acts little of his will.
>
> (4.5.120–22)

These scenes would have been enough to excite a London audience shaken by the events of 1601, but they do not actually constitute a direct reference to them, and they could be easily explained away. After all, political upheaval, betrayal, and assassination were Shakespeare's theatrical stock-in-trade—witness *Richard III, Julius Caesar, Richard II, Henry V,* and so on. Essex and the imprisonment of Southampton must have preyed on Shakespeare's mind, but it is difficult to attribute anything in *Hamlet* specifically to these events, and it is particularly difficult to attribute what is startling and innovative about the play to them. Though the links to the insurrection are intriguing, some version of Shakespeare's *Hamlet* was, in all likelihood, being performed before Essex took his fateful steps. Shakespeare may have ventured to add some lines or scenes to heighten the connection between the play and contemporary events, but the key elements of the play must already have been in place, as suggested by a marginal note that Gabriel Harvey (the Cambridge academic entangled in disputes with Nashe and Greene) jotted down in his copy of Chaucer. "The Earl of Essex much commends *Albion's England*," Harvey writes, in an account of contemporary literary fashions, and then continues, "The younger sort takes much delight in Shakespeare's *Venus and Adonis*; but his *Lucrece* and his *Tragedy of Hamlet, Prince of Denmark* have it in them to please the wiser sort." The present tense suggests that Essex was alive when Harvey penned the first clear reference to Shakespeare's tragedy.

Something deeper must have been at work in Shakespeare, then, something powerful enough to call forth the unprecedented representation of tormented inwardness. "To be, or not to be": as audiences and readers have long instinctively understood, these suicidal thoughts, provoked by the death of a loved one, lie at the heart of Shakespeare's tragedy. They may well have been the core of the playwright's own inward disturbance. The Shakespeares had named their twins, Judith and Hamnet, after their Stratford neighbors Judith and Hamnet Sadler. The latter appears in Stratford records as both Hamnet and Hamlet Sadler; in the loose orthography of the time, the names were virtually interchangeable. Even if the decision to redo the old tragedy were a strictly commercial one, the coincidence of the names—the act of writing his own son's name again and again—may well have reopened a deep wound, a wound that had never properly healed.

But, of course, in *Hamlet*, it is the death not of a son but of a father that provokes the hero's spiritual crisis. If the tragedy swelled up from Shakespeare's own life—if it can be traced back to the death of Hamnet—something must have made the playwright link the loss of his child to the imagined loss of his father. I say "imagined" because Shakespeare's father was buried in Holy Trinity Churchyard on September 8, 1601: the handwriting may have been on the wall, but he was almost certainly still alive when the tragedy was written and first performed. How did the father's death become bound up so closely in Shakespeare's imagination with the son's?

Shakespeare undoubtedly returned to Stratford in 1596 for his son's funeral. The minister, as the regulations required, would have met the corpse at the entry to the churchyard and accompanied it to the grave. Shakespeare must have stood there and listened to the words of the prescribed Protestant burial service. While the earth was thrown onto the body—perhaps by the father himself, perhaps by friends—the minister intoned the words, "Forasmuch as it hath pleased Almighty God of his great mercy to take unto himself the soul of our dear brother here departed, we therefore commit his body to the ground, earth to earth, ashes to ashes, dust to dust; in sure and certain hope of the Resurrection to eternal life."

Did Shakespeare find this simple, eloquent service adequate, or was he tormented with a sense that something was missing? "What ceremony else?" cries Laertes, by the grave of his sister Ophelia; "What ceremony else?" (5.1.205, 207). Ophelia's funeral rites have been curtailed because she is suspected of the sin of suicide, and Laertes is both shallow and rash. But the question he repeatedly asks echoes throughout *Hamlet*, and it articulates a concern that extends beyond the boundaries of the play. Within living memory, the whole relationship between the living and the dead had been changed. In Lancashire, if not closer to home, Shakespeare could have seen the remnants of the old Catholic practice: candles burning night and day, crosses everywhere, bells tolling constantly, close relatives wailing and crossing themselves, neighbors visiting the corpse and saying over it a Paternoster or a De Profundis, alms and food distributed in memory of the dead, priests paid to say Masses to ease the soul's perilous passage through purgatory. All of this had come under attack; everything had been scaled back or eliminated outright. Above all, it was now illegal to pray for the dead.

The first Protestant prayer books had retained the old formula: "I commend thy soul to God the father almighty, and thy body to the ground, earth to earth, ashes to ashes, dust to dust." But vigilant reformers felt that these words had too much of the old Catholic faith hidden within them, and so a simple change was made: "We therefore commit his body to the ground. . . ." The dead person is no longer directly addressed, as if he retained some contact with the living. The small revision makes a large point: the dead are completely dead. No prayers can help them; no messages can be sent to them or received from them. Hamnet was beyond reach.

Catholics believed that after death, while wicked souls went directly to hell and saintly souls to heaven, the great majority of the faithful, neither completely good nor completely bad, went to purgatory. Purgatory was a vast prison house under the earth where souls would suffer torments until they had paid for the sins they had committed during life. (Some thought there was an entry to it in Ireland, through a cave in the county of Donegal discovered by Saint Patrick.) These sins were not so wicked as to entail an eternity of woe, but they had left a stain that needed to be burned away before the soul could enter heaven. All of the souls in purgatory, without exception, were saved and would eventually ascend to bliss. That was the good news. The bad news was that purgatorial sufferings, painted on church walls and described in hallucinatory detail by preachers, were horrible. One instant of fiery pain in the afterlife was worse, churchmen taught, than the worst pain a person could suffer in life. Indeed, the torments of souls imprisoned in purgatory were identical, except in their duration, to the torments of the damned in hell. And this duration, though limited, was not inconsiderable. One Spanish theologian calculated that an average Christian would have to spend approximately one to two thousand years in purgatory.

Fortunately, the Catholic Church taught, there was a way to help your loved ones and yourself. Certain good works—prayers, alms, and above all special Masses—could significantly ease the suffering, reduce the purgatorial prison term, and hasten the soul's passage to heaven. You could prudently arrange for these good works on your own behalf, during your lifetime, and you could bestow them on those who had passed away. The wealthy and powerful endowed chantries where priests would say prayers in perpetuity for the dead, and they founded civic institutions—almshouses, hospitals, schools—designed to generate an abundant supply of prayers for the founder. Poorer people saved their pennies to pay for sets of Masses, available in different packages. The most effective was said to be the trental, a sequence of thirty Masses, but even one or two could help.

What evidence was there for the efficacy of these measures? In addition to church doctrine, there was the testimony of the dead themselves. Many stories were told of ghosts who had returned to earth from purgatory, desperately pleading for help. And after the help was given, these same ghosts would often return to thank the giver and bear witness to the immense comfort that their charitable donations had provided. The ghostly apparitions that people actually encountered were almost always terrifying. They could be harbingers of catastrophe, signs of madness, or manifestations of evil, for the devil could assume the shape of a dead person and sow wicked ideas in the minds of the unsuspecting. But the church's teachings helped make sense of what was happening when people were haunted by the spirits of those whom they had loved: the dead in their purgatorial suffering were simply pleading to be remembered. "Remember our thirst while ye sit and drink," the Catholic Thomas More heard the voices of the dead crying; remember "our hunger while ye be feasting; our restless watch while ye be sleeping; our sore and grievous pain while ye be playing; our hot, burning fire while ye be in pleasure and sporting. So might God make your offspring after remember you." And with remembrance, in the form of the appropriate rituals, would come relief.

Zealous Protestants regarded this whole set of beliefs and institutional practices as an enormous confidence game, a racket designed to extract money from the credulous. Purgatory, they said, was "a poet's fable," an elaborate fantasy that had been imposed upon the whole society, top to bottom, so that king and fishwife alike were being ruthlessly exploited. Persuaded by these arguments or, more plausibly, simply eager to seize church wealth, Henry VIII dissolved the monasteries and chantries that had been the ritual centers of the Catholic cult of the dead. Under his Protestant successors, Edward VI and Elizabeth I, reformers in Parliament abolished the whole system of intercessory foundations created to offer prayers for souls in purgatory. The authorities kept many of the hospitals, almshouses, and schools, of course, but stripped them of their ritual functions. And through sermons and homilies and the church service itself, the clergy made a systematic effort to reeducate the populace, urging their flock to reimagine the whole relationship between this life and the beyond.

This was not an easy task. Belief in purgatory may well have been abused—plenty of pious Catholics thought it was—but it addressed fears and longings that did not simply vanish when people were told by the officials of the church and the state that the dead were beyond all earthly contact. Ceremony was not the only or even the principal issue. What mattered was whether the dead could continue to speak to the living, at least for a short time, whether the living could help the dead, whether a reciprocal bond remained. When Shakespeare stood in the churchyard, watching the dirt fall on the body of his son, did he think that his relationship with Hamnet was gone without a trace?

Perhaps. But it is also possible that he found the service, with its deliberate refusal to address the dead child as "thou," its reduction of ritual, its narrowing of ceremony, its denial of any possibility of communication, painfully inadequate. And if he could make his peace with the Protestant understanding of these things, others close to him assuredly could not. Nothing is known of his wife Anne's beliefs about death, though there may be a very small hint in the strange inscription that was placed on her grave in 1623 by her daughter Susanna. "A mother's bosom you gave, and milk and life," the inscription begins; "for such bounty, alas! I can only render stones!" The lines that follow imply the radical idea that the dead woman's soul, as well as her body, is imprisoned in the grave: "Rather would I pray the good angel to roll away the stone from the mouth of the tomb, that thy spirit, even as the body of Christ, should go forth." But these may be Susanna's heterodox views and not at all those of Anne Hathaway Shakespeare, let alone ones she might have held back in 1596, the year of Hamnet's death.

Shakespeare's parents, John and Mary, also presumably stood by Hamnet's grave. Indeed, they had spent far more time with the boy than his father had, for while Shakespeare was in London, they were all living together in the same house with their daughter-in-law and the three grandchildren. They had helped to raise Hamnet, and they tended Hamnet through his last illness. And about his parents' beliefs with regard to the afterlife, specifically about his father's beliefs, there is some evidence. This evidence strongly suggests that John Shakespeare would have wanted something done for Hamnet's soul, something that he perhaps appealed urgently to his son to do or that he undertook to do on his own. The arguments, or pleading, or tears that may have accompanied such appeals are irrevocably lost. But at least there is a trace of what Shakespeare's father (and, presumably, his mother as well) would have thought necessary, proper, charitable, loving, and, in a single word, Christian.

Back in the 1580s, while Thomas Lucy was combing the neighborhood of Stratford for Catholic subversives and Catholics were said to be hiding the evidence of their dangerous loyalties, John Shakespeare (if the papers discovered in the eighteenth century were authentic) put his name to something seriously incriminating: the "spiritual last will and testament" that the Jesuits had circulated among the faithful. At the time William may have known nothing about this—his father probably slipped the papers between the rafters and roof tiles of the Henley Street house in secrecy—but the faith and anxiety that led to the signing of the document would probably have come up at the funeral of Hamnet. For what John Shakespeare had hidden away had specifically to do with death.

The "spiritual testament" was a kind of insurance policy for the Catholic soul, and it must have seemed particularly important to those who could not practice their faith openly or who were under pressure to collaborate with the Protestants. The signer declares that he is a Catholic, but he adds that if at any time he should chance "by suggestion of the devil to do, say, or think" anything contrary to his faith, he formally revokes his sin and wills "that it be held for neither spoken or done by me." So too if he should happen not to receive the proper Catholic last rites—confession, anointing, and communion—he wishes that they be performed "spiritually." He knows that he "is born to die, without knowing the hour, where, when, or how" and fears that he could be "surprised on a sudden." Hence he is grateful, he declares, for the opportunity to experience penance now, for he knows that he could be taken out of this life "when I least thought thereof: yea even then, when I was plunged in the dirty puddle of my sins."

Catholics were taught in this period to be particularly fearful of a sudden death, a death that would prevent the ritual opportunity to settle the sinner's accounts with God and to show the appropriate contrition. Any stains that had not been removed in this life would have to be burned away in the afterlife. The "spiritual testament" was an attempt to address this fear, and it went on to enlist family and friends as allies:

> I John Shakespeare do . . . beseech all my dear friends, parents, and kinsfolk, by the bowels of our Savior Jesus Christ, that since it is uncertain what lot will befall me, for fear notwithstanding lest by reason of my sins I be to pass and stay a long while in Purgatory, they will vouchsafe to assist and succor me with their holy prayers and satisfactory works, especially with the holy Sacrifice of the Mass, as being the most effectual means to deliver souls from their torments and pains.

Those who set their name to such a document (and it is at least plausible that John Shakespeare was among them, and probable that he shared their concerns) were not speaking solely for themselves; they were asking those who loved them to do something crucially important for them, something that the state had declared illegal.

In 1596, at the funeral of Hamnet, the issue would almost certainly have surfaced. The boy's soul needed the help of those who loved and cared for him. John Shakespeare, who had virtually raised his grandson, may well have urged his prosperous son William to pay for masses for the dead child, just as he likely wanted masses to be said for his own soul. For he was getting old and would soon be in need of the "satisfactory works" that could shorten the duration of his agony in the afterlife.

If this delicate subject was broached, did William angrily shake his head or instead quietly pay for clandestine Masses for Hamnet's soul? Did he tell his father that he could not give his son—or, looking ahead, that he would not give him—what he craved? Did he say that he no longer believed in the whole story of the terrible prison house, poised between heaven and hell, where the sins done in life were burned and purged away?

Whatever he determined at the time, Shakespeare must have still been brooding over it in late 1600 and early 1601, when he sat down to write a tragedy whose doomed hero bore the name of his dead son. His thoughts may have been intensified by news that his elderly father was seriously ill back in Stratford, for the thought of his father's death is deeply woven into the play. And the death of his son and the impending death of his father—a crisis of mourning and memory—constitute a psychic disturbance that may help to explain the explosive power and inwardness of *Hamlet*.

A ghost comes back to earth to demand revenge: this is the thrilling theatrical device that everyone remembered from the earlier Elizabethan play about Hamlet, and Shakespeare invests the scene with incomparable power. "If thou didst ever thy dear father love . . . ," the ghost says to his groaning son, "Revenge his foul and most unnatural murder" (1.5.23–25). But, strangely enough, the spectral injunction that Shakespeare's Hamlet dwells upon is not this stirring call to action but something quite different: "Adieu, adieu, Hamlet. Remember me." "Remember thee?" Hamlet echoes, clutching his head.

> Ay, thou poor ghost, while memory holds a seat
> In this distracted globe. Remember thee?
>   (1.5.91, 95–97)

On the face of things, as Hamlet's tone of incredulity suggests, the request is absurd: the son is hardly likely to forget the return of his father from the grave. But in fact Hamlet does not sweep to his revenge, and it turns out that remembering his father—remembering him in the right way, remembering him at all—is far more difficult to do than he imagined. Something interferes with the straightforward plan, an interference whose emblem is the feigned madness that makes no sense in the plot. And it turns out that this interference springs from the same sources that may have led Shakespeare's own father to sign the Catholic "spiritual testament," with its desperate plea to his family and friends: Remember me.

"I am thy father's spirit," the ghost tells his son,

> Doomed for a certain term to walk the night,
> And for the day confined to fast in fires

Till the foul crimes done in my days of nature
Are burnt and purged away. But that I am forbid
To tell the secrets of my prison-house
I could a tale unfold whose lightest word
Would harrow up thy soul.

(1.5.9–16)

Shakespeare had to be careful: plays were censored, and it would not have been permissible to refer to purgatory as a place that actually existed. There is thus a sly literalness in the ghost's remark that he is forbidden "To tell the secrets of my prison-house." But virtually everyone in Shakespeare's audience would have understood what this prison-house was, a location Hamlet himself signals when he swears, a few moments later, "by Saint Patrick" (1.5.140), the patron saint of purgatory.

The ghost has suffered the fate so deeply feared by pious Catholics. He has been taken suddenly from this life, with no time to prepare ritually for his end. "Cut off even in the blossoms of my sin," he tells his son, adding in one of the play's strangest lines, "Unhouseled, dis-appointed, unaneled" (1.5.76–77). "Unhouseled"—he did not receive last communion; "dis-appointed"—he did not undertake deathbed confession or appointment; "unaneled"—he did not receive extreme unction, the anointing (or aneling) of his body with holy oil. He went into the afterlife without having undertaken any preparatory penance, and now he is paying the full price: "O horrible, O horrible, most horrible!" (1.5.80).

What does it mean that a ghost from purgatory erupts into the world of *Hamlet* pleading to be remembered? Even setting aside for a moment the fact that purgatory, according to the Protestant church, did not exist, the allusions to it here are an enigma, for spirits in God's great penitentiary could not by definition ask anyone to commit a crime. After all, they are being purged of their sins in order to ascend to heaven. Yet this ghost is not asking for Masses and alms; he is preempting God's monopoly on revenge by demanding that his son kill the man who murdered him, seized his crown, and married his widow. Audiences then as now would not necessarily worry about this—the play is not, after all, a theology lesson. But Hamlet worries about it, and his paralyzing doubts and anxieties displace revenge as the center of the play's interest.

The official Protestant line in Shakespeare's time was that there were no ghosts at all. The apparitions that men and women encountered from time to time—apparitions that uncannily bore the appearance of loved ones or friends—were mere delusions, or, still worse, they were devils in disguise, come to tempt their victims to sin. Hamlet at first declares that he has seen an "honest ghost" (1.5.142), but his initial confidence gives way to uncertainty:

> The spirit that I have seen
> May be the devil, and the devil hath power
> T'assume a pleasing shape; yea, and perhaps,
> Out of my weakness and my melancholy—
> As he is very potent with such spirits—
> Abuses me to damn me.
>
> (2.2.575–80)

Such thoughts lead to a cycle of delay, self-reproach, continued failure to act, and renewed self-reproach. They account for the play-within-the-play—Hamlet's device to get some independent confirmation of the ghost's claims—and for the hero's queasy sense of groping in the dark. And they are linked to a broader sense of doubt and disorientation in a play where the whole ritual structure that helped men and women deal with loss has been fatally damaged.

Shakespeare would have experienced the consequences of this damage as he stood by the grave of his son or tried to cope with his father's pleas for help in the afterlife. The Protestant authorities had attacked the beliefs and outlawed the practices that the Catholic Church had offered as a way to negotiate with the dead. They said that the whole concept of purgatory was a lie and that all one needed was robust faith in the saving power of Christ's sacrifice. There were those who firmly possessed such faith, but nothing in Shakespeare's works suggests that he was among them. He was instead part of a very large group, probably the bulk of the population, who found themselves still grappling with longings and fears that the old resources of the Catholic Church had served to address. It was because of those longings and fears that people like John Shakespeare secretly signed "spiritual testaments."

All funerals invite those who stand by the grave to think about what, if anything, they believe in. But the funeral of one's own child does more than this: it compels parents to ask questions of God and to interrogate their own faith. Shakespeare must have attended the regular services in his Protestant parish; otherwise his name would have turned up on lists of recusants. But did he believe what he heard and recited? His works suggest that he did have faith, of a sort, but it was not a faith securely bound either by the Catholic Church or by the Church of England. By the late 1590s, insofar as his faith could be situated in any institution at all, that institution was the theater, and not only in the sense that his profoundest energies and expectations were all focused there.

Shakespeare grasped that crucial death rituals in his culture had been gutted. He may have felt this with enormous pain at his son's graveside. But he also believed that the theater—and his theatrical art in particular—could tap into the great reservoir of passionate feelings that, for him and for thousands of his contemporaries, no longer had a satisfactory outlet.

The Reformation was in effect offering him an extraordinary gift— the broken fragments of what had been a rich, complex edifice—and he knew exactly how to accept and use this gift. He was hardly indifferent to the success he could achieve, but it was not a matter of profit alone. Shakespeare drew upon the pity, confusion, and dread of death in a world of damaged rituals (the world in which most of us continue to live) because he himself experienced those same emotions at the core of his being. He experienced them in 1596, at the funeral of his child, and he experienced them with redoubled force in anticipation of his father's death. He responded not with prayers but with the deepest expression of his being: *Hamlet*.

In the early eighteenth century, the editor and biographer Nicholas Rowe, trying to find out something about Shakespeare's career as an actor, made inquiries, but memories had faded. "I could never meet with any further account of him this way," Rowe noted, "than that the top of his performance was the Ghost in his own *Hamlet*." Enacting the purgatorial spirit who demands that the living listen carefully to his words—"lend thy serious hearing / To what I shall unfold" (1.5.5–6)—Shakespeare must have conjured up within himself the voice of his dead son, the voice of his dying father, and perhaps too his own voice, as it would sound when it came from the grave. Small wonder that it would have been his best role.

CHAPTER 11

Bewitching the King

HAMLET MARKED AN EPOCH for Shakespeare as a writer as well as an actor. With this play, he made a discovery by means of which he relaunched his entire career. Already, prior to 1600, he had amassed considerable experience as a writer of tragedy. In *Titus Andronicus, Richard III, Romeo and Juliet, Richard II,* and *Julius Caesar,* he had explored the lust for revenge, the pathological ambition and fatal irresponsibility of monarchs, the murderous enmity of households, and the fatal consequences of political assassination. The crucial breakthrough in *Hamlet* did not involve developing new themes or learning how to construct a shapelier, tighter plot; it had to do rather with an intense representation of inwardness called forth by a new technique of radical excision. He had rethought how to put a tragedy together—specifically, he had rethought the amount of causal explanation a tragic plot needed to function effectively and the amount of explicit psychological rationale a character needed to be compelling. Shakespeare found that he could immeasurably deepen the effect of his plays, that he could provoke in the audience and in himself a peculiarly passionate intensity of response, if he took out a key explanatory element, thereby occluding the rationale, motivation, or ethical principle that accounted for the action that was to unfold. The principle was not the making of a riddle to be solved, but the creation of a strategic opacity. This opacity, Shakespeare found, released an enormous energy that had been at least partially blocked or contained by familiar, reassuring explanations.

Shakespeare's work had long been wryly skeptical of official explanations and excuses—the accounts, whether psychological or theological, of why people behave the way they do. His plays had suggested that the choices people make in love are almost entirely inexplicable and irrational, which is the conviction that generates the comedy in *A Midsummer Night's Dream* and the tragedy in *Romeo and Juliet*. But at least love was the clearly identifiable motive. With *Hamlet*, Shakespeare found that if he refused to provide himself or his audience with a familiar, comforting rationale that seems to make it all make sense, he could get to something immeasurably deeper. The key is not simply the creation of opacity, for by itself that would only create a baffling or incoherent play. Rather, Shakespeare came increasingly to rely on the inward logic, the poetic coherence that his genius and his immensely hard work had long enabled him to confer on his plays. Tearing away the structure of superficial meanings, he fashioned an inner structure through the resonant echoing of key terms, the subtle development of images, the brilliant orchestration of scenes, the complex unfolding of ideas, the intertwining of parallel plots, the uncovering of psychological obsessions.

This conceptual breakthrough in *Hamlet* was technical; that is, it affected the practical choices Shakespeare made when he put plays together, starting with the enigma of the prince's suicidal melancholy and assumed madness. But it was not only a new aesthetic strategy. The excision of motive must have arisen from something more than technical experimentation; coming in the wake of Hamnet's death, it expressed Shakespeare's root perception of existence, his understanding of what could be said and what should remain unspoken, his preference for things untidy, damaged, and unresolved over things neatly arranged, well made, and settled. The opacity was shaped by his experience of the world and of his own inner life: his skepticism, his pain, his sense of broken rituals, his refusal of easy consolations.

In the years after *Hamlet*, Shakespeare wrote a succession of astonishing tragedies—*Othello* in 1603 or 1604, *King Lear* in 1604 or 1605, and *Macbeth* in 1606—that drew upon his discovery. Repeatedly, he took his source and deftly sliced away what would seem indispensable to a coherent, well-made play. Thus though *Othello* is constructed around the remorseless desire of the ensign Iago to destroy his general, the Moor, Shakespeare refused to provide the villain with a clear and convincing explanation for his behavior. That explanation would not have been difficult to find: it was already there, fully articulated, in Shakespeare's source for his play, a short story by the Italian university teacher and writer Giambattista Giraldi (known to contemporaries as "Cinthio.") "The wicked Ensign," Cinthio writes of Iago, "taking no account of the faith he had pledged to his wife, and of the friendship, loyalty, and obligations he owed the Moor, fell ardently in love with Desdemona, and bent all his thoughts to see if he could manage to enjoy her." Afraid to show his love openly, the ensign does everything he can to hint to the lady that he desires her, but Desdemona's thoughts are entirely focused upon her husband. She does not merely reject the ensign's advances; she does not even notice them. Incapable of conceiving such purity of love, Cinthio's ensign concludes that Desdemona must be in love with someone else. The likeliest candidate, he concludes, is the Moor's handsome corporal, and he plots to get rid of him. But that is not all, Cinthio explains: "Not only did he turn his mind to this, but the love which he had felt for the Lady now changed to the bitterest hate, and he gave himself up to studying how to bring it about that, once the Corporal were killed, if he himself could not enjoy the Lady, then the Moor should not have her either." Everything neatly follows.

But not in Shakespeare's play. His villain does not dream of possessing Desdemona, nor is she the particular object of his hatred. To be sure, there is a moment in which he seems about to rehearse the motive that Cinthio had provided:

> That Cassio loves her, I do well believe it,
> That she loves him, 'tis apt and of great credit.
> The Moor—howbe't that I endure him not—
> Is of a constant, loving, noble nature,

> And I dare think he'll prove to Desdemona
> A more dear husband. Now I do love her too.
>   (2.1.273–78)

Since Shakespeare's Iago thinks only that his slander will be a plausible one—"'tis apt and of great credit"—this is not quite Cinthio's Iago, who genuinely believes that Desdemona must be in love with the handsome corporal. But the two versions of the villain seem to converge in those last words: "Now I do love her too." Yet it is precisely here that Shakespeare can be caught in the act of creating his special effect:

> Now I do love her too,
> Not out of absolute lust—though peradventure
> I stand accountant for as great a sin—
> But partly led to diet my revenge
> For that I do suspect the lusty Moor
> Hath leapt into my seat, the thought whereof
> Doth, like a poisonous mineral, gnaw my inwards.
>   (2.1.278–84)

What in Cinthio was simple and clear, in Shakespeare becomes opaque: "Not out of absolute lust." A further motivation—Iago's fear that he has been cuckolded by Othello—displaces the first, but neither is convincing, and the addition of further layers only weakens the explanatory force of all of them, leaving intact the terrible inner torment. Iago's murky attempt to account for his obsessive, unappeasable hatred—in Coleridge's memorable phrase, "the motive-hunting of motiveless malignity"—is famously inadequate. And, crucially, this inadequacy becomes an issue in the tragedy itself. Near the play's end, when Othello has finally understood that he has been tricked into believing that his wife was unfaithful, that he has murdered the innocent woman who loved him, and that his reputation and whole life have been destroyed, he turns to Iago and demands an explanation. Exposed as a moral monster, caught, and pinioned, Iago's terrible reply—his last utterance in the play—is a blank refusal to supply the missing motive:

Demand me nothing. What you know, you know.
From this time forth I never will speak word.
                                        (5.2.309–10)

The words are specific to *Othello* and to the fathomless cruelty of its villain, but the opacity extends to crucial elements in each of Shakespeare's
great tragedies.

Perhaps the greatest instance of strategic opacity comes in the play
Shakespeare wrote shortly after *Othello*, *King Lear*. Lear's story—his mis-
guided anger at the one daughter who truly loves him; his betrayal by the
two wicked daughters upon whom he has bestowed all of his wealth and
power—had often been told before. Shakespeare could have heard it
recounted from the pulpit or seen it mentioned briefly in Spenser's *Faerie
Queene* or read a fuller account in the chronicles to which he was
addicted. He had almost certainly seen a version of it performed onstage.
He could have been struck by its resemblance to one or more of the old
folktales he clearly loved as a child: to "Cinderella," perhaps, with its one
sweet daughter set against her wicked sisters, and, still more, to the story
of the virtuous daughter who falls into disfavor for telling her splenetic
father she loves him as much as salt. But the fate of Lear was principally
rehearsed in Shakespeare's time both as a piece of authentic British history from the very ancient past (c. 800 B.C.E.) and as a warning to contemporary fathers not to put too much trust in the flattery of their
children. Lear foolishly sets a love test: "Which of you," he asks his three
daughters, "shall we say doth love us most?" (1.1.49). In some versions of
the story, including Shakespeare's, this test occurs at the moment when
the father feels he can no longer manage his affairs and decides to retire.

But why does Lear, who has, as the play begins, already drawn up the
map equitably dividing the kingdom among his three daughters, stage
the love test at all? In Shakespeare's principal source, an old Queen's Men
play called *The True Chronicle History of King Leir* (eventually published
in 1605 but dating from 1594 or earlier), there is a gratifyingly clear
answer. Leir's strong-willed daughter Cordella has vowed that she will
only marry a man whom she herself loves; Leir wishes her to marry the
man he chooses for his own dynastic purposes. He stages the love test,

anticipating that in competing with her sisters, Cordella will declare that she loves her father best, at which point Leir will demand that she prove her love by marrying the suitor of his choice. The stratagem backfires, but its purpose is clear.

Once again, as he did in *Hamlet* and *Othello*, Shakespeare simply cut out the motive that makes the initiating action of the story make sense. Lear says he wants an answer to his question so that he can divide the kingdom according to the level of each daughter's love, but the play opens with characters discussing the map of the division—it has already been drawn up—and noting that the portions are exactly equal. And Lear makes matters still stranger by proceeding to test Cordelia, as if there were something still at stake, after he has already given away, with a great show of precision, the first two-thirds of his realm.

By stripping his character of a coherent rationale for the behavior that sets in motion the whole ghastly train of events, Shakespeare makes Lear's act seem at once more arbitrary and more rooted in deep psychological needs. His Lear is a man who has determined to retire from power but who cannot endure dependence. Unwilling to lose his identity as absolute authority both in the state and in the family, he arranges a public ritual— "Which of you shall we say doth love us most?"—whose aim seems to be to allay his own anxiety by arousing it in his children. But Cordelia refuses to perform: "What shall Cordelia speak? Love and be silent" (1.1.60). Lear demands an answer: "Speak." When she says "Nothing" (1.1.85–86), a word that echoes darkly throughout the play, Lear hears what he most dreads: emptiness, loss of respect, the extinction of identity.

At the end of the play, extinction comes to Lear in a more terrible form than he had imagined. The old Queen's Men play and all the other versions of the story concluded with Lear's reconciliation with Cordelia and with his restoration to the throne. Shakespeare's original audience must have expected some version of this upbeat ending, though perhaps they anticipated that the play's final moments would show the death of the aged Lear and the ascent to the throne of his virtuous daughter. What they would not have foreseen was that Shakespeare would cut out the triumph of Cordelia—the vindication that made moral sense of the whole narrative— and instead depict the ruined king holding his murdered daughter in his arms and howling with grief. "Is this the promised end?" asks one of the bystanders, voicing what must have been the audience's incredulity. In this unprecedented climax, the theatrical effect we have been calling opacity seems to be made literal—"All's cheerless, dark, and deadly"—as the dying Lear swings wildly from the delusive hope that Cordelia is still alive to the impossibly bleak recognition that she is dead:

> No, no, no life!
> Why should a dog, a horse, a rat, have life,
> And thou no breath at all? Thou'lt come no more,
> Never, never, never, never, never!
>
> (5.3.262, 289, 304–7)

These words, the tragedy's climactic imagining of what it feels like to lose a child, are the most painful that Shakespeare ever wrote.

They were written, however, not about Hamnet but about Cordelia, and not in the immediate wake of the playwright's loss but almost a decade later, at a time of prosperity and success. Shakespeare's career was flourishing. Queen Elizabeth's death in 1603, bringing to an end a remarkable forty-five-year reign, had not harmed him or his company. Quite the contrary: within a matter of weeks the new ruler, James VI of Scotland, who became James I of England, acted to make the Lord Chamberlain's Men his own theater company, the King's Men.

The king and his family evidently found his new troupe marvelously entertaining. The troupe performed eight plays at court in the winter of 1603–4. The next season, they had eleven court performances, including *The Spanish Maze* (now lost), two satiric comedies by Ben Jonson (*Every Man in His Humour* and *Every Man out of His Humour*), and fully seven plays by Shakespeare: *Othello, The Merry Wives of Windsor, Measure for Measure, The Comedy of Errors, Henry V, Love's Labour's Lost,* and *The Merchant of Venice*. Indeed, the king enjoyed *The Merchant of Venice* enough to order it performed twice in three days, on February 10 and 12, 1605. The late queen had taken pleasure in the theater, but this new royal patronage represented an unprecedented level of success, both for the company and for its principal playwright.

Shakespeare not only had a share in the profits from all the company's court and public performances, but as part owner of the Globe, he also received a portion of the rent that all of the sharers paid (that is, he was in effect in the happy position of paying rent to himself). Imagination, entrepreneurial skill, and unremitting labor had made him a wealthy man; he had, as Juliet's nurse says, thinking of the sound of coins in money sacks, "the chinks" (*Romeo and Juliet*, 1.5.114). There is no evidence—as there is, for example, with Ben Jonson or John Donne—that Shakespeare laid out his money for books (let alone for paintings, or antique coins, or small bronzes, or indeed for any other object of learning or art). What interested him was real estate in and around Stratford.

He could easily have afforded a place for his wife and children to live in London, but they—or he—evidently preferred that they remain in the country. In late 1597, about a year after Hamnet's death, Shakespeare settled Anne and the two girls, fourteen-year-old Susanna and twelve-year-old Judith, at New Place, the large, three-story brick and timber house he had purchased in Stratford. The house had been built late in the fifteenth century by the town's leading citizen, and though it was demolished in the eighteenth century, surviving sketches and other records suggest that it bore witness to the playwright's remarkable success in the world. With five gables, ten rooms heated by fireplaces, gardens and orchards on three sides, two barns and other outbuildings, New Place was a residence fit for a gentleman of means. In May 1602 and again in July 1605, Shakespeare made very substantial investments in "yardlands" and leases of tithes in the Stratford area. He was now, in addition to a successful playwright and actor, a significant local rentier and one of Stratford's leading citizens.

Transactions of this size would have required one or more visits home, in addition to those he customarily made—once a year, the seventeenth-century biographer John Aubrey noted—to see his family. The obvious place to break the long journey by horseback was in Oxford, where Shakespeare customarily frequented, according to early gossips, a winehouse called the Taverne. The Taverne was owned by a vintner named John Davenant, who lived there with his wife, Jane, and a growing family, including the son William who later became the distinguished Restoration playwright. John Davenant was said to be an intensely serious fellow—no one ever saw him smile—but he was prosperous and highly respected, so much so that he was elected mayor of Oxford. Jane Davenant was said to be "a very beautiful woman, and of a very good wit and of conversation extremely agreeable."

Shakespeare seems to have been close to the family. William Davenant's older brother Robert, a parson, recalled that when he was a child Shakespeare "gave him a hundred kisses." William claimed that he was named after Shakespeare, and among his intimate friends he hinted that Shakespeare was something more than his godfather. It seemed to him, he would say over a glass of wine, that he wrote "with the very spirit" of Shakespeare. Then as now, ambitious playwrights in their most exuberant bursts of narcissistic self-confidence may have been tempted to make this extravagant claim, but Davenant's drinking friends believed him "contented enough to be thought" Shakespeare's son. It is perhaps the most striking tribute to Shakespeare's exalted reputation in the late seventeenth century that a distinguished gentleman—William was an ardent royalist who was imprisoned during the Interregnum for his adherence to the monarchy and later knighted—would boast that he was a humbly born playwright's illegitimate child. Certainly, some contemporaries were shocked: it seemed to them a bit much for Davenant to enhance his artistic reputation by making his mother, as they put it, a whore.

William Davenant was christened on March 3, 1606, so if there is any truth to his heavy hints, Shakespeare would have been in Oxford at various times in the late spring and summer of 1605, perhaps in connection with the substantial real estate purchase he finalized in July. The possibility that Shakespeare was making visits to Oxford during this period is intriguing for reasons other than speculation about his secret love life. From August 27 to 31, 1605, King James, accompanied by his queen, Anne of Denmark, and his son Henry, paid Oxford his first official visit. During these four days, the university mounted four plays, three in Latin and the fourth, for the sake of the ladies (and for those gentlemen whose Latin was shakier than they were inclined to admit), in English. These were hardly casual or impromptu affairs: theatrical costumes were hired from the King's Revels company in London, and the great stage designer Inigo Jones was employed to construct special machinery to change the scenes. If he were anywhere near Oxford at the time, Shakespeare would have had the strongest professional reason to see how the performances were received.

Things apparently did not go well. The queen and the ladies took offense at an almost naked man who performed in the first of the plays, *Alba* (written in part by the great scholar Robert Burton). The king was apparently bored by this play and the next; actually fell asleep during the third, *Vertumnus*; and did not even bother to attend the fourth. The one play of the four to survive, *Vertumnus*, tends to bear out the king's critical judgment, but its failure must have been a particular disappointment. The officials had turned to Matthew Gwinn, a former fellow of St. John's College who had in 1603 published a Latin tragedy on the life of Nero and, more important, had been one of the overseers for the plays performed at the visit of Queen Elizabeth to Oxford in 1592. In the early seventeenth century Gwinn was practicing as a physician in London (he was, among other things, the physician of the prisoners in the Tower), but, as a person of distinction and experience, he was brought back to write a play for the scholarly king. He was also commissioned to stage a welcoming event, one that seems to have particularly interested Shakespeare.

As the king, arriving with his entourage, reached St. John's College, he was greeted with a "device"—a kind of pageant or miniature play— written by Gwinn. Three "sibyls," that is, three boys dressed to look like ancient prophetesses, greeted James. They approached him, the text says, "as if from a wood"; carrying branches in their hands, perhaps, they emerged, in one observer's account, from "a castle made all of ivy." The first sibyl's words recalled a legendary event that had befallen Banquo, an eleventh-century Scot from whom James traced his descent: Banquo encountered the "fatal Sisters," who foretold "power without end" not to him but to his descendants. "We three same Fates so chant to thee and thine," the speaker went on to tell James, launching into a series of antiphonal salutations:

Hail, whom Scotland serves!
Whom England, hail!
Whom Ireland serves, all hail!
Whom France gives titles, lands besides, all hail!
Hail, whom divided Britain join'st in one!
Hail, mighty Lord of Britain, Ireland, France!

From this distance, the greeting ceremony seems an unpromising bit of fluff, but it was carefully calculated to please the king. The invocation of the distant ancestor Banquo reached comfortably back before the terrible awkwardness of his more recent forbears. James was, after all, the son of Mary, Queen of Scots, the restless intriguer whom Elizabeth had imprisoned and then, under intense pressure from incensed members of Parliament shouting "Kill the witch," reluctantly executed. It assured James that his loyal English subjects regarded him not as a Scottish interloper, son of the scarlet whore of Babylon, but as the destined ruler of the united realm. And it extended the vision of fame and grandeur and stability to James's children, Henry and Charles: "We set no times nor limits to the fates."

James was nervous, deeply nervous. He could relax, toy with abstruse scholarly questions, get drunk, fondle his handsome male favorites, lose himself in the peculiar joy of killing animals. He could, in the right mood, laugh at himself and be teased, even quite coarsely. But he could never entirely escape the terror that haunted him. Attempts to delight him with fireworks displays or surprises tended to go awry; chance events could conjure up horrible memories of his past; and though he was an ardent hunter, he could never learn to fence, because the sight of a drawn sword would suddenly send him into a panic.

He had good reason for fear. Not only had his mother been executed by the queen on whose throne he now sat, but his father had died at an assassin's hand. He himself had narrowly escaped assassination on at least one and perhaps more than one occasion. He believed that his enemies would stop at nothing in their attempts to harm him and his children: he feared not sharp steel alone but also wax figurines stuck with pins and the mumbled charms of toothless old women. Like Elizabeth and Henry

VIII, he was made intensely anxious by prognostications: attempts to predict the future by sorcery or other magical means were felonies. Hence even Matthew Gwinn's innocuous little ceremony of greeting had a slight element of daring. Still, it must have been deeply reassuring for James to be told that his rule and the rule of his descendents had been prophesied centuries before—the boys of St. John's were a kind of theatrical charm to ward off the sick fear at the pit of his stomach. The king's pleasure must have been evident, for the little ceremony of greeting—whether Shakespeare stood in the crowd watching it or heard about it from one of the bystanders—seems to have stuck in the playwright's imagination.

A year later, in the summer of 1606, the king of Denmark came to England to visit his sister, Queen Anne. "There is nothing to be heard at court," writes one observer of the visit, "but sounding of trumpets, hautboys, music, revelings, and comedies." It was probably on one of these festive occasions that James sat down with his guests to see *Macbeth*, a new tragedy performed by his company, the King's Men. When the three weird sisters appeared onstage, did the king recall the pleasant little pageant outside of St. John's College? Probably not. He had, after all, seen many extravagant shows since his accession to the English throne, and there were other things to occupy his mind.

But Shakespeare must have seen, or heard about, those three boys dressed up as ancient sibyls, and he had not forgotten them. He conjured them up in *Macbeth* to restage the reassuring vision of unbroken dynastic succession. Midway through the play, Macbeth goes out to talk with the "secret, black, and midnight hags." "My heart / Throbs to know one thing," Macbeth says to them,

> Tell me, if your art
> Can tell so much, shall Banquo's issue ever
> Reign in this kingdom?
>
> (4.1.64, 116–19)

The witches urge him to content himself with what he already knows, but Macbeth insists on an answer. He cannot endure the uncertainty—"I will be satisfied," he shouts (4.1.120)—and he gets in response a strange spectacle, a pageant that resembles the entertainments mounted to reassure kings.

It is the general pattern of Shakespeare's tragedies that when the hero gets what he wants, the result is devastating. Macbeth wins a great battle for his king, Duncan, and is handsomely honored, but the honor only whets his restless discontent. He kills Duncan and seizes the crown, but the treason initiates an unending nightmare of suspicion and anxiety. He orders the assassination of his friend Banquo, but the ghost of the murdered man haunts him, and he is dismayed by the escape of Banquo's son. He longs to feel secure, unconstrained, and "perfect," as he puts it, "Whole as the marble, founded as the rock." Instead he feels "cabined, cribbed, confined, bound in / To saucy doubts and fears" (3.4.20–21, 23–24). It is to relieve these doubts and fears that he turns to the witches and demands that they show him what lies ahead. But the answer Macbeth sees is for him a singularly bitter one, since it is not his own line of succession that is on display in the witches' pageant but the heirs of a man he has murdered, Banquo. Eight kings pass before him, the last bearing a glass that shows many more to follow. The magic mirror is a familiar device from witch lore, and it may in the court production in 1606 have served a further purpose: the actor could have approached the throne and held the glass so that Banquo's heir James would see his own reflection. Here, as in the Oxford device, the fatal sisters prophesy "power without end." "What," asks the despairing Macbeth, "will the line stretch out to th' crack of doom?" (4.1.133).

Shakespeare constructed *Macbeth* around, or perhaps as, a piece of flattery. The flattery is not direct and personal, the fulsome praise characteristic of many other royal entertainments in the period, but indirect and dynastic. That is, James is honored not for his wisdom or learning or statecraft but for his place in a line of legitimate descent that leads all the way from his noble ancestor in the distant past to the sons that promise an unbroken succession. In order to enhance this point Shakespeare had to twist the historical record. Gwinn's pageant probably took Banquo from Raphael Holinshed's *Chronicle*, a book Shakespeare had used heavily in his English histories. But when, following Gwinn's lead, Shakespeare opened to the Scottish section of Holinshed, he would have found that Banquo figures as one of the murderous Macbeth's chief allies, not as his moral alternative. ("At length therefore, communicating his purposed intent with his trusty friends, amongst whom Banquo was the chiefest, upon confidence of their promised aid, he slew the king.") Shakespeare's Banquo, by contrast, is a figure of probity and decency. When Macbeth cautiously asks for his assistance, without specifying what action he has in mind, the upright thane delicately but firmly declares his allegiance to the reigning king. Shakespeare transforms James's ancestor, then, from a collaborator into a resister. It must have been agreeable to James—whose immediate past was a sickening tangle of conspiracy and betrayal—to be told that his line was founded on a rock of rectitude.

The vision of stable rule and secure dynastic succession would have appealed to more than the king alone. A few months earlier, the whole country had been deeply shaken by the discovery—at the last possible minute—of a plot to destroy James, his entire family and court, and virtually all the political leaders of the realm. On November 4, 1605, the night before King James I was due to appear in person to open a new session of Parliament, officers of the Crown, alerted some days before by a hint in an anonymous letter, apprehended Guy Fawkes in a cellar that extended beneath the Parliament House. The cellar was loaded with barrels of gunpowder and iron bars, concealed by a load of lumber and coal. Carrying a watch, a fuse, and tinder, Fawkes intended to put into execution a desperate plot devised by a small group of conspirators, embittered by what they perceived as James's unwillingness to extend toleration to Roman Catholics. Under ferocious torture, Fawkes revealed the names of those who had conspired with him to blow up the entire government. The conspirators were hunted down. Those who resisted were killed on the spot; others were arrested and, after a trial that the king watched in secret, were hanged, cut down while they were still alive, slit open, and hewed in quarters.

Among those arrested and brought to trial for the Gunpowder Plot was Father Henry Garnet, the head of the clandestine Jesuit mission in England. Garnet, against whom there was very little hard evidence, pleaded innocent, but the government prosecutors made much of the fact that he was the author of *A Treatise of Equivocation*, a book defending the morality of giving misleading or ambiguous answers under oath. Once again James watched the trial from a secret vantage point. Convicted of treason, Garnet was dragged on a hurdle to Saint Paul's Churchyard for execution, his severed head then joining the others displayed on pikes on London Bridge.

"The King is in terror," wrote the Venetian ambassador; " he does not appear nor does he take his meals in public as usual. . . . The Lords of the Council also are alarmed and confused by the plot itself and (by) the King's suspicions; the city is in great uncertainty; Catholics fear heretics, and vice-versa; both are armed, foreigners live in terror of their houses being sacked by the mob." If the bloody denouement of what the prosecutor, Sir Edward Coke, called a "heavy and doleful tragedy" was meant to bring calm to the nation, it did not entirely succeed. On March 22, a rumor quickly spread that the king had been stabbed with an envenomed knife, some said by English Jesuits, some by Scots in women's apparel, some by Spaniards and Frenchmen. Gates were locked, soldiers were levied, courtiers looked pale, women began to wail—until the king issued a proclamation insisting that he was alive. The country had experienced a nightmare from which it had not yet completely awakened.

The King's Men, like the other theater companies, would have had to think hard about what would best suit this moment, both for the general London audience and for the court. In *Macbeth*, Shakespeare seems to have set out to write a play that would function as a collective ritual of reassurance. Everyone had been deeply shaken: the whole of the ruling elite, along with the king and his family, could have been blown to bits, the kingdom ripped apart and plunged into the chaos of internecine religious warfare. The staging of the events of eleventh-century Scotland— the treacherous murder of the king, the collapse of order and decency, the long struggle to wrest the realm from the bloody hands of traitors— allowed its seventeenth-century audience to face a symbolic version of this disaster and to witness the triumphant restoration of order.

The plot of *Macbeth*, to be sure, is very far from the Gunpowder Plot: there is no Catholic conspiracy, no threatened explosion, no last-minute reprieve for the kingdom. But Shakespeare plants subtle allusions of which the most famous is a joke that must have provoked a ripple of shuddering laughter through its original audiences. The strangely comic moment comes in the immediate wake of one of the most harrowing scenes of dread and soul sickness that Shakespeare ever wrote. Macbeth has just treacherously murdered the sleeping king Duncan, a guest in his castle. Deeply shaken by the deed and gripped by fear and remorse, he and his ambitious wife are exchanging anxious words when they hear a loud knocking at the castle gate. The knocking is a simple device, but in performance it almost always has a thrilling effect, an effect subtly antic-ipated by Macbeth's horrified sense before the murder that the very image of what he is about to do makes "my seated heart knock at my ribs" (1.3.135). As the insistent knocking continues, the conspirators exit to wash the blood off their hands and to change into their nightgowns. Lady Macbeth is—or strives to seem—icily calm, calculating, and confi-dent: "A little water clears us of this deed" (2.2.65). Not so the appalled Macbeth: "Wake Duncan with thy knocking. I would thou couldst," he declares in horror or despair, longing or bitter irony (2.2.72). At this point, a porter, roused by the noise but half-drunk from the evening's rev-elry, appears. As he grumblingly goes to unlock the gate, he seems to be still in a dream state. He imagines that he is the gatekeeper in hell, open-ing the door to new arrivals. "Here's an equivocator," he says of one of these imaginary sinners, "that could swear in both the scales against either scale, who committed treason enough for God's sake, yet could not equivocate to heaven. O, come in, equivocator" (2.3.8–11). This treason-ous equivocator knocking on hell's gate is almost certainly an allusion to the recently executed Jesuit Henry Garnet.

Why didn't Shakespeare, or any other playwright, represent more directly the supremely dramatic events of November 1605? After all, those events not only formed a perfect story of national danger and sal-vation but even—as carefully stage-managed by James's principal adviser, the Earl of Salisbury—gave the king himself a crucial role in uncovering the diabolical plot. The anonymous letter of warning said only that "they shall receive a terrible blow this Parliament, and yet they shall not see who hurts them." Salisbury claimed that he and the Privy Council were not sure what to make of these opaque phrases until the king brilliantly deciphered them and sent them searching the cellar. The statute making

November 5 a day of national thanksgiving proclaimed that the ruinous plot would have succeeded "had it not pleased Almighty God, by inspiring the King's most excellent Majesty with a divine spirit, to interpret some dark phrases of a letter showed his Majesty, above and beyond all ordinary construction." This melodramatic account seems like a gift specially prepared for a theater company; why couldn't the King's Men accept it?

The answer lies in part in a long-term history of official wariness, a history that extends back before the public theaters in London were even built. In 1559, the first year of Elizabeth's reign, the queen instructed her officers not to permit any "interlude" to be "played wherein either matters of religion or of the governance of the estate of the commonweal shall be handled or treated." While it would have been almost impossible to enforce such a prohibition in the broadest sense, without simply banning the theater, the censors were alert to anything that came too close to contemporary controversies. Moreover, the monarch and the ruling elite were uneasy about being represented onstage, no matter how flattering the portrayal. By allowing such representations, they would in effect be ceding control of their own persons, and they feared that the theater would only succeed, as the queen put it, in "making greatness familiar."

Nonetheless, in the wake of the national near catastrophe and the last-minute redemption, it is surprising that the text of *Macbeth* does not contain so much as a prologue, written to the king, celebrating the recent escape; or a complimentary allusion to James's role as the special enemy of Satan and the beloved of God; or a grateful acknowledgment of the happiness of being ruled by Banquo's wise heir. That Shakespeare limited himself to dark hints about an equivocator who belongs in hell may be linked to a disturbing experience that his company had had the previous winter. The King's Men were by all measures a great success: between November 1, 1604, and February 12, 1605, they gave no fewer than eleven performances at court, all but three of them plays by Shakespeare. But one of these performances ran into the kind of trouble that could have had disastrous consequences. Buoyed by the monarch's patronage and secure in their place as the premier company, they evidently decided to test the conventional limits of representation. They thought they might interest the king and please their larger audience with a play based on a dramatic event in James's life: his narrow escape from assassination, or so he claimed, in August 1600 at the hands of the Earl of Gowrie and his brother Alexander.

As with the Gunpowder Plot, the official account of the event reads like a melodrama: out hunting in Scotland with his retinue, the king was induced by a strange story of a pot of gold coins to ride off to Gowrie House. There he was lured by Alexander Gowrie to ascend without attendants into the turret. Left behind in the hall and increasingly anxious, the king's followers were led to believe that their master had slipped away and ridden off, but just as they were about to go in search of him, they were startled by the sight of James leaning from a window of the turret and shouting, "I am murdered! Treason!" The door of the turret was locked, but John Ramsay, one of the king's men, managed to ascend by a different stair and break into the chamber, where he found James struggling with Alexander. Ramsay stabbed the king's assailant in the face and neck, while downstairs other followers of the king dispatched the assailant's brother, the Earl of Gowrie.

It is probably no accident that the story seems too good to be true. Many disinterested observers must have smelled a rat—a treacherous political killing of two powerful nobles whom the king distrusted and to whom he was in debt to the tune of eighty thousand pounds. The state evidently felt it had to shore up the story of a treasonous attempt on the king's life. Not only did the Earl of Gowrie betray a subject's obligation of loyalty to his sovereign, according to the official account, not only did he trample on a host's obligation to his guest, but he also violated the worship of God: a "little close parchment bag, full of magical characters and words of enchantment" was found on the earl's body at his death. It was only when the bag was removed from him that his body began to bleed. The Hebrew characters proved that its bearer was a "cabbalist," the magistrates declared, "a studier of magic, and a conjuror of devils." The torture of several witnesses with the "boot"—a device that crushed the bones of the feet—produced the full array of evidence that the state required, and a flurry of executions, along with the king's seizure of the Gowrie property, brought the episode to a close. Scottish ministers were instructed "to

praise God for the King's miraculous delivery from that vile treason."
Several refused, whether because they doubted the story or thought the
instruction idolatrous, and were promptly dismissed from their posts.
Most grudgingly complied.

Some playwright affiliated with the King's Men—perhaps Shakespeare
himself—grasped that this story would make an exciting play. The company
knew, of course, that they would be violating the Elizabethan taboo on representing living magnates and contemporary or near-contemporary events,
since someone (and here too Shakespeare is a possibility) would have had
to play the part of James. But they may have wanted to test whether the
restriction would be continued into the new regime. Moreover, they may
have noted that the king had gone out of his way to reward anyone who
actively supported his version of the bloody events at Gowrie House, and
they calculated that an English audience would find these events fascinating. They were at least partly right: in December 1604 *The Tragedy of
Gowrie* was twice performed before large crowds. But, as a court spy
noted, the play did not please everyone: "whether the matter or manner
be not well handled, or that it be thought unfit that Princes should be
played on the Stage in their Life-time, I hear that some great Councilors
are much displeased with it, and so 'tis thought shall be forbidden." The
company did not fall from favor as a consequence of their miscalculation,
but the play was evidently banned. There is no record of other performances, and the text did not survive.

A year later, in the wake of the Gunpowder Plot, the King's Men
thought once again about doing a Scottish play, but they knew that they
had to be more careful this time. If they wanted to stage a Scottish tale
of treason—the story of a noble host who, corrupted by black magic,
attempts to murder his royal guest—they would have to push it far back
in time. And if they wanted to perform something that would capture
the king's imagination, they had to study his mind more attentively.
That mind, as James's English subjects were discovering, was extremely
strange.

Queen Elizabeth's godson, a celebrated wit named John Harington,
recounted an audience with the king in 1604. James began in a pedantic
vein—he showed off his learning, Harington wrote, "in such sort as made

me remember my examiner at Cambridge"—and went on to literature, with a discussion of the Italian epic poet Ariosto. Then the conversation took a strange turn: "His Majesty did much press for my opinion touching the power of Satan in matter of witchcraft, and . . . why the Devil did work more with ancient [i.e., old] women than others." Harington tried to deflect the odd urgency of the king's question with an off-color joke: he reminded the king that Scripture says the devil has a preference for "walking in dry places." But James did not simply laugh and move on to other matters. There was, he said, a weird apparition in the heavens in Scotland before his mother's death, "a bloody head dancing in the air." The English courtier restrained himself and made no further attempt at comedy.

James's anxiety about witches and apparitions was no laughing matter, and it obviously behooved anyone interested in the king's favor—a playwright as much as a courtier—to take its full measure. There may have been an understanding among the King's Men that their principal playwright would undertake to do some research into James's fantasy life, with a view toward writing a play specifically designed to please him. No formal agreement would have been necessary, for the desirability of understanding James in order to please him—particularly after the debacle of *The Tragedy of Gowrie*—was obvious enough. Shakespeare may not have been merely passing through Oxford by chance in August 1605; he may have been there on assignment, watching James's reactions the way Horatio in *Hamlet* watches the king.

Observing how the king responded to the shows put on for him would have been useful (it would in this case have given a clear indication of the sort of thing that put him to sleep), but it did not answer the key questions: What would keep the king awake? What would catch his attention without triggering his fear? What would excite his interest, gratify his curiosity, arouse his generosity, make him long for more? The King's Men needed to enter the king's head. Staring at James from the midst of the cheering crowd was no substitute for the kind of conversational insight that Harington had, a privilege from which a mere player would have been excluded. There were, however, other means of access into the king's interests and imagination. James had taken the unusual step of publishing a learned dialogue on witchcraft in 1597, the *Dae-*

monologie. This work, which went through two London editions in 1603 and which Shakespeare could easily have encountered, acknowledges the existence of skepticism—"many can scarcely believe that there is such a thing as witchcraft"—but argues that disbelief is a step toward atheism and damnation. Witches do indeed exist and are a significant danger to the whole realm.

Shakespeare knew about witches long before the Scottish king lectured his subjects on them. He would have heard of the ecclesiastical commissions that traveled through the country seeking out necromancers, conjurers, and magical healers; the parliamentary statutes repeatedly passed making "witchcrafts, enchantments, and sorceries" punishable by death; the laws forbidding anyone from attempting through charms or other illicit means to know "how long her Majesty shall live or continue, or who shall reign as King or Queen of this Realm of England after her Highness's decease." He may well have read the act passed in 1604 against anyone who

> shall consult, covenant with, entertain, employ, feed, or reward any evil and wicked Spirit to or for any intent or purpose; or take up any dead man, woman, or child out of his, her, or their grave, or any other place where the dead body resteth, or the skin, bone, or any other part of any dead person, to be employed or used in any manner of witchcraft, sorcery, charm, or enchantment; or shall use, practice, or exercise any witchcraft, enchantment, charm, or sorcery, whereby any person shall be killed, destroyed, wasted, consumed, pined, or lamed in his or her body.

As a person with deep roots in country life, Shakespeare would have heard of and perhaps directly known cases where sick cattle or damaged crops or children dying of lingering illnesses were blamed upon the malevolent magic of neighbors. People could attribute such catastrophes to natural causes as well, but an unexpected blow—a violent storm; a mysterious, wasting sickness; an inexplicable case of impotence—set them grumbling menacingly at the poor, ugly, defenseless old woman in the hovel at the end of the lane. "Many witches are found there," a German visitor to England noted in 1592, "who frequently do much mischief by means of hail and tempests."

An ambitious, self-aggrandizing justice of the peace named Brian Darcy published an account of the pretrial examinations of accused witches that he conducted in Essex in 1582. His account provides a close-up, eerily detailed glimpse of a rural community grappling with everyday concerns, and in this case a community being prodded by its magistrate toward violent persecution. Using the testimony of small children and quarreling neighbors to ferret out the occult crimes he knew he would discover, the zealous magistrate identified a whole network of witches who conspired with demonic spirits—"familiars" in the form of dogs, cats, and toads, with names like Tiffin, Titty, and Suckin—to wreak havoc. After she had a falling-out with Mrs. Thurlow, Ursula Kemp sent her spirit Tiffin ("like a white lamb") to rock Thurlow's infant's cradle, until the infant almost fell onto the ground. "Mother Mansfield" came to Joan Cheston's house and asked for some curds. Joan said she had none, "and within a while after some of her cattle were taken lame." "Lynd's wife" reported that Mother Mansfield came to her and asked for a "mess of milk"; she refused, explaining that "she had but a little, not so much as would suckle her calf." That night her calf died. It is all at a similarly local level: a small uncharitable act, a few harsh words—and then the nasty consequences. A farmer's wife churns and churns but can get no butter; thread breaks in the spindle, even though the spindle was perfectly smooth; a child who has been robust begins to languish. This was the everyday world of places like Snitterfield and Wilmcote and Shottery, the villages near Stratford that Shakespeare knew from the inside. What was missing, if they were lucky, was a Brian Darcy to transform the ordinary tension, frustration, and grief of early modern village life into judicial murder.

From James's *Daemonologie*, Shakespeare would have learned that though the king was struck by the fact that so many of the people accused of witchcraft were old women from small villages, he was not at all interested in the local hatreds and heartbreaks that generated most of the accusations. Unlike Brian Darcy's, the king's mind soared away from the familiar rancors of rural life. As befitted a monarch of wide reading,

James had grand metaphysical theories, complex political strategies, the subtle ideas of an intellectual and a statesman. He was, moreover, well aware that many of the charges of witchcraft were mere fantasies and lies, and he was proud of his perspicacity.

By themselves, James thought, witches have no magical powers. But they have made a pact with the devil, a pact solemnized in the nightmarish assemblies known as sabbats. In order to lure Christians away from the true faith, the devil deludes his followers into thinking that they have been granted special gifts and that they possess the ability to harm their neighbors. Hence what appear to be the effects of magic are for the most part counterfeits, illusions cunningly crafted to deceive "men's outward senses." These illusions are often startlingly impressive, to be sure, but their effectiveness is not surprising, "since we see by common proof that a simple juggler will make a hundred things seem both to our eyes and ears otherwise than they are." The devil's power has limits, set down before the foundations of the world were laid—he cannot create actual miracles, he cannot destroy godly magistrates, he cannot read thoughts— but he is more accomplished than the greatest mountebank. Indeed, the devil teaches his disciples "many jugglery tricks at cards, dice, and such like, to deceive men's senses" with false miracles; he is an exceptionally subtle corrupter of anyone with moral weaknesses; and if he cannot read thoughts, he is learned enough in physiognomy to guess at men's thoughts by studying their faces.

The devil's goal is the ruin not of a tiny hamlet but of a whole kingdom, and hence his principal target is not this or that local villager but God's own representative on earth, the king. It is to ensnare princes that the devil teaches his disciples, his "scholars," as the owlish James calls them, his tricks. And, as one might expect of a malevolent being who has lived for centuries, closely observed men and beasts and the natural world, and thoroughly mastered the arts of deception, the devil's tricks are impressive. "He will make his scholars to creep in credit with Princes," James writes, "by fore-telling them many great things"—the outcome of battles, the fate of commonwealths, and the like—"part true, part false." If Satan's scholars only spoke lies, their master would soon lose credit, and if they straightforwardly told the truth, they could scarcely do the devil's work. So their prognostications are "always doubtsome, as his Oracles were." Through his astonishing agility Satan provides other means for witches to please princes, "by fair banquets and dainty dishes, carried in short space from the farthest part of the world." And he seems to confer upon his agents spectral forces, "which all are but impressions in the air, easily gathered by a spirit," in order to delude men's senses.

Ambiguous and deceptive prophecies; seductive pleasures; airy, insubstantial illusions—these are among the devices witches employ, James thought, when they set out to destroy someone. Shakespeare, as *Macbeth* shows, took careful note. He may also have gone out of his way to acquaint himself with the king's actual dealings with witches. He could have inquired about these dealings from anyone who had been in Scotland during James's reign there, and there were many potential informants, since a great number of his compatriots followed James to London. He could also have read about them in a sensational pamphlet, *News from Scotland*, published in 1591. Two years before, a storm had disrupted James's marriage arrangements; his bride-to-be, Anne of Denmark, was supposed to sail from Denmark to Scotland in 1589, but thunder, lightning, and rain forced the ship to take refuge in Oslo. James impetuously sailed there and married her. When he returned some months later to Scotland, he became convinced that the tempest had been the result of diabolical intervention. He became directly involved in an unprecedented series of witchcraft investigations, investigations that claimed to discover a network of witches in North Berwick—about twenty miles from Edinburgh, on the Firth of Forth—involved in communal devil worship.

One of the accused, Agnes Thompson, confessed to the king and his council that on Halloween 1590 some two hundred witches had sailed to the town in sieves. Then, while one of the coven, Geillis Duncane, played a tune on a small instrument, a "Jew's trump," they sang and danced their way into the kirk (church) where Satan impatiently awaited them. The devil put his buttocks over the pulpit railing for the witches to kiss, as a sign of fealty, and then made his "ungodly exhortations," focusing his malice against "the greatest enemy he hath in the world," namely, the king of Scotland. James thus found himself the direct object of attack in the satanic sermon, no doubt a satisfying confirmation of the sanctity of his royal person, but also unnerving. For during interrogation—and James was an enthusiastic user of torture to obtain confessions—Agnes Thompson disclosed some of the devices that had been used against him: "She confessed that she took a black toad, and did hang the same up by the heels three days, and collected and gathered the venom as it dropped and fell from it in an oyster shell, and kept the same venom close covered, until she should obtain any part or piece of foul linen cloth that had appertained to the King's Majesty." If she had been able to get hold of a fragment of his shirt or handkerchief, she told the king, and had anointed it with the venom, then she would have "bewitched him to death." And though this plot was frustrated, she and her companions had succeeded in causing at least some harm. They had christened a cat, tied body parts from a dead man to its limbs, and then thrown it into the sea. The effect was to raise "such a tempest in the sea as a greater hath not been seen" and to provoke a contrary wind against the king's ship, coming from Denmark. "His Majesty had never come safely from the sea, if his faith had not prevailed above their intentions."

Disposed though he was to believe every one of these absurd charges, James was eager not to seem naive, and he declared that the miserable women he was interrogating, stripping, prodding obscenely, and torturing were all "extreme liars." But one of them, Agnes Sampson, took him aside and told him "the very words" that he had exchanged with his bride on their wedding night in Norway. James was astonished "and swore by the living God that he believed that all the devils in hell could not have discovered the same, acknowledging her words to be most true." The king was then convinced that the witches were present not only on the tempest-tossed sea and in the graveyard where they dug up corpses and performed their obscene rites, but also in the bedroom, where they somehow overheard the most intimate moments of marital conversation.

These beliefs, and both the political pretensions and the deep fears they bespoke, were not hidden away in some dark place where only James's intimates knew of them; they were matters of public record.

Shakespeare seems to have noted them carefully, and he may have observed something still more germane to his purpose. When James heard that the witches had danced into the North Berwick kirk to the sound of a reel played on a small trumpet by Geillis Duncane, he was struck with "a wonderful admiration." He sent for the witch and commanded her to play the same dance before him.

Poor Geillis Duncane: a maidservant, she had originally aroused her master's suspicions because she had proved all too successful in her efforts "to help all such as were troubled or grieved with any kind of sickness." Though she first protested that she was innocent, a series of brutal body searches and tortures—"the Pilliwinks upon her fingers, which is a grievous torture, and binding or wrenching her head with a cord or rope"—had elicited from her the desired confession. Now she found herself performing the fatal role that had been violently imposed upon her before the fascinated, horrified, and pleased king. "In respect of the strangeness of these matters," *News from Scotland* reports, James "took great delight to be present at their examinations." Witchcraft was not only a frightening danger; it was also a wonderful show.

As Shakespeare grasped, the king was aroused by witches to "a wonderful admiration"—precisely the effect that the King's Men were hoping to achieve. Hence the astonishing spectacle with which Shakespeare opened his new Scottish show:

> When shall we three meet again?
> In thunder, lightning, or in rain?
> (*Macbeth*, 1.1.1–2)

Taking over Gwinn's device—three sibyls stepping forward as if from a wood and prophesying the future—Shakespeare recapitulates the promise to Banquo's heirs of stable dynastic rule. Yet the pretty civilities of St. John's College are altogether swept away. Once again Shakespeare radically altered his source, literally introducing opacity—"fog and filthy air"—where there was once simple transparency. The play begins with three strange creatures all right:

> What are these,
> So withered, and so wild in their attire,
> That look not like th'inhabitants o'th' earth
> And yet are on't?. . .
>
> . . . .
>
> You should be women,
> And yet your beards forbid me to interpret
> That you are so—
>
> (1.3.37–44)

But the scene is a wild heath. When Macbeth enters, the "weird sisters" greet him in terms that startlingly recall, virtually as a quotation, Gwinn's entertainment:

> FIRST WITCH: All hail, Macbeth! Hail to thee, Thane of Glamis
> SECOND WITCH: All hail, Macbeth! Hail to thee, Thane of Cawdor.
> THIRD WITCH: All hail, Macbeth, that shalt be king hereafter!
>
> (1.3.46–48)

But what was reassuring is now turned inside out, what was warmly welcoming is made chilling. Even within the world of the play, Macbeth, to whom the ostensibly happy prophecy is made, registers the disturbance. "Good sir," asks his friend Banquo, "why do you start and seem to fear / Things that do sound so fair?" (1.3.49–50).

Shakespeare was burrowing deep into the dark fantasies that swirled about in the king's brain. It is all here: the ambiguous prophecies designed to lure men to their destruction, the "Shipwrecking storms and direful thunders" (1.2.26) that once threatened Anne of Denmark, the murderous hatred of anointed kings, the illusory apparitions, the fiendish equivocations, the loathsome concoction of body parts, even the witches' sailing in a sieve to do their diabolical mischief—

> But in a sieve I'll thither sail,
> And like a rat without a tail

I'll do, I'll do, and I'll do.
(1.3.7–9)

If James had been fascinated by a command performance of diabolical
music, the King's Men would give him that and more:

> Come, sisters, cheer we up his sprites,
> And show the best of our delights.
> I'll charm the air to give a sound
> While you perform your antic round,
> That this great king may kindly say
> Our duties did his welcome pay.
> (4.1.143–48)

"This great king"—the witches are referring to Macbeth, but it is not the
imagined usurper who craved demonic entertainment; it is the living
king of England and Scotland.

Why should Shakespeare have risked the irony of this transformation? Why, for that matter, did he risk the transformation of Gwinn's
reassuring compliment into a nightmarish tragedy of betrayal and
destruction? *Macbeth* does not represent disaster miraculously averted; it
does not confirm the belief that a divinity hedges an anointed king; it
does not support James's fantasy that a truly good man is invulnerable to
the malice of witchcraft. Trust is violated, families are destroyed, nature
itself is poisoned. To a king who paled at the sight of sharp steel, it offered
the insistent spectacle of a bloody dagger, both a real dagger and what
Macbeth calls a dagger of the mind. True, the pageant promises the throne
to an endless succession of Banquo's heirs. True as well, the restoration of
order in the tragedy's final moments could be seen as a representation
of the order that had been restored to the realm after the Gunpowder Plot:
the severed head of Macbeth, carried onstage at the concluding moment
by the victorious Macduff, was a reminder of the conspirators' heads that
members of the audience could see every time they walked across London Bridge. Yet *Macbeth* hardly sits comfortably with the functions of
prince-pleasing or popular reassurance. The materials Shakespeare

worked with touched off something extremely peculiar in him, something that does not fit the overarching scheme.

Shakespeare was a professional risk-taker. He wrote under pressure—judging from its unusual brevity, *Macbeth* was composed in a very short time—and he went where his imagination took him. If the cheerful sibyls of St. John's became the weird sisters dancing around a cauldron bubbling with hideous contents—

> Scale of dragon, tooth of wolf,
> Witches' mummy, maw and gulf
> Of the ravined salt-sea shark,
> Root of hemlock digged i'th' dark,
> Liver of blaspheming Jew,
> Gall of goat, and slips of yew
> Slivered in the moon's eclipse,
> Nose of Turk, and Tartar's lips,
> Finger of birth-strangled babe
> Ditch-delivered by a drab
>
> (4.1.22–31)

—then Shakespeare was obliged to pursue the course. The alternative was to write the kind of play that would put James to sleep and send the thrill-seeking crowds to rival theaters. But this explanation still leaves open the question of why Shakespeare's imagination took the peculiar turn that it did.

Something comparable to the potent blend of opportunism and imaginative generosity, appropriation and moral revulsion aroused in Shakespeare by the crowd's laughter at Lopez's execution may have been at work. When Shakespeare learned about the king's wonder and delight at Geillis Duncane's performance, he grasped what could be done to gratify the king's fantasies, and at the same instant his imagination began to enter into the figure of the condemned. He and his company would perform in the place, as it were, of the witch and her coven. They would sing the songs and chant the charms and provide the fascination that James desired. And they would complicate that fascination, moving through the figures of the weird sisters to the larger, more familiar world of domestic intimacy and court intrigue.

It is the general gift of the imagination to enter into the lives of others, but in the case of witches there is a special and particular bond: witches are the progeny of the imagination. The witchmongers of the Middle Ages and the Renaissance—the men who thought that there should be more denunciations of neighbors, more body searches, tortures, trials, and, above all, executions—believed that witches trafficked in fantasy. According to the famous witchcraft manual, the *Malleus maleficarum*, devils provoke and shape fantasies by direct corporeal intervention in the mind. Demonic spirits can incite what the authors, the Dominican inquisitors Heinrich Kramer and James Sprenger, call a "local motion" in the minds of those awake as well as asleep, stirring up and exciting the inner perceptions, "so that ideas retained in the repositories of their minds are drawn out and made apparent to the faculties of fancy and imagination, so that such men imagine these things to be true." This process of making a stir in the mind and moving images from one part of the brain to another is, they write, called "interior temptation." It can lead men to see objects before their eyes—daggers, for example— that are not in fact there; conversely, it can lead men *not* to see other objects—their own penises, for example—that are still there, though concealed from view by what the inquisitors term a "glamour." Hence, Kramer and Sprenger write, "a certain man tells that, when he had lost his member, he approached a known witch to ask her to restore it to him. She told the afflicted man to climb a certain tree, and that he might take which he liked out of a nest in which there were several members. And when he tried to take a big one, the witch said: You must not take that one; adding because it belonged to a parish priest."

Reading this and other passages in the *Malleus maleficarum*, an older contemporary of Shakespeare's, an English country gentleman named Reginald Scot, said that he was tempted to regard the whole work as a "bawdy discourse," a kind of obscene joke book. But he checked the impulse: "these are no jests," he writes, "for they be written by them that were and are judges upon the lives and deaths of those persons." Scot's response in 1584 was to publish *The Discovery of Witchcraft*, the greatest

English contribution to the skeptical critique of witchcraft. On his accession to the English throne, James ordered all copies of Scot's book to be
burned. But it seems, from allusions that he made to it, that Shakespeare
got hold of a copy and read it when he wrote *Macbeth*.

Scot argues that it is the masters of language, the poets, who have
been the principal sources of the murderous fantasies that lead to witch
hunts. The poet Ovid affirms, writes Scot, that witches

> can raise and suppress lightening and thunder, rain and hail,
> clouds and winds, tempests and earthquakes. Others do write,
> that they can pull down the moon and the stars. Some write that
> with wishing they can send needles into the livers of their ene-
> mies. Some that they can transfer corn in the blade from one
> place to another. Some, that they can cure diseases supernatu-
> rally, fly in the air, and dance with devils. . . . They can raise spir-
> its (as others affirm) dry up springs, turn the course of running
> waters, inhibit the sun, and stay both day and night, changing
> the one into the other. They can go in and out at auger holes, and
> sail in an egg shell, a cockle or muscle shell, through and under
> the tempestuous seas. They can go invisible, and deprive men of
> their privities, and otherwise of the act and use of venery. They
> can bring souls out of the graves.

Such are the visions that poets have given us, and they have led people
to torture and kill their innocent neighbors. But, Scot concludes, there is
a defense against this ghastly mistake: do not believe the songs that
poets sing.

The King's Men did not preach anything of the kind: dressing themselves up as witches, they were determined to profit from those obsessions. The weird sisters in Shakespeare's play apparently traffic in bad
weather: "When shall we three meet again? / In thunder, lightning, or in
rain?" (1.1.1–2). They seem to cause unnatural darkness: "By th' clock 'tis
day, / And yet dark night strangles the travelling lamp" (2.4.6–7). They
make themselves invisible, fly in the air, dance with devils, sail in a sieve,
cast spells, and drain men dry. But, though many of the demonic powers

listed by Scot as the inventions of poets are alluded to in *Macbeth*, it is oddly difficult to determine what, if anything, the witches actually do in the play.

The opacity in *Macbeth* is not produced by the same radical excision of motivation Shakespeare so strikingly employed in *Hamlet, Othello,* and *King Lear.* If the audience does not know exactly why Hamlet assumes his madness or Iago hates Othello or Lear puts the love test to his daughters, it most assuredly knows why Macbeth plots to assassinate King Duncan: spurred on by his wife, he wishes to seize the crown for himself. But in a tortured soliloquy, Macbeth reveals that he is deeply baffled by his own murderous fantasies:

> My thought, whose murder yet is but fantastical,
> Shakes so my single state of man that function
> Is smothered in surmise, and nothing is
> But what is not.
>
> (1.3.138–41)

At the center of the familiar and conventional motive there is a dark hole—"nothing is / But what is not." And this hole that is inside Macbeth is linked to the dark presence, within his consciousness and within the play's world, of the witches. Do they actually arouse the thought of murdering Duncan in Macbeth's mind, or is that thought already present before he encounters them? Do they have some affinity with Lady Macbeth—who calls upon the spirits that attend on mortal thoughts to "unsex" her (1.5.38–39)—or is their evil completely independent of hers? Does the witches' warning—"beware Macduff" (4.1.87)—actually induce Macbeth to kill Macduff's family, or has he already waded too deep in bloodshed to turn back? Do their ambiguous prophecies lead him to a final, fatal overconfidence, or is his end the result of his loss of popular support and the superior power of Malcolm's army? None of the questions are answered. At the end of the play the weird sisters are left unmentioned, their role unresolved. Shakespeare refuses to allow the play to localize and contain the threat in the bodies of witches.

Macbeth leaves the weird sisters unpunished but manages to impli-

cate them in a monstrous threat to the fabric of civilized life. The genius
of the play is bound up with this power of implication, by means of which
the audience can never quite be done with them, for they are most suggestively present when they cannot be seen, when they are absorbed in
the ordinary relations of everyday life. If you are worried about losing
your manhood and are afraid of the power of women, it is not enough to
look to the bearded hags on the heath, look to your wife. If you are worried about temptation, fear your own dreams. If you are anxious about
your future, scrutinize your best friends. And if you fear spiritual desola-
tion, turn your eyes on the contents not of the hideous cauldron but of
your skull: "O, full of scorpions is my mind, dear wife!" (3.2.37).

   The witches—eerie, indefinable, impossible to locate securely or to
understand—are the embodiment of the principle of opacity that Shakespeare embraced in his great tragedies. Shakespeare's theater is the equiv-
ocal space where conventional explanations fall away, where one person
can enter another person's mind, and where the fantastic and the bodily
touch. This conception of his art is what it meant for him to take the
place of Geillis Duncane and perform his theatrical witchcraft before the
wondering gaze of the king. There is no record of the king's response, but
Shakespeare's company never fell from its position as the King's Men.

CHAPTER 12

The Triumph of the Everyday

S HAKESPEARE SEEMS TO HAVE begun contemplating the
possibility of retirement—not so much planning for it as brooding
about its perils—as early as 1604, when he sat down to write *King
Lear*. The tragedy is his greatest meditation on extreme old age; on
the painful necessity of renouncing power; on the loss of house, land, authority, love, eyesight, and sanity itself. This vision of devastating loss surged up
not in an eccentric recluse and not in a man facing the onset of his own decay,
but in a hugely energetic and successful playwright who had just turned forty.
Even at a time when life expectancy was short, forty years old was not
regarded as ancient. It was the middle of the passage, not the moment of
reckoning. Shakespeare was in age closer to the play's young people—
Goneril, Regan, and Cordelia; Edgar and Edmund—than he was to the two
old men, Lear and Gloucester, whose terrible fates he depicts.

Once again, there is no easy, obvious link between what Shakespeare
wrote—here a tremendous explosion of rage, madness, and grief—and
the known circumstances of his own life. His father had died in 1601,
probably in his sixties. In 1604 his mother was still alive and not, as far as
we know, either mad or tyrannical. He had two daughters, but he could

hardly claim that he had given them everything or that they had attempted to turn him out of his own house. He had, it is true, a younger brother named Edmund, the name of the villainous plotter in *King Lear*, but Edmund Shakespeare—an aspiring actor in London—was obviously no match for the bastard son of Gloucester, any more than Shakespeare's brother Richard could conjure up, in anything but name, England's homicidal hunchback king.

Shakespeare might well have been set to thinking about the story of Lear by a widely discussed lawsuit that had occurred in late 1603. The two elder daughters of a doddering gentleman named Sir Brian Annesley attempted to get their father legally certified as insane, thereby enabling themselves to take over his estate, while his youngest daughter vehemently protested on her father's behalf. The youngest daughter's name happened to be Cordell, a name almost identical to Cordella, the name of the daughter in the venerable legend of King Leir who tried to save her father from the malevolent designs of her two older sisters. The uncanny coincidence of the names and the stories must have been hard to resist.

Whether or not the Annesley case actually triggered the writing of the tragedy, Shakespeare was singularly alert to the way in which the Leir legend was in touch with ordinary family tensions and familiar fears associated with old age. For his play's central concerns, Shakespeare simply looked around him at the everyday world. This seems at first an odd claim: of all of his tragedies, *King Lear* seems the wildest and the strangest. The old king swears by Apollo and Hecate and calls upon the thunder to "Smite flat the thick rotundity o' the world!" (3.2.7). His friend, the Earl of Gloucester, thinks he is the victim of divine malevolence: "As flies to wanton boys are we to the gods; / They kill us for their sport" (4.1.37–38). The Bedlam beggar Poor Tom screams that he is possessed by a legion of exotic devils: Modo, Mahu, and Flibbertigibbet. But despite the constant invocation of a grand metaphysical frame, the play's events, terrible and trivial alike, occur in a universe in which there seems to be no overarching design at all. The devils are altogether fictional, and the gods on whom Lear and Gloucester call are conspicuously, devastatingly silent. What surrounds the characters with their loves and hatreds and torments is the most ordinary of worlds—"low farms, / Poor pelting

villages, sheep-cotes, and mills" (2.3.17–18)—and the action that trig-
gers the whole hideous train of events is among the most ordinary of
decisions: a retirement.

In the culture of Tudor and Stuart England, where the old
demanded the public deference of the young, retirement was the focus of
particular anxiety. It put a severe strain on the politics and psychology of
deference by driving a wedge between status—what Lear at society's pinnacle calls "The name, and all the additions to a king" (1.1.136)—and
power. In both the state and the family, the strain could be somewhat
eased by transferring power to the eldest legitimate male successor, but as
the families of both the legendary Lear and the real Brian Annesley
show, such a successor did not always exist. In the absence of a male heir,
the aged Lear, determined to "shake all cares and business" from himself
and confer them on "younger strengths," attempts to divide his kingdom
among his daughters so that, as he puts it, "future strife / May be prevented now" (1.1.37–38, 42–43). But this attempt, centered on a public
love test, is a disastrous failure, since it leads him to banish the one child
who truly loves him.

Shakespeare contrives to show that the problem with which his characters are grappling does not simply result from the absence of a son and
heir. In his most brilliant and complex use of a double plot, he intertwines
the story of Lear and his three daughters with the story of Gloucester and
his two sons, a story he adapted from an episode he read in Philip Sidney's
prose romance, *Arcadia*. Gloucester has a legitimate heir, his elder son,
Edgar, as well as an illegitimate son, Edmund, and in this family the tragic
conflict originates not in an unusual manner of transferring property from
one generation to another, such as Lear is attempting, but rather in the
reverse: Edmund seethes with murderous resentment at the disadvantage
entirely customary for someone in his position, both as a younger son and
as what was called a base or natural child.

In the strange universe of *King Lear*, nothing but precipitous ruin
lies on the other side of retirement, just as nothing but a bleak, feature-
less heath lies on the other side of the castle gate. In Shakespeare's imagination, the decision to withdraw from work—"To shake all cares and
business from our age," as Lear says, "Conferring them on younger

strengths" (1.1.37–38)—is a catastrophe. To be sure, the work in question here is ruling a kingdom, and Shakespeare's age had every reason to fear the crisis in authority that inevitably accompanied the debility of the ruler and the transfer of power. But the play is not only a warning to monarchs. It taps into a far more pervasive fear in this period, a period that had very few of the means that our society (itself hardly a model of virtue) now routinely employs to ease the anxieties and relieve the needs of the old.

Shakespeare's world constantly told itself that authority naturally inhered in the elderly. At stake, they said, was not simply a convenient social arrangement—convenient, in any case, for the old and for anyone who hoped someday to become old—but rather the moral structure of the universe, the sanctified, immemorial order of things. But at the same time, they nervously acknowledged that this order of things was unstable and that age's claim to authority was pathetically vulnerable to the ruthless ambitions of the young. Once a father had turned over his property to his children, once he had lost his ability to enforce his will, his authority would begin to crumble away. Even in the house that had once been his own, he would become what was called a sojourner. There could even be a ritualized acknowledgment of this drastic change in status, as testimony in a contemporary lawsuit suggests: having agreed to give his daughter in marriage to Hugh, with half of his land, the widower Anseline and the married couple were to live together in one house. "And the same Anseline went out of the house and handed over to them the door by the hasp, and at once begged lodging out of charity."

Retelling the Leir story was one way that Shakespeare and his contemporaries articulated their anxiety, but they had other, more practical ways to deal with the fragility of custom. Parents facing retirement frequently hired a lawyer to draw up what were called maintenance agreements, contracts by which, in return for the transfer of family property, children undertook to provide food, clothing, and shelter. The extent of parental anxiety may be gauged by the great specificity of many of these requirements—so many yards of woolen cloth, pounds of coal, or bushels of grain—and by the pervasive fear of being turned out of the house in the wake of a quarrel. Maintenance agreements stipulated that the children were only legal guardians of their parents' well-being, "depositaries" of the parental property. The parents could "reserve" some rights over this property, and, theoretically at least, if their "reservation" was not honored, they could move to reclaim what they had given away.

King Lear, set in a pagan Britain roughly contemporary with the prophet Isaiah, is very far from the Renaissance world of customary arrangements and legal protections—the world of the yeomen, artisans, and tradesmen from whose midst Shakespeare had emerged. But, notwithstanding the play's archaic setting, at the core of the tragedy is the great fear that haunted the playwright's own class: the fear of humiliation, abandonment, and a loss of identity in the wake of retirement. Lear's maddened rage is a response not only to his daughters' vicious ingratitude but also to the horror of being turned into an ordinary old man, a sojourner begging his children for charity:

> Ask her forgiveness?
> Do you but mark how this becomes the house:
> "Dear daughter, I confess that I am old;
> Age is unnecessary. On my knees I beg
> That you'll vouchsafe me raiment, bed, and food."
> (2.4.145–49)

His cruel daughter, in response, unbendingly proposes that he "return and sojourn with my sister" (2.4.198).

Near the climax of this terrible scene in which the wicked Goneril and Regan, by relentlessly diminishing his retinue, in effect strip away his social identity, Lear speaks as if he had actually drawn up a maintenance agreement with his daughters:

> LEAR: I gave you all—
> REGAN: And in good time you gave it.
> LEAR: Made you my guardians, my depositaries;
>   But kept a reservation to be followed
>   With such a number.
> (2.4.245–48)

But there is no maintenance agreement between Lear and his daughters; there could be none in the world of absolute power—of all or nothing—that he inhabits.

Shakespeare had no intention of someday going to the door of New Place, stepping across the threshold, and then asking his daughters to take him back in as a sojourner. It was not a matter of mistrust—he seems to have loved and trusted one of his daughters at least. It was a matter of identity. If *King Lear* is any indication, he shared with his contemporaries a fear of retirement and dread of dependence upon children. And from the surviving evidence, he could scarcely be expected to find comfort in the enduring bond with his wife. His way of dealing with this fear was work—the enormous labors that enabled him to accumulate a small fortune—and then the investment of his capital in land and tithes (an agricultural commodities investment), so that he could assure himself a steady annual income. He could not count on acting and touring and turning out two plays a year forever; someday it would have to come to a stop. What then? From 1602 to 1613, in the midst of astonishingly creative years, Shakespeare carefully accumulated and laid out his money so that in his old age he would never have to depend upon his daughters—or upon the theater.

Shakespeare had made his fortune virtually entirely on his own. His mother's inheritance, such as it was, had been first mortgaged and then forfeited through his father's incompetence or improvidence; his father's standing in Stratford had been compromised by debt and possibly by recusancy; his brothers amounted to little or nothing, his sister, Joan, married a poor hatter; and he himself had married a woman of very modest means. No convenient bequests had come his way; no wealthy relations had provided assistance at key moments; and no local magnate had spotted his brilliant promise when he was still a boy and helped him to a start in life. New Place was the tangible fruit of his own imagination and his hard work.

To acquire such a house meant that Shakespeare had had to save his money. The limited evidence that survives suggests that in London he lived frugally. He rented rooms in relatively modest surroundings: records from a minor lawsuit show that in 1604—the year he wrote part or all of

Measure for Measure, All's Well That Ends Well, and *King Lear*—he lived above a French wig-maker's shop on the corner of Mugwell and Silver Streets in Cripplegate, at the northwest corner of the city walls. He seems to have had an affinity for neighborhoods—Shoreditch, Bishopsgate, Cripplegate, and the Clink in Surrey—inhabited by artisans, many of whom were émigrés from France or the Low Countries. These were not disreputable haunts, but they were modest, and the rents were low. How many rooms he rented, or how spacious they were, is unknown, but he seems to have furnished them sparsely. His personal property in London, assessed for tax purposes, was only five pounds. (The property of the most affluent inhabitant of the parish was assessed at three hundred pounds.) Of course, Shakespeare could have hidden things away—books, paintings, plate—to reduce his liability, but the assessors at least saw very few signs of wealth.

Generations of scholars have combed the archives for more details, but the principal records are a succession of notices for the nonpayment of taxes. In 1597, the year Shakespeare bought the handsome New Place, the tax collectors for Bishopsgate ward affirmed that William Shakespeare, assessed the sum of thirteen shillings fourpence on his personal property, had not paid. The next year he was again delinquent, and a further notice, in 1600, when he was living on the Surrey side of the river, suggests that he was still in arrears. He may in the end have paid his taxes—the records are incomplete—but it does not seem likely. Shakespeare was someone who not only lived a modest London life but also hated to let even small sums of money slip through his fingers.

Perhaps he was worrying about the financial security of his wife and daughters back in Stratford, perhaps he hated the example of his father's embarrassments, perhaps he told himself that he would do anything not to end up like the wretched Greene. For whatever the reason, Shakespeare seems to have treated money—his money at least—with considerable seriousness. No one refers to him as a skinflint, but he did not like to waste his substance, and he was clearly determined not to be an easy mark for anyone. In 1604 he was storing more malt in his barn in Stratford than he (or, more to the point, his wife) needed for domestic consumption. He sold twenty bushels of it to a neighboring apothecary, Philip Rogers, who had a sideline brewing ale. Rogers's debt, including another two shillings he borrowed from Shakespeare, amounted to a little over two pounds. When the debtor returned only six shillings, Shakespeare hired a lawyer and took his neighbor to court to recover the remaining thirty-five shillings tenpence and damages. Thirty-five shillings tenpence was not a trivial sum at the time, but neither was it a king's ransom. It took energy to pursue the matter, just as it took energy a few years later when Shakespeare once again went to court to recover the six pounds, plus damages, that he said was owed to him by John Addenbrooke.

Shakespeare was hardly alone in pursuing such small sums; he lived in a litigious age, and the courts were flooded with suits of this kind. But no one forced him to go through the process, made all the more time-consuming by the fact that in some of these cases he probably had to travel to Stratford to do so. No, the odd pounds and shillings and pence must have mattered to him, and not, strictly speaking, because the owner of New Place needed them to live on.

Standing in the graveyard at Elsinore, Hamlet contemplates a skull that the gravedigger has dislodged with his dirty shovel: "This fellow might be in 's time a great buyer of land," he remarks to Horatio,

> with his statutes, his recognizances, his fines, his double vouchers, his recoveries. Is this the fine of his fines and the recovery of his recoveries, to have his fine pate full of fine dirt? Will his vouchers vouch him no more of his purchases, and double ones too, than the length and breadth of a pair of indentures? The very conveyances of his lands will hardly lie in this box; and must th'inheritor himself have no more, ha? (5.1.94–102)

It is altogether fitting that Hamlet should speak with such wry disdain. For on the one hand, he is the prince of Denmark, far above mere moneygrubbing, and on the other hand, as he has made overwhelmingly clear, he is indifferent to all worldly ambition. But where did Prince Hamlet, we might wonder, get his technical knowledge of the property law he despises—recognizances, double vouchers, recoveries, and the like? From

someone who had a lively interest in land purchases: the playwright himself. Is this hypocrisy? Not at all. Shakespeare could imagine what it
would feel like to be a melancholy prince and conjure up his brooding
laughter at the vanity of human striving, but he himself could not afford
to be indifferent to the everyday enterprise of making a living.

At the time he was writing Hamlet's lines about the "great buyer of
land," Shakespeare's interest in real estate investments was apparently
becoming known to his fellow townsmen, who must, in any event, have
been struck by his worldly success. In 1598 Abraham Sturley of Stratford
wrote to a friend, then in London, that according to information he had
received, "our countryman Mr. Shaksper is willing to disburse some
money upon some odd yardland or other at Shottery or near about us."
These are Stratford businessmen consulting with each other about the
best way to get their "countryman" to invest in some scheme of theirs—
the playwright was evidently regarded as both wealthy enough and canny
enough to make a careful, coordinated approach to him worthwhile.

In May 1602 Shakespeare paid £320 for four "yardlands"—well over
one hundred acres—of arable land in Old Stratford, north of Stratford-
upon-Avon. A few months later he acquired title to a quarter-acre parcel,
comprising a garden and a cottage, just opposite his garden at New Place.
And in July 1605, a year after he took Rogers to court for thirty-five
shillings, Shakespeare paid the very substantial sum of £440 for a half
interest in a lease of "tithes of corn, grain, blade, and hay" in and around
Stratford. The lease—in effect an annuity—brought him £60 per annum.
He was planning for his future: the profit from the tithes would continue
through his lifetime and into the lives of his heirs.

An investment of this size reflected the exceptionally large income
that Shakespeare was earning in the early years of the reign of James I.
The suppression of *The Tragedy of Gowrie* could have harmed both
Shakespeare's company and his career, but it did not. James displayed a
peculiar quality that contemporaries would repeatedly note: he was nervous, sensitive, and on occasion dangerously paranoid, but then unexpectedly he could ignore or even laugh uproariously at what others—and not
only absolute monarchs—could have taken as gross insults. In the case of
the premier theater company of his new kingdom, he may simply have

regarded the players as too insignificant to care about, for good or ill. Or perhaps he regarded the players as a collective version of the court jester, whom Shakespeare depicts with such wry sympathy in *Twelfth Night*, *King Lear*, and elsewhere: the master can on occasion be annoyed with or even threaten his clown—"Take heed, sirrah; the whip" (*King Lear*, 1.4.94)—but it would be vulgar to get more seriously nettled.

The King's Men were exceptionally busy, both at court and at the Globe, and Shakespeare must have been heavily involved as writer, director, and actor, as well as principal business partner. His workload must have been staggering. He would have had to keep track of the receipts and expenditures; rewrite some of the scenes; help with the casting; decide on cuts; weigh in on interpretive decisions; consult on the properties, costumes, and music; and of course memorize his own parts. We have no idea in how many of the plays he actually appeared in the frenetic 1604–5 season, but it must have been more than a few. In such circumstances, the companies were not large enough to exempt one of its named actors from the stage, even if that particular actor was busy with a dozen other things. His name appears as one of the ten "principal comedians" in a 1598 performance of *Every Man In his Humour*. Presumably, he appeared in this play again at its court revival, and he probably made appearances in at least some of his own plays, many of which, notwithstanding the doubling of parts, require large casts.

Even for actors extraordinarily well trained in the arts of memory—and even for the playwright who wrote the plays—it must have been exhausting to mount so many complex productions in such a short time. But, of course, the invitation to perform before the king and the court was a signal honor, as well as a rich source of income: receiving a handsome £10 per performance, the company made £100 in the Christmas and New Year's season of 1605–6, £90 in that of 1606–7, £130 in 1608–9 and again in 1609–10, and £150 in 1610–11. These are very large sums of money, earned in the short holiday season. Meanwhile, the company continued to perform a full repertoire of plays at the Globe, and they still on many occasions packed their gear and went on tour: Oxford in May and June 1604; Barnstaple and Oxford again in 1605; Oxford, Leicester, Dover, Saffron Walden, Maidstone, and Marlborough in 1606. We do not know if Shakespeare went on all of these trips; by the early fall it was already time for him to think hard about the coming season, when the company would introduce new plays, revive still others, perform again at court, keep their public audience happy at the Globe.

As always, Shakespeare had a special, grim reason to throw himself into a frenzy of work: one morning someone—it could be a lackey in an attic room or a great lady in her curtained bed—would wake up with the telltale buboes in the groin or the armpits. The plague would have announced its return, and in a matter of days or weeks the theaters would be shut down. It must have seemed crucially important to all of the company members always to be putting money in their purses, while there was money to be had. They could not afford to miss any occasion for profit, and, plague permitting, the regime of James I provided many occasions.

Shakespeare and his company had not been forced to choose one venue or another and let the others slip away: they had not been frozen out of the new Scottish-dominated court; they had not alienated their London popular audience; they had not lost touch with the cities and towns where they would perform on tour. On the contrary, they had consolidated their grip on each of these key constituencies and were busily trying to add yet another venue. The plan did not originate with Shakespeare, but it must have become part of his long-term strategy. The strategy was to dominate the market—the market here being the performance of plays to the court and to the public at large, in London and in the provinces—or to come as close to doing so as possible.

During the reign of Elizabeth, in 1596, the entrepreneur James Burbage (the father of the famous actor) paid six hundred pounds for property that had, until the dissolution of the monasteries, been part of a large friary, belonging to the order known as the Friars Preachers or Black Friars. The location was a desirable one: though it was within the city walls, it was a "liberty" and hence outside the jurisdiction of the city fathers. A theater had already been established twenty years earlier in one of the Blackfriars halls, where a succession of children's companies had performed. But this enterprise had collapsed after eight financially troubled years, and the indoor theater had gone silent. The enterprising

Burbage smelled a profit, if he could reopen it for performances by what was then the Lord Chamberlain's Men. He had built the Theater, one of England's first outdoor playhouses; now, by reconstructing the hall where the children's companies had played, he would open England's first indoor playhouse for adult actors. The location was prestigious—not in the suburbs, hard by the bearbaiting arenas and execution grounds, but right in the heart of the city. The Blackfriars hall was much smaller than the Globe, but it had the great advantage, given the vagaries of the English weather, of being roofed and enclosed. It was, at least by comparison with the open amphitheaters, a place of decorum and even luxury. Disorderly crowds would not stand restlessly around the stage; instead, everyone would be seated. Hence admission prices could be greatly increased—from the mere pennies at the Globe to as high as two shillings in Blackfriars—and, as it was possible to illuminate the hall by candlelight, there could be evening as well as afternoon performances.

Everything to do with the theater was a high-risk speculation, but given the popularity of the Lord Chamberlain's Men, the scheme would probably have begun to pay off at once, had it not been for an unexpected complication: the neighbors found out about Burbage's plan and vehemently objected. A petition was signed by thirty-one residents of the precinct, including Shakespeare's printer friend, Richard Field, and the company's own noble patron, the lord chamberlain himself, who happened to live in the same complex of buildings. They argued that the theater would be a traffic nightmare, that it would attract "all manner of vagrant and lewd persons," that the crowds would increase the risk of plague, and, an all-but-irresistible clincher, that the players' drums and trumpets would disrupt services and drown out sermons in nearby churches. The government blocked the reopening of the theater, and James Burbage soon after died. His death was probably not caused, as some have said, by a broken heart—in his late sixties, he had weathered many similar crises, and nothing in his career suggests that he had a sensitive heart. Still, anxiety about the huge investment must have clouded his last days and would certainly have preoccupied his heirs. The hall was rented out for forty pounds per year to the Children of the Chapel Royal—one of the companies of boy actors—so at least there was some income. But it was not until 1608, twelve years after the original investment, that the company, now the King's Men, finally succeeded in performing in the Blackfriars Theater. The fact that they managed to do so, against deep-seated opposition, is a sign of how powerful they had become.

It was James Burbage's son, Richard, who brought his father's plan to fruition. The brilliant actor, who created many of the great Shakespearean roles, proved to be a canny, resourceful, and tenacious businessman as well. Following the model of the Globe Theater, Burbage organized a syndicate to hold and administer the new playhouse. Its seven equal partners each held a one-seventh share in the Blackfriars playhouse for a term of twenty-one years. Shakespeare, already a sharer in the Globe, was one of the partners in the new venture, the culmination of an elaborate entrepreneurial strategy.

The King's Men were firmly established as the court's favorite entertainers; they carried the royal stamp of favor upon them when they traveled; they attracted huge London audiences to their Bankside amphitheater, the Globe; and they would now cater as well to a more exclusive clientele at the Blackfriars, which could accommodate some five hundred higher-paying spectators. Gallants eager to show off their clothes could even pay to sit on the Blackfriars stage and become part of the spectacle. The practice—not permitted at the Globe—must have annoyed the actor in Shakespeare: later in the century a riot broke out during a performance of *Macbeth* when a nobleman slapped an actor who had remonstrated with him for crossing directly in front of the action in order to greet a friend on the other side of the stage. And it must have annoyed the playwright in him as well, since the stage-sitters could conspicuously get up and walk out during the play. But the businessman in Shakespeare must have found the extra profit irresistible.

Somehow, in the midst of this frenzy of activity—the relocation of the Globe; the adjustment to the new Scottish regime; the recruitment of new actors; the rush of court performances; the learning of new roles; the exhausting provincial tours; the harried negotiations over the reopening of Blackfriars; and the hurried trips back to Stratford to see his wife and children, bury his mother, celebrate the marriage of his daughter, purchase real estate, and conduct petty lawsuits—Shakespeare also found the time to write. Small wonder that as early as 1604 he had begun to brood about retirement.

To make retirement a viable option, it was not only a matter of accumulation and investment; the author of *King Lear* had to rethink his relation to the world. To judge from the plays, his mind was fantastically restless—"an extravagant and wheeling stranger," as Othello is described (1.1.137). His imagination swooped from archaic Britain to contemporary Vienna, from ancient Troy to France's Roussillon, from medieval Scotland to Timon's Athens and Coriolanus's Rome. The scene in the sprawling *Antony and Cleopatra* moves back and forth from the queen's palace in Alexandria to Rome, with detours to Sicily, Syria, Athens, Actium, and assorted military camps, battlefields, and monuments. The strange play *Pericles,* which he co-authored with the very minor writer George Wilkins, is even more unmoored, shifting from Antioch to Tyre to Tarsus to Pentapolis (in what is now Libya) to Ephesus to Mytilene (on the island of Lesbos). It is as if, more than anything else, Shakespeare's mind feared—or defied—enclosure.

But the problem posed by retirement was not enclosure. "I could be bounded in a nutshell," Hamlet says, "and count myself a king of infinite space, were it not that I have bad dreams" (2.2.248–50). Shakespeare's bad dream, or so at least *King Lear* suggests, had to do with a loss of power and the threat of dependency posed by age. As his career progressed, he shifted the principal focus of his plays away from ardent young men and women, impatient to get on with their lives, to the older generation. This shift is obvious in *King Lear,* with its tormented old men, but it can also be seen, though more subtly, in the character of Othello, who worries about his age, and in Macbeth, whose vitality ebbs away before our eyes:

> My way of life
> Is fall'n into the sere, the yellow leaf,
> And that which should accompany old age,
> As honour, love, obedience, troops of friends,
> I must not look to have.
>
> (5.3.23–27)

And instead of Romeo and Juliet or Rosalind and Orlando, as Shake-speare's quintessential vision of what it means to be in love, he gives us "grizzled" Antony and his wily Cleopatra, "wrinkled deep in time" (3.13.16, 1.5.29).

It will not do to force the point: Shakespeare's last play, *The Two Noble Kinsmen*, which he probably wrote in 1613–14 with the playwright John Fletcher, fifteen years his junior, is a tragicomic story of young lovers. Another product of this collaboration, the lost *Cardenio* (based on a source in *Don Quixote*), was probably also about the perils and pleasures of youthful passion. But it is striking that *The Two Noble Kinsmen* contains a grotesque description of a very old man, as if Shakespeare were contemplating with a shudder what he feared might lie ahead:

> The agèd cramp
> Had screwed his square foot round,
> That gout had knit his fingers into knots,
> Torturing convulsions from his globy eyes
> Had almost drawn their spheres, that what was life
> In him seemed torture.
>
> (5.2.42–47)

And, more significant, the greatest of these late plays, *The Winter's Tale* and *The Tempest*, both have a distinctly autumnal, retrospective tone. Shakespeare seems to be self-consciously reflecting upon what he has accomplished in his professional life and coming to terms with what it might mean to leave it behind.

From very early in his career, Shakespeare recycled and transformed what he had already tried out, but the ghosts of his past accomplishments haunt the late plays to an exceptional degree. *The Winter's Tale* is a rework-ing in particular of *Othello*, as if Shakespeare had set himself the task once again of staging a story of male friendship and homicidal jealousy, but this time without any tempter at all. The effect is the most extreme version in his work of the radical excision of motive: there is no reason at all why King Leontes should suspect his beautiful wife, nine months pregnant, of adultery with his best friend; no reason why he should cause the death of his only son, order his newborn daughter to be abandoned, and destroy his own happiness; and there is no reason why he should, after sixteen years, recover the daughter and the wife whom he has believed long dead. The fatal madness comes upon him suddenly and without provocation; and the restoration takes the conspicuously irrational and dangerous form of magic: a statue brought to life.

Where is Shakespeare in this strange story, a story lifted from his old rival Robert Greene? In part, he seems playfully to peer out at us behind the mask of a character he added to Greene's story, the rogue Autolycus, the trickster and peddler and "snapper-up of unconsidered trifles" (4.3.25–26). As a fragment of wry authorial self-representation, Autolycus is the player stripped of the protection of a powerful patron and hence revealed for what he is: a shape-changing vagabond and thief. He embodies the playwright's own sly consciousness of the absurdity of his trade: extracting pennies from the pockets of naive spectators gaping at the old statue trick stolen from a rival. And if the spectacular finale is not simply a trick, akin to a cardsharp's sleight of hand, if the playwright manages to give it an eerie power, then Shakespeare is somewhere else onstage, peering out from behind a different mask—that of the old woman who arranges the whole scene of the statue's coming-to-life. There is something deliberately witchlike about the dead queen's friend Paulina, for there is something potentially illicit about this resurrection, something akin to the black art of necromancy: "those that think it is unlawful business / I am about, let them depart" (5.3.96–97).

A peculiar queasiness comes over the play's end. It is as if not this one play alone but the whole of Shakespeare's enterprise—the bringing of the dead to life, the conjuring up of the passions, the effacement of rational motives, and the exploration of secret places in the soul and in the state—were being called into question. Either it is a fraud, set up to extract money from the gullible, or it is witchcraft. If the audience stays in the theater, it is because of the wonder of the spectacle and because of the reassuring hope, articulated by Leontes, that its causes and effects are simply those of the ordinary world:

> O, she's warm!
> If this be magic, let it be an art
> Lawful as eating.
>
> (5.3.109–11)

And with this, the play moves quickly to its end, running just ahead of the mockery it knows is close behind: "That she is living," says Paulina,

> Were it but told you, should be hooted at
> Like an old tale. But it appears she lives.
>
> (5.3.116–18)

The Winter's Tale hints, for those in the audience listening carefully enough to pick up the suggestion, that Leontes' queen was not dead but that she lived hidden for sixteen years in a house that Paulina has visited "privately twice or thrice a day" (5.2.95). Nothing is made of the hint; it may be there to reassure spectators who might have been otherwise reluctant to applaud necromancy, but it is so brief that it is difficult to see how it could have worked in performance. Perhaps instead it was a personal reassurance, the playwright's tiny superstitious note to himself, as if he were warding off the intimation that what he did was a form of magic.

Shakespeare had revealed this intimation before, in *A Midsummer Night's Dream* and *Macbeth*. Now, at the end of his career, he returned to it, at first playing with it obliquely in *The Winter's Tale* and then finally facing it directly and embracing it. The protagonist of *The Tempest* is a prince and a powerful magician, but he is also unmistakably a great playwright—manipulating characters, contriving to set them up in relation to one another, forging memorable scenes. Indeed, his princely power is precisely the playwright's power to determine the fate of his creations, and his magical power is precisely the playwright's power to alter space and time, create vivid illusions, cast a spell. Shakespeare's plays are rarely overtly self-reflexive: he wrote as if he thought that there were more interesting (or at least more dramatic) things in life to do than write plays. Though from time to time he seems to peer out, somewhere within Richard III or Iago or Autolycus or Paulina, for the most part he keeps himself hidden. But at last in *The Tempest*, he comes if not directly to the surface, then at least so close that his shadowy outline can be discerned.

The Tempest is not, strictly speaking, Shakespeare's last play. Written probably in 1611, it was followed by *All Is True* (now more often called *Henry VIII*), *The Two Noble Kinsmen*, and the lost *Cardenio*. But none of these latter plays is a wholly personal vision; each was written in collaboration with John Fletcher, whom Shakespeare seems to have handpicked as his successor as principal playwright for the King's Men. *The Tempest* is the last play Shakespeare wrote more or less completely on his own— no collaborator and, as far as is known, no direct literary source—and it has the air of a farewell, a valediction to theatrical magic, a retirement.

Though in exile, the magician Prospero has the kind of power that an absolute monarch could never actually possess, the power that only a great artist has over his characters. The power, as Shakespeare represents it, is hard-won—the result of deep learning and of a trauma in the distant past, "the dark backward and abyss of time" (1.2.50). Prospero had been the Duke of Milan, but, absorbed in his occult studies and inattentive to practical affairs, he was overthrown by his usurping brother. Cast adrift and shipwrecked with his daughter on an ocean island, he has used his secret arts to enslave the deformed and brutish Caliban and to take under his command the spirit Ariel. Then, as the play opens, fate and his own magical powers bring onto the island his enemies. His brother and his brother's principal ally, along with their dependents, are in his hands. Audiences accustomed to walking by gibbets on their way to the theater had a very good idea of their likely fate. Prospero does not even have the nominal restraints imposed upon Renaissance rulers by institutions; on the island he rules there are none. If Shakespeare's principal model for the magician's realm is the theater, with its bare stage and its experimental openness—a world where anything is possible—another model invoked by the play is one of the islands encountered by European voyagers to the New World. On such islands, as many contemporary reports made clear, restraint tended to melt away, and, for those in command, anything was possible. With years of isolation to brood on his injuries and plan his revenge, Prospero is free to do with his hated enemies entirely as he chooses.

What he chooses to do—at least by the standards of Renaissance princes and playwrights alike—is next to nothing. For *The Tempest* is a play not about possessing absolute power but about giving it up. Lear also gives up his power, of course, but that renunciation is a disaster. Prospero reclaims what was his by birthright—the dukedom of Milan, that is, his social authority and wealth in an ordinary, familiar world. But he abandons everything that has enabled him to bring his enemies under his control, to force them to submit to his designs, to manipulate them and the world into which he has introduced them. In short, he abandons the secret wisdom that has made him godlike.

> I have bedimmed
> The noontide sun, called forth the mutinous winds,
> And 'twixt the green sea and the azured vault
> Set roaring war—to the dread rattling thunder
> Have I given fire, and rifted Jove's stout oak
> With his own bolt; the strong-based promontory
> Have I made shake, and by the spurs plucked up
> The pine and cedar; graves at my command
> Have waked their sleepers, oped, and let 'em forth
> By my so potent art. But this rough magic
> I here abjure.
>
> (5.1.41–51)

If these words belong not only to Prospero but also to Prospero's creator, if they reflect what Shakespeare felt in contemplating retirement, then they mark a sense both of personal loss and of personal evolution. In *King Lear* retirement had seemed an unmitigated catastrophe; in *The Tempest* it seems a viable and proper action. In both cases, to be sure, the action is understood as an acknowledgment of mortality: Lear says that he will "Unburthened crawl toward death" (1.1.39); Prospero says that when he returns to Milan, "Every third thought shall be my grave" (5.1.315). Although, as his investment in long-term annuities suggests, Shakespeare himself expected that he would live much longer than in fact he did, he was clear-eyed about what lay on the far side of his decision. Yet in *The Tempest*, Prospero's decision to give up his "potent art" and return to the place of his origin is not only or even principally about exhaustion and the anticipation of death. The magician in fact knows that he is at the height of his powers: "My high charms work" (3.3.88). His choice—the breaking of the staff, the drowning of the book "deeper than did ever plummet sound" (5.1.56), and the voyage home—is represented not as weakness but as a moral triumph.

It is a triumph in part because it marks Prospero's decision not to exact vengeance against those who have injured him—"The rarer action is / In virtue than in vengeance" (5.1.27–28)—and in part because something about the power that Prospero wields, though wielded in the name of justice and legitimacy, order and restoration, is dangerous. In what does the power consist? Creating and destroying worlds. Bringing men and women into an experimental space and arousing their passions. Awakening intense anxiety in all the creatures he encounters and forcing them to confront what is hidden within them. Bending people to serve him. Prospero's charms do not work on everyone—his brother Antonio seems singularly unaffected—but for those on whom it does work, it is potentially destructive as well as redemptive. In any case, it is an excess of power, more than an ordinary mortal should have.

The clearest sign of that excess comes in the tremendous speech abjuring his "rough magic." Since the play opens with Prospero arousing an enormous storm, his specific allusion to that particular magical power makes theatrical sense, but he goes on at once to claim and to renounce something else:

> graves at my command
> Have waked their sleepers, oped, and let 'em forth
> By my so potent art.
>
> (5.1.48–50)

This was for Shakespeare's culture the most feared and dangerous form of magic, the sign of diabolical powers. It is not something Prospero, the benign magus, has actually done in the course of *The Tempest*, nor it is something that his own account of his life would lead us to imagine him doing. But as a description of the work of the playwright, rather than the magician, it is unnervingly accurate. It is not Prospero but Shakespeare who has commanded old Hamlet to burst from the grave and who has brought back to life the unjustly accused Hermione. Shakespeare's business throughout his career had been to awaken the dead.

At the end of *The Tempest*, in an epilogue rare in Shakespeare's work, Prospero steps forward, still in character, but stripped of his magical powers:

> Now my charms are all o'erthrown,
> And what strength I have's mine own,
> Which is most faint.
> (lines 1–3)

He has become an ordinary man, and he needs help. He is asking for applause and cheers—the theatrical premise, still tied by a thread to the plot, is that the audience's hands and breath will fill his sails and enable him to return home—but the terms in which he does so are peculiarly intense. The appeal for applause turns into an appeal for prayer:

> Now I want
> Spirits to enforce, art to enchant;
> And my ending is despair
> Unless I be relieved by prayer,
> Which pierces so, that it assaults
> Mercy itself, and frees all faults.
> As you from crimes would pardoned be,
> Let your indulgence set me free.
> (lines 13–20)

For Prospero, whose morality and legitimacy are repeatedly insisted upon, this guilt does not make entire sense, but it might have made sense for the playwright who peers out from behind the mask of the prince. What did it mean to do what Shakespeare had done? Why, if he is implicated in the figure of his magician hero, might he feel compelled to plead for indulgence, as if he were asking to be pardoned for a crime he had committed? The whiff of criminality is just a fantasy, of course, but it is a peculiar fantasy, of a piece with the hint of necromancy—"Th'expense of spirit," to use a phrase from the sonnets, "in a waste of shame" (129.1).

Against a background of personal caution, prudential calculation, and parsimoniousness, Shakespeare had built his career on acts of compulsive identification, the achievement of petty thefts coupled with an immense imaginative generosity. Though he had in his own affairs kept himself from the fate of Marlowe or Greene, he had in the playhouse trafficked in reckless passion and in subversive ideas. He had turned everything life had dealt him—painful crises of social standing, sexuality, and religion—into the uses of art and had turned that art into profit. He had managed even to transform his grief and perplexity at the death of his son into an aesthetic resource, the brilliant practice of strategic opacity. Is it surprising that his pride in what he had accomplished—he comes before us not as one of what *A Midsummer Night's Dream* calls "rude mechanicals" (3.2.9) but as prince and a learned magician—was mingled at the end with guilt?

Perhaps too he had slowly wearied of his own popular success or had come to question its worth. He had, as a performer and a playwright, appealed again and again for applause, and he must have been gratified that he generally received it. But if he fully knew who he was—and the figure of the princely magician suggests that Shakespeare understood what it meant to be Shakespeare—then he may have decided that he had had enough. He would finally be able to turn away from the crowd.

To judge from the pattern of Shakespeare's investments, the thought that he would leave the theater someday must have been with him for a long time. And because virtually all of these investments, apart from those in the playhouse, were in and around Stratford, he must have long harbored the dream that he eventually attempted to realize: he would leave London and return home. He had gone back again and again over the years, of course, but this return would be decisively different. He would give up his rented rooms, pack up his belongings, and actually take possession of the fine house and the barns and the arable lands he had purchased. He would pull back from the peddling of fantasies, or, rather, such playwriting as he might continue to do would now become a sideline, as the real estate had once been a sideline. Living with his aging wife and unmarried daughter, Judith; spending time with his beloved daughter Susanna, her husband, John Hall, and his granddaughter, Elizabeth; watching over his property, participating in local quarrels; visiting with old friends, he would be a respected Stratford gentleman, no more nor less.

But the closer he came to making this decision, the more his whole lifework seemed to flood back over him. The central preoccupations of almost all his plays are there in *The Tempest*: the story of brother betraying brother; the corrosive power of envy; the toppling of a legitimate ruler; the dangerous passage from civility to the wilderness; the dream of restoration; the wooing of a beautiful young heiress in ignorance of her social position; the strategy of manipulating people by means of art, especially through the staging of miniature plays-within-plays; the cunning deployment of magical powers; the tension between nature and nurture; the father's pain at giving his daughter to her suitor; the threat of social death and the collapse of identity; the overwhelming, transformative experience of wonder. The startling revelation of this very late play is that nothing of Shakespeare's immense imaginative life was actually lost. There is a famous song in *The Tempest* about the body of a drowned man:

> Full fathom five thy father lies.
>   Of his bones are coral made;
> Those are pearls that were his eyes;
>   Nothing of him that doth fade
> But doth suffer a sea-change
> Into something rich and strange.
>   (1.2.400–405)

The same is true of Shakespeare's poetic imagination: nothing had faded—all that had happened over the decades was that the bones of his works had suffered a sea change into something rich and strange.

How could Shakespeare give all of this up? The answer is that he couldn't, at least not entirely. When he actually left London is not known. He may have moved back to Stratford as early as 1611, just after he finished *The Tempest*, but he did not cut all of his ties. He was no longer over-whelmingly present, but he collaborated with John Fletcher on at least three plays. And in March 1613 he made the last of his real estate investments, not this time in Stratford, but in London. For the large sum of £140 (£80 of which was in cash), he purchased a "dwelling house or tenement" built over one of the great gatehouses of the old Blackfriars priory. This was precisely the kind of dwelling that he could have bought, had he wished his wife and children to live with him in London, during the long years of his professional life there. But it was only now that he had returned to Stratford that he decided he wanted to own something in the city. Though his Blackfriars house was in hailing distance of the Blackfriars Theater and close too to Puddle Wharf, where boats could take him quickly across the river to the Globe, Shakespeare does not seem to have bought it to live in. He may have arranged to stay there during his trips back to London—to see the plays on which he had collaborated or to conduct business—but he rented it to someone named John Robinson. Still, he owned something in the place where he had wielded his magical powers.

The transaction by which Shakespeare acquired title to the Blackfriars property was an odd and very complex one, involving three official co-purchasers who put up no money—it was Shakespeare alone who did so—but who were appointed as trustees. The only plausible explanation that has ever been offered is that the arrangement was an elaborate contrivance designed to keep his wife, Anne, from having any dower rights to the property should she outlive him. Did Anne know that her husband had set up the purchase in this way, or was it to be an unpleasant surprise, along with the second-best bed? We do not know, but all signs indicate that Shakespeare's return to Stratford, his decision to embrace the ordinary, was not an easy one.

At the very beginning of July 1613, only a few months after he completed the expensive Blackfriars purchase, news would have reached Shakespeare of a disaster that must have had a powerful impact upon him: on June 29, during a performance of the new play he had co-authored with Fletcher, the Globe Theater—the structure he himself had helped to build back in the winter of 1599—had burned to the ground.

Here, in a letter written three days after the event, is a version of the account that would have quickly been brought to Stratford:

> The King's players had a new play, called *All is true*, representing some principal pieces of the reign of Henry VIII, which was set forth with many extraordinary circumstances of pomp and majesty, even to the matting of the stage; the Knights of the Order with their Georges and garters, the Guards with their embroidered coats, and the like: sufficient in truth within a while to make greatness very familiar, if not ridiculous. Now, King Henry making a masque at the Cardinal Wolsey's house, and certain chambers [i.e., small cannons] being shot off at his entry, some of the paper, or other stuff, wherewith one of them was stopped, did light on the thatch, where being thought at first an idle smoke, and their eyes more attentive to the show, it kindled inwardly, and ran round like a train, consuming within less than an hour the whole house to the very grounds.
>
> This was the fatal period of that virtuous fabric, wherein yet nothing did perish but wood and straw, and a few forsaken cloaks; only one man had his breeches set on fire, that would perhaps have broiled him, if he had not by the benefit of a prov-ident wit put it out with bottle ale.

No injuries or deaths, then, but a severe financial blow to the sharers in the King's Men and to the "housekeepers" of the playhouse, a blow that fell with particular force upon Shakespeare himself, who was both a sharer and a housekeeper. It could have been much worse: the company's costumes and its jealously guarded playbooks were saved. If these had not been quickly carried out of harm's way, the King's Men might well have been ruined, for the costumes represented a huge investment and many of the playbooks may well have been the sole complete copies. A more rapidly moving fire could have meant that half of Shakespeare's plays—those that had not already appeared in quartos—would never have found their way into print.

Still, it was bad enough. This was a world without disaster insurance, and the cost of rebuilding the playhouse would have to be shouldered by

Shakespeare and the other owners. Even though he was a relatively wealthy man, this was precisely the kind of outlay of capital that Shakespeare, having left London and distanced himself from the daily operation of the King's Men, would not have wished to make, and he may well have decided to get out there and then. As there is no mention in his last will and testament of the valuable shares he held in the playing company and the Globe, he must have liquidated those assets earlier, though the record of the transaction, and hence the precise date, is lost. If, as seems likely, he sold the shares in the wake of the fire, Shakespeare would have made still more decisive his act of retirement.

Near the end of *The Tempest*, Prospero, declaring that "Our revels now are ended," abruptly breaks off the wedding masque he has, through his magical powers, created for his daughter and son-in-law. The actors, he explains,

> were all spirits, and
> Are melted into air, into thin air;
> And like the baseless fabric of this vision,
> The cloud-capped towers, the gorgeous palaces,
> The solemn temples, the great globe itself,
> Yea, all which it inherit, shall dissolve;
> And, like this insubstantial pageant faded,
> Leave not a rack behind.
>
> (4.1.148–56)

In the summer of 1613, these lines must have seemed in retrospect eerily prophetic: the great Globe itself had indeed dissolved. Shakespeare had been haunted all his life by a sense of the insubstantiality of things—it is the almost inescapable burden of the actor's profession—and the fire only made literal what he already knew and what his magician hero had declared:

> We are such stuff
> As dreams are made on, and our little life
> Is rounded with a sleep.
>
> (4.1.56–58)

The building itself, of course, could always be rebuilt—the Globe was up and running again in a year's time—but its fragility was one sign among many that Shakespeare, reaching his fiftieth birthday in 1614, could read in himself and in his world. His brother Gilbert died in 1612, at the age of forty-five; a year later his brother Richard died just shy of his fortieth birthday. Shakespeare's mother, Mary, had brought eight children into the world; only two of them, Will and his younger sister Joan, were still alive. For us, fifty is an age of undiminished vigor, and even then it was hardly ancient, but Shakespeare seems to have thought of himself as well struck in years and may have drawn from his own inner life Prospero's strange remark: "Every third thought shall be my grave."

Perhaps it was precisely this acknowledgment of evanescence that made Shakespeare hold on all the more tenaciously to the very substantial assets he had accumulated in the course of his life. Three wealthy landowners, Arthur Mainwaring, William Replingham, and William Combe, came up with a scheme to enclose substantial acreage near Stratford, including some of the land in which Shakespeare was a titheholder. Enclosure—rationalizing the jumble of small holdings and common fields, concentrating holdings, building fences, taking some of the land out of tillage to allow systematic, profitable sheep grazing—was a popular economic strategy for the very rich, but it was generally hated by those less wealthy. It tended to make grain prices rise, overturn customary rights, reduce employment, take away alms for the poor, and create social unrest. To its credit, the Stratford Corporation vigorously opposed the enclosure scheme. Since Shakespeare's tithes were potentially at risk, he could have been expected to join the opposition, which was led by his cousin Thomas Greene, the town clerk.

A memo Greene jotted down of a conversation held on November 17, 1614, provides a vivid glimpse of the ordinary world, in its grainy detail, in which Shakespeare was fully immersed. He had imagined kings and princes carving up huge territories:

> Of all these bounds, even from this line to this,
> With shadowy forests and with champains riched,

With plenteous rivers and wide-skirted meads,
We make thee lady.
(King Lear, 1.1.61–64)

But it was now on a far different scale and for different stakes that he was operating.

> At my cousin Shakespeare, coming yesterday to town, I went to see him how he did. He told me that they assured him they meant to enclose no further than to Gospel Bush and so up straight (leaving out part of the dingles to the field) to the gate in Clopton hedge, and take in Salisbury's piece. And that they mean in April to survey the land and then to give satisfaction, and not before. And he and Mr. Hall say they think there will be nothing done at all.

Seconded by his son-in-law John Hall, Shakespeare told Greene that he was not going to back the corporation in protesting the proposed enclosure; indeed, he thought, or claimed to think, that "there will be nothing done at all." Either Shakespeare was lied to ("they assured him . . .") or he was lying, for less than two months later, in early January, the work began. The encloser Combe, who seems to have been a nasty and pugnacious fellow, ordered a ditch to be dug; there were arguments, harsh words, and blows. Women and children from Stratford and nearby Bishopton organized themselves, went out, and filled in the ditch; and a long court fight began. Shakespeare stayed out of it, indifferent to its outcome perhaps. For already back in October, he had reached an agreement with the enclosers that if his tithe interests were at all compromised, he would have "reasonable satisfaction . . . in yearly rent or a sum of money." He did not stand to lose anything, and he did not choose to join his cousin Greene in a campaign on behalf of others who might be less fortunate. Perhaps, as some have said, Shakespeare believed in modernizing agriculture and thought that in the long run everyone would prosper; more likely, he simply did not care. It is not a terrible story, but it is not uplifting either. It is merely and disagreeably ordinary.

The same can be said perhaps about the difficulties surrounding the marriage of his daughter Judith, the ill-fated twin sister of Hamnet. His elder daughter, Susanna, had wed someone Shakespeare liked, but Judith's proposed match, Thomas Quiney, was designed to make any father of the bride wince. At least he would not have come as a complete surprise. The Shakespeares and the Quineys had been acquainted for many years—as one of the rare surviving letters to the playwright shows, the groom's father had once asked Will for a loan. Young Quiney was twenty-seven years old, a vintner by trade; Judith was thirty-one: not quite the age difference between William and Anne, but enough perhaps to trigger a twinge of uneasiness if Shakespeare had come to feel that a husband should be older than his wife. The initial problem, in any case, was not the age difference; it was a matter of the marriage license. The couple wanted to marry in 1616 during the Lenten season, when weddings were officially prohibited without special permission. Failing to obtain this permission, they were married anyway and then got caught. When Thomas failed to show up on the appointed day at the consistorial court in Worcester, where he would have faced a fine, he was promptly excommunicated. Judith may have shared in this punishment. Shakespeare was hardly a paragon of piety, but he had always been rather careful to avoid trouble—it was a strategy that went back a long way in his life—and this unpleasantness may have upset him.

He was in for something far more upsetting. A month after the wedding between Judith and Thomas, an unmarried Stratford woman named Margaret Wheeler died in childbirth, and her child died with her. Sexual transgressions—"whoredom, fornication, and uncleanness," in the words of the official homily—were routinely investigated and punished in this period, and the death of the unwed mother and child did not close the case. It would in any event have been difficult, in a town the size of Stratford, to keep such secrets for long. On March 26, 1616, the newlywed Thomas Quiney confessed in the vicar's court that he was responsible and was sentenced to a humiliating public penance, which he evaded by donating five shillings to the poor.

Shakespeare may have had very limited physical and psychological strength to deal with the crisis: in less than a month's time, he would be dead. The public disgrace of his son-in-law no doubt came at the worst possible moment for him. Indeed, some biographers have gone so far as to attribute Shakespeare's decline to the shock of Quiney's confession and the public humiliation. This seems highly implausible: Shakespeare was hardly a rigid Victorian moralist. In *The Tempest*, he had Prospero urge strict chastity before marriage, but he had also written *Measure for Measure* and other plays that depict sexual appetite with compassion or wry amusement. For that matter, Anne Hathaway had been pregnant when he stood with her at the altar. Shakespeare may have felt some version of the sentiments of the old shepherd in *The Winter's Tale*—"I would there were no age between ten and three-and-twenty, or that youth would sleep out the rest; for there is nothing in the between but getting wenches with child, wronging the ancientry, stealing, fighting. . . ." (3.3.58–61)—but he is unlikely to have fallen apart at the revelation of his son-in-law's behavior. Still, this was an ugly story, and it was his own daughter, not some imaginary Audrey or Jaquenetta, who must have felt the full force of the humiliation.

Shakespeare had probably been feeling unwell for some months, for already in January, just at the time he must have learned of the proposed wedding, he had called for his attorney, Francis Collins, and asked him to draft his last will and testament. The document, for reasons unknown, was not completed at that time, but on March 25, the day before Thomas Quiney's sentencing in the ecclesiastical court, Collins returned, and Shakespeare finished his will, signing the pages with a very shaky hand. The will was both cursory and sour in relation to his wife, Anne, the recipient of the famous second-best bed. But in relation to his daughter Judith it was much more careful and canny. The great bulk of the estate would go to Susanna and her husband, but Judith would not be excluded entirely. She would be given immediately the reasonably handsome marriage portion of a hundred pounds and could, under highly restrictive conditions, receive more money. Collins, or the clerk who was writing down the words dictated by the dying man, made a telling correction. "I give and bequeath unto my son-in-law," Shakespeare evidently began and then, at the thought of Thomas Quiney, abruptly changed course: "son-in-law" is crossed out and replaced with "daughter Judith." There would, the will stipulates, be another £50 in the marriage portion, but only if Judith renounced her claim to one of the properties she might have expected to inherit. And if she or any children she might bear should still be alive after three years, another £150 would be theirs; if Judith were dead and there were no children, then £100 would go to Susanna's daughter, Elizabeth Hall, and £50 to Shakespeare's surviving sister, Joan. Not a penny then to Judith's husband, Thomas Quiney. Indeed, Judith herself, should she live (as in fact she did), would only get the annual interest from the £150, not the principal, and Quiney could claim the sum only if he came up with the equivalent amount in land. In other words, his daughter Judith was not getting much of her father's wealth, and her husband—not mentioned by name—would not get his hands on any of it.

That is not quite all. Among the numerous small bequests—his sword to Thomas Combe; five pounds to Thomas Russell; money to buy rings for "my fellows" John Heminges, Richard Burbage, and Henry Condell; and so forth—there was a token of remembrance for his younger daughter: Judith was to receive "my broad silver-gilt bowl." But virtually everything else of value—money, New Place, the Blackfriars gatehouse, and "all my barns, stables, orchards, gardens, lands, tenements," etc., etc.—went to Susanna and her husband and to their children and children's children. To the poor of Stratford, this very wealthy man left the modest sum of ten pounds. Nothing for the church; nothing for the local school; no scholarship for a deserving child; no bequest to a worthy servant or apprentice. Beyond the family and a very small circle of friends, there was no extended world of concern. And even within the family, almost everything had contracted to the single line Shakespeare hoped to establish and maintain. Anne and Judith would have understood exactly what it all meant for them.

The contraction of his world helps perhaps to explain how quietly he passed from it. His burial on April 25, 1616, is noted in the Stratford register, but there are no contemporary accounts of his last hours. He was not at all slighted: he was buried, as befitted such an important person, in the chancel of Holy Trinity Church, and already by the 1630s, the painted funerary monument, familiar to innumerable tourists to Stratford, had been erected. But no one at the time thought to record the details of his illness or his passing, or at least no documents doing so have survived. The earliest known account of Shakespeare's death was jotted down in the early 1660s by John Ward, vicar of Stratford from 1662 to 1681. Ward dutifully reminded himself to read the works of Stratford's most famous writer—"Remember to peruse Shakespeare's plays, and be versed in them, that I may not be ignorant in that matter"—and then noted what he had heard about the great man's end: "Shakespeare, Drayton, and Ben Jonson had a merry meeting, and it seems drank too hard, for Shakespeare died of a fever there contracted."

That such a merry meeting could have taken place is not inconceivable: Michael Drayton, an accomplished poet, was from Warwickshire, and perhaps, as some have thought, he and Jonson came to Stratford to celebrate Judith's wedding. But there are certainly no corroborating signs of paternal joy in Judith's marriage, and fevers are not ordinarily contracted from hard drinking. Ward's brief note is probably not to be trusted, any more than is the still briefer comment from the late seventeenth century about Shakespeare's end: "He died a papist." This comment, penned by a chaplain of Corpus Christi College, Oxford, named Richard Davies, is intriguing, given Shakespeare's complex relationship to Catholicism, but, as Davies provides no further evidence, it may only reflect a sense that he had returned at the end of his life to the point from which he had begun.

Even if we strip away the machinations over the enclosures, the probable sense of disappointment in his younger daughter, the disgrace of Thomas Quiney, the sour anger toward his wife; even if we imagine his Stratford life as a sweet idyll—the great poet watching the peaches ripen on the espaliered trees or playing with his granddaughter—it is difficult to escape a sense of constriction and loss. The magician abjures his astonishing, visionary gift; retires to his provincial domain; and submits himself to the crushing, glacial weight of the everyday.

He who had imagined the lives of kings and rebels, Roman emperors and black warriors, he who had fashioned a place for himself in the wild world of the London stage, would embrace ordinariness. Shakespeare would enact a final, fantastic theatrical experiment: the everyday life of a country gentleman, the role he had been slowly constructing for years through the purchase of the coat of arms, the investments, the decision to keep his family in Stratford, the careful maintenance of old social networks. Why would he have done such a thing? In part, perhaps, because of a lingering sense of lack. Shakespeare began his life with questions about his faith, his love, and his social role. He had never found anything equivalent to the faith on which some of his contemporaries had staked their lives. If he himself had once been drawn toward such a commitment, he had turned away from it many years before. To be sure, he had infused his theatrical vision with the vital remnants of that faith, but he never lost sight of the unreality of the stage and never pretended that his literary visions could simply substitute for the beliefs that led someone like Campion to his death. And though he may have had brief glimpses of bliss, he had never found or could never realize the love of which he wrote and dreamed so powerfully. From the perspective of this sense of lack—a skeptical intimation of hollowness in faith and in love—his performance of the role of the ordinary gentleman might be seen as a crucial achievement.

But the embrace of the everyday is surely not only a question of lack and compensation; it is a question of the nature of his whole magnificent imaginative achievement. Throughout his career Shakespeare was fascinated by exotic locations, archaic cultures, and larger-than-life figures, but his imagination was closely bound to the familiar and the intimate. Or rather, he loved to reveal the presence of ordinariness in the midst of the extraordinary. Shakespeare has been criticized from time to time for this quality: pedants have sourly observed that his toga-wearing Romans throw up their hats in the air, as if they are London workmen; critics concerned with decorum have complained that a handkerchief—something you blow your nose in—is too vulgar an object to be mentioned, let alone to serve at the center of a tragedy; and at least one great writer—Tolstoy—thought that an aged Lear who walks about raving wildly was an appropriate object not of awe but of moral revulsion and aesthetic contempt.

It is true: Shakespeare's imagination never soared altogether above the quotidian, never entered the august halls of the metaphysical and shut the door to the everyday. In *Venus and Adonis*, we see the sweat on the face of the goddess of love. In *Romeo and Juliet*, while the grieving parents weep over Juliet's lifeless body, the musicians who have been hired for the wedding quietly joke with each other while they put away their instruments—and then decide to linger for the funeral dinner. In *Antony and Cleopatra*, the same observer who describes sultry Cleopatra on her gorgeous barge also paints a very different picture: "I saw her once / Hop forty paces through the public street" (2.2.234–35).

He made a decision early in his life, or perhaps a decision was made for him: he had something amazing in him, but it would not be the gift of the Demiurge; rather, it would be something that would never altogether lose its local roots. There is a letter that was written by Machiavelli shortly after he had lost his position in Florence and had been forcibly rusticated. He writes with disgust of the vulgar arguments and stupid games he was forced to watch at the local taverns. His only relief came in the evenings, when he could put off the clothes sullied by the banalities of the daylight hours. Dressed in a rich gown, he would take down from his shelves his beloved authors—Cicero, Livy, Tacitus—and feel that at last he had companions fit for his intellect. Nothing could be further from Shakespeare's sensibility. He never showed signs of boredom at the small talk, trivial pursuits, and foolish games of ordinary people. The highest act of his magician Prospero is to give up his magical powers and return to the place from which he had come.

Perhaps Shakespeare was drawn home by something else, a motive that—unlike all the others in his very private life—seems to lie in plain sight. Everyone has noticed the slight in his will to his wife, Anne, along with the slights to his daughter Judith and to her scapegrace of a husband. But that will is also, in its quiet way, a remarkable declaration of love, a declaration that may help to explain what drew him back to Stratford. The woman who most intensely appealed to Shakespeare in his life was twenty years younger than he: his daughter Susanna. It cannot be an accident that three of his last plays—*Pericles*, *The Winter's Tale*, and *The Tempest*—are centered on the father-daughter relationship and are so deeply anxious about incestuous desires. What Shakespeare wanted was only what he could have in the most ordinary and natural way: the pleasure of living near his daughter and her husband and their child. He understood that this pleasure had a strange, slightly melancholy dimension, a joy intimately braided together with renunciation—that is the burden of those last plays. But it is a strangeness that hides within the boundaries of the everyday. And that is where he was determined to end his days.

Bibliographical Notes

❧ ALL BIOGRAPHICAL STUDIES of Shakespeare necessarily build on the assiduous, sometimes obsessive archival research and speculation of many generations of scholars and writers. The long history of this enterprise is the subject of Samuel Schoenbaum's *Shakespeare's Lives* (New York: Oxford University Press, 1970) and Gary Taylor's *Reinventing Shakespeare: A Cultural History from the Restoration to the Present* (New York: Weidenfeld and Nicolson, 1989). Schoenbaum delights in chronicling the mythmaking extravagances and absurdities of Shakespeare biography, but there is at least as much to admire as to ridicule.

I have profited greatly not only from recent research, which has painstakingly winkled out some intriguing new details about the playwright's life and times, but also from nineteenth- and early-twentieth-century studies. These studies came under fierce attack from C. J. Sisson in 1934 in an influential essay, "The Mythical Sorrows of Shakespeare" (in *Studies in Shakespeare: British Academy Lectures*, ed. Peter Alexander [London: Oxford University Press, 1964], 9–32), but recent scholarship, including Marjorie Garber's *Shakespeare's Ghost Writers: Literature as Uncanny Causality* (New York: Methuen, 1987), Leah Marcus's *Puzzling Shakespeare: Local Reading and Its Discontents* (Berkeley: University of California Press, 1988), and Richard Wilson's *Will Power: Essays on Shakespearean Authority* (Detroit: Wayne State University Press,

1993), has reassessed their significance and usefulness. Foremost among them is J. O. Halliwell-Phillipps's two-volume *Outlines of the Life of Shakespeare*, 10th ed. (London: Longmans, 1898). Also useful and suggestive are Edward Dowden, *Shakspere: A Critical Study of His Mind and Art* (London: Henry King, 1876); Frederick Fleay, *A Chronicle History of the Life and Work of William Shakespeare, Player, Poet, and Playmaker* (London: Nimmo, 1886); Sidney Lee, *A Life of William Shakespeare* (New York: Macmillan, 1898); George Brandes, *William Shakespeare: A Critical Study* (New York: Frederick Unger, 1898); Charles Elton, *William Shakespeare, His Family and Friends* (London: John Murray, 1904); Charlotte Stopes, *Shakespeare's Warwickshire Contemporaries* (Stratford-upon-Avon: Shakespeare Head Press, 1907); and David Masson, *Shakespeare Personally* (London: Smith, Elder, 1914). Edgar Fripp's two-volume *Shakespeare, Man and Artist* (London: Oxford University Press, 1938) is a chaotic treasure trove of valuable information, which I have repeatedly mined.

Among more recent biographies, the most thorough, informative, and steadily thoughtful is Park Honan's *Shakespeare: A Life* (Oxford: Oxford University Press, 1998), which I have frequently consulted. Jonathan Bate's fine collection of essays, *The Genius of Shakespeare* (London: Picador, 1997), contains important biographical insights, as does Katherine Duncan-Jones's *Ungentle Shakespeare: Scenes from His Life* (London: Arden Shakespeare, 2001). Among the other biographical studies upon which I have drawn are Marchette Chute's lively *Shakespeare of London* (New York: Dutton, 1949); M. M. Reese's *Shakespeare: His World and His Work* (London: Edward Arnold, 1953); Stanley Wells's *Shakespeare: A Dramatic Life* (London: Sinclair-Stevenson, 1994); Eric Sams's *The Real Shakespeare: Retrieving the Early Years, 1564–1594* (New Haven: Yale University Press, 1995); I. L. Matus's *Shakespeare, In Fact* (New York: Continuum, 1999); Anthony Holden's *William Shakespeare* (Boston: Little, Brown, 1999); and Michael Wood's *In Search of Shakespeare* (London: BBC, 2003), written to accompany a BBC television series.

Though by definition unreliable and often wildly inaccurate, some of the most searching reflections on Shakespeare's life have come in the form of fiction: *Nothing Like the Sun: A Story of Shakespeare's Love-Life* (London: Heinemann, 1964), by Anthony Burgess, who also wrote a lively straightforward biography (*Shakespeare* [Hammondsworth: Penguin, 1972]); Edward Bond's play *Bingo* (London: Methuen, 1974); Marc Norman and Tom Stoppard's screenplay for the film *Shakespeare in Love* (New York: Hyperion, 1998); and, above all, the brilliant "Scylla and Charybdis" chapter of James Joyce's *Ulysses*.

At the other end of the spectrum from fiction, several important volumes make available the crucial historical documents upon which all Shakespeare biographies are based. These volumes, upon which I have drawn heavily throughout this book, include B. R. Lewis, *The Shakespeare Documents: Facsimiles, Transliterations, and Commentary*, 2 vols. (Stanford: Stanford University Press, 1940); Samuel Schoenbaum, *William Shakespeare: Records and Images* (New York: Oxford University Press, 1981); David Thomas, *Shakespeare in the Public Records* (London: HMSO, 1985); Robert Bearman, *Shakespeare in the Stratford Records* (Phoenix Mill, UK: Alan Sutton, 1994); and, above all, Schoenbaum, *William Shakespeare: A Documentary Life* (New York: Oxford University Press, 1975; also available in a 1977 compact edition).

Equally indispensable is the scholarship of the indefatigable E. K. Chambers: the two-volume *William Shakespeare: A Study of Facts and Problems* (Oxford: Clarendon, 1930), rich in significant details often buried in footnotes, asides, and appendices; the two-volume *Medieval Stage* (London: Oxford University Press, 1903); and the monumental four-volume *Elizabethan Stage* (Oxford: Clarendon, 1923). Geoffrey Bullough's eight-volume *Narrative and Dramatic Sources of Shakespeare* (New York: Columbia University Press, 1957–75) usefully brings together almost all of the known sources of Shakespeare's plays and thereby provides a suggestive guide to Shakespeare's wide and restless reading.

The evidence painstakingly gathered, edited, and appraised in Schoenbaum, Chambers, and Bullough is present throughout every chapter of this book. In the bibliographical notes below, I have listed the other principal sources, both primary and secondary, upon which I have drawn. I have, wherever possible, grouped these sources together by topic, in the order in which the particular topic appears in each chapter, so that readers eager to pursue one or another aspect of Shakespeare and his age can find their way through the immense forest of critical resources.

Convenient orientation to contemporary Shakespeare scholarship can be found in two valuable collections of essays, upon which I have repeatedly drawn: *A Companion to Shakespeare*, ed. David Scott Kastan (Oxford: Blackwell, 1999), and *New History of Early English Drama*, ed. John D. Cox and David Scott Kastan (New York: Columbia University Press, 1997). Many individual essays in these volumes bear on the topics I have treated.

All quotations from Shakespeare's works in *Will in the World* are from *The Norton Shakespeare*, ed. Stephen Greenblatt, Walter Cohen, Jean E. Howard, and Katharine Eisaman Maus (New York: W. W. Norton, 1997). (Citations to *King Lear* are from the conflated text version.) The Oxford edition of Shakespeare's plays, upon which *The Norton Shakespeare* is based, has an extraordinarily detailed *Textual Companion*, ed. Stanley Wells and Gary Taylor, which I have found valuable, as I have the individual volumes of the Arden Shakespeare series.

CHAPTER 1: PRIMAL SCENES

On Shakespeare's schooling, William Baldwin's bulky two-volume *William Shakspere's Small Latine and Lesse Greeke* (Urbana: University of Illinois Press, 1944) is comprehensive but dull and daunting. C. R. Thompson's *School in Tudor England* (Ithaca: Cornell University Press, 1958) is a helpful introduction. Joel Altman's *The Tudor Play of Mind* (Berkeley: University of California Press, 1978) suggestively links school exercises and the writing of plays. Roger Ascham's *The Schoolmaster* (1570), a key Elizabethan educational text in which the teaching of Latin plays a central role, is available in a modern edition, ed. Lawrence Ryan (Ithaca: Cornell University Press, 1967).

On the love of verbal display in Elizabethan culture, a classic work is Rosemond Tuve, *Elizabethan and Metaphysical Imagery* (Chicago: University of Chicago Press, 1947). On the whole scope of literary production in this period, C. S. Lewis's brilliant and opinionated *English Literature in the Sixteenth Century, Excluding Drama* (Oxford: Clarendon, 1954) remains indispensable. Among the immense number of critical studies of Shakespeare's relation to language, Frank Kermode's *Shakespeare's Language* (New York: Farrar, Straus and Giroux, 2000) is an illuminating place to begin.

On the mystery plays, see V. A. Kolve, *The Play Called Corpus Christi* (Stanford: Stanford University Press, 1966); Rosemary Woolf, *The English Mystery Plays* (Berkeley: University of California Press, 1972); and Glynne Wickham, *Early English Stages: 1300 to 1660*, 2nd ed. (New York: Routledge, 1980). Two earlier books, Willard Farnham, *The Medieval Heritage of Elizabethan Tragedy* (Berkeley: University of California Press, 1935), and H. C. Gardiner, *Mysteries' End: An Investigation of the Last Days of the Medieval Religious Stage* (New Haven: Yale University Press, 1946), remain particularly valuable. Bernard Spivack, *Shakespeare and the Allegory of Evil* (New York: Columbia University Press, 1958), and Robert Weimann, *Shakespeare and the Popular Tradition in the Theater: Studies in the Social Dimension of Dramatic Form and Function* (Baltimore:

Johns Hopkins University Press, 1978), are useful guides to the "morality" backgrounds of Shakespeare's plays. Andrew Gurr, "The Authority of the Globe and the Fortune," in *Material London, ca. 1600,* ed. Lena Cowan Orlin (Philadelphia: University of Pennsylvania Press, 2000), 250–67, is illuminating on the magistrate's power to license plays. On seasonal rituals, see C. L. Barber, *Shakespeare's Festive Comedy: A Study of Dramatic Form and Its Relation to Social Custom* (Princeton: Princeton University Press, 1959), and François Laroque, *Shakespeare's Festive World: Elizabethan Seasonal Entertainment and the Professional Stage* (Cambridge: Cambridge University Press, 1993).

Hostility to performances of plays, whether by schoolboys or professionals, is explored in Jonas Barish, *The Antitheatrical Prejudice* (Berkeley: University of California Press, 1981). For a close look at the important traveling company with which Shakespeare may have been associated, see Scott McMillan and Sally-Beth MacLean, *The Queen's Men and Their Plays* (Cambridge: Cambridge University Press, 1998).

The principal accounts of Elizabeth's royal progresses are found in John Nichols, ed., *The Progresses and Public Processions of Queen Elizabeth*, 3 vols. (London, 1823). Robert Langham's letter describing the Kenilworth festivities is available in a modern edition by R. J. P. Kuin, *Robert Langham: A Letter* (Leiden: Brill, 1983).

CHAPTER 2: THE DREAM OF RESTORATION

On Shakespeare's provincial environment, Mark Eccles, *Shakespeare in Warwickshire* (Madison: University of Wisconsin Press, 1961), provides a brief, yet surprisingly rich initiation. C. L. Barber and Richard Wheeler have suggestive psychoanalytic reflections on Shakespeare's relation to his father in *The Whole Journey: Shakespeare's Power of Development* (Berkeley: University of California Press, 1986) and in "Shakespeare in the Rising Middle Class," in *Shakespeare's Personality*, ed. Norman Holland, Sidney Homan, and Bernard Paris (Berkeley: University of California Press, 1989). On the presence of technical vocabularies in Shakespeare, see David Crystal and Ben Crystal, *Shakespeare's Words: A Glossary and Language Companion* (London: Penguin, 2002). On the pattern of loss and recovery in Shakespeare's late plays, see Northrop Frye, *A Natural Perspective: The Development of Shakespearean Comedy and Romance* (New York: Harcourt, Brace and World, 1965).

L. B. Wright's *Middle-Class Culture in Elizabethan England* (Ithaca: Cornell University Press, 1935) is a classic, if contested, guide to Elizabethan social structures, as is Lawrence Stone's *The Crisis of the Aristocracy: 1558–1641* (London: Oxford University Press, 1986). See also Felicity Heal and Clive Holmes, *The Gentry in England and Wales, 1500–1700* (Basingstoke, UK: Macmillan, 1994), and Joyce Youings, *Sixteenth Century England: The Penguin Social History of Britain* (London: Penguin, 1984). On yeomen, the social class from which Shakespeare descended, see Mildred Campbell, *The English Yeoman under Elizabeth and the Early Stuarts* (New Haven: Yale University Press, 1942). On the wool trade, see Peter J. Bowden, *The Wool Trade in Tudor and Stuart England* (London: Macmillan, 1962). On Stratford, see *Minutes and Accounts of the Corporation of Stratford-upon-Avon and Other Records, 1553–1620*, ed. Richard Savage and Edgar Fripp (Dugdale Society, 1921–30), supplemented by a volume of the same title edited by Levi Fox (Dugdale Society, 1990).

Prices and wages in Shakespeare's time are difficult to weigh in relation to the modern world, but for an initial glimpse, see the royal proclamation governing London wages, reprinted in Ann Jennalie Cooke, *The Privileged Playgoers of Shakespeare's London: 1576–1642* (Princeton: Princeton University Press, 1981). E. A. J. Honigmann and Susan Brock produced an edition of wills by Shakespeare and his contemporaries in the London theater, *Playhouse Wills, 1558–1642* (Manchester: Manchester University Press, 1993).

CHAPTER 3: THE GREAT FEAR

On the struggle between Catholics and Protestants in the sixteenth century, see Patrick Collinson, *The Birthpangs of Protestant England* (Houndmills, UK: Macmillan, 1988); Debora Shuger, *Habits of Thought in the English Renaissance* (Berkeley: University of California Press, 1990); and Eamon Duffy, *The Stripping of the Altars: Traditional Religion in England c. 1400–c. 1580* (New Haven: Yale University Press, 1992); all provide useful and usefully different points of orientation.

On the religion of Shakespeare and his family, there continues to be lively debate. Against the claim by Fripp, in *Shakespeare, Man and Artist*, that Shakespeare's father was a Puritan, Peter Milward's *Shakespeare's Religious Background* (London: Sidgwick and Jackson, 1973) summarizes arguments for his Catholicism. That John Shakespeare was a Catholic would seem to be confirmed by his "spiritual last will and testament," but the original is lost and its authenticity has been challenged. There are useful articles by James McManaway, "John Shakespeare's 'Spiritual Testament'" in *Shakespeare Survey* 18 (1967): 197–205, and F. W. Brownlow, "John Shakespeare's Recusancy: New Light on an Old Document," in *Shakespeare Quarterly* 40 (1989): 186–91. The case against authenticity is summarized in J. O. Halliwell-Phillips, *Outlines of the Life of Shakespeare* (1898), 2:399–404 and has been vigorously resumed by Robert Bearman in "John Shakespeare's 'Spiritual Testament': a Reappraisal" in *Shakespeare Survey* 56 (2003): 184–203, but more recent scholarship has cautiously tended to confirm its authenticity.

E. A. J. Honigmann's important *Shakespeare: The Lost Years* (Manchester: Manchester University Press, 1985) focused attention on the young Shakespeare's possible Lancashire connection, which continues to be intensely investigated and debated. Christopher Haigh's *Reformation and Resistance in Tudor Lancashire* (London: Cambridge University Press, 1975) provides a useful account of the religious stuggle in that region. Some of the most tantalizing findings for Shakespeare studies are reported in Richard Wilson's "Shakespeare and the Jesuits," in *The Times Literary Supplement* (December 19, 1997): 11–13, and explored in *Shakespeare and the Culture of Christianity in Early Modern England*, ed. Dennis Taylor and David N. Beauregard (New York: Fordham University Press, 2003). Here too there are dissenting views, including those presented by Robert Bearman in "'Was William Shakespeare William Shakeshafte?' Revisited," *Shakespeare Quarterly* 53 (2002): 83–94. Bearman's arguments are countered by Honigmann in "The Shakespeare/Shakeshafte Question, Continued," *Shakespeare Quarterly* 54 (2003): 83–86. Jeffrey Knapp, in *Shakespeare's Tribe* (Chicago: University of Chicago Press, 2002), strenuously argues that the adult Shakespeare was committed to a broad-based Erasmian Christianity, carefully limited in its central doctrinal tenets, tolerant of the range of beliefs and practices that lay outside those tenets, and steadfastly communitarian. I have also had the benefit of reading in manuscript Wilson's book *Secret Shakespeare: Studies in Theatre, Religion, and Resistance* (Manchester: Manchester University Press, 2004). In Wilson's view, the young Shakespeare was linked in some way to the Jesuits' "terrorist cells" in Lancashire. Though he became wary of fanaticism, Wilson argues, Shakespeare remained a Catholic throughout his life and coded many cryptic Catholic messages in his plays.

On Campion, Richard Simpson's 1867 biography, *Edmund Campion*

(London: Williams and Norgate), remains authoritative; Evelyn Waugh's *Edmund Campion* (Boston: Little, Brown, 1935) is eloquent and highly partisan. See also E. E. Reynolds, *Campion and Parsons: The Jesuit Missions of 1580–1* (London: Sheed and Ward, 1980); Malcolm South, *The Jesuits and the Joint Mission to England during 1580–1581* (Lewiston, NY: Mellen, 1999); and James Holleran, *A Jesuit Challenge: Edmund Campion's Debates at the Tower of London in 1581* (New York: Fordham University Press, 1999).

CHAPTER 4: WOOING, WEDDING, AND REPENTING

On Shakespeare's marriage, the principal source remains J. W. Gray, *Shakespeare's Marriage* (London: Chapman and Hall, 1905). David Cressy's *Birth, Marriage, and Death: Ritual, Religion, and the Life-Cycle in Tudor and Stuart England* (New York: Oxford University Press, 1997) is an illuminating guide to the contemporary conduct of the major life-cycle events. For the demographic estimates, I have relied on E. A. Wrigley and R. S. Schofield, *The Population History of England, 1541–1871* (Cambridge, MA: Harvard University Press, 1981). Anthony Burgess's amusing novel, *Nothing Like the Sun*, is built around the presumption that Anne Whatley of Temple Grafton was a real person, Shakespeare's lost love, rather than the trace of a clerical error.

For the sentimental picture of Shakespeare in the bosom of his family, see the nineteenth-century lithograph, by an unknown artist, reproduced in Schoenbaum, *William Shakespeare: Records and Images*, 199. The idea that sonnet 145 might be an early poem to Anne Hathaway is discussed in Andrew Gurr, "Shakespeare's First Poem: Sonnet 145," *Essays in Criticism* 21 (1971): 221–26.

The second-best bed is interpreted as a "tender remembrance" in Lewis, *The Shakespeare Documents*, 2:491, who cites Joseph Quincy Adams. For a more realistic reading of Shakespeare's last will and testament, see E. A. J. Honigmann, "Shakespeare's Will and Testamentary Traditions," in *Shakespeare and Cultural Traditions: The Selected Proceedings of the International Shakespeare Association World Congress, Tokyo, 1991*, ed. Tetsuo Kishi, Roger Pringle, and Stanley Wells (Newark: University of Delaware, 1994), 127–37. Frank Harris, in *The Man Shakespeare and His Tragic Life-Story* (New York: Michael Kennerley, 1909), depicts a Shakespeare consumed with loathing for his wife; it is from Harris that I take the suggestion that the curse on the person who moves his bones was

Shakespeare's way of keeping his wife from being laid, at her death, by his side. On the late seventeenth-century visitor to the grave who was told that the curse was Shakespeare's last poem, see Chambers, *William Shakespeare*, 2:259.

CHAPTER 5: CROSSING THE BRIDGE

On hunting (and its illegal cousin, poaching), see Edward Berry, *Shakespeare and the Hunt: A Cultural and Social Study* (Cambridge: Cambridge University Press, 2001). Samuel Schoenbaum's irenic view of Thomas Lucy's character is found in *William Shakespeare: A Documentary Life*, 107. There is a suggestive chapter on Somerville in Stopes, *Shakespeare's Warwickshire Contemporaries*. In *Secret Shakespeare* Richard Wilson revives the theory, first advanced by the Victorian critic Richard Simpson, that Somerville was not an isolated lunatic but rather a participant in a serious conspiracy. He did not commit suicide in the Tower, the theory goes, but was murdered by fellow conspirators in order to prevent his revealing incriminating evidence at the moment of his execution. (Why he should have waited until that moment is not readily apparent.) At some point before he wrote *Hamlet* (1600–1601), Shakespeare probably read Luis de Granada's *Of Prayer and Meditation* (1582), but the link to Somerville should not be exaggerated: there was another edition of Luis's work, published in 1599, without the incendiary dedicatory letter by Richard Harris that led Somerville to his fatal resolution.

On touring, the ongoing volumes of the *Records of Early English Drama* (Toronto: University of Toronto Press, 1979–) are invaluable. Peter Greenfield, "Touring," in *New History of Early English Drama*, ed. John D. Cox and David Scott Kastan (New York: Columbia University Press, 1997), 251–68; and Sally-Beth MacLean," The Players on Tour," in *Elizabethan Theatre*, vol. 10, ed. C. E. McGee (Port Credit, Ontario: P. D. Meany, 1988), 55–72, are useful and suggestive. On the possible connection of Shakespeare to the Queen's Men, see McMillan and MacLean, *The Queen's Men and Their Plays*.

For the impression London made upon first-time visitors, the place to begin is William Rye, *England as Seen by Foreigners* (London: John Russell Smith, 1865). See also A. L. Beier and Roger Finlay, eds., *London 1500–1700: The Making of a Metropolis* (London: Longman, 1986); N. L. Williams, *Tudor London Visited* (London: Cassell, 1991); Lawrence Manley, *Literature and Culture in Early Modern London* (Cambridge: Cambridge University Press, 1995);

and David Harris Sacks, "London's Dominion: The Metropolis, the Market Economy, and the State," in *Material London, ca. 1600*, 20–54. The characterization of London as "the Fair that lasts all year" is cited in Sacks.

A crucial primary source for this and the following chapter is John Stow's 1598 *Survey of London*, available in a modern edition, ed. C. L. Kingsford (Oxford: Clarendon, 1971).

On the legal concept of benefit of clergy, see my "What Is the History of Literature?" *Critical Inquiry* 23 (1997): 460–81. On the concept of "moral luck," see Bernard Williams, *Moral Luck: Philosophical Papers, 1973–1980* (Cambridge: Cambridge University Press, 1981).

CHAPTER 6 : LIFE IN THE SUBURBS

Ian Archer has a useful account of "Shakespeare's London," in *A Companion to Shakespeare*, ed. David Scott Kastan (Oxford: Blackwell, 1999), 43–56. On London's "entertainment zone," see Steven Mullaney, *The Place of the Stage: License, Play, and Power in Renaissance England* (Chicago: University of Chicago Press, 1987). On bearbaiting, see S. P. Cerasano, "The Master of the Bears in Art and Enterprise," *Medieval and Renaissance Drama in England* 5 (1991): 195–209; and Jason Scott-Warren, "When Theaters Were Bear-Gardens; or, What's at Stake in the Comedy of Manners," *Shakespeare Quarterly* 54 (2003): 63–82. The contemporary amused by the spectacle of the ape on the pony was the Spanish secretary to the Duke of Najera, who visited Henry VIII in 1544 (cited in Chambers, *Elizabethan Stage*, from whence the Dekker quotation and the account of the Southwark spectacle also come).

A mid-sixteenth-century undertaker kept a gruesome contemporary record of London's "theater of punishments": *The Diary of Henry Machyn, Citizen and Merchant-Taylor of London, from A.D. 1550 to A.D. 1563*, ed. John Gough Nichols (London: Camden Society, 1848). Machyn's diary stops before Shakespeare's birth, but there is no sign in the later sixteenth century of a substantial reduction in the punishments he so assiduously notes.

On the design and operation of the principal London playhouses in Shakespeare's time, see, in addition to Chambers's *Elizabethan Stage*, Herbert Berry, *Shakespeare's Playhouses* (New York: AMS Press, 1987); Andrew Gurr, *The Shakespearean Stage, 1574–1642*, 3rd ed. (Cambridge: Cambridge University Press,

1992); William Ingram, *The Business of Playing: The Beginnings of Adult Professional Theater in Elizabethan London* (Ithaca: Cornell University Press, 1992); and Arthur Kinney, *Shakespeare by Stages* (Oxford: Blackwell, 2003). Many of the finer details of theatrical architecture and finance remain in dispute.

A famous resource for Elizabethan theater studies is the detailed account book kept by the impresario Philip Henslowe. The book, *Henslowe's Diary*, has been edited by R. A. Foakes (2nd ed.; Cambridge: Cambridge University Press, 2002). One problem, even with this remarkably detailed record, is to understand the contemporary significance of the charges and payments. Helpful guidance may be found in Roslyn L. Knutson, *Playing Companies and Commerce in Shakespeare's Time* (Cambridge: Cambridge University Press, 2001); G. E. Bentley, *The Profession of Dramatist in Shakespeare's Time, 1590–1642* (Princeton: Princeton University Press, 1971); and Peter Davison, "Commerce and Patronage: The Lord Chamberlain's Men's Tour of 1597," in *Shakespeare Performed*, ed. Grace Ioppolo (London: Associated University Presses, 2000), 58–59.

The attacks on the stage by Northbrooke and Gosson, along with the ironic dialogue by Florio, are conveniently assembled in Chambers, *Elizabethan Stage*. There is an excellent account of the anxieties of Elizabethan officials in Lacey Baldwin Smith, *Treason in Tudor England: Politics and Paranoia* (Princeton: Princeton University Press, 1986). On the government's attempts to regulate the theater, see Richard Dutton, *Mastering the Revels* (London: Macmillan, 1991), and Janet Clare, *"Art Made Tongue-Tied by Authority": Elizabethan and Jacobean Dramatic Censorship* (New York: St. Martin's, 1990).

All citations of the plays of Christopher Marlowe, with the exception of *2 Tamburlaine*, are from *English Renaissance Drama*, ed. David Bevington, Lars Engle, Katharine Eisaman Maus, and Eric Rasmussen (New York: W. W. Norton, 2002). *2 Tamburlaine* is cited from Christopher Marlowe, *Plays*, ed. David Bevington and Eric Rasmussen (Oxford: Oxford University Press, 1998). The large critical literature on the impact of Marlowe on Shakespeare includes an illuminating article by Nicholas Brooke, "Marlowe as Provocative Agent in Shakespeare's Early Plays," in *Shakespeare Survey* 14 (1961): 34–44.

On Edward Alleyne, see S. P. Cerasano, "Edward Alleyn: 1566-1626," in *Edward Alleyn: Elizabethan Actor, Jacobean Gentleman*, ed. Aileen Reid and Robert Maniura (London: Dulwich Picture Gallery, 1994), 11–31. There is no proof that Edward Alleyne was the first Tamburlaine, but he was famous for the part, and Nashe's reference to him in 1589 as the Roscius of the contemporary players suggests that Alleyne created the role.

On Shakespeare's relation to the printing press, see David Scott Kastan, *Shakespeare and the Book* (Cambridge: Cambridge University Press, 2001), and Peter W. M. Blayney, *The First Folio of Shakespeare*, 2nd ed. (New York: W. W. Norton, 1996). On Shakespeare's reading, in addition to Bullough's eight-volume *Narrative and Dramatic Sources of Shakespeare*, I have found useful Henry Anders, *Shakespeare's Books: A Dissertation on Shakespeare's Reading and the Immediate Sources of His Works* (Berlin: Reimer, 1904); Kenneth Muir, *The Sources of Shakespeare's Plays* (London: Methuen, 1977); Robert S. Miola, *Shakespeare's Reading* (Oxford: Oxford University Press, 2000); and Leonard Barkan, "What Did Shakespeare Read?" in *Cambridge Companion to Shakespeare*, ed. Margareta de Grazia and Stanley Wells (Cambridge: Cambridge University Press, 2001), 31–47.

CHAPTER 7: SHAKESCENE

On the competitive world in which Shakespeare worked, see James Shapiro, *Rival Playwrights: Marlowe, Jonson, Shakespeare* (New York: Columbia University Press, 1991), and James Bednarz, *Shakespeare and the Poets' War* (New York: Columbia University Press, 2001). On the collaborations that coexisted with the rivalries, see Jeffrey Masten, *Textual Intercourse: Collaboration, Authorship, and Sexualities in Renaissance Drama* (Cambridge: Cambridge University Press, 1997), Jonathan Hope, *The Authorship of Shakespeare's Plays: A Socio-Linguistic Study* (Cambridge: Cambridge University Press, 1994), and Brian Vickers, *Shakespeare, Co-Author: A Historical Study of Five Collaborative Plays* (Oxford: Oxford University Press, 2002). It is striking that the five plays to which Vickers devotes his lengthy study—*Titus Andronicus, Timon of Athens, Pericles, Henry VIII*, and *The Two Noble Kinsmen*—are, by a wide consensus, among the weakest to bear Shakespeare's name. The odd effect, then, of the most recent account of collaboration is to reinforce a highly traditional account of Shakespeare's singular creative genius.

Helpful and informative on the way in which Shakespeare and his contemporaries organized and conducted their professional lives are Bentley, *The Profession of Dramatist in Shakespeare's Time, 1590–1642*; Peter Thomson, *Shakespeare's Professional Career* (Cambridge: Cambridge University Press, 1992); Andrew Gurr, *The Shakespearian Playing Companies* (Oxford:

Clarendon, 1996); and Knutson, *Playing Companies and Commerce in Shakespeare's Time*. Though not always reliable, T. W. Baldwin, *The Organization and Personnel of the Shakespearean Company* (Princeton: Princeton University Press, 1927), lays out most of the key information. T. J. King, *Casting Shakespeare's Plays: London Actors and Their Roles, 1590–1642* (Cambridge: Cambridge University Press, 1992); Tiffany Stern, *Rehearsal from Shakespeare to Sheridan* (Oxford: Oxford University Press, 2000); and David Bradley, *From Text to Performance in the Elizabethan Theatre: Preparing the Play for the Stage* (Cambridge: Cambridge University Press, 1992), are illuminating, along with G. E. Bentley, *The Profession of Player in Shakespeare's Time, 1590–1642* (Princeton: Princeton University Press, 1984). In *Shakespeare as Literary Dramatist* (Cambridge: Cambridge University Press, 2003), Lukas Erne argues that Shakespeare was more interested than scholars have usually recognized in the printed as well as the performance aspect of his plays.

On Shakespeare as performer, see Meredith Skura, *Shakespeare the Actor and the Purposes of Playing* (Chicago: University of Chicago Press, 1993). David Wiles, *Shakespeare's Clown: Actor and Text in the Elizabethan Playhouse* (Cambridge: Cambridge University Press, 1987), and David Mann, *The Elizabethan Player: Contemporary Stage Representation* (London: Routledge, 1991), are useful, as is Jean Howard, *The Stage and Social Struggle in Early Modern England* (London: Routledge, 1994).

Shakespeare's extraordinary talent was not ignored by his contemporaries and rivals. For some of their responses, see E. A. J. Honigmann, *Shakespeare's Impact on His Contemporaries* (London: Macmillan, 1982), and the two-volume *Shakspere Allusion-Book: A Collection of Allusions to Shakspere from 1591 to 1700*, ed. John Munro (London: Oxford University Press, 1932). Emrys Jones, *The Origins of Shakespeare* (Oxford: Clarendon, 1977), is illuminating on the first flowering of this talent.

Marlowe's strange and violent life has been the subject of many biographies, including Charles Nicholl's engagingly speculative *The Reckoning: The Murder of Christopher Marlowe* (London: Jonathan Cape, 1992), Constance Kuriyama's *Christoper Marlowe: A Renaissance Life* (Ithaca: Cornell University Press, 2002), and David Riggs, *The World of Christopher Marlowe* (London: Faber, 2004). *Greene's Groatsworth of Wit, Bought with a Million of Repentance* (1592) is available in an informative edition by D. Allen Carroll (Binghamton: Center for Medieval and Early Renaissance Studies, 1994).

CHAPTER 8: MASTER-MISTRESS

On Southampton's claim to be the fair young man of the sonnets, see, especially, G. P. V. Akrigg, *Shakespeare and the Earl of Southampton* (Cambridge, MA: Harvard University Press, 1968). On the career of the possible go-between, see Frances Yates, *John Florio: The Life of an Italian in Shakespeare's England* (Cambridge: Cambridge University Press, 1934).

Joel Fineman, who had little or no interest in Shakespeare's biography, has, in my view, written the most psychologically acute study of the sonnets, *Shakespeare's Perjured Eye* (Berkeley: University of California Press, 1986). The editions of the sonnets by Stephen Booth (New Haven: Yale University Press, 1977), Katherine Duncan-Jones (Arden Shakespeare, 1997), and Colin Burrow (Oxford Shakespeare, 2002) each provide abundant commentaries, as does Helen Vendler's *The Art of Shakespeare's Sonnets* (Cambridge, MA: Harvard University Press, 1997); and Duncan-Jones rehearses in detail the competing identifications of the principal figures in the sequence. In *Shakespeare and the Goddess of Complete Being* (London: Faber and Faber, 1992), Ted Hughes has brilliant pages on *Venus and Adonis*, which he views as the key to unlocking Shakespeare's whole poetic achievement. Leeds Barroll's *Politics, Plague, and Shakespeare's Theater: The Stuart Years* (Ithaca: Cornell University Press, 1991) describes the circumstances that led to the periodic closing of the theaters on public health grounds. In "Elizabethan Protest, Plague, and Plays: Rereading the 'Documents of Control,'" *English Literary Renaissance* 26 (1996): 17–45, Barbara Freedman argues against the view that plague closures were always enforced.

The homoeroticism of Shakespeare's sonnet sequence was registered with shock at least as early as the eighteenth century, when the editor George Steevens remarked, "It is impossible to read [it] without an equal mixture of disgust and indignation." On the complex erotic environment in which Shakespeare lived, worked, and (presumably) loved, see Stephen Orgel, *Impersonations: The Performance of Gender in Shakespeare's England* (Cambridge: Cambridge University Press, 1996); Alan Bray, *Homosexuality in Renaissance England*, 2nd ed. (New York: Columbia University Press, 1995); and Bruce R. Smith, *Homosexual Desire in Shakespeare's England: A Cultural Poetics* (Chicago: University of Chicago Press, 1991), as well as his *Shakespeare and Masculinity* (New York: Oxford University Press, 2000). Eve Kosofsky Sedgwick's chapter on the sonnets in her book *Between Men: English Literature and Male Homosocial Desire* (New York: Columbia University Press, 1985) is also extremely interesting.

CHAPTER 9: LAUGHER AT THE SCAFFOLD

In *Shakespeare and the Jews* (New York: Columbia University Press, 1996), James Shapiro argues that there was a significant, if clandestine, Jewish community in London in Shakespeare's time. Though this claim is debatable, Shapiro provides ample evidence for a widespread Elizabethan and Jacobean interest in Jews. See also David S. Katz, *The Jews in the History of England, 1485–1850* (New York: Oxford University Press, 1994), and Laura H. Yungblut, *Strangers Settled Here Amongst Us: Policies, Perceptions, and the Presence of Aliens in Elizabethan England* (London: Routledge, 1996).

In " 'There Is a World Elsewhere': William Shakespeare, Businessman," in *Images of Shakespeare: Proceedings of the Third Congress of the International Shakespeare Association, 1986*, ed. Werner Habich, D. J. Palmer, and Roger Pringle (Newark: University of Delaware Press, 1988), 40–46, E. A. J. Honigmann analyzes Shakespeare's own involvement in moneylending and other mercantile enterprises, as does William Ingram, "The Economics of Playing," in *A Companion to Shakespeare*, ed. David Scott Kastan (Oxford: Blackwell, 1999) 313–27.

On the single surviving manuscript play that may contain scenes in Shakespeare's handwriting, see Scott McMillin, *The Elizabethan Theatre and "The Book of Sir Thomas More"* (Ithaca: Cornell University Press, 1987), and T. H. Howard-Hill, ed., *Shakespeare and* Sir Thomas More: *Essays on the Play and Its Shakespearian Interest* (Cambridge: Cambridge University Press, 1989). The dating of *Sir Thomas More* and of Shakespeare's own participation in the project is uncertain. The script may have been drafted by Anthony Munday and others in 1592–93 or 1595, at the time of the agitation against "strangers"; Shakespeare could have been involved from the beginning or could, as seems more likely, have made his additions as late as 1603 or 1604 during a further attempt to have it approved for performance.

Direct evidence of Shakespeare's personal involvement with the community of "strangers" living in London dates from the early seventeenth century. In 1604, and probably for some time before, he was living in rented rooms on the corner of Mugwell and Silver Streets. His neighbors in the tenement were Christopher Mountjoy, a French Protestant, and his wife, Marie. Mountjoy had fled to England in the wake of the St. Bartholomew's Day massacre in 1572 and had prospered as a manufacturer of ladies' wigs and other headgear. In 1612 Shakespeare was deposed as a witness in a lawsuit between Mountjoy and his son-in-law Stephen Belott. The latter claimed that his father-in-law had pledged to give him sixty pounds on marrying and to leave him a legacy of two hundred pounds. Both parties to the suit agreed that in 1604 Shakespeare had helped, at the parents' request, to persuade the young man to marry Mountjoy's daughter and therefore knew the terms that had to be agreed upon. In his testimony Shakespeare spoke well both of the Mountjoys and of Belott, whom he had known, he said, "for the space of ten years or thereabouts," but he declared under oath that he did not remember the precise financial terms of the marriage settlement. The documents from the lawsuit were unearthed in 1909; there is a good account of them in Samuel Scheonbaum's *Records and Images* and in Park Honan's *Shakespeare: A Life.*

CHAPTER 10: SPEAKING WITH THE DEAD

For the development of the Shakespearean soliloquy, see Wolfgang Clemen, *Shakespeare's Soliloquies*, trans. C. S. Stokes (London: Methuen, 1987). On Shakespeare's working and reworking of *Hamlet* and other plays, see John Jones, *Shakespeare at Work* (Oxford: Clarendon, 1995). On the impact on Shakespeare of the death of Hamnet, see the sensitive psychoanalytic account by Richard P. Wheeler, "Death in the Family: The Loss of a Son and the Rise of Shakespearean Comedy," in *Shakespeare Quarterly* 51 (2000): 127–53. In *Hamlet in Purgatory* (Princeton: Princeton University Press, 2001), I have written at length on the consequences for Shakespeare of the change in the relationship between the living and the dead. See also Roland M. Frye, *The Renaissance Hamlet: Issues and Responses in 1600* (Princeton: Princeton University Press, 1984). On the larger historical, cultural, and theological issues, see Theo Brown, *The Fate of the Dead: A Study of Folk-Eschatology in the West Country after the Reformation* (Ipswich, UK: D. S. Brewer, 1979); Clare Gittings, *Death, Burial, and the Individual in Early Modern England* (London: Croom Helm, 1984); Julian Litten, *The English Way of Death: The Common Funeral since 1450* (London: R. Hale, 1991); Cressy, *Birth, Marriage, and Death;* and Duffy, *The Stripping of the Altars.*

CHAPTER 11: BEWITCHING THE KING

Alvin Kernan's *Shakespeare, the King's Playwright: Theater in the Stuart Court, 1603–1613* (New Haven: Yale University Press, 1995) discusses Shakespeare's relation to James.

On the relation of *Macbeth* to the Gunpowder Plot, see Henry Paul, *The Royal Play of Macbeth* (New York: Macmillan, 1950), and Garry Wills, *Witches and Jesuits: Shakesepare's Macbeth* (New York: Oxford University Press, 1995). On the Gowrie conspiracy, see Louis Barbé, *The Tragedy of Gowrie House* (London: Alexander Gardner, 1887). Kramer and Sprenger's *Malleus maleficarum* is available in an English translation and edition (1928; repr., New York: Dover, 1971) by Montague Summers, who also edited Reginald Scot's *Discoverie of Witchcraft* (1930; repr., New York: Dover, 1972). Keith Thomas, *Religion and the Decline of Magic* (London: Weidenfeld and Nicolson, 1971), and Stuart Clark, *Thinking with Demons: The Idea of Witchcraft in Early Modern Europe* (Oxford: Clarendon, 1997), are particularly helpful on the place of the occult in the mentality of the period. In "Shakespeare Bewitched," in *New Historical Literary Study: Essays on Reproducing Texts, Representing History*, ed. Jeffrey N. Cox and Larry J. Reynolds (Princeton: Princeton University Press, 1993), 108–35, I discuss at greater length Shakespeare's relation to witch hunting.

CHAPTER 12: THE TRIUMPH OF THE EVERYDAY

Bernard Beckerman, *Shakespeare at the Globe* (New York: Macmillan, 1962), and Irwin Smith, *Shakespeare's Blackfriars Playhouse: Its History and Its Design* (New York: New York Universitiy Press, 1964), are both extremely useful introductions to Shakespeare's principal theaters in the latter part of his career. On staging, Alan Dessen and Leslie Thomson's *A Dictionary of Stage Directions in English Drama, 1580–1642* (Cambridge: Cambridge University Press, 1999) is illuminating, as is Dessen's *Elizabethan Stage Conventions and Modern Interpreters* (Cambridge: Cambridge University Press, 1984). The account of the burning of the Globe, from a letter, dated July 2, 1613, written by Sir Henry Wotton to his nephew Sir Edmund Bacon, is cited in Chambers, *Elizabethan Stage*, 4:419–20.

Index

Aaron the Moor (char.), 34
ABC with the Cathechism, The, 25
actors, 166
    Greene's disdain for, 204–6, 213
    Lancashire troupes of, 104–5
    low social standing of, 74–75, 79, 204, 205–6
    memory and improvisation among, 163, 295
    "rolls" and, 294–95
    skills and talents of, 73–74
    theatrical apprenticeships and, 73
    touring, 28–33, 40, 184, 188, 289, 365–66
    as vagabonds, 77–78, 88
    see also specific actors and companies
Acts and Monuments (Foxe), 91, 159
Adams, Joseph Quincy, 146
Addenbrooke, John, 363
Adonis (char.), 126, 241–45
Adriana (char.), 130
adultery:
    in court life, 234

    in sonnets, 143, 255
Aesop, 213
Agincourt, 223, 298, 309
Aglionby, Edward, 42–43
Aguecheek, Sir Andrew (char.), 70
Alba (Burton et al.), 332
Albany (char.), 127
Albion's England, 311
Alchemist, The (Jonson), 167
alderman
    John Shakespeare as, 60–61
    jurisdiction of, 60, 165, 182
Aldgate, 164, 165
Allen, Giles, 291–92
Allen, William, Cardinal, 110
Alleyn, Edward, 190–91, 198, 213, 273
All is True, see Henry VIII
All's Well That Ends Well (Shakespeare), 123, 136, 221, 361
America, 73
Amleth (char.), 303, 305
Angelo (char.), 33, 110, 136
Anne, Lady (char.), 126